Social Policy for Children and Families

Third Edition

SAGE was founded in 1965 by Sara Miller McCune to support the dissemination of usable knowledge by publishing innovative and high-quality research and teaching content. Today, we publish more than 750 journals, including those of more than 300 learned societies, more than 800 new books per year, and a growing range of library products including archives, data, case studies, reports, conference highlights, and video. SAGE remains majority-owned by our founder, and after Sara's lifetime will become owned by a charitable trust that secures our continued independence.

Los Angeles | London | Washington DC | New Delhi | Singapore | Boston

Social Policy for Children and Families

A Risk and Resilience Perspective

Third Edition

Edited by

Jeffrey M. Jenson
University of Denver

Mark W. Fraser
University of North Carolina at Chapel Hill

Los Angeles | London | New Delhi
Singapore | Washington DC | Boston

Los Angeles | London | New Delhi
Singapore | Washington DC | Boston

FOR INFORMATION:

SAGE Publications, Inc.
2455 Teller Road
Thousand Oaks, California 91320
E-mail: order@sagepub.com

SAGE Publications Ltd.
1 Oliver's Yard
55 City Road
London EC1Y 1SP
United Kingdom

SAGE Publications India Pvt. Ltd.
B 1/I 1 Mohan Cooperative Industrial Area
Mathura Road, New Delhi 110 044
India

SAGE Publications Asia-Pacific Pte. Ltd.
3 Church Street
#10–04 Samsung Hub
Singapore 049483

Publisher: Kassie Graves
Editorial Assistant: Carrie Montoya
Production Editor: Jane Haenel
Copy Editor: Allan Harper
Typesetter: C&M Digitals (P) Ltd.
Proofreader: Jeff Bryant
Indexer: Jean Casalegno
Cover Designer: Gail Buschman
Marketing Manager: Shari Countryman

Printed in the United States of America

Library of Congress Cataloging-in-Publication Data

Social policy for children and families : a risk and resilience perspective / edited by Jeffrey M. Jenson, Mark W. Fraser. — Third edition.

pages cm
Includes bibliographical references and index.

ISBN 978–1–4833–4455–3 (pbk. : alk. paper)

1. Children—Government policy—United States.
2. Child welfare—United States. 3. Youth—Government policy—United States. 4. Family policy—United States.
5. Developmental psychology. 6. Child development.
I. Jenson, Jeffrey M. II. Fraser, Mark W., 1946–

HV741.S623 2016
362.82'5610973—dc23   2014048506

This book is printed on acid-free paper.

19 20 21 22 23 10 9 8 7 6 5

Contents

Acknowledgments

The ideas expressed in the third edition of this volume address many of the most pressing problems confronting children, youth, and families in American society. We thank each of the chapter authors for providing important new information about innovative approaches to public policy in their respective service delivery sectors. Each author's commitment to expanding the application of principles of risk, protection, and resilience to the design, implementation, and evaluation of social policies for young people and their families is exemplary. A book such as this one owes a great debt to many people behind the scenes. Thanks to Diane Wyant of the University of North Carolina at Chapel Hill and Jenifer Rinner of the University of Denver for administrative and technical support in manuscript preparation. Finally, special thanks to Mary, Nils, and Anna Jenson and to Mary, Alex, and Katy Fraser for the daily reminders of what it means to be a family.

—Jeffrey M. Jenson
—Mark W. Fraser

SAGE Publications acknowledges the contributions of the following reviewers:

Lisa R. Caya, University of Wisconsin–La Crosse

Michael Cheang, University of Hawaii at Manoa

Jennifer Cornish Genovese, Syracuse University

Angela Fontes, NORC at the University of Chicago

Clinton G. Gudmunson, Iowa State University

Ivan L. Page, Albany State University

Carlos Perez, Lubbock Christian University

Wendy Thompson, Andrews University

Introduction

Much has been written about risk and protective factors associated with social and health problems. Begun some 35 years ago, research to trace the causes of behavior problems in young people has led to a new understanding of the individual, interpersonal, and environmental factors that affect developmental and, indeed, life course outcomes. In recent years, attention has been directed to increasing our understanding of the concept of resilience, which is commonly thought of as a child's capacity to overcome adverse life circumstances (Fraser, Kirby, & Smokowski, 2004). Knowledge of risk and resilience has been widely used to improve the efficacy of prevention and treatment programs for vulnerable children and families (Catalano et al., 2012; Jenson & Bender, 2014).

In the first and second editions of this book, we argued that the principles of risk, protection, and resilience held great promise for the design of social policies and the delivery of social programs for children and families. We also noted that knowledge gained from longitudinal investigations of risk, protection, and resilience in children and youth was rarely applied to social policy. Our view has not changed. We still have much to learn about the etiological processes of risk and resilience and about the application of these principles to social interventions and programs. However, considerable progress in understanding principles of risk, protection, and resilience has been made since the publication of the first two editions of this book. Equally important, advances in fields such as public health and prevention science—in which research-based knowledge is used to design prevention interventions—are now having a practical and significant effect on social policies. Innovative policies and programs based on risk and resilience are all the more evident in each of the chapters in the third edition. Clearly, one dramatic example of change and innovation lies in health-care reform, exemplified by the implementation of the Patient Protection and Affordable Care Act (PL 11–148). This legislation and other new policies affecting the nation's children and families are reviewed in this edition. We hope that this book will help students, practitioners, policymakers, and researchers apply principles of risk and resilience to the design of social and health policies.

ORGANIZATION OF THE BOOK

The core section of the book is formed by eight chapters devoted to poverty, child welfare, education, mental health, health, developmental disabilities, substance abuse, and juvenile justice policies. Chapter authors identify key policies in their respective areas and evaluate the extent to which the principles of risk, protection, and resilience can be used

1

to improve existing programs and services. Recommended readings, questions for discussion, and Web-based resources are provided for each of the core chapters. In this regard, authors follow a similar outline in which they

- trace the purpose of social policy in a substantive area;

- describe the incidence and prevalence of problems;

- articulate common risk and protective factors associated with the onset or persistence of the relevant problem behavior;

- identify historical and current policies that have been developed to address these problems;

- evaluate the extent to which policies have been based on the principles of risk, protection, and resilience;

- identify strategies for incorporating elements of risk, protection, and resilience in new policy directives; and

- discuss ways of integrating social policy for children, youth, and families across policy and service domains.

Trina Williams Shanks and Sandra Danziger identify critical approaches to combating poverty in Chapter 2. Past and current income-maintenance policies are reviewed in the context of risk, protection, and resilience. Williams Shanks and Danziger describe several innovative programs to illustrate the promise of recent policy approaches to reducing poverty and social disadvantage.

Peter Pecora and Markell Harrison-Jackson examine child welfare policies and programs aimed at children, youth, and families in Chapter 3. In describing a key service domain for children, youth, and families, Pecora and Harrison-Jackson trace the history and evolution of American child welfare policy and offer suggestions about ways to incorporate principles of risk, protection, and resilience in a key service domain.

Public schools touch the lives of a majority of American children and families. Changes in educational policy and practice that have been made since the publication of the first edition of this book are having a profound effect on teachers, parents, and children and youth in elementary, middle, and high schools. In Chapter 4, Andy Frey, Myrna Mandlawitz, Armon Perry, and Hill Walker update their discussion of the landmark No Child Left Behind Act and its sweeping implications for the character of public education across the country. They note that educational reform is closely linked to political ideology and societal values pertaining to educational access and opportunity. Frey and colleagues conclude by offering an agenda for reform.

In Chapter 5, Mary Fraser and Paul Lanier review the effectiveness of mental health policies for children, youth, and families. Key among the promising policy and program directives that they identify is the *system of care* approach. Fraser and Lanier note the frequency of co-occurring problems among youth and suggest making the integration of mental health, juvenile justice, and substance abuse policies a public policy priority.

Kathleen Rounds, William Hall, and Guadalupe Huitron trace the development of key U.S. public health policies in Chapter 6. The authors highlight important changes reflected in the implementation of the Patient Protection and Affordable Care Act (PL 11–148) and assess the impact of those changes on young people and their families. Recommendations for integrated health policy based on risk, protection, and resilience are offered.

In recent years, recognizing and understanding developmental disabilities that are commonly found among children and youth has become a focus of policy debate. In Chapter 7, Susan Parish, Alison Saville, Jamie Swaine, and Leah Igdalsky discuss changes in policy for children with developmental disabilities in the past several decades. Using a risk and protective factor perspective, they offer recommendations for improving service delivery to children and youth with developmental disabilities.

In Chapter 8, Elizabeth Anthony, Jeffrey Jenson, and Matthew Howard review current trends in the prevalence, etiology, prevention, and treatment of adolescent substance abuse. The authors trace the origins of policies aimed at young substance abusers and comment on the relative effectiveness of alternate policy approaches. Implications of the Patient Protection and Affordable Care Act on funding streams for substance abuse prevention and treatment are noted. Anthony and colleagues conclude that principles of risk, protection, and resilience have been influential in improving the efficacy of prevention and treatment programs for young people and reflect on the implications of these findings for substance abuse policy.

In Chapter 9, William Barton traces major changes in juvenile justice policy since the creation of the juvenile court. He identifies the tension found in public policy between the competing program goals of rehabilitation and punishment. Barton concludes with cautious optimism about the application of public health principles to juvenile justice policies and programs.

In the final chapter of the book, we expand on our framework for using principles of risk, protection, and resilience to develop more fully integrated policies for children, youth, and families. We argue that integration of policy and programs across service domains should be a goal of future policy directives targeting children, youth, and families. Considerations are given to the developmental processes of children and youth in the design of this framework. Recommendations for ways to advance a public health framework based on risk, protection, and resilience in policy design, implementation, and evaluation are offered.

SUMMARY

We hope that the interdisciplinary framework described in this book stimulates innovative ideas about the design of policies for vulnerable children and families. Principles of risk, protection, and resilience—too often ignored in policy discussions—hold great promise for improving the efficacy of social policies. We believe that an increased focus on risk and protection will lead to policies that are more likely to produce services and programs that effectively help children and families to prevail over adversities.

REFERENCES

Catalano, R. F., Fagan, A. A., Gavin, L. E., Greenberg, M. T., Irwin, Jr., C. E., Ross, D. A., & Shek, D. T. (2012). *Lancet, 379,* 1653–1664. doi:10.1016/S0140-6736(12)60238-4.

Fraser, M. W., Kirby, L. D., & Smokowski, P. R. (2004). Risk and resilience in childhood. In M. W. Fraser (Ed.), *Risk and resilience in childhood: An ecological perspective* (2nd ed., pp. 13–66). Washington, DC: NASW Press.

Jenson, J. M., & Bender, K. A. (2014). *Preventing child and adolescent behavior. Evidence-based strategies in schools, families, and communities.* New York: Oxford University Press.

A Risk and Resilience Framework for Child, Youth, and Family Policy

Jeffrey M. Jenson

Mark W. Fraser

Over the past 100 years or more, social policies and programs for American children, youth, and families have undergone frequent shifts in philosophy and direction. Many policy frameworks, such as universal prevention, selective eligibility, rehabilitation, and punishment, have contributed to the conceptual bases for services, programs, and interventions designed for young people. However, the most consistent characteristic of American social policy for children and families may be the sheer inconsistency of efforts aimed at helping the nation's most vulnerable populations.

Recent advances in understanding the developmental processes associated with the onset and persistence of child and adolescent problems warrant new thinking about policies and programs. Since the second edition of this book was published in 2011, we have learned more about why some children and adolescents develop social and health problems, and—in the case of such problems as sexually transmitted diseases, drug use, and delinquency—why some youths make choices that lead to poor outcomes at home and in school and the community. Unfortunately, this knowledge is not yet systematically applied to policy or program design, which results in poorly specified, inadequately integrated, and wastefully duplicated services for children and families. The motivation for the third edition of this volume comes from the growing recognition that knowledge gained from understanding the developmental trajectories of children who experience social and health problems must be used to craft more effective policies and programs.

COMING OF AGE IN AMERICA

Children, youth, and families face enormous challenges in American society. At no time in the country's history have young people and their parents been confronted simultaneously by such a wide array of positive and negative influences and opportunities. Most children and youth become healthy adults who participate in positive—or prosocial—activities guided by interests that lead to meaningful and fulfilling lives. However, for some American children and youth, the path to adulthood is a journey filled with risk and uncertainty. Because of the adversities these young people face, the prospect of a successful future is often bleak.

If we were to draw a picture depicting the current health of America's children and youth, it would be a portrait of contrasts. On a positive note, young people between 16 and 24 years old are volunteering and becoming more involved in social causes than in the past (Center for Information and Research on Civic Learning and Engagement, 2014). In addition, the prevalence of some problem behavior—most notably, violent offending—has decreased considerably in recent years. For example, following a period of rapid increase between the late 1980s and 1995, violent juvenile crime rates reached historically low levels in 2011 (Puzzanchera, 2013).

Juxtaposed against this promising news are the disturbing accounts of school shootings, persistently high rates of school dropout and drug use, and increases in childhood poverty (for reviews of school shootings, see Bockler, Seeger, Sitzer, & Heitmeyer, 2013; Vossekuil, Fein, Reddy, Borum, & Modzeleski, 2002; Wike & Fraser, 2009). Nearly 40% of public schools in the United States reported at least one violent incident to police in the 2009–2010 school year (U.S. Department of Education, 2014). Sporadic acts of school violence have occurred in virtually every region of the country in the years following the horrific 1999 shootings at Columbine High School in Colorado (Centers for Disease Control and Prevention, 2008a). The deaths of 20 young children and six adults at Sandy Hook Elementary School in Newtown, Connecticut, was a jolting reminder that students and teachers are not always safe in their own schools and communities (Swanson, 2013).

Academic failure and school dropout have become profound social problems. About 4% of all youth between the ages of 16 and 19 years old dropped out of school in 2012. Particularly troubling is evidence indicating that youth of color drop out of school at much higher rates than Caucasian students. In 2012, 7% of Latino, 10% of American Indian, and 6% of African American students dropped out of school as compared with only 3% of Caucasian youth (Annie E. Casey Foundation, 2014). As the world moves to greater globalization of markets and demands a more educated workforce, these young people face lives of limited opportunities and high unemployment, bringing consequential high societal costs.

Drug use among American youth also imposes considerable individual and societal costs on the nation. In 2013, nearly 50% of the nation's senior high school students reported lifetime use of any illicit drug, and 25% indicated they had used an illicit drug other than marijuana (Johnston, O'Malley, & Bachman, 2013). Despite a recent leveling in drug use trends, more than 20% of eighth-grade students reported lifetime use of any illicit drug in 2013. Particularly worrisome is evidence indicating that 7% of the nation's high school seniors have tried dangerous drugs such as ecstasy (Johnston et al., 2013). These unacceptably high rates of drug use among children and youth are the focus of multifaceted policy and practice efforts at the federal, state, and local levels.

Poverty is related to many social and health problems. Nearly 23% of U.S. children younger than 18 years old live in poverty, which significantly affects individuals, families, and communities (Annie E. Casey Foundation, 2014). In the United States, children are more likely than all other age groups to be poor (Cauce, Stewart, Rodriguez, Cochran, & Ginzler, 2003), and children of color are disproportionately represented in poverty. Among all U.S. children younger than 18 years, 40% of African Americans, 37% of American Indians, and 34% of Latino children were poor in 2012. Those rates are more than double the rates for Asian and Pacific Islanders (15%) and non-Latino Caucasians (14%) living in poverty (Annie E. Casey Foundation, 2014).

These statistics are important because living in poverty has both short- and long-term effects. Poverty has negative effects on several key outcomes during childhood and adolescence, including school achievement and delinquency (Brooks-Gunn & Duncan, 1997; Hannon, 2003; Yoshikawa, Aber, & Beardslee, 2012). Poverty is also associated with adverse consequences during adulthood and later stages of life (Duncan, Ziol-Guest, & Kalil, 2010; McCord, 1997; Nikulina, Widom, & Czaja, 2011). The social and environmental conditions created by poverty give rise to a variety of public health problems that require well-reasoned evidence-based policy and program responses.

POLICY AND PROGRAM RESPONSES TO CHILDHOOD AND ADOLESCENT PROBLEMS

Experts from the fields of criminology, education, medicine, nursing, psychology, public health, social work, and sociology agree that no single pathway leads to school failure, drug use, delinquency, and other social and health problems. Rather, it is the accumulation of risk—the sheer number of adversities and traumas confronted by children and families— that seems to disrupt normal developmental trajectories (Rutter, 2001). In the mid-1970s, Jessor and Jessor (1977) asserted that a small group of youth simultaneously engaged in a variety of dangerous and costly problem behaviors; that assertion has been well supported by the research evidence over the past three decades. Indeed, the same academically marginalized youths who are involved in drug use may also be the youths who are at risk of sexually transmitted diseases and violent victimization by family members or partners. Despite the fact that we know far more about these high-risk youths, their friends, and their families (e.g., Catalano et al., 2012; Elliott et al., 2006; Fraser, 2004; Jenson & Bender, 2014), we have seen few innovative policy strategies being introduced to reduce the number of children and adolescents who experience these problems. A looming challenge for both advocates and experts is to find ways to incorporate and translate new knowledge (i.e., the product of research) into public policies and programs. *challenge*

One barrier to the uptake of research knowledge is that current social policies and programs intended to meet the needs of U.S. children, youth, and families are highly fragmented. Many policies aimed at improving conditions for vulnerable and high-risk populations have failed to consider the number, nature, or severity of problems experienced by American families. Other policies and resultant programs are duplicated among agencies, leading to a host of eligibility and implementation conflicts in child welfare, developmental disability, mental health, substance abuse, education, and juvenile justice services.

Moreover, the application of theoretical and empirical evidence to the design of social policies and programs aimed at improving the lives of children, youth, and families is limited. Social policy is often hurriedly created in the context of galvanizing community events—such as the rush to implement safety policies in the aftermath of the shootings at Sandy Hook Elementary School in 2012—or trends that have attracted public attention and compelled legislation. In some cases, policies developed in reaction to specific events lead to decisions that fail to account adequately for unforeseen or unintended long-term consequences. A case in point is that of the extensive juvenile justice reforms implemented across the country in the early to mid-1990s. Faced with increased rates of gang activity and violent youth crime, nearly all states enacted reforms emphasizing strict sanctions and punishments for young offenders. Many of these reforms—most notably, boot camp programs and the extensive use of judicial waivers for serious offenders (with some juvenile offenders being prosecuted in criminal courts and exposed to adult rather than juvenile sanctions)—subsequently produced mixed or ineffective results (Bernard & Kurlychek, 2010; Jenson, Potter, & Howard, 2001).

Over the past several decades, we have learned much about the causes and progression of child and adolescent problems. However, advances in understanding the life-course development of problem behaviors among children and youth primarily have been used to enhance prevention and treatment strategies rather than to inform theory development (Biglan, Brennan, Foster, & Holder, 2004; Farrington, 2011). Aside from Bronfenbrenner's (1979, 1986) ecological perspective, the field lacks conceptual models that inform social and health policies for children, youth, and families. In this book, we argue that a public health framework—rooted in ecological theory and based on principles of risk and resilience—is defining a new and useful conceptual model for the design of public policy across the substantive areas of child welfare, education, income assistance, mental health, health, developmental disabilities, substance use, and juvenile justice.

PUBLIC HEALTH FRAMEWORKS FOR SOCIAL POLICY

In the field of prevention science, public health frameworks for understanding and preventing child and adolescent problems have become widely used to promote positive youth outcomes (Biglan et al., 2004; Catalano et al., 2012; Hawkins, 2006; Jenson & Bender, 2014). When designing or selecting interventions to ameliorate youth problems, social scientists give first consideration to the presence or absence of risk and protective factors affecting youth outcomes. Another concept closely related to those of risk and protection is the concept of resilience, which is the ability to overcome adverse conditions and to function normatively in the face of risk. A public health perspective guiding policy development aimed at children, youth, and families must incorporate these key concepts of risk, protection, and resilience.

Risk and Protection

Risk factors are individual, school, peer, family, and community influences that increase the likelihood that a child will experience a social or health problem. Although the idea of identifying risk factors to better understand childhood and adolescent problems has gained widespread acceptance in the prevention field (Catalano, 2007; Jenson, 2006; O'Connell, Boat, & Warner, 2009; Romer, 2003; Woolf, 2008), its origins are relatively recent. The early work on identifying risk factors dates only to the 1970s, when researchers began placing greater importance on understanding the individual, family, and community correlates of mental illness (Rutter, 1979, 1987). Stimulated in part by advances in research design and statistical analysis (e.g., the development of path analysis and structural equation modeling), a new emphasis on modeling underlying causes led investigators to identify specific factors that were associated with the occurrence of delinquency, drug use, suicide, school dropout, and other problems. This approach, adapted from public health efforts to identify risk factors associated with problems such as smoking and heart disease, led to the use of "risk-based" strategies to prevent social problems in childhood and adolescence (Hawkins, Catalano, & Miller, 1992).

Risk Factors

The earliest risk factor models were simple lists of the correlates of adolescent problems (e.g., Garmezy, 1971). These models were drawn from previous research that identified risk factors for adolescent problem behaviors such as substance abuse and delinquency (e.g., Hawkins, Jenson, Catalano, & Lishner, 1988). Early models often failed to consider the temporal relationship of risk factors to the occurrence of specific behaviors or to examine the additive and interactive effects of risk factors. However, recent reviews of risk factors for adolescent problem behaviors have improved on earlier efforts by limiting their selection of studies to those in which the risk factor clearly preceded a problem behavior (e.g., Fraser, Kirby, & Smokowski, 2004; Fraser & Terzian, 2005; Herrenkohl, Aisenberg, Williams, & Jenson, 2011; Herrenkohl, Chung, & Catalano, 2004). In addition, longitudinal studies have been conducted to better understand the processes by which risk factors influence behavior over the course of childhood and adolescence (e.g., Hawkins, Kosterman, Catalano, Hill, & Abbott, 2005; Loeber, Farrington, Stouthamer-Loeber, & Van Kammen, 1998; Spoth, Redmond, & Shin, 1998). In this book, we adopt Fraser and Terzian's (2005) definition of a risk factor: "Broadly defined, the term *risk factor* relates to any event, condition, or experience that increases the probability that a problem will be formed, maintained, or exacerbated" (p. 5).

This definition recognizes that the presence of one or more risk factors in a person's life has the potential to increase the likelihood that a problem behavior will occur at a later point in time. However, the presence of a risk factor does not ensure or guarantee that a specific outcome, such as school failure, will inevitably occur. Rather, the presence of a risk factor suggests an increased chance or probability that such a problem might develop. Table 1.1 presents common risk factors for childhood and adolescent problems arranged by level of influence. These and other factors are discussed in relation to specific topics presented in Chapter 2 through Chapter 9. In addition, the discussions address protective factors, which are closely related to risk factors. *Protective factors* are those influences, characteristics, and conditions that buffer or mitigate a person's exposure to risk.

Table 1.1 Common Risk Factors for Childhood and Adolescent Problems by Level of Influence

Environmental Factors
Laws and norms favorable to antisocial behavior Availability and access to illicit drugs and firearms Poverty and limited economic development Neighborhood and community disorganization Low neighborhood attachment Media portrayals of antisocial behavior
Interpersonal and Social Factors
Favorable parental attitudes toward problem behavior Family history of involvement in problem behavior Family and parent–child conflict Poor attachment with parents Inconsistent parental monitoring, supervision, and discipline Poor academic performance in early grades Low commitment to school Rejection by conforming peer groups Association with antisocial peers
Individual Factors
Early behavior problems Favorable attitudes toward problem behaviors Sensation-seeking orientation Impulsivity Attention deficits Genetic and other biological factors

Source: Adapted from Fraser et al. (2004); Jenson and Bender (2014); and O'Connell et al. (2009).

Protective Factors

Researchers began to notice that some apparently high-risk youths did not engage in problem behaviors. Studies showed that these youths were protected from risk. That is, they seemed to have personal resources that helped them prevail over adversities. These resources came to be called *protective factors*. Still today, there is ongoing debate about the exact definition of *protection* as well as how to put knowledge about protective factors into practice (Fletcher & Sarkar, 2013; Fraser et al., 2004; Rossa, 2002). Most investigators agree that protective factors are attributes or characteristics that lower the probability of an undesirable outcome (Benard, 2004; Rutter, 1987; Werner & Smith, 1992). However, whether protective factors are independent of risk factors remains in contention.

The knowledge base associated with the concept of protection emerged in the 1980s, when investigators such as Rutter (1979) and Werner and Smith (1982) observed that

interesting

certain positive attributes appeared to operate in the presence of risk or adversity. However, the exact definition of a protective factor quickly became a topic of debate. Most of this debate has centered on the confusion created when risk and protective factors are thought of as opposite ends of a single continuum (Pollard, Hawkins, & Arthur, 1999). For example, researchers have often identified consistent family management practices as important in producing positive outcomes in children, whereas a style of inconsistent family management is construed as a factor leading to poor outcomes. In some studies, consistent family management is identified as a protective factor and inconsistent family management is seen as a risk factor. Using risk and protection in this manner establishes the two concepts as polar opposites, with one pole representing positive outcomes and the other pole representing negative outcomes. Therein lies the ongoing debate among social scientists, which can be briefly summarized as two questions:

very interesting

1. Do risk factors and protective factors represent measurable levels of an attribute or characteristic that has two poles along a single continuum?

2. Are risk factors and protective factors separate and independent constructs?

Our concept of protection holds that protective factors operate as a buffering agent to moderate exposure to risk. We offer the following definition from Fraser and Terzian (2005): "protective factors [are] resources—individual or environmental—that minimize the impact of risk" (p. 12).

This definition is important because it views protective factors as individual characteristics and environmental conditions, and it emphasizes that those conditions or characteristics interact with specific risk factors present in either the child or the child's environment. We argue that protective factors operate in three ways, by serving to

- reduce or buffer the impact of risk in a child's life,

- interrupt a chain of risk factors that may be present in a young person's life (e.g., disrupt a potential chain of risk that begins with peer rejection and leads to involvement with antisocial peers and then to delinquency), and

- prevent or block the onset of a risk factor (Fraser & Terzian, 2005).

Table 1.2 shows common protective factors discussed by authors in subsequent chapters.

Resilience: When a Child Prevails Over Adversity

Resilience is characterized by successful adaptation in the presence of risk or adversity (Garmezy, 1986; Luthar, 2003; Olsson, Bond, Burns, Vella-Brodrick, & Sawyer, 2003; Ungar, 2011). Fortunately, we have numerous examples of young people and adults who have "overcome the odds" of the negative effects of risks identified in areas of child welfare (Festinger, 1984), juvenile justice (Grunwald, Lockwood, Harris, & Mennis, 2010; Vigil, 1990), and substance abuse (Werner & Smith, 2001). Rather than a single influence or

Table 1.2   Common Protective Factors for Childhood and Adolescent Problems
by Level of Influence

Environmental Factors
Opportunities for education, employment, and other prosocial activities Caring relationships with adults or extended family members Social support from non-family members Physical and psychological safety
Interpersonal and Social Factors
Reliable support and discipline from parents or caregivers Attachment to parents or caregivers Caring relationships with siblings Low parental conflict Support for early learning High levels of commitment to school Positive teacher expectations Effective classroom management Ability to make friends and get along with others Relationships with positive and prosocial peers Involvement in conventional activities Belief in prosocial norms and values
Individual Factors
Emotional self-regulation Social and problem-solving skills Positive attitude Temperament High intelligence Low childhood stress

Source: Adapted from Fraser et al. (2004); Jenson and Bender (2014); and O'Connell et al. (2009).

factor we conceptualize resilience as the outcome of a process that takes into account both the level of risk exposure and the presence of protective factors. When exposure to risk is high, evidence suggests that most children and adolescents experience some type of problem or developmental difficulty (Cicchetti & Rogosch, 1997; Pollard et al., 1999). In circumstances in which the risk level is high, protective factors exert their influence on developmental outcomes; however, in circumstances in which the risk level is low, protective factors are more likely to have a neutral or relatively benign effect (Fraser, Richman, & Galinsky, 1999).

Sameroff and colleagues (Sameroff, 1999; Sameroff & Fiese, 2000; Sameroff & Gutman, 2004) have used the phrase *promotive* factor to refer to attributes or characteristics that have *direct protective* effects on people's lives, irrespective of the level of risk exposure (for a discussion of direct versus interactive protective effects, see Lösel & Farrington, 2012). Researchers have observed that some factors (e.g., high intelligence, low delinquency among peers) have positive effects on child and adolescent outcomes independent of risk. Whether protection operates principally as a buffer that interacts with risk exposure or whether protection has both interactive and direct promotive effects on life course outcomes is the focus of ongoing discussion and research. To date, tests of the impact of direct protective effects have been relatively limited (see, e.g., Gutman, Sameroff, & Eccles, 2002; Lösel & Farrington, 2012; Pardini, Loeber, Farrington, & Stouthamer-Loeber, 2012; Sameroff, Bartko, Baldwin, Baldwin, & Siefer, 1999; Youngblade, Theokas, Schulenberg, Curry, Huang, & Novak, 2007).

On balance, experts are viewing resilience as the outcome of an interactive process involving risk and protection. Thus, *adaptation,* which is expressed through individual behavior, is interpreted as an interactive product involving the presence or absence of a specific risk; the level of exposure to risk; and the strength of the specific risk and protective factors present in a child's life.

APPLYING PRINCIPLES OF RISK AND RESILIENCE TO SOCIAL POLICY

Applications of public health principles primarily have been used to develop preventive interventions in school and community settings (Catalano et al., 2012; Durlak, Weissberg, Dymnicki, Taylor, & Schellinger, 2011; Jenson & Bender, 2014; Luthar & Cicchetti, 2000). The results have been impressive. Recent research has identified a number of efficacious risk-oriented programs aimed at preventing child and adolescent problems such as substance abuse (Botvin & Griffin, 2004; Foxcroft, Ireland, Lister-Sharp, Lowe, & Breen, 2003; Gottfredson & Wilson, 2003) and delinquency (Catalano, Loeber, & McKinney, 1999; Limbos et al., 2007; Wilson & Lipsey, 2007). Research and governmental entities, which are concerned with improving the dissemination of effective programs, have made lists of effective interventions available to practitioners, educators, and the general public (Campbell Collaboration Library, 2014; Center for the Study and Prevention of Violence, 2014; Substance Abuse and Mental Health Administration, 2014). Prevention and treatment strategies using a risk and protective perspective are now widely recognized by public and private entities (at both the state and federal levels) as the dominant approach to preventing and treating childhood and adolescent problems (Center for the Study and Prevention of Violence, 2014; Centers for Disease Control and Prevention, 2008b; National Institute on Drug Abuse, 1997; O'Connell et al., 2009; Schinke, Brounstein, & Gardner, 2002).

A logical next step in the application of the risk and resilience model requires extending the framework to the development of a broader cross-section of programs and public policies (Fraser & Galinsky, 2004). To date, only a few examples of this process exist.

Investigators in the public health field have applied principles of risk, protection, and resilience to their design of prevention strategies targeting risk factors for AIDS. Evidence suggests that the implementation of this approach has led to reductions in the spread of AIDS in many parts of the world (Sorenson, Masson, & Perlman, 2002).

A second example of using a public health framework to effect program and policy change comes from innovations in substance abuse prevention. Hawkins, Catalano, and colleagues at the Social Development Research Group (Hawkins, Catalano, & Associates, 1992) created the Communities That Care (CTC) program, which is a theoretically based prevention system designed to help community leaders develop and implement effective substance abuse prevention programs. The CTC program is based on the social development model (SDM), which is a general theory of human behavior that integrates perspectives from social control theory (Hirschi, 1969), social learning theory (Bandura, 1989), and differential association theory (Matsueda, 1982; Sutherland, 1973). SDM specifies the mechanisms and causal pathways by which risk and protective factors interact in the etiology of various behaviors, including adolescent drug use (Catalano & Hawkins, 1996). The SDM proposes that four protective factors inhibit the development of antisocial behaviors in children: (1) *bonding,* defined as attachment and commitment to family, school, and positive peers (Garmezy, 1986); (2) *belief in the shared values or norms* of these social units; (3) *external constraints* such as clear, consistent standards against drug use (Hansen, Malotte, & Fielding, 1988; Scheier & Botvin, 1998); and (4) *social, cognitive, and emotional skills* that provide protective tools allowing children to solve problems (Rutter, 1987), to perform in social situations (Werner & Smith, 1982), and to resist influences and impulses to violate their norms for behavior (Hansen, Graham, Sobel, Shelton, Flay, & Johnson, 1987).

In the CTC model, communities form coalitions to engage in systematic prevention planning, which requires them to identify risk and protective factors for adolescent problems that are prevalent in their localities. Following the assessment of such factors, communities are encouraged to select prevention strategies based on available empirical evidence (Brown, Hawkins, Arthur, Briney, & Fagan, 2011). Recent findings from the Community Youth Development Study, which is a longitudinal, randomized trial that uses principles of the CTC model, have revealed significantly lower rates of delinquency and drug use among students in experimental communities as compared with control communities (Hawkins et al., 2008; Hawkins et al., 2012). These groundbreaking findings suggest that well-organized and well-implemented community planning efforts that focus on risk and protection can lead to positive outcomes for young people. Although the CTC model falls short of satisfying the criteria for a formal policy, it successfully initiates a process whereby knowledge of risk and protective factors becomes an integral part of program design. As implied in the preceding examples, applying principles of risk and resilience to policy design requires an understanding of the developmental trajectories associated with the onset or persistence of child and adolescent problems. Figure 1.1 illustrates the process involved in applying a public health perspective to policy and program design for children, youth, and families.

Two additional elements in the risk and resilience model, ecological theory and life-course development, are outlined briefly in the next section.

Figure 1.1   A Risk and Resilience Framework for Child, Youth, and Family Policy

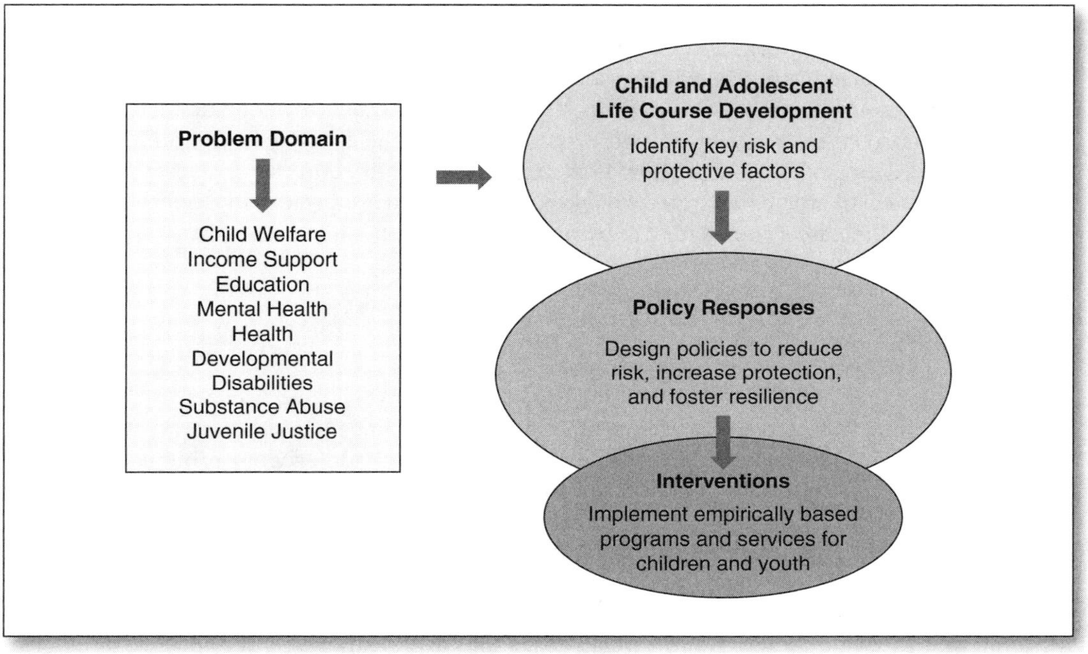

ECOLOGICAL THEORY AND LIFE-COURSE DEVELOPMENT

As we mentioned earlier, we use an ecological perspective to provide a context for thinking about principles of risk, protection, and resilience over the course of child development. The ecological perspective is well known and widely applied in education, practice, and research across many disciplines and professions (Bronfenbrenner, 1979, 1986; Fraser, 2004; Germain, 1991). Ecological theory posits that development is deeply affected by interactions between the biological and psychological characteristics of the individual child and conditions in his or her environment. Environmental conditions are usually described as the developmental context, as layers of family, peer, school, and community influences (Bronfenbrenner, 1979, 1986). An ecological perspective holds that child development is a product of transactions between an organism and these layers of contextual influence. In the vernacular of practice, child development is influenced by events that occur in the lives of young people within their family, peer, school, and community settings.

We believe social policies for children, youth, and families must be framed in an ecological perspective that considers the influence of context. For example, a child who is referred to the juvenile justice system is also a child who lives within some type of family unit, attends a local school, and has a network of peers. Evidence indicates that both unique and interrelated risk and protective factors increase or decrease the likelihood of problem behavior within each of these domains (Fraser, 2004; Herrenkohl et al., 2011; Jenson & Howard, 1999). Therefore, social policies are most likely to be effective when they address the myriad influences that lead to and may sustain problem behavior for young people. In earlier work, we discussed risk and protective factors in the context of the ecological perspective as a way to explain the onset and prevention of childhood and adolescent problems (Fraser, 2004; Jenson, 2004). However, the knowledge of such factors has seldom been used as a lens through which to examine social policy for children, youth, and families. Our intention is to show how principles contained in the ecological perspective can be used to create integrated policies that may cut across traditional policy boundaries found within care systems for American children, youth, and families.

SUMMARY

Knowledge gained from studies of risk, protection, and resilience has significantly affected our understanding of the onset and persistence of childhood and adolescent problems. Principles of risk, protection, and resilience also have been helpful in improving the conceptual and methodological rigor of prevention and treatment programs for children and youth (Jenson & Bender, 2014; Kaftarian, Robinson, Compton, Davis, & Volkow, 2004; Limbos et al., 2007; Wilson & Lipsey, 2007). However, to date, these principles have not been systematically applied to social policies for children and families. This chapter has outlined a public health framework for child and family policy based on risk, protection, and resilience. Principles of ecological theory and life-course development were introduced as essential parts of the framework. In subsequent chapters, we more fully examine the utility of a public health framework for child and family policy.

REFERENCES

Annie E. Casey Foundation. (2014). *Kids count data center.* Retrieved from http://datacenter.kidscount.org

Bandura, A. (1989). Human agency in social cognitive theory. *American Psychologist, 14,* 1175–1184. doi:10.1037/0003–066X.44.9.1175

Bernard, T. J., & Kurlychek, M. C. (2010). *The cycle of juvenile justice reform* (2nd ed.). New York: Oxford University Press.

Biglan, A., Brennan, P. A., Foster, S. L., & Holder, H. D. (2004). *Helping adolescents at risk. Prevention of multiple problem behaviors.* New York: Guilford Press.

Bockler, N., Seeger, T., Sitzer, P., & Heitmeyer, W. (2013). *School shootings. International research, case studies, and concepts for prevention.* New York: Springer.

Botvin, G. J., & Griffin, K. W. (2004). Life skills training: Empirical findings and future directions. *The Journal of Primary Prevention, 25,* 211–232. doi:10.1023/B:JOPP.0000042391.58573.5b

Bronfenbrenner, U. (1979). *The ecology of human development: Experiments by nature and design.* Cambridge, MA: Harvard University Press.

Bronfenbrenner, U. (1986). Ecology of the family as a context to human development: Research perspectives. *Development Psychology, 22,* 723–742. doi:10.1037/0012–1649.22.6.723

Brooks-Gunn, J., & Duncan, G. J. (1997). The effects of poverty on children. *Future of Children, 7,* 55–71. doi:10.2307/1602387

Brown, E. C., Hawkins, J. D., Arthur, M. W., Briney, J. S., & Fagan, A. A. (2011). Prevention service system transformation using Communities That Care. *Journal of Community Psychology, 39,* 183–201. doi:10.1002/jcop.20426

Campbell Collaboration Library. (2014). [Database]. Retrieved from http://www.campbellcollaboration .org

Catalano, R. F. (2007). Prevention is a sound public and private investment. *Criminology and Public Policy, 6,* 377–398. doi:10.1111/j.1745-9133.2007.00443.x

Catalano, R. F., Fagan, A. A., Gavin, L. E., Greenberg, M. T., Irwin, Jr., C. E., Ross, D. A., & Shek, D. T. (2012). Worldwide application of prevention science in adolescent health. *Lancet, 379,* 1653–1664. doi:10.1016/S0140-6736(12)60238-4

Catalano, R. F., & Hawkins, J. D. (1996). The social development model: A theory of antisocial behavior. In J. D. Hawkins (Ed.), *Delinquency and crime: Current theories* (pp. 149–197). New York: Cambridge University Press.

Catalano, R. F., Loeber, R., & McKinney, K. (1999). *School and community interventions to prevent serious and violent offending* (NCJ 177624). Washington, DC: Office of Juvenile Justice and Delinquency Prevention, U.S. Department of Justice. Retrieved from http://www.ncjrs.gov/pdffiles1/ojjdp/177624.pdf

Cauce, A. M., Stewart, A., Rodriguez, M. D., Cochran, B., & Ginzler, J. (2003). Overcoming the odds? Adolescent development in the context of urban poverty. In S. S. Luthar (Ed.), *Resilience and vulnerability: Adaptation in the context of childhood adversities* (pp. 343–363). Cambridge, UK: Cambridge University Press. doi:10.1017/CB09780511615788.016

Center for Information and Research on Civic Learning and Engagement. (2014). Volunteering and community service. Retrieved from http://www.civicyouth.org/quick-facts/volunteering community-service/.

Center for the Study and Prevention of Violence. (2014). *Blueprints for healthy youth development.* Retrieved from http://www.colorado.edu/cspv/blueprints/index.html

Centers for Disease Control and Prevention. (2008a). *School-associated student homicides—United States, 1992–2006.* Washington, DC: Author.

Centers for Disease Control and Prevention. (2008b). *Understanding youth violence. Fact sheet.* Atlanta, GA: Author. Retrieved from http://www.cdc.gov/ncipc/pub-res/YVFact Sheet.pdf

Cicchetti, D., & Rogosch, F. A. (1997). The role of self-organization in the promotion of resilience in maltreated children. *Development and Psychopathology, 9,* 787–815. doi:10.1017/S0954579497001442

Duncan, G. J., Ziol-Guest, K. M., & Kalil, A. (2010). Early childhood poverty and adult attainment, behavior, and health. *Child Development, 81,* 306-325. doi: 10.1111/j.1467-8624.2009.01396.x

Durlak, J. A., Weissberg, R. P., Dymnicki, A. B., Taylor, R. D., & Schellinger, K. B. (2011). The impact of enhancing students' social and emotional learning: A meta-analysis of school-based universal interventions. *Child Development, 82,* 405–432. doi: 10.1111/j.1467-8624.2010.01564.x

Elliott, D. S., Menard, S., Rankin, B., Elliott, A., Huizinga, D., & Wilson, J. W. (2006). *Good kids from bad neighborhoods: Successful development in social context.* Cambridge: Cambridge University Press.

Farrington, D. P. (Ed). (2011). *Integrated developmental and life-course theories of offending.* Piscataway, NJ: Transaction Publishers.

Festinger, T. (1984). *No one ever asked us: A postscript to the foster care system.* New York: Columbia University Press.

Fletcher, D., & Sarkar, M. (2013). Psychological resilience: A review and critique of definitions, concepts, and theory. *European Psychologist, 18*(1), 12–23. doi:10.1027/1016-9040/a000124

Foxcroft, D. R., Ireland, D., Lister-Sharp, D. J., Lowe, G., & Breen, R. (2003). Longer term primary prevention for alcohol misuse in young people: A systematic review. *Addiction, 98,* 397–411. doi:10.1046/j.1360-0443.2003.00355.x

Fraser, M. W. (2004). The ecology of childhood: A multisystems perspective. In M. W. Fraser (Ed.), *Risk and resilience in childhood: An ecological perspective* (2nd ed., pp. 1–12). Washington, DC: NASW Press.

Fraser, M. W., & Galinsky, M. J. (2004). Risk and resilience in childhood: Toward an evidence-based model of practice. In M. W. Fraser (Ed.), *Risk and resilience in childhood: An ecological perspective* (2nd ed., pp. 385–402). Washington, DC: NASW Press.

Fraser, M. W., Kirby, L. D., & Smokowski, P. R. (2004). Risk and resilience in childhood. In M. W. Fraser (Ed.), *Risk and resilience in childhood: An ecological perspective* (2nd ed., pp. 13–66). Washington, DC: NASW Press.

Fraser, M. W., Richman, J. M., & Galinsky, M. J. (1999). Risk, protection, and resilience: Towards a conceptual framework for social work practice. *Social Work Research, 23,* 131–144.

Fraser, M. W., & Terzian, M. A. (2005). Risk and resilience in child development: Practice principles and strategies. In G. P. Mallon & P. McCartt Hess (Eds.), *Handbook of children, youth, and family services: Practice, policies, and programs* (pp. 55–71). New York: Columbia University Press.

Garmezy, N. (1971). Vulnerability research and the issue of primary prevention. *American Journal of Orthopsychiatry, 41,* 101–116.

Garmezy, N. (1986). On measures, methods, and models. *Journal of the American Academy of Child and Adolescent Psychiatry, 25,* 727–729. doi:10.1016/S0002-7138(09)60303-4

Germain, C. B. (1991). *Human behavior in the social environment: An ecological view.* New York: Columbia University Press.

Gottfredson, D. C., & Wilson, D. B. (2003). Characteristics of effective school-based substance abuse prevention. *Prevention Science, 4,* 27–38. doi:10.1023/A:1021782710278

Grunwald, H. E., Lockwood, B., Harris, P. W., & Mennis, J. (2010). Influences of neighborhood context, individual history, and parenting behavior on recidivism among juvenile offenders. *Journal of Youth and Adolescence, 39,* 1067–1079. doi: 10.1007/s10964-010-9518-5

Gutman, L., Sameroff, A. J., & Eccles, J. S. (2002). The academic achievement of African American students during early adolescence: An examination of multiple risk, promotive, and protective factors. *American Journal of Community Psychology, 30*(3), 367–400. doi:10.1023/A:1015389103911

Hannon, L. (2003). Poverty, delinquency, and educational attainment: Cumulative disadvantage or disadvantage saturation? *Sociological Inquiry, 73,* 576–594. doi:10.1111/1475-682X.00072

Hansen, W. B., Graham, J. W., Sobel, J. L., Shelton, D. R., Flay, B. R., & Johnson, C. A. (1987). The consistency of peer and parent influences on tobacco, alcohol, and marijuana use among young adolescents. *Journal of Behavioral Medicine, 10,* 559–579. doi:10.1007/BF00846655

Hansen, W. B., Malotte, C. K., & Fielding, J. E. (1988). Evaluation of a tobacco and alcohol abuse prevention curriculum for adolescents. *Health Education Quarterly, 15,* 93–114.

Hawkins, J. D. (2006). Science, social work, prevention: Finding the intersection. *Social Work Research, 30,* 137–152. doi:10.1093/swr/30.3.137

Hawkins, J. D., Brown, E. C., Oesterle, S., Arthur, M. W., Abbot, R. D., & Catalano, R. F. (2008). Early effects of Communities That Care on targeted risks and initiation of delinquent behavior and substance use. *Journal of Adolescent Health, 43,* 15–22. doi:10.1016/j.jadohealth.2008.01.022

Hawkins, J. D., Catalano, R. F., & Associates. (1992). *Communities That Care: Actions for drug abuse prevention.* San Francisco: Jossey-Bass.

Hawkins, J. D., Catalano, R. F., & Miller, J. Y. (1992). Risk and protective factors for alcohol and other drug problems in adolescence and early adulthood: Implications for substance abuse prevention. *Psychological Bulletin, 112,* 64–105. doi:10.1037/0033-2909.112.1.64

Hawkins, J. D., Jenson, J. M., Catalano, R. F., & Lishner, D. L. (1988). Delinquency and drug abuse: Implications for social services. *Social Service Review, 62,* 258–284. doi:10.1086/644546

Hawkins, J. D., Kosterman, R. Catalano, R. F., Hill, K. G., & Abbott, R. D. (2005). Promoting positive adult functioning through social development intervention in childhood: Long-term effects from the Seattle Social Development Project. *Archives of Pediatrics and Adolescent Medicine, 159,* 25–31. doi:10.1001/archpedi.159.1.25

Hawkins, J. D., Oesterle, S., Brown, E. C., Monahan, K. C., Abbott, R. D., Arthur, M. W., & Catalano, R. F. (2012). Sustained decreases in risk exposure and youth problem behaviors after installation of the Communities That Care prevention system in a randomized trial. *Archives of Pediatrics and Adolescent Medicine, 166,* 141–148. doi:10.1001/archpediatrics.2011.183

Herrenkohl, T. I., Aisenberg, E., Williams, J. H., & Jenson, J. M. (2011). *Violence in context: Current evidence on risk, protection, and prevention.* New York: Oxford University Press.

Herrenkohl, T. I., Chung, I. J., & Catalano, R. F. (2004). Review of research on predictors of youth violence and school-based and community-based prevention approaches. In P. Allen-Meares and M.W. Fraser (Eds.), *Intervention with children and adolescents: An interdisciplinary perspective* (pp. 449–476). Boston: Pearson Education.

Hirschi, T. (1969). *Causes of delinquency.* Berkeley: University of California Press.

Jenson, J. M. (2004). Risk and protective factors for alcohol and other drug use in adolescence. In M. W. Fraser (Ed.), *Risk and resiliency in childhood: An ecological perspective* (2nd ed., pp. 183–208). Washington, DC: NASW Press.

Jenson, J. M. (2006). Advances and challenges in preventing childhood and adolescent problem behavior. *Social Work Research, 30,* 131–134. doi:10.1093/swr/30.3.131

Jenson, J. M., & Bender, K. A. (2014). *Preventing child and adolescent behavior. Evidence-based strategies in schools, families, and communities.* New York: Oxford University Press.

Jenson, J. M., & Howard, M. O. (1999). *Youth violence. Current research and recent practice innovations.* Washington, DC: NASW.

Jenson, J. M., Potter, C. C., & Howard, M. O. (2001). American juvenile justice: Recent trends and issues in youth offending. *Social Policy and Administration, 35,* 48–68. doi:10.1111/1467-9515.00219

Jessor, R., & Jessor, S. L. (1977). *Problem behavior and psychosocial development: A longitudinal study of youth.* New York: Academic Press.

Johnston, L. D., O'Malley, P. M., & Bachman, J. G. (2013). *Drug use, drinking, and smoking: National survey results from high school, college, and young adult populations.* Washington, DC: Government Printing Office. Retrieved from http://monitoringthefuture.org.

Kaftarian, S., Robinson, E., Compton, W., Davis, B. W., & Volkow, N. (2004). Blending prevention research and practice in schools: Critical issues and suggestions. *Prevention Science, 5,* 1–3. doi:10.1023/B:PREV.0000013975.74774.bc

Limbos, M. A., Chan, L. S., Warf, C., Schneir, A., Iverson, E., Shekelle, P., & Kipke, M. D. (2007). Effectiveness of interventions to prevent youth violence. A systematic review. *American Journal of Preventive Medicine, 33,* 65–74. doi:org/10.1016/j.amepre.2007.02.045

Loeber, R., Farrington, D. P., Stouthamer-Loeber, M., & Van Kammen, W. B. (1998). *Antisocial behavior and mental health problems.* Mahwah, NJ: Lawrence Erlbaum.

Lösel, F., & Farrington, D. P. (2012). Direct protective and buffering protective factors in the development of youth violence. *American Journal of Preventive Medicine, 43*(2, Suppl 1), S8–S23. doi:10.1016/j.amepre.2012.04.029

Luthar, S. S. (2003). *Resilience and vulnerability: Adaptation in the context of childhood adversities.* Cambridge, UK: Cambridge University Press. doi:10.1017/CB09780511615788

Luthar, S. S., & Cicchetti, D. (2000). The construct of resilience: Implications for interventions and social policies. *Development and Psychopathology, 12,* 857–885. doi:10.1017/S0954579400004156

Matsueda, R. L. (1982). Testing control theory and differential association: A causal modeling approach. *American Sociological Review, 47,* 489–504. doi:10.2307/2095194

McCord, J. (1997). *Violence and childhood in the inner city.* Cambridge, UK: Cambridge University Press.

National Institute on Drug Abuse. (1997). *Preventing drug use among children and adolescents: A research guide to what works* (NIH Publication Number 97–4212). Bethesda, MD: National Institutes of Health.

Nikulina, V., Widom, S. C., & Czaja, S. (2011). The role of childhood neglect and childhood poverty in predicting mental health, academic achievement and crime in adulthood. *American Journal of Community Psychology, 48,* 309–321. doi:10.1007/s10464-010-9385-y

O'Connell, M. E., Boat, T., & Warner, K. E. (Eds.). (2009). *Preventing mental, emotional, and behavioral disorders among young people: Progress and possibilities.* Washington, D.C.: National Research Council and Institute of Medicine. The National Academies Press.

Olsson, C. A., Bond, L., Burns, J. M., Vella-Brodrick, D. A., & Sawyer, S. M. (2003). Adolescent resilience: A concept analysis. *Journal of Adolescence, 26,* 1–11. doi:10.1016/S0140-1971(02)00118-5

Pardini, D. A., Loeber, R., Farrington, D. P., & Stouthamer-Loeber, M. (2012). Identifying direct protective factors for nonviolence. *American Journal of Preventive Medicine, 43*(2, Suppl 1), S28–S40.

Pollard, J. A., Hawkins, J. D., & Arthur, M. W. (1999). Risk and protection: Are both necessary to understand diverse behavioral outcomes in adolescence? *Social Work Research, 23,* 145–158.

Puzzanchera, C. (2013). *Juvenile arrests, 2011* (NCJ 244476): Washington DC: U.S. Department of Justice, Office of Juvenile Justice and Delinquency Prevention. Retrieved from http://www.ncjj.org/pdf/Juvenile%20Arrests%20Bulletins/244476.pdf

Romer, D. (2003). Prospects for an integrated approach to adolescent risk reduction. In D. Romer (Ed.), *Reducing adolescent risk: Toward an integrated approach* (pp. 1–9). Thousand Oaks, CA: Sage.

Rossa, M. W. (2002). Some thoughts about resilience versus positive development, main effects, versus interaction effects and the value of resilience. *Child Development, 71,* 567–569. doi:10.1111/1467-8624.00166

Rutter, M. (1979). Protective factors in children's responses to stress and disadvantage. In M. W. Kent & J. E. Rolf (Eds.), *Primary prevention of psychopathology: Vol. 3. Social competence in children* (pp. 49–74). Lebanon, NH: University Press of New England.

Rutter, M. (1987). Psychosocial resilience and protective mechanisms. *American Journal of Orthopsychiatry, 57,* 316–331. doi:10.1111/j.1939-0025.1987.tb03541.x

Rutter, M. (2001). Psychosocial adversity: Risk, resilience, and recovery. In J. M. Richman & M. W. Fraser (Eds.), *The context of youth violence: Resilience, risk, and protection* (pp. 13–41). Westport, CT: Praeger.

Sameroff, A. J. (1999). Ecological perspectives on developmental risk. In J. D. Osofsky & H. E. Fitzgerald (Eds.), *WAIMH handbook of infant mental health: Vol. 4. Infant mental health groups at risk* (pp. 223–248). New York: Wiley.

Sameroff, A. J., Bartko, W. T., Baldwin, A., Baldwin, C., & Siefer, R. (1999). Family and social influences on the development of child competence. In M. Lewis & C. Feiring (Eds.), *Families, risk, and competence* (pp. 161–186). Mahwah, NJ: Lawrence Erlbaum.

Sameroff, A. J., & Fiese, B. H. (2000). Transactional regulation: The developmental ecology of early intervention. In J. P. Shonkoff & S. J. Meisels (Eds.), *Handbook of early childhood intervention* (2nd ed., pp. 135–159). New York: Cambridge University Press.

Sameroff, A. J., & Gutman, L. M. (2004). Contributions of risk research to the design of successful interventions. In P. Allen-Meares & M. W. Fraser (Eds.), *Intervention with children and adolescents: An interdisciplinary approach* (pp. 9–26). Boston: Allyn & Bacon.

Scheier, L. M., & Botvin, G. J. (1998). Relations of social skills, personal competence, and adolescent drug use: A developmental exploratory study. *Journal of Early Adolescence, 18,* 77–114. doi:10.1177/0272431698018001004

Schinke, S., Brounstein, P., & Gardner, S. (2002). *Science-based prevention programs and principles, 2002* (DHHS Pub No. SMA 03–3764). Rockville, MD: Substance Abuse and Mental Health Services Administration.

Sorenson, J. L., Masson, C. L., & Perlman, D. C. (2002). HIV/Hepatitis prevention in drug abuse treatment programs: Guidance from research. *NIDA Science and Practice Perspectives, 1,* 4–12. Washington, DC: National Institute on Drug Abuse.

Spoth, R., Redmond, C., & Shin, C. (1998). Direct and indirect latent variable parenting outcomes of two universal family-focused preventive interventions: Extending a public-health oriented research base. *Journal of Consulting and Clinical Psychology, 66,* 385–399. doi:10.1037/0022-006X.66.2.385

Substance Abuse and Mental Health Administration. (2014). *National registry of effective programs.* Retrieved from http://www.nrepp.samhsa.gov/

Sutherland, E. H. (1973). Development of the theory [Private paper published posthumously]. In K. Schuessler (Ed.), *Edwin Sutherland on analyzing crime* (pp. 13–29). Chicago: University of Chicago Press.

Swanson, J. (2013). Mental illness and new gun law reforms. The promise and peril of crisis-driven policy. *Journal of the American Medical Association, 309,* 1233–1234. doi:10.1001/jama.2013.1113.

Ungar, M. (2011). The social ecology of resilience. Addressing contextual and cultural ambiguity of a nascent construct. *American Journal of Orthopsychiatry, 81,* 1–17. doi: 10.1111/j.1939-0025.2010.01067.x

U.S. Department of Education. (2014). *Indicators of school crime and safety 2013* (NCES 2014-042). Washington, DC: Author. Retrieved from http://nces.ed.gov/pubs2014/2014042.pdf

Vigil, J. D. (1990). Cholos and gangs: Culture change and street youth in Los Angeles. In R. Huff (Ed.), *Gangs in America: Diffusion, diversity, and public policy* (pp. 142–162). Thousand Oaks, CA: Sage.

Vossekuil, B., Fein, R. A., Reddy, M., Borum, R., & Modzeleski, W. (2002). *The final report and findings of the Safe School Initiative: Implications for the prevention of school attacks in the United States.* Washington, DC: U.S. Secret Service and U.S. Department of Education.

Werner, E. E., & Smith, R. S. (1982). *Vulnerable but invincible: A longitudinal study of resilient children and youth.* New York: Adams, Bannister, & Cox.

Werner, E. E., & Smith, R. S. (1992). *Overcoming the odds: High risk children from birth to adulthood.* New York: Cornell University Press.

Werner, E. E., & Smith, R. S. (2001). *Journeys from childhood to the midlife: Risk, resilience, and recovery.* New York: Cornell University Press.

Wike, T. L., & Fraser, M. W. (2009). School shootings: Making sense of the senseless. *Aggression and Violent Behavior, 14,* 162–169. doi: 10.1010/j.avb.2009.01.005

Wilson, S. J., & Lipsey, M. W. (2007). School-based interventions for aggressive and disruptive behavior: Update of a meta-analysis. *American Journal of Preventive Medicine, 33,* S130–S143. doi:10.1016/j.amepre.2007.04.011

Woolf, S. H. (2008). The power of prevention and what it requires. *Journal of the American Medical Association, 299,* 2437–2439. doi:10.1001/jama.299.20.2437

Yoshikawa, H., Aber, J. L., & Beardslee, W. R. (2012). The effects of poverty on the mental, emotional, and behavioral health of children and youth. Implications for prevention. *American Psychologist, 67,* 272–284. doi:10.1037/a0028015.

Youngblade, L. M., Theokas, C., Schulenberg, J., Curry, L., Huang, I., & Novak, M. (2007). Risk and promotive factors in families, schools, and communities: A contextual model of positive youth development in adolescence. *Pediatrics, 119* (Supplement 1), S47–S53. doi: 10.1542/peds.2006-2089H

CHAPTER 2

Antipoverty Policies and Programs for Children and Families

Trina R. Williams Shanks

Sandra K. Danziger

Poverty is acknowledged as a risk factor for many problems experienced by children and youth. Evidence from various disciplines indicates that children growing up in low-income households experience social and health conditions that place them at risk for later academic, employment, and behavioral problems (Conley, 1999; Davis-Kean, 2005; Duncan & Brooks-Gunn, 1997; Guo & Harris, 2000; McLoyd, 1998; Sampson, Morenoff, & Gannon-Rowley, 2002; Williams Shanks & Robinson, 2013). Indeed, the detrimental influence of poverty is apparent in all of the substantive policy areas discussed in this book.

Children are poor because they reside in households and/or communities that are poor. Thus, a principal goal of antipoverty policies is to break the link between poor resources of parents or caregivers and adverse child outcomes. To achieve this goal, some antipoverty policies and programs provide material support to parents. Other antipoverty initiatives offer resources and opportunities directly to children. Evidence suggests that the specific targets of social policy should not be an "either-or" proposition or strategy. That is, studies show that it is important both to support low-income parents and to promote child well-being (Waldfogel, 2006; Waters Boots, Macomber, & Danziger, 2008; Haskins, Garfinkel, & McLanahan, 2014).

In this chapter, we examine risk and protective factors associated with childhood and adolescent poverty. Major income-assistance and income-maintenance policies for children and families are reviewed. Trends in antipoverty policy are noted; particular emphasis is paid to the Great Recession of 2007 to 2009 and its impact on children and families. We conclude with a brief discussion of how American social policies aimed at ameliorating

AUTHORS' NOTE: The authors would like to thank Megan Gilster and Pinghui Wu for their diligent research assistance in preparing this chapter.

childhood poverty compare with approaches in other industrialized countries. Finally, policy and program directives that may help improve the comprehensiveness and integration of services and promote positive outcomes for children and families are identified.

PREVALENCE AND TRENDS IN POVERTY

The debate about the best way to measure poverty is long and ongoing (Blank, 2008; Couch & Pirog, 2010). To bring some unity to the study of poverty, the U.S. Census Bureau in the 1960s established income thresholds based on before-tax cash sources to determine whether a household is officially poor. These thresholds are updated annually. As shown in Figure 2.1, child poverty rates reached a low during the late 1960s to early 1970s. Since then, child poverty rates have fluctuated with periodic increases and decreases. Nearly 23% of all children under the age of 18 lived in poverty in 1993; child poverty declined between 1993 and 2002 but increased in the last decade. By 2012, 22.3% of children lived in poverty. Since 2011, the Census Bureau also has reported an alternate measure, the Supplemental Poverty Measure, which includes the value of noncash benefits for basic needs and subtracts taxes and other expenses. By this measure, 18% of children were poor in 2012 (Short, 2013).

Figure 2.1   Child Poverty Rates in the United States by Race and Ethnicity, 1960–2012

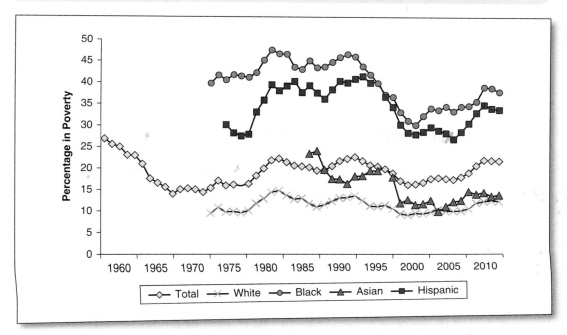

Source: U.S Census Bureau (2012). http://www.census.gov/hhes/www/poverty/data/historical/hstpov3.xls

However, the average poverty rate hides considerable variation by race and ethnicity, as shown in Figure 2.1. Black and Hispanic children continue to be twice as likely to be poor compared with Asian and non-Hispanic White children. As shown in Figure 2.2, children residing in female-headed households experience poverty at four times the rate of all other households. These poverty disparities remain high in the post–Great Recession period.

Figure 2.2   Child Poverty Rates by Household Type, 1960–2012

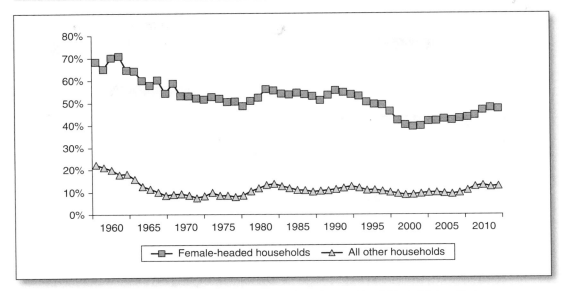

Source: U.S Census Bureau (2012). http://www.census.gov/hhes/www/poverty/data/historical/hstpov10.xls

In spite of the widespread use of the Census Bureau definition and its use of the new measure, the measurement of poverty continues to be debated. Critics charge that the majority of surveys that measure income flows into a household miss an important aspect of a household's financial situation because they fail to consider family assets. For example, a family with housing equity, savings, and investments is in a better situation and has more favorable long-term prospects than a family of equal income but no assets. Although there is no official approach to measuring assets, researchers typically calculate assets by using household net worth (Brandolini, Magri, & Smeeding, 2010; Haveman & Wolff, 2004; Shapiro, Oliver, & Meschede, 2009).

Data reflecting household net worth reveal that racial and ethnic disparities in assets are even greater than disparities in income (Lui, Robles, Leondar-Wright, Brewer, & Adamson, 2006; Oliver & Shapiro, 1995; Shapiro, 2004). As shown in Figure 2.3, Black and Hispanic households at times own about a tenth, respectively, of the median net worth of non-Hispanic White households. Although most households faced declines in net worth after the recession of 2007 to 2009, households of color fared worse and now have less than five cents for every dollar of wealth owned by non-Hispanic White households. Furthermore, as depicted in Figure 2.4, households with children have the lowest levels of net worth. Couples with no children have the most wealth, followed by couples with children, followed by single-parent households with children at a distant third. The situation is even worse when considering financial net worth, which excludes home equity and the value of vehicles. Over half of families with children are asset-poor according to this measure, meaning that they lack sufficient financial assets to sustain the household at the poverty line for three months. In fact, female-headed households with children had asset poverty rates as high as 77% in 2007 (Aratani & Chau, 2010).

Figure 2.3 Median Household Net Worth by Race and Ethnicity, 1983–2010 (in Thousands, 2010 dollars)

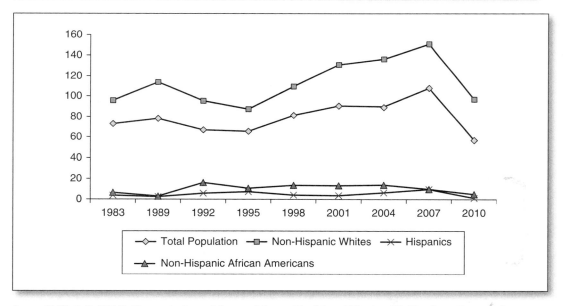

Source: Wolff, E. N. (2012). *The asset price meltdown and the wealth of the middle class* (Working Paper No. 18559). Cambridge, MA: National Bureau of Economics Research.

Another way to think about poverty is at the neighborhood or community level. Neighborhood poverty refers to the spatial concentration of poor households in neighborhoods, which are measured by census tracts. Generally, a poor neighborhood is one in which 20% to 40% of residents live below the poverty line. The concentration of the poor in high-poverty census tracts in the United States increased dramatically between 1970 and 1990. Since that time, as shown in Figure 2.5, the number of people living in poor neighborhoods and the number of poor neighborhoods fell in the first decade and rose again in the 2000s (Jargowsky, 2013).

Figure 2.4 Median Net Worth by Household Types, 1989–2010 (in Thousands, 2010 dollars)

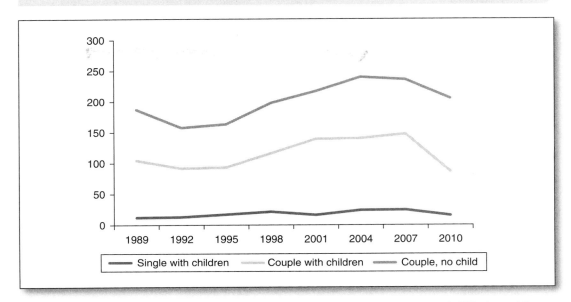

Source: 2010 Survey of Consumer Finances Chart Book. http://www.federalreserve.gov/econresdata/scf/files/2010_SCF_Chartbook.pdf

In the early period, the growing concentration of poverty resulted from two main macroeconomic changes. First, a decline in manufacturing markets negatively impacted inner cities and resulted in an increase in urban poverty rates. Second, factors such as discrimination in the housing and lending markets and rapid suburban development increased racial and socioeconomic segregation such that inner-city neighborhoods became predominantly Black and poor (Jargowsky, 1997; Massey & Denton, 1993). The 1990s were also characterized by an increase in the suburbanization of neighborhood poverty. That is, although poverty declined in all other areas, rates of suburban poverty experienced almost no change (Jargowsky, 2003; Kingsley & Pettit, 2007).

The decline in neighborhood poverty between 1990 and 2000 may be explained by neighborhood fluctuations in moderate, high, and extreme poverty rates (Kingsley & Pettit, 2007) and by decreases in overall poverty caused by the improving economy of the late 1990s (Jargowsky, 2003). Recent evidence suggests that the economic decline since 2000 and especially during the Great Recession has led to a new increase in poverty—both nationally and in isolated neighborhood settings. Suburban poverty has continued to grow, especially in western and Sun Belt states (Kneebone, 2009), and neighborhood poverty has also increased in midwestern cities and suburbs in recent years (Kneebone & Garr, 2010).

People of color experience poverty at much higher rates than Whites; this disparity is most evident among children (Jargowsky, 2003; Sharkey, 2009). Only 1 % of White children

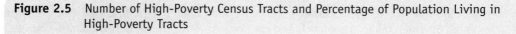

Figure 2.5 Number of High-Poverty Census Tracts and Percentage of Population Living in High-Poverty Tracts

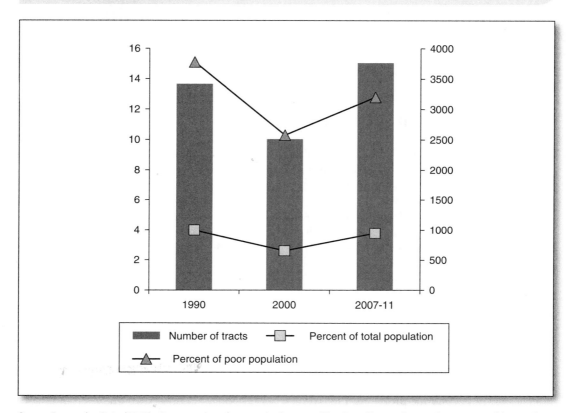

Source: Jargowsky, P. A. (2013). *Concentration of poverty in the new millennium. Changes in prevalence, composition, and location of high poverty neighborhoods.* A Report by the Century Foundation and the Rutgers Center for Urban Research and Education. Retrieved from: http://tcf.org/bookstore/detail/concentration-of-poverty-in-the-new-millennium

born between 1955 and 1970 lived in poor neighborhoods, whereas 29% of Black children born during this time lived in poor neighborhoods at some point in their childhood. About 31% of Black children born between 1985 and 2000 experienced neighborhood poverty (Sharkey, 2009). Inequality and poverty in neighborhood contexts for children expose them to serious risks that often compromise normal and healthy development.

POVERTY, RISK, AND PROTECTION

Poverty stems from interpersonal, social, and environmental factors that occur at all levels of a child's life (Bronfenbrenner, 1979). Figure 2.6 depicts the increasingly wide spheres of influence related to the onset, persistence, and consequences of poverty. Poverty and low income are due in part to economic conditions and policies regarding jobs, housing, and stocks, all of which fell to crisis levels and created economic loss and instability for families and children during the Great Recession (see text box). Clearly, efforts to prevent or reduce poverty should include state and federal policies and programs that target the multiple levels of influence, from socioeconomic conditions to community and family resources. We discuss interpersonal, social, and environmental risk and protective factors associated with poverty in the following section.

INTERPERSONAL AND SOCIAL RISK FACTORS

Material hardships such as food insufficiency, unstable housing, and lack of basic health care are consistently associated with poverty. Material hardship is particularly important because it adversely affects many aspects of child development. In 1999, findings from a national sample of children revealed that 23% of families below the federal poverty level had experienced *food insecurity* (they were unable to afford balanced meals, had to cut the size of meals, or had too little money for food) in the past year (Gershoff, 2003). A 2006 survey revealed that 25% of children in families with income below the poverty level had experienced food insecurity in the past year (Nord, 2009). Since the Great Recession, food insecurity has risen, such that, in 2012, 20% of households with children across the income spectrum were food insecure at some point in the year (Coleman-Jenson, Nord, & Singh, 2013).

Qualitative researchers have detailed the many stressors and negative outcomes experienced by children residing in low-income families that are trying to meet basic needs (Edin & Lein, 1998; Newman, 1999). Parenting practices and behaviors that are created as a result of economic strain and material hardship also indirectly affect children. Conger and colleagues (1991) proposed a family process model that considers the influence of a family's economic problems and parental depression on child and youth development. In this model, a low-income mother's and father's depression is hypothesized to increase marriage hostility and decrease nurturing and involved parenting (Conger et al., 1991; Conger et al., 2002). Studies have also found that material hardship and financial stress are related to low self-esteem, a decreased sense of control over one's life, and feelings of helplessness among parents, which in turn adversely affects their ability to use effective parenting skills (Bradley & Corwyn, 2002; Conger & Donnellan, 2007; Gershoff, Aber, Raver, & Lennon, 2007; McLoyd, 1990, 1998).

Parent and family investment in children's education and development—including educational materials in the home, engagement with school, and facilitation of extracurricular activities—is another way in which poverty influences child development. Mayer found that parental education, attitudes, and behaviors were more important than income in explaining child outcomes, once basic material needs are met (Mayer, 1997). Cognitive stimulation in the home both in terms of the availability of learning materials and parental teaching and conversations is correlated with household income and is predictive of positive educational outcomes and fewer behavior problems (Bradley & Corwyn, 2002, 2003; Guo & Harris, 2000; Shonkoff & Phillips, 2000). A positive home environment is especially important for children's academic growth during the summer, when school resources are not available (Downey, von Hippel, & Broh, 2004; Entwisle & Alexander, 1992). Clearly, poor parents often lack the resources, skills, and opportunities to help their children succeed in school.

Recent findings from investigators interested in promoting asset-based policies suggest that a family's assets offer protection for children, particularly those residing in low-income households (Grinstein-Weiss, Williams Shanks, & Beverly, 2014; Huang, Sherraden, Kim, & Clancy, 2014; Williams Shanks, Kim, Loke, & Destin, 2010). Assets appear to operate as an important protective factor in relation to standardized test scores, school performance, and certain types of antisocial conduct and behaviorial problems (Conley, 1999; Orr, 2003; Williams Shanks, 2007). Equally important, studies have found positive relationships between household assets and children's academic outcomes across racial groups (Williams Shanks & Destin, 2009) and among female-headed households (Zhan, 2006; Zhan & Sherraden, 2003).

Figure 2.6   Circles of Influence on Childhood Family Poverty

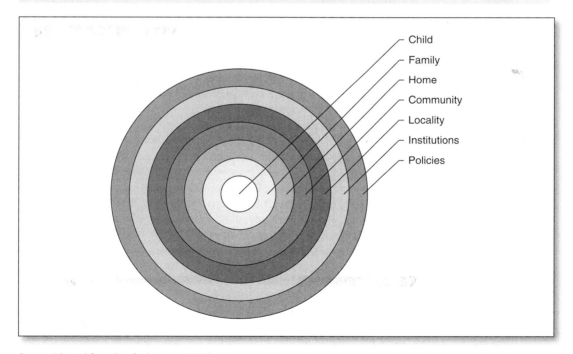

Source: Adapted from Bronfenbrenner (1979).

ENVIRONMENTAL RISKS

Wilson (1987, 2009) suggested that concentrated neighborhood poverty isolates poor residents and limits their exposure to positive role models, employment networks, and community resources. A large body of research has examined the direct and indirect effects of neighborhood poverty on child and adolescent outcomes (Harding, 2003; Hart, Atkins, & Matsuba, 2008; Kling, Ludwig, & Katz, 2005; Leventhal & Brooks-Gunn, 2000; Pachter, Auinger, Palmer, & Weitzman, 2006). Many investigators have emphasized the significant and adverse effects of limited local resources and opportunities on children's development. Poor neighborhoods tend to lack quality institutions and social services (Leventhal & Brooks-Gunn, 2000; Sampson et al., 2002). Children growing up in poor neighborhoods witness frequent acts of violence and experience considerable chaos, disorder, and isolation. In such communities, parental stress and a lack of support services negatively affect developmental outcomes in children and youth (Klebenov, Brooks-Gunn, & Duncan, 1994; Kohen, Leventhal, Dahinten, & McIntosh, 2008; McLoyd, 1998; Patton, Woolley & Hong, 2012; Williams Shanks & Robinson, 2013).

Much research has documented the escalating trend in mass incarceration and its unequal impacts on poor and especially urban communities of color. Loury (2010), for example, noted the "ubiquity" of this experience, reporting that in some neighborhoods, one in five adult men may be behind bars on any given day. According to Clear, having so many young men go in and out of jails and prisons is "a central factor determining the social ecology of poor neighborhoods" (Clear, 2009, p.10). Research has attempted to disentangle the effects of parental incarceration from the effects of other family and community risk factors in terms of the impact on children (e.g., Wildeman and Western, 2010; Wildeman and Turney, 2014). In addition to the impacts of parental incarceration on parent involvement, family resources, and family structure, many poor outcomes for children have been linked to this experience, including future criminality and incarceration, child health, child behaviorial problems associated with mental health and cognitive risks, homelessness, and foster care placement (Wildeman and Western, 2010). The impacts of disproportionate incarceration are also likely felt at the neighborhood, school, and community levels and should be considered when mapping strategies for service intervention to increase support for affected families and to prevent the more deleterious effects on children.

Children and families living in poor neighborhoods are doubly disadvantaged by frequent exposure to numerous interpersonal, social, and environmental risk factors. These factors interact in complex ways and lead to a number of adverse outcomes for children. Youth exposed to neighborhood and household poverty encounter negative influences and antisocial environments that place them at risk for a number of adverse individual and social outcomes. These risks are particularly influential during early childhood (Shonkoff & Phillips, 2000). Policies and programs such as asset building and income support, which target the upstream economic strain of poverty, along with initiatives to enhance parenting skills and home environments, which target the downstream processes of social disadvantage, are necessary to set a course for children to escape poverty. While it is important that interventions take place during early childhood, it is also crucial to develop and sustain policies and programs aimed at reducing risk and fostering resilience across the life course.

ANTIPOVERTY POLICIES AND PROGRAMS

The United States has never instituted a comprehensive federal response to child poverty. In fact, no federal role in cash aid to poor children and families existed prior to 1935; only assistance from state, local, and private charities was available. Even today, with an array of federal antipoverty programs, no policy or program reaches everyone who is eligible, and typically no priority is given to social development or economic mobility (Williams Shanks, 2014). Although critically important to child well-being, we exclude health insurance, medical care, and educational programs because these topics are covered in other chapters. Table 2.1 provides an overview of some of the major federal programs that offer support for the basic needs of low-income children; funding levels for major antipoverty programs between 1960 and 2012 are shown in Figure 2.7.

The first federal welfare program, Aid to Dependent Children, was part of the 1935 Social Security Act. The name of the program changed at midcentury to Aid to Families with Dependent Children (AFDC). The Personal Responsibility and Work Opportunity Reconciliation Act (PRWORA, Public Law No. 104–93), signed by President Bill Clinton in August 1996, ended AFDC's 60-year history and resulted in major changes in the structure of the program and its diminished role as a resource for the poor. Compared with AFDC, the new Temporary Assistance for Needy Families (TANF) plays a smaller role as a resource for families.

Several rules restrict participation in TANF, including lifetime time limits for receipt of benefits and a mandatory work requirement. States are required to impose sanctions in the form of benefit reduction or case closure to families who do not comply with requirements. States can implement diversion programs to deter or deflect applicants from entering the program (e.g., providing a one-time lump-sum payment to families who agree not to seek cash benefits for a set period of time). TANF disallows parents with a drug felony conviction from receiving benefits and requires teenage parents under the age of 18 to live with an adult and attend school as a condition of receiving benefits. New legal immigrants are not allowed to receive means-tested public benefits, including TANF, for the first 5 years after entry (Fix, 2006).

Neither the critics' dire predictions of increased child poverty nor the proponents' rosy forecasts that children would directly benefit from seeing their mothers take jobs came true in the first decade after welfare reform (Danziger, 2010). Studies did not find that welfare leavers had improvements in terms of stress levels and mental health status as they exited the rolls, nor did the lives of children improve as a result of welfare reform and increases in the employment of mothers (Danziger, 2010; Edin & Kissane, 2010).

Welfare reform has dramatically reduced nationwide reliance on cash assistance, even while participation in other antipoverty programs has grown, as shown in Figure 2.7 (Danziger, 2010). Welfare caseloads have fallen precipitously since the mid-1990s and did not increase during the Great Recession (see text box). The failure of the welfare system to respond to increased poverty during the recession raises concern for how single mothers and their children will fare in the coming years.

The food stamp program became the Supplemental Nutrition Assistance Program (SNAP) in 2008 (H.R. 2419, the Food, Conservation, and Energy Act of 2008). SNAP provides food assistance in the form of electronic benefit transfer (EBT) cards, which function like debit cards at retail grocery stores. SNAP program participation increased to an estimated 11% of U.S. households in 2009 (U.S. Department of Agriculture, 2010a). The rise in program participation is associated with the deep recession and the rise in unemployment and poverty. A federal entitlement program, SNAP is open to anyone who is income-eligible and helps to ease the family budget by covering food costs. The average monthly per person benefit in 2009 was $125.31(Food and Nutrition Service, 2009). The maximum monthly benefit for a family of four in 2014 is $632. As shown in Figure 2.7, the rate of participation in SNAP is quite high. However, only 37.9% of low-income (<185% poverty level) children experiencing food insecurity receive SNAP. Similarly, the Special Supplemental Nutrition Program for Women, Infants, and Children (WIC) is a federal food-support program for low-income pregnant and postpartum women and their young children (U.S. Department of Agriculture, 2010b). However, states administer WIC and set the eligibility requirements, and the program is funded through the mechanism of a limited block grant to states rather than as an open-ended entitlement.

An increasingly important addition to antipoverty efforts is the Earned Income Tax Credit (EITC), a refundable tax credit to low-income workers and their families. In 2010, more than 27 million families received income support through the federal EITC. It is estimated that the program lifts 2.5 million children with working parents out of poverty each year (U.S. Department of the Treasury, 2010). For most individuals filing without children, the maximum annual benefit in 2013 was $487, but for a single person with two dependent children, the maximum benefit was $5,372. The maximum allowable income to receive any benefit is just above $51,500 (married filing jointly with three children or more), which is more than 200% of the federal poverty line. Some states and localities also have tax credits for working low-income families that supplement this program (Purmort, 2010). As Figure 2.7 shows, the number of households receiving the EITC began to exceed Temporary Assistance for Needy Families (TANF) participation in the early 1990s, when EITC federal policy expanded. EITC has now outstripped TANF as a source of income support, but it only is available for children with employed parents.

The 1996 Personal Responsibility and Work Opportunity Reconciliation Act (PRWORA) expanded and consolidated federal funding for child care for employed parents into the Child Care and Development Block Grant (CCDBG). Under this act, states are provided flexibility in determining income and work eligibility, structuring the voucher program, and determining which types and standards of care will be reimbursed at what rates. There is consistent evidence that subsidies facilitate employment of low-income and welfare recipient families (Blau & Tekin, 2007; Danziger, Ananat, & Browning, 2004; Bainbridge, Meyers, & Waldfogel, 2003; Meyers, Heintze, & Wolf, 2002; Press, Fagan, & Laughlin, 2006). Between 1997 and 2006, public funding more than doubled from $3.7 billion to $9 billion (U.S. House of Representatives, 2008). During the recession of 2007 to 2009, The American Recovery and Reinvestment Act expanded funds for child-care subsidies and for quality improvements in child-care services. Although the majority of low-income families rely on child care that is developmentally inadequate or minimally adequate (Levine Coley, Li-Grining, & Chase-Lansdale, 2006), it is unclear whether subsidy receipt leads to higher quality care (Antle et al., 2008). Subsidies could be structured to promote use of higher quality care, but the issue of greatest priority is access as only 20% of those who are eligible receive assistance with child care.

Supplemental Security Income (SSI) is a program of the Social Security Administration. Unlike retirement income from social security, which is funded by social security taxes, SSI is funded by general federal tax revenues. Families with children who have a disability are eligible to receive SSI support; in 2010, 15.7% of recipients were under 18 (Social Security Administration, 2010). Eligibility requirements were made more stringent with the passing of PRWORA in 1996. The average monthly benefit for a child recipient (under the age of 18) was $597 in 2010 (Social Security Administration, 2010). Although a relatively high rate of those who qualify are served, many people who are unemployed for long periods because of illness or disability experience long delays in the application and review process (U.S. General Accounting Office, 2009).

The federal government also supports the employment of youth and adults through training and education programs designed to ensure that participants are job-ready. Although job-training programs were originally designed to assist dislocated workers, they became a part of federal antipoverty strategies by the 1960s (LaLonde, 1995). Just as PRWORA shifted the focus of welfare toward "work first," the approach of job-training programs has also shifted toward employment. The Workforce Investment Act of 1998 (WIA) was enacted to replace the Job Training Partnership Act (JTPA), with an emphasis on job placement before training or education (Holzer, 2008). With the changes from JTPA to WIA, substantially fewer low-income youth and adults received training. About 95% of program leavers reported receiving training in JTPA, compared with 68.4% of exiters from WIA in 2003 (Frank & Minoff, 2005).

Federal housing assistance is funded through the U.S. Department of Housing and Urban Development (HUD) and is administered by local housing authorities. It takes two main forms: (1) Section 8 housing vouchers for private units and (2) subsidized public housing units. Both programs serve a small fraction of low-income renters and have long waiting lists of families who have applied for assistance. About half of those served in these programs are families with children. Moreover, 5.6 million eligible households with children experience serious housing needs (Turner & Kingsley, 2008). The character of public housing in the United States has been changing in the last 20 years as a result of efforts such as Moving to Opportunity (MTO) and Hope VI. These initiatives attempt to disperse concentrated neighborhood poverty. Although the goal of the program was to improve outcomes for individuals, the development of new mixed-income housing units decreased the amount of housing generally available to poor residents (Sharkey, 2009). Once again, access has been a key concern, with few eligible households receiving needed assistance.

Finally, a federal program that is not shown in Table 2.1 provides another source of assistance to low-income families and their children. In 1998, the Assets for Independence Act (AFIA) was enacted and funded with $125 million over 5 years. Annual appropriations for the program from 1999 through 2009 have ranged between $10 million and $25 million. The AFI program provides federal funding to support Individual Development Account (IDA) programs at the community level. Paired with local match funding, the program offers incentives for those earning below 200% of the Federal Poverty line to save for a home, pursue higher education, or capitalize a small business. The program is still very small and,

Table 2.1 Characteristics of Current Federal Antipoverty Programs

Program	When Began	Participation (FY 2012)	Percentage of Eligible Served	Eligibility	Purpose (and Site for Further Information)	Discretionary/ Entitlement
Subsidized Housing	1937	2.51 million families[a]	9%[b]	Very low income families. Income limits vary from Housing Authority Area.	Subsidized housing units located in buildings that are publicly managed (i.e., public housing) or privately owned and managed under government contracts. http://portal .hud.gov/portal/page/portal/HUD/ topics/rental_assistance/phprog	Discretionary
Supplemental Nutrition Assistance Program (SNAP)	1964	46.61 million people (2011)[c]	79%[d]	Gross monthly income <130% Federal Poverty level (FPL). Net monthly income <100% FPL.	Provides poor families with assistance purchasing food they need. http://www.fns.usda.gov/snap	Entitlement
Women, Infants, and Children (WIC)	1972	8.91 million women and children[e]	61%[f]	States set income eligibility (between 185% and 100% FPL) and nutrition risk eligibility.	Provides food, health-care referrals, and nutrition education for low-income pregnant and postpartum women and to infants and children up to age 5. http://www.fns.usda .gov/wic	Discretionary
Supplemental Security Income (SSI)	1974	9.18 million people[g]	68%[h]	Age 65 or older, or blind, or disabled and limited income and resources (e.g., monthly income <$674 and resources <$2,000 for a single person).	Income assistance for aged, blind, and disabled people, who have little or no income. http://www .socialsecurity.gov/ssi	Entitlement

Program	When Began	Participation (FY 2012)	Percentage of Eligible Served	Eligibility	Purpose (and Site for Further Information)	Discretionary/ Entitlement
Section 8	1974	2.33 million families[a]	15%[b]	Household income up to 80% of the area median.	A housing vouchers program that allows participants to rent privately owned residences from participating owners. Renters pay 30% of family income toward housing costs. http://portal.hud.gov/portal/page/portal/HUD/topics/rental_assistance http://portal.hud.gov/portal/page/portal/HUD/topics/housing_choice_voucher_program_section_8	Discretionary
Earned Income Tax Credit (EITC)	1975	27 million households[i]	79%[j]	Income limits based on family size (e.g., <$48,279 for married filing jointly with 3+ children).	A refundable tax credit to low-income workers (especially targeted at those with qualifying, dependent children). http://www.eitc.irs.gov	Entitlement
Hope VI	1993	See Subsidized Housing.	See Subsidized Housing.	Current residents of public housing are affected/new housing is open to those residents, other low income, and moderate income families.	Redevelopment of large-scale public housing sites to create mixed income housing in order to deconcentrate poverty. http://www.hud.gov/hopevi	Discretionary
Child Care and Development Block Grant (CCDBG)	1996	1.50 million children in 0.9 million families[k]	20%[l]	States determine income and work status eligibility.	Child care vouchers provided to families who choose the type of care (including formal centers, family care homes, relative care, and care by nonrelatives).	Discretionary

(Continued)

35

Table 2.1 (Continued)

Program	When Began	Participation (FY 2012)	Percentage of Eligible Served	Eligibility	Purpose (and Site for Further Information)	Discretionary/ Entitlement
Temporary Assistance to Needy Families (TANF)	1996	4.02 million people[m]	40%[h]	States determine eligibility of families with children.	Cash assistance with a work requirement. Five-year limited term of lifetime federal assistance. http://www.doleta.gov/programs/	Discretionary
Workforce Investment (WIA)	1998	1.23 million exiters (in 2008)[n]	Not Available	Adults, dislocated workers, and youth aged 14 to 21 who face employment challenges and are primarily low income.	Job search and placement assistance and labor market information ("core" services) then career counseling and assessment ("intensive" services) before job training or education. http://www.doleta.gov/programs/	Discretionary

a. U.S. Department of Housing and Urban Development (2012) http://www.huduser.org/portal/datasets/picture/yearlydata.html#data-display-tab

b. Turner & Kingsley (2008).

c. U.S. Department of Agriculture (2012). http://www.fns.usda.gov/pd/SNAPsummary.htm

d. U.S. Department of Agriculture (2011). http://www.fns.usda.gov/sites/default/files/Reaching2011_Summary.pdf

e. U.S. Department of Agriculture (2012). http://www.fns.usda.gov/pd/wisummary.htm

f. U.S. Department of Agriculture (2009). http://www.fns.usda.gov/sites/default/files/WICEligibles2000-2009Summary_0.pdf

g. Social Security Administration (2012). http://www.ssa.gov/policy/docs/statcomps/ssi_asr/2012/ssi_asr12.pdf

h. Waters Boots (2010).

i. Internal Revenue Service (2012). http://www.eitc.irs.gov/EITC-Central/eitcstats

j. Internal Revenue Service (2010). http://www.eitc.irs.gov/EITC-Central/Participation-Rate

k. U.S Department of Health and Human Services (2012). http://www.acf.hhs.gov/programs/occ/resource/fy-2012-ccdf-data-tables-preliminary-table-1

l. U.S. House of Representatives (2008).

m. U.S. Department of Health and Human Services (2012). https://www.acf.hhs.gov/sites/default/files/ofa/2012trec_tan.pdf?nocache-135895977

n. Social Policy Research Associates (2010).

over the first decade of its existence, has supported the opening of fewer than 100,000 accounts. However, AFI provides an example of a policy that intentionally seeks to improve the long-term economic condition of low- to moderate-income households (U.S. Department of Health and Human Services, 2010; Williams Shanks, 2014).

Another way to think about the degree to which social policy assists children and families is to compare child poverty in the United States with that in other industrialized countries. The U.S. child poverty rate is more than four times higher than rates in such European countries as Sweden, Norway, Finland, and Denmark (Lindsey, 2004; Rainwater & Smeeding, 2003a, 2003b). The low child-poverty rates in these nations are realized not because earnings are higher but because a large proportion of children are being lifted from poverty through government intervention (Rainwater & Smeeding, 2003a). The reduction in child poverty resulting from governmental programs and income transfers in the United States is less than 25%, compared with more than 75% in Sweden and Norway (Lindsey, 2004; Rainwater & Smeeding, 2003a, 2003b).

In sum, a variety of antipoverty programs provide assistance through cash, food support, tax credits, childcare, workforce development, and housing. However, despite all of these programs, many eligible low-income at-risk families are not served. In some cases,

Figure 2.7   Federal Antipoverty Program Participation, 1965 to 2012

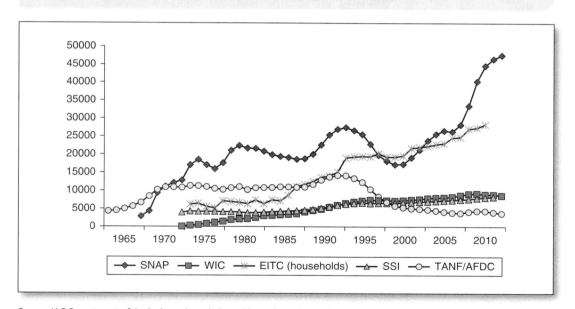

Source: U.S Department of Agriculture (2012). http://www.fns.usda.gov/pd/SNAPsummary.htm; U.S Department of Agriculture (2012). http://www.fns.usda.gov/pd/wisummary.htm; Tax Policy Center (2012). http://www.taxpolicycenter .org/taxfacts/displayafact.cfm?DocID=37&Topic2id=40&Topic3id=42; Social Security Administration (2012). http://www .ssa.gov/policy/docs/statcomps/supplement/2013/7a.html#table7.a9; Social Security Administration (2005–2013). http:// www.ssa.gov/policy/docs/statcomps/supplement/

mothers with work requirements may be able to increase earnings through employment but subsequently risk losing eligibility for other forms of assistance, resulting in little aggregate benefit in terms of poverty status (Currie, 2006). Moreover, when parents are required to work outside the home, parental well-being may not improve and children actually may receive less attention. Indeed, there could be an increase in the number of poorly supervised or unsupervised, latchkey children and little reduction in family poverty. There are many gaps in the existing safety net, particularly when viewed from the broader goal of improving outcomes for children and youth.

Impacts of the Great Recession of 2007 to 2009 on Children and Youth

The Great Recession of 2007 to 2009 was the most severe economic crisis in the U.S. since the 1930s. During these 18 to 24 months, incomes declined by an average of 8%, the number of jobs declined by 6%, and unemployment peaked at 10% (Danziger, 2013). Housing and stock prices collapsed, creating widespread residential instability, declining wealth, and wider racial and ethnic disparities in income (Danziger, 2013). According to the Bureau of Labor Statistics, the percentage of parents with children age 18 years of age or under who were employed (the employment:population ratio) fell from 79% in 2001 to 74% in 2010; it recovered to only 75% by 2013.

Estimates of extreme poverty among households with children have been even more alarming. Shaefer and Edin (2013) found a significant increase in families with children living on $2 a day per person or less. The authors reported that by "mid-2011, 1.65 million households with 3.55 million children were living in extreme poverty in a given month . . . constituting 4.3 percent of all nonelderly households with children" (p. 265). This reflects a 159% increase since 1996, but, when taking into consideration the receipt of public food assistance, housing subsidies, and tax credit, the growth in extreme poverty since 2007 has been 50%. Shaefer and Edin (2013) argued that the disappearance of the cash safety net, slow economic growth during the 2000s, and major job losses of the Great Recession are contributing to the growing population of children who experience spells of little to no family income.

Many studies have examined the direct and indirect effects of the Great Recession on family economic loss, material hardship and stress, and parent and child well-being (e.g., Ananat, Gassman-Pines, Francis, & Gibson-Davis, 2013; Leininger & Kalil, 2014). Sudden and large drops in income, home foreclosures, and general housing instability have increased debt and spending cutbacks since the recession. Many indicators of child well-being, from health to child behavior to cognitive skills, may be adversely affected by these economic shocks. Furthermore, parents with severe economic loss and instability tend to live in poor and jobless communities characterized by low-quality early childhood education and inadequate public schools. The combination of low income, difficult living conditions, and poor-quality education significantly increases risk for adverse outcomes during childhood and adolescence.

Economic factors are especially harmful during infancy. Johnson and Schoeni (2007) used data from the *Panel Study of Income Dynamics* to analyze the impact of early life experiences on later behavior. They found that poor health at birth *and* limited parental resources (including low income, lack of health insurance, and unwanted pregnancy) interfered with cognitive development and health outcomes in childhood, led to reduced educational attainment during adolescence, and led to worse labor-market and health outcomes in adulthood. These effects suggest that socioeconomic factors have both immediate and long-term negative effects on the lives of young people.

Studies of the recession are raising long-term danger signs. Ananat and colleagues (2013) found that variation in a state's job losses among adults were related to the state's average math scores. This relationship was strong even when the findings for students whose parents lost jobs were compared with those for students whose parents remained employed. The authors showed that the recent economic recession affected all students, not just those whose parents had lost jobs. Children were also affected by job losses among family friends and neighbors and by resulting changes to their communities and classrooms. Leininger and Kalil (2014) used data from the *Michigan Recession and Recovery Study*, a random survey of households in the three-county Metropolitan Detroit Area in 2009 to 2011, to examine the effect of parental economic strain and perceived financial worries on childhood behaviorial problems. The authors found that financial strain was significantly related to internalizing behavior problems among White children. In contrast, the relationship between financial strain and internalizing behaviors among Black children was of small magnitude and was not significant once objective measures of economic hardship were considered.

Research also illustrates the positive impacts of having an economic safety net before and/or during the recent recession. For example, Short (2013) found that 18% of children who were 18 years of age or younger were poor in 2010. She estimated that this rate would have increased by four percentage points had the Earned Income Tax Credit (EITC) not been in place at the time. Short also suggested that food assistance through SNAP and housing subsidies and school-lunch participation reduced poverty by several percentage points. She concluded by noting that poverty would decline if more people had access to antipoverty programs.

Analysts from the Center on Budget and Policy Priorities examined the effects of the expansion of safety net programs (e.g., child tax credit, EITC, food stamps, and unemployment) that were included in the American Recovery and Reinvestment Act of 2009 (ARRA) (Sherman, 2011). They found that, in 2011, 9 million poor children were lifted out of poverty when these benefits were considered. However, while the official child poverty rate increased from 18% to 22% during the Great Recession, evidence suggests that income from these programs helped keep this increase from being even higher (Sherman, 2011). This finding suggests that the increase in child poverty was partially offset by supports found in the ARRA. Unfortunately, these supports expired at the end of the recent recession.

Many analysts question the decision not to expand effective safety net programs during difficult economic conditions. They argue against policies that promote budget cuts to programs for families hit hardest by the recession. Furthermore, beyond poverty reduction and lessening the exposure to poverty, new studies point to beneficial outcomes for high-risk children who live in communities with

(Continued)

(Continued)

available safety net services. In a recent paper, Almond and colleagues (Almond, Hoynes, & Schanzenbach, 2011) found positive long-term impacts on adult health and economic well-being for high-risk infants born in counties where the early Food Stamp program had begun compared with those born in areas where the federal program had not yet started. Using data from the *Panel Study of Income Dynamics* and administrative data, the authors found that exposure to the program before the age of 5 years led to greater long-term economic self-sufficiency and lower risk for diabetes and heart disease. Findings such as these suggest that cutbacks in safety net programs could have long-term adverse consequences for children.

USING KNOWLEDGE OF RISK, PROTECTION, AND RESILIENCE TO ACHIEVE SERVICE INTEGRATION

In recent years, investigators and policy officials have begun to promote positive social development as a means to ameliorate childhood poverty. Such a focus represents an alternative to emphasizing the relationship between poverty and adverse child outcomes in policies and programs. Sen (1993, 1999) suggested that a person's functional capabilities and the freedom to attain what is valued for one's own welfare should form the basis of antipoverty policies and programs. Similarly, Sherraden (1991) argued that income-support policies provide an important safety net but are insufficient for long-term growth and development. He suggested that helping low-income households build tangible financial assets can lead to positive changes in self-efficacy and civic participation and to improvements in child well-being (Sherraden, 2005). Sherraden's work suggests that the accumulation of resources in the form of savings and assets promotes investment for long-term security either by increasing human capital or by anticipating future circumstances (e.g., expanding a business or planning for retirement). Although there has been experimentation at the local and state levels to incorporate these social-development and asset-building ideas, they currently receive very little federal expenditure. Yet, demonstration projects and local initiatives that promote social mobility and increase economic security for vulnerable children and households are receiving greater attention and are contributing to policy conversations (Cramer & Williams Shanks, 2014).

Integrated and systems-level interventions represent one important approach to preventing and ameliorating childhood poverty. Systems-level approaches focus on better coordination across service sectors. Thus, rather than creating public policies composed of separate streams of money to address particular needs or problems, a systems approach argues for a comprehensive community-change strategy that addresses the full array of problems facing families. One cross-system policy and program example that has received considerable attention recently is the Harlem Children's Zone (HCZ) in New York City (Tough, 2008). In the HCZ, Geoffrey Canada and colleagues have developed an array of community programs and educational innovations (including two charter schools) in a 97-block area of Harlem. Services are designed to support children and families in a meta-phorical "conveyor belt" from birth to college (Tough, 2008). Specific interventions include parenting classes in *The Baby College,* pre-kindergarten instruction in *Harlem Gems,* and an array of afterschool, health, college-preparatory, employment-training, and substance-abuse programs and services. Initial evidence shows that children who are enrolled in the HCZ schools have better attendance, more time in classroom instruction, and better achievement scores in math and English than those who are not enrolled (Dobbie & Fryer, 2009; Tough, 2008). Although it is hard to disentangle school and community effects, HCZ intentionally bundled a high-quality school experience with complementary wrap-around services to improve achievement and reduce gaps that have traditionally existed between low-income minority children and their better-off peers (Dobbie & Fryer, 2009). In 2010, the federal government launched a Promise Neighborhood initiative based on the HCZ model. As of 2012, Promise Neighborhood planning and implementation grants have been given to communities in 20 states and the District of Columbia (U.S. Department of Education, 2014).

Others have created and supported similar comprehensive community-building strate-gies. For example, the Annie E. Casey Foundation has funded a series of neighborhood-change initiatives aimed at childhood poverty, including the Rebuilding Communities and Making Connections programs (Annie E. Casey Foundation, 2010). The Skillman Foundation has launched comprehensive community-building initiatives in six local neighborhoods in Detroit through its Good Neighborhoods Initiative (Skillman Foundation, 2010). Efforts to assess and evaluate these long-term comprehensive change projects face major research challenges (Kubisch et al., 2002; Stone, 1996). Although much has been learned, no clear blueprint for how to successfully make low-income communities safe and healthy places for children has emerged.

In a similar vein, some also argue for greater expansion of programs with a two-generation approach that offer comprehensive services simultaneously for adults and their young children. Such programs seek to encourage human capital in the same family across gen-erations by combining education or job training for low-income parents and early child-hood education for their young children (Chase-Lansdale & Brooks-Gunn, 2014). One strategy is to offer high-quality early-childhood education based on proven models. A second approach is to provide comprehensive education and employment services that eventually lead to family-supporting wages for parents along with appropriate guidance and support. The idea is to increase the likelihood of a quality learning-focused environ-ment for children both at school and at home as well as to provide parental resources so that participating families avoid many of the stressors typically encountered by children living in poverty (Chase-Lansdale & Brooks-Gunn, 2014).

Another promising approach to promoting positive development among low-income youth incorporates an asset-building strategy to establish a child development account (CDA) system (Elliott, 2012; Goldberg, 2005; Williams Shanks et al., 2010). The vision is that every child from birth gets a subsidized account in her or his own name with an initial deposit that also matches additional savings. The deposit is intended to provide a founda-tion for family financial capability and tangible resources that can be invested in a child's future. A primary use of the account is initially to save for college or postsecondary education. However, money also could be used for other purposes in early adulthood. The intent of this strategy is to provide young people with resources to support whatever choices might help them build personal capabilities and get started in life, regardless of their parents' financial situation. An example of this approach, the Saving for Education, Entrepreneurship, and Downpayment (SEED) initiative, has been tested in the United States (Center for Social Development, 2010), and similar programs are beginning to emerge at the state and municipal levels (Cramer, Black, and King, 2014).

The concept of child development accounts has already been established as policy internationally. In the United Kingdom, the Child Trust Fund (CTF) has provided a certificate for at least £250 to the parents of every baby born in the country, with additional funds offered to the parents of low-income children (Child Trust Fund, 2010). Parents use these certificates to open an account on their child's behalf, which can grow tax-exempt until the child reaches age 18. The U.K. government imposes no restrictions on use once a child reaches 18 but plans to offer financial information and counseling within schools as part of its national education curriculum. When the program launched in 2005, it opened 3 million CTFs. In 2007, about one quarter of these accounts received additional contributions beyond the initial government deposit (Bennett, Chávez Quezada, Lawton, & Perun, 2008). With a change in government in 2010, the U.K. no longer guarantees an initial deposit for these CTFs, but children with existing accounts are allowed to keep them.

Singapore has introduced child development accounts that can be used for preschool and other education- or health-related expenses from birth to age 6 (Loke & Sherraden, 2007). The government has also created the Post-Secondary Education Account (PSEA) to cover approved education-related expenses between the ages of 7 and 20. Unused balances from the child accounts can roll over to a child's PSEA, and unused balances from PSEAs can be rolled over to the adult child's Central Provident Fund. Thus, Singapore essentially has a lifelong system of accounts to help its citizens build assets and meet personal and financial goals (Loke & Cramer, 2009). These examples may provide important lessons to policymakers in the United States.

SUMMARY

This chapter has provided evidence that income poverty, asset poverty, and neighborhood poverty, alone and in combination, are associated with profound disadvantages for children and families, particularly since the Great Recession of 2007 to 2009. From our review, it is also apparent that existing antipoverty policies and programs in the United States, although providing crucial supports to many, are not sufficient to lift large numbers of children out of poverty or to greatly shift developmental outcomes for poor children. However, if the will and resources to make systemic change could be found, a variety of programs, including comprehensive community-change and asset-building strategies, are showing promise.

To realize long-term success in breaking the link between household poverty and child well-being, a few observations can be made. A "family security approach"—like that called for by Waters Boots et al. (2008)—is crucial in that multiple generations within a family and multiple levels of influence must be targeted concomitantly. No single program is likely to be enough. Although the most concrete issue for a family may be insufficient income, "fixing" income-support policies alone might not take us far enough along in a risk and protection framework. We have seen the failure of the current array of antipoverty programs to reach and respond to those experiencing poverty and economic shocks. Families with children, especially those headed by young single women, undoubtedly could use better-designed cash assistance and financial help with housing, child care, food, and job training to make ends meet. However, to prevent a lifetime of poverty and dead-end jobs, a host of other resources—education, parenting support, services to provide children with a nurturing home environment, and high-quality early child care—are needed. Given that families may experience spells in and out of poverty throughout the life course, it would be strategic to assist parents of young children, both women and men, to increase their educational attainment and plan a better life for themselves and for their children. Work-related support services and training might be part of a broader goal to improve long-term outcomes for entire families.

Finally, American antipoverty policies and programs have failed to reduce racial and ethnic inequities in income, wealth, and neighborhood poverty. Income and, indeed, health disparities by race and ethnicity have not narrowed over time (see Chapter 6). This situation warrants targeted supports and interventions for diverse communities at highest risk, particularly Hispanic-origin and Black families. Benchmarks for a successful policy approach would be both improved outcomes for poor children and decline in racial and ethnic disparities.

QUESTIONS FOR DISCUSSION

1. What risk and protective factors are associated with poverty?

2. Some experts point to income inequality itself as a cause of poor child-development outcomes. What are the relative advantages and potential disadvantages of focusing policy attention on reducing poverty (i.e., income inequality) versus assisting children and families in need?

3. How do current public-assistance programs target supports for low-income families with children? What are their limitations from a risk and resilience framework?

4. What new social-development and system-level approaches have been developed to prevent or reduce poverty? How do these approaches aim to break the link between poverty and child well-being?

5. How has the Great Recession of 2007 to 2009 affected the number of poor children and families in the United States?

6. What impacts did safety net programs have on children and families affected by poverty during the years of the recession?

7. How much can government and community-based partners do for families in need? What is the role of personal, parental, and community responsibility in antipoverty policies and programs?

REFERENCES

Almond, D., Hoynes, H. & Schanzenbach, D.W. (2011) Inside the war on poverty: The impact of the food stamp program on birth outcomes. *Review of Economics and Statistics 93*(2): 387–403.

Ananat, E.O., Gassman-Pines, A., Francis, D. and Gibson-Davis, C. (2013). *Children left behind: The effects of statewide job loss on student achievement.* NBER Working Papers.

Annie E. Casey Foundation. (2010). *Helping vulnerable kids and families succeed.* Retrieved from http://www.aecf.org

Antle, B., Frey, A., Barbee, A., Frey, S., Grisham-Brown, J., & Cox, M. (2008). Child care subsidy and program quality revisited. *Early Education and Development, 19,* 560–573.

Aratani, Y. & Chau, M. (2010). *Asset poverty and debt among families with children.* New York: National Center for Children in Poverty, Columbia University.

Bainbridge, J., Meyers, M. K., & Waldfogel, J. (2003). Child care policy reform and the employment of single mothers. *Social Science Quarterly, 84,* 771–791. doi:10.1046/j.0038–4941.2003.08404002.x

Bennett, J., Chávez Quezada, E., Lawton, K., & Perun, P. (2008). *The U.K. Child Trust Fund: A successful launch.* London: Institute for Public Policy Research and Aspen Institute.

Blank, R. M. (2008). Presidential address: How to improve poverty measurement in the United States. *Journal of Policy Analysis and Management, 27,* 233–254. doi:10.1002/pam.20323

Blau, D., & Tekin, E. (2007). The determinants and consequences of child care subsidies for single mothers in the USA. *Journal of Population Economics, 20,* 719–741. doi:10.1007/s00148–005–0022–2

Bradley, R. H., & Corwyn, R. F. (2002). Socioeconomic status and child development. *Annual Review of Psychology, 53,* 371–399. doi:10.1146/annurev.psych.53.100901.135233

Bradley, R. H., & Corwyn, R. F. (2003). Age and ethnic variations in family process mediators of SES. In M. H. Bornstein & R. H. Bradley (Eds.), *Socioeconomic status, parenting, and child development* (pp. 161–188). New York: Lawrence Erlbaum.

Brandolini, A., Magri, S., & Smeeding, T. M. (2010). Asset-based measurement of poverty. *Journal of Policy Analysis and Management, 29*(2), 267–284. doi:10.1002/pam.20491

Bronfenbrenner, U. (1979). *The ecology of human development.* Cambridge, MA: Harvard University Press.

Center for Social Development, Washington University in St. Louis. (2010). *Saving for Education, Entrepreneurship, and Downpayment national initiative.* Retrieved from http://csd.wustl.edu/AssetBuilding/SEED

Chase-Lansdale, P. L., & Brooks-Gunn, J. (2014). Two-generation programs in the twenty-first century. *The Future of Children, 24*(1), 13–39.

Child Trust Fund. (2010). *About the child trust fund.* Retrieved from http://www.childtrustfund.gov.uk

Clear, T. R. (2009). *Imprisoning communities: How mass incarceration makes disadvantaged neighborhoods worse.* New York: Oxford University Press.

Coleman-Jensen, A., Nord, M., & Singh, A. (2013). *Household food security in the United States in 2012.* (ERR-155). Washington, D.C.: U.S. Department of Agriculture, Economic Research Service. http://www.ers.usda.gov/media/1183208/err-155.pdf

Conger, R. D., & Donnellan, M. B. (2007). An interactionist perspective on the socioeconomic context of human development. *Annual Review of Psychology, 58,* 175–199. doi:10.1146/annurev.psych.58.110405.085551

Conger, R. D., Lorenz, F. O., Elder, G. H., Jr., Melby, J. N., Simons, R. L., & Conger, K. J. (1991). A process model of family economic pressure and early adolescent alcohol use. *The Journal of Early Adolescence, 11*(4), 430–449. doi:10.1177/0272431691114003

Conger, R. D., Wallace, L. E., Sun, Y., Simons, R. L., McLoyd, V. C., & Brody, G. H. (2002). Economic pressure in African American families: A replication and extension of the family stress model. *Developmental Psychology, 38*(2), 179–193. doi:10.1037/0012-1649.38.2.179

Conley, D. (1999). *Being Black, living in the red: Race, wealth, and social policy in America.* Berkeley: University of California Press.

Couch, K. A., & Pirog, M. A. (2010). Poverty measurement in the U.S., Europe, and developing countries. *Journal of Policy Analysis and Management, 29*(2), 217–226. doi:10.1002/pam.20488

Cramer, R. Black, R. & King, J. (2014). *Children's savings accounts: Research, practice, and implications for policy design.* Washington, DC: New America Foundation.

Cramer, R. & Williams Shanks, T. R. (2014). *The assets perspective: The rise of asset building and its impact on social policy.* New York, NY: Palgrave Macmillan.

Currie, J. M. (2006). *The invisible safety net: Protecting the nation's poor children and families.* Princeton, NJ: Princeton Univ. Press.

Danziger, S. (2013). Evaluating the effects of the Great Recession. *Annals of the American Academy of Political and Social Science, 650,* 6–24.

Danziger, S. K. (2010). The decline of cash welfare and implications for social policy and poverty. *Annual Review of Sociology, 36,* 523–545. doi:10.1146/annurev.soc.012809.102644

Danziger, S. K., Ananat, E., & Browning, K. (2004). Child care subsidies and the transition from welfare to work. *Family Relation, 53,* 219–228.

Davis-Kean, P. E. (2005). The influence of parent education and family income on child achievement: The indirect role of parental expectations and the home environment. *Journal of Family Psychology, 19*(2), 294–304. doi:10.1037/0893-3200.19.2.294

Dobbie, W., & Fryer, R. G. (2009). *Are high quality schools enough to close the achievement gap? Evidence from a social experiment in Harlem* (NBER Working Paper 15473). Cambridge, MA: National Bureau of Economic Research.

Downey, D. B., von Hippel, P. T., & Broh, B. A. (2004). Are schools the great equalizer? Cognitive inequality during the summer months and the school year. *American Sociological Review, 69*(5), 613–635. doi:10.1177/000312240406900501

Duncan, G. J., & Brooks-Gunn, J. (Eds.). (1997). *Consequences of growing up poor.* New York: Russell Sage Foundation.

Edin, K. and Kissane, R. J. (2010), Poverty and the American family: A decade in review. *Journal of Marriage and Family, 72:* 460–479. doi: 10.1111/j.1741-3737.2010.00713.x

Edin, K., & Lein, L. (1998). The private safety net: The role of charitable organizations in the lives of the poor. *Housing Policy Debate, 9*(3), 541–573.

Elliott, W. (2012). *Ideas for refining children's savings account proposals.* Washington, D.C.: New America Foundation & Center for Social Development.

Entwisle, D. R., & Alexander, K. L. (1992). Summer setback: Race, poverty, school composition, and mathematics achievement in the first two years of school. *American Sociological Review, 57*(1), 72–84. doi:10.2307/2096145

Fix, M. (2006). *Immigrants' costs and contributions: The effects of reform.* Washington, DC: Migration Policy Institute.

Food and Nutrition Service. (2009). *Characteristics of supplementary assistance program households: Fiscal year 2008* (No. SNAP-09-CHAR). Washington, DC: United States Department of Agriculture.

Frank, A., & Minoff, E. (2005, December 14). *Declining share of adults receiving training under WIA are low-income or disadvantaged.* Washington, DC: Center for Law and Social Policy.

Gershoff, E. T. (2003). *Low income and hardship among America's kindergarteners in living at the edge* (Research Brief No. 3). New York: National Center for Children in Poverty.

Gershoff, E. T., Aber, J. L., Raver, C. C., & Lennon, M. C. (2007). Income is not enough: Incorporating material hardship into models of income associations with parenting and child development. *Child Development, 78,* 70–95. doi:10.1111/j.1467–8624.2007.00986.x

Goldberg, F. (2005). The universal piggy bank: Designing and implementing a system of savings accounts for children. In M. Sherraden (Ed.), *Inclusion in the American dream* (pp. 303–322). Oxford, UK: Oxford University Press.

Grinstein-Weiss, M., Williams Shanks, T.R. & Beverly, S. (2014). Family assets and child outcomes: Evidence and directions. *Future of Children, 24*(1), pp.147–170.

Guo, G., & Harris, K. M. (2000). The mechanisms mediating the effects of poverty on children's intellectual development. *Demography, 37*(4), 431–447. doi:10.1353/dem.2000.0005

Harding, D. J. (2003). Counterfactual models of neighborhood effects: The effect of neighborhood poverty on dropping out and teenage pregnancy. *American Journal of Sociology, 109*(3), 676–719. doi:10.1086/379217

Hart, D., Atkins, R., & Matsuba, M. K. (2008). The association of neighborhood poverty with personality change in childhood. *Journal of Personality and Social Psychology, 94,* 1048–1061.

Haskins, R., Garfinkel, I., & McLanahan, S. (2014). Introduction: Two-generation mechanisms of child development. *The Future of Children, 24*(1), 3–12.

Haveman, R. H., & Wolff, E. N. (2004). The concept and measurement of asset poverty: Levels, trends and composition for the U.S., 1983–2001. *Journal of Economic Inequality, 2,* 145–169. doi:10.1007/s10888–005–4387–y

Holzer, H. J. (2008). *Workforce development and the disadvantaged: New directions for 2009 and beyond* (Brief No. 7). Washington, DC: The Urban Institute.

Huang, J., Sherraden, M., Kim, Y., & Clancy, M. (2014). Effects of child development accounts on early social-emotional development: An experimental test. *JAMA Pediatrics, 168*(3), 265–271. doi:10.1001/jamapediatrics.2013.4643.

Jargowsky, P. A. (1997). *Poverty and place: Ghettos, barrios, and the American city.* New York: Russell Sage Foundation.

Jargowsky, P. A. (2003). *Stunning progress, hidden problems: The dramatic decline in concentrated poverty in the 1990s.* Washington, DC: The Brookings Institution.

Jargowsky, P. A. (2013). *Concentration of poverty in the new millennium. Changes in prevalence, composition, and location of high poverty neighborhoods.* A Report by the Century Foundation and the Rutgers Center for Urban Research and Education. Retrieved from: http://tcf.org/bookstore/detail/concentration-of-poverty-in-the-new-millennium

Johnson, R.C., & Schoeni, R. F. (2007). *The influence of early-life events on human capital, health status, and labor market outcomes over the life course.* PSC Research Report No. 07-616.

Kingsley, G. T., & Pettit, K. L. S. (2007). *Concentrated poverty: Dynamics of change* (Neighborhood Change in Urban America No. 5). Washington, DC: Urban Institute.

Klebanov, P. K., Brooks-Gunn, J., & Duncan, G. J. (1994). Does neighborhood and family poverty affect mothers' parenting, mental health, and social support? *Journal of Marriage and Family, 56*(2), 441–455. doi:10.2307/353111

Kling, J. R., Ludwig, J., & Katz, L. F. (2005). Neighborhood effects on crime for female and male youth: Evidence from a randomized housing voucher experiment. *Quarterly Journal of Economics, 120,* 87–130.

Kneebone, E. (2009). *The suburbanization of American poverty* (Metropolitan Opportunity Series No. 2). Washington, DC: The Brookings Institution.

Kneebone, E., & Garr, E. (2010). *The suburbanization of poverty: Trends in metropolitan America, 2000 to 2008* (Metropolitan Opportunity Series No. 3). Washington, DC: The Brookings Institution.

Kohen, D. E., Leventhal, T., Dahinten, V. S., & McIntosh, C. N. (2008). Neighborhood disadvantage: Pathways of effects for young children. *Child Development, 79*(1), 156–169. doi:10.1111/j .1467–8624.2007.01117.x

Kubisch, A. C., Auspos, P., Brown, P., Chaskin, R., Fulbright-Anderson, K., & Hamilton, R. (2002). *Voices from the field II: Reflections on comprehensive community change.* Washington, DC: Aspen Institute.

LaLonde, R. J. (1995). The promise of public sector–sponsored training programs. *The Journal of Economic Perspectives, 9*(2), 149–168.

Leininger, L., & Kalil, A. (2014). Parents' financial strain and children's behavior problems in the aftermath of the Great Recession. *Journal of Marriage and the Family, 76 (October)*, 998–1010. doi:10.1111/jomf.12140.

Leventhal, T., & Brooks-Gunn, J. (2000). The neighborhoods they live in: The effects of neighborhood residence on child and adolescent outcomes. *Psychological Bulletin, 126*(2), 309–337. doi:10.1037/0033–2909.126.2.309

Levine Coley, R., Li-Grining, C. P., & Chase-Lansdale, P. L. (2006). Low-income families' child care experiences: Meeting the needs of children and families. In N. J. Cabrera, R. Hutchens, & H. E. Peters (Eds.), *From welfare to child care* (pp. 149–170). Mahwah, NJ: Lawrence Erlbaum.

Lindsey, D. (2004). *The welfare of children.* New York: Oxford University Press.

Loke, V., & Cramer, R. (2009). *Singapore's Central Provident Fund: A national policy of life-long asset accounts.* Washington, DC: New America Foundation.

Loke, V., & Sherraden, M. (2007). *Building children's assets in Singapore: The Post-Secondary Education Account policy* (CSD Policy Brief 07–36). St. Louis, MO: Center for Social Development.

Loury, G.C. (2010). Crime, inequality and social justice. *Daedalus 139.3*, 134–140, 146.

Lui, M., Robles, B., Leondar-Wright, B., Brewer, R., & Adamson, R. (2006). *The color of wealth: The story behind the U.S. racial wealth divide.* New York: New Press.

Massey, D. S., & Denton, N. A. (1993). *American apartheid: Segregation and the making of the underclass.* Cambridge, MA: Harvard University Press.

Mayer, S. E. (1997). *What money can't buy: Family income and children's life chances.* Cambridge, MA: Harvard University Press.

McLoyd, V. C. (1990). The impact of economic hardship on Black families and children: Psychological distress, parenting, and socioemotional development. *Child Development, 61*, 311–346. doi:10.2307/1131096

McLoyd, V. C. (1998). Socioeconomic disadvantage and child development. *American Psychologist, 53*, 185–204. doi:10.1037/0003–066X.53.2.185

Meyers, M. K., Heintze, T., & Wolf, D. A. (2002). Child care subsidies and the employment of welfare recipients. *Demography, 39*, 165–179. doi:10.1353/dem.2002.0008

Newman, K. S. (1999). *No shame in my game: The working poor in the inner city.* New York: Russell Sage Foundation.

Nord, M. (2009). *Food insecurity in households with children: Prevalence, severity, and household characteristics* (Economic Information Bulletin No. 56). Washington, DC: United States Department of Agriculture Economic Research Service.

Oliver, M. L., & Shapiro, T. M. (1995). *Black wealth/White wealth: A new perspective on racial inequality.* New York: Routledge.

Orr, A. (2003). Black–White differences in achievement: The importance of wealth. *Sociology of Education, 76*(4), 281–304.

Pachter, L. M., Auinger, P., Palmer, R., & Weitzman, M. (2006). Do parenting and the home environment, maternal depression, neighborhood, and chronic poverty affect child behavioral problems differently in different racial-ethnic groups? *Pediatrics, 117*, 1329–1338.

Patton, D.U., Woolley, M.E. & Hong, J. (2012). Exposure to violence, student fear, and low academic achievement: African American males in the critical transition to high school. *Children and Youth Services Review, 34,* 388–395.

Press, J., Fagan, J., & Laughlin, L. (2006). Taking pressure off families: Child-care subsidies lessen mothers' work-hour problems. *Journal of Marriage and Family, 68,* 155–171. doi:10.1111/j.1741-3737 .2006.00240.x

Purmort, J. (2010). *Making work supports work: A picture of low wage workers in America.* New York: National Center for Children in Poverty.

Rainwater, L., & Smeeding, T. M. (2003a). Doing poorly: U.S. child poverty in cross-national context. *Children, Youth and Environments, 13.* Retrieved from http://colorado.edu/journals/cye

Rainwater, L., & Smeeding, T. M. (2003b). *Poor kids in a rich country: America's children in comparative perspective.* New York: Russell Sage Foundation.

Sampson, R. J., Morenoff, J. D., & Gannon-Rowley, T. (2002). Assessing "neighborhood effects": Social processes and new directions in research. *Annual Review of Sociology, 28,* 443–478. doi:10.1146/ annurev.soc.28.110601.141114

Sen, A. (1993). Capability and well-being. In M. Nussbaum & A. Sen (Eds.), *The quality of life* (pp. 30–53). Oxford, UK: Clarendon Press. doi:10.1093/0198287976.003.0003

Sen, A. (1999). *Development as freedom.* New York: Knopf.

Shaefer, H.L. & Edin, K. (2013). Rising extreme poverty in the United States and the response of federal means-tested transfer programs. *Social Service Review, 87*(2), 250–268.

Shapiro, T. M. (2004). *The hidden cost of being African American: How wealth perpetuates inequality.* New York: Oxford University Press.

Shapiro, T. M., Oliver, M. L., & Meschede, T. (2009). *The Asset Security and Opportunity Index.* Waltham, MA: Brandeis University.

Sharkey, P. (2009). *Neighborhoods and the Black–White mobility gap.* Washington, DC: Pew Charitable Trusts.

Sherman, A. (2011). *Poverty and financial stress would have been substantially worse in 2010 without government action.* Washington, D.C. Center on Budget and Policy Priorities

Sherraden, M. (2005). Assets and public policy. In M. Sherraden (Ed.), *Inclusion in the American dream: Assets, poverty, and public policy* (pp. 3–19). Oxford, UK: Oxford University Press.

Sherraden, M. W. (1991). *Assets and the poor: A new American welfare policy.* Armonk, NY: M. E. Sharpe.

Shonkoff, J. P., & Phillips, D. A. (2000). *From neurons to neighborhoods: The science of early childhood development.* Washington, DC: National Academies Press.

Short, K. (2013). *The Research Supplemental Poverty Measure 2012.* U.S. Census Bureau Current Population Reports P-60 247

Skillman Foundation (2010). *About the Skillman Foundation.* Retrieved from www.skillman.org

Social Policy Research Associates. (2010). *PY 2008 WIASRD data book* (Project No. 1382). Washington, DC: U.S. Department of Labor, Office of Performance Technology, Employment and Training Administration.

Social Security Administration. (2010). *Monthly statistical snapshot, May 2010.* Retrieved from http:// www.socialsecurity.gov/policy/docs/quickfacts/stat_ snapshot/#table3

Stone, R. (1996). *Core issues in comprehensive community-building initiatives.* Chicago: Chapin Hall.

Tough, P. (2008). *Whatever it takes: Geoffrey Canada's quest to change Harlem and America.* New York: Houghton Mifflin.

Turner, M. A., & Kingsley, G. T. (2008). *Federal programs for addressing low-income housing needs: A policy primer.* Washington, DC: The Urban Institute.

U.S. Department of Agriculture. (2010a). *Supplemental nutrition assistance program*. Retrieved from http://www.fns.usda.gov/snap

U.S. Department of Agriculture. (2010b). *Women, infants and children program*. Retrieved from http://www.fns.usda.gov/wic/

U.S. Department of Education (2014). *Promise Neighborhoods*. Retrieved from http://www2.ed.gov/programs/promiseneighborhoods

U.S. Department of Health and Human Services. Administration for Children and Families. Office of Community Services. 2010. *Assets for Independence Program: Status at the conclusion of the tenth year*. Report to Congress.

U.S. Department of the Treasury. (2010). *The earned income tax credit*. Retrieved from http://www.eitc.irs.gov

U.S. General Accounting Office. (2009). *Social Security Administration: Further actions needed to address disability claims and service delivery challenges* (GAO 09–511T). Washington, DC: U.S. Government Printing Office.

U.S. House of Representatives. (2008). Background material and data on the programs within the jurisdiction of the Committee on Ways and Means. *2008 Green Book*. Washington, DC: Government Printing Office. Retrieved from http://waysandmeans.house.gov/singlepages.aspx?NewsID = 10490

Waldfogel, J. (2006). *What children need*. Cambridge MA: Harvard University Press.

Waters Boots, S. (2010). *Improving access to public benefits: Helping eligible individuals and families get the income supports they need*. Baltimore: The Ford Foundation, Open Society Institute, and Annie E. Casey Foundation.

Waters Boots, S., Macomber, J., & Danziger, A. (2008). *Family security: Supporting parents' employment and children's development* (New Safety Net Paper No. 3). Washington, DC: Urban Institute.

Wildeman, C., & Western, B. (2010). Incarceration in fragile families. *The Future of Children 20* (2), 187–177.

Wildeman, C., & Turney, K. (2014). Positive, negative, or null? The effects of maternal incarceration on children's behavioral problems. *Demography* doi:10.1007/s13524-014-0291-z

Williams Shanks, T. R. (2007). The impact of household wealth on child development. *Journal of Poverty, 11*(2), 93–116. doi:10.1300/J134v11n02_05

Williams Shanks, T. R. (2014). The evolution of anti-poverty policies and programs. In R. Cramer & T. R. Williams Shanks (Eds). *The Assets Perspective: The Rise of Asset Building and its Impact on Social Policy* (p. 13–31). New York, NY: Palgrave Macmillan.

Williams Shanks, T. R., & Destin, M. (2009). Parental expectations and educational outcomes for young African American adults: Do household assets matter? *Journal of Race and Social Problems, 1*(1), 27–35. doi:10.1007/s12552-009-9001-7

Williams Shanks, T. R., Kim, Y., Loke, V., & Destin, M. (2010). Assets and child well-being in developed countries. *Children and Youth Services Review*. doi:10.1016/j.childyouth.2010.03.011

Williams Shanks, T. R. & Robinson, C. (2013). Assets, economic opportunity and toxic stress: A framework for understanding child and educational outcomes. *Economics of Education Review,33,*154–170. http://dx.doi.org/ 10.1016/j.econedurev.2012.11.002.

Wilson, W. J. (1987). *The truly disadvantaged: The inner city, the underclass, and public policy*. Chicago: University of Chicago Press.

Wilson, W. J. (2009). *More than just race: Being Black and poor in the inner city*. New York: W. W. Norton.

Wolff, E. N. (2012). *The asset price meltdown and the wealth of the middle class* (Working Paper No. 18559). Cambridge, MA: National Bureau of Economics Research.

Zhan, M. (2006). Assets, parental expectations and involvement, and children's educational performance. *Children and Youth Services Review, 28*(8), 961–975. doi:10.1016/j.childyouth.2005.10.008

Zhan, M., & Sherraden, M. (2003). Assets, expectations, and children's educational achievement in female-headed households. *Social Service Review, 77*(2), 191–211. doi:10.1086/373905

ADDITIONAL READING

Bane, M. J., & Zenteno, R. (Eds.). (2009). *Poverty and poverty alleviation strategies in North America.* Cambridge, MA: Harvard University Press.

Cancian, M., & Danziger, S. (Eds.). (2009). *Changing poverty.* New York: Russell Sage Foundation.

Cramer, R. & Williams Shanks, T.R. (2014). *The assets perspective: The rise of asset building and its impact on social policy.* New York, NY: Palgrave Macmillan.

Currie, J. M. (2006). *The invisible safety net: Protecting the nation's poor children and families.* Princeton, NJ: Princeton University Press.

Lindsey, D. (2004). *The welfare of children.* New York: Oxford University Press.

Sherraden, M. (Ed.). (2005). *Inclusion in the American dream: Assets, poverty, and public policy.* Oxford, UK: Oxford University Press.

Tough, P. (2008). *Whatever it takes: Geoffrey Canada's quest to change Harlem and America.* New York: Houghton Mifflin.

Waldfogel, J. (2006). *What children need.* Cambridge MA: Harvard University Press.

WEB-BASED RESOURCES

Center for Social Development, George Warren Brown School of Social Work, Washington University in St. Louis, http://csd.wustl.edu

Institute for Research on Poverty, University of Wisconsin–Madison, http://www.irp.wisc.edu/

National Center for Children in Poverty, http://www.nccp.org/

National Poverty Center, Gerald R. Ford School of Public Policy, University of Michigan, http://www.npc.umich.edu/

CHAPTER 3

Child Welfare Policies and Programs

Peter J. Pecora

Markell Harrison-Jackson

PURPOSE AND OVERVIEW OF CHILD WELFARE POLICY

The child welfare system provides a variety of child and family social services. About 3.4 million referrals for alleged maltreatment were reported to U.S. child protection services in 2012 (U.S. Department of Health and Human Services [DHHS], 2013a). Compared with 1990, this is a profound increase in the number of children being referred as victims of maltreatment.[1] Notwithstanding these long-term increases, there is some evidence that both reporting and incidence rates of child maltreatment have decreased significantly over the past ten years (Finkelhor & Jones, 2006; Sedlak et al., 2010; U.S. DHHSa).

For the analyses included in a recent report from the National Center on Child Abuse and Neglect Data System, a perpetrator is the person who is responsible for the abuse or neglect of a child. In 2012, 80.3% of perpetrators of child maltreatment were parents, and another 6.1% were other relatives of the victim. Of the perpetrators who were parents, 88.5% were the biological parent of the victim. Women are slightly more likely than men to be perpetrators, accounting for 53.5% of perpetrators. And approximately four out of five perpetrators (82.2%) were between the ages of 18 and 44 years (U.S. DHHS, 2013a).

AUTHORS' NOTE: This chapter draws from material in the third edition of *The Child Welfare Challenge*. We appreciate the advice from that textbook's co-authors, James Whittaker, Anthony Maluccio, Richard Barth, Diane DePanfilis, and Robert Plotnick. Special thanks to the policy staff of the American Public Human Services Association and Child Welfare League of America for the policy briefs and position statements that informed the legislative policy section. Finally, foster care alumni, practitioners, and foster parents have taught us much about the real impacts of policy; we appreciate the time they have devoted to improving the child welfare system.

In the United States during 2012, about 399,546 children were in out-of-home protective placements in foster care and nonfamily settings, and 748,000 children were served by child welfare agencies[2] (see Table 3.1). Overall, the number of children in placement rose steadily between 1980 and 2000. However, as a result of changes in public policies and programs, the number of children in out-of-home care has slowly decreased since 2000 (U.S. DHHS, 2013b, 2013c). This decline in out-of-home care is likely due also to decreases in the incidence rates of child maltreatment in some communities (Sedlak et al., 2010).

Child maltreatment is clearly a major social and health problem. The purpose of this chapter is to describe public policies in the field of child welfare. In this field, public policymakers, practitioners, and scholars are working to devise new ways to deal with maltreatment. Indeed, new resources and ideas are reshaping child welfare practices across the country. Notably, agencies in Florida, Illinois, and New York City are making successful efforts to reduce children's lengths of stay in out-of-home care, to reduce the level of restrictiveness of child placements, and to increase the proportion of children placed with kin who are not blood relatives. In addition, the number of children being adopted or securing a permanent placement through guardianship has increased over the last two decades because some states have substantially decreased the time to adoption (Avery, 1998; U.S. DHHS, 2003a, 2013c).

These innovations may expand further with new initiatives designed to reduce time in care and increase permanency. These initiatives include child welfare demonstration waivers,[3] "permanency roundtables,"[4] expedited adoptive parent assessments, expedited approvals of subsidy applications, increased judicial personnel, and heightened attention by the agencies and courts to the need for more timely permanency planning. Although the child welfare system is burdened, professionals, families, and advocates across the country are experimenting with new policies and procedures designed to find safe and enduring living arrangements for children.

In this chapter, we review risk and protective factors related to the reasons that children and their families become involved in the child welfare system, as well as the major social policies that are directed toward these families. In addition, we examine the ways in which the concepts of risk and protection are implemented in those policies. Drawing from innovative projects and programs across the country, we conclude with a discussion of current policy issues and recommendations for improving child welfare services.

MISSION AND GOALS OF CHILD WELFARE SERVICES

Early childhood development, neuroscience, and epigenetic research are underscoring the importance of communities paying careful attention to nurturing children via supporting the adults raising them (Biglan, Flay, Embry, & Sandler, 2012). Developmentally, maltreatment often results in delayed physical growth, neurological damage, and mental and emotional/psychological problems, such as violent behavior, depression, and posttraumatic stress disorder. Research has shown that maltreatment is positively associated with a variety of social and health problems, including substance abuse, eating disorders, obesity, depression, suicide, and sexual promiscuity in transition to adulthood

Table 3.1   Children in America: Selected Facts and Figures

National Child Demographics	
Child population 0–17 years old in 2012 in the United States	77,844,222[a]
Racial/ethnic diversity of children 0–17 years old in the United States in 2013[b]	
• White	52.4%
• Black or African American	13.8%
• American Indian & Alaska Native	0.9%
• Asian	4.6%
• Hispanic or Latino	24.1%
• Native Hawaiian & Other Pacific Islander	0.2%
• Two or more races	4.0%
Who Cared for America's Children?	
Estimated number of "stay-at-home" parents (2012 data):	
• Mothers	Mothers: 5 million (about 24%)[c]
• Fathers	Fathers: 189,000 in 2012 (<1%)
(*Note.* Nearly 2 million fathers (16%) were stay-at-home fathers if they had children under 18.)[d]	
Percentage of children living with one parent varied by race and origin (2012 data): (*Note.* The presence of a cohabitating partner ranged from 0.9% to 3.6% in single-parent households.)[e]	
• All children	24.9%
• Asian children	12%
• White non-Hispanic children	19.9%
• Hispanic (any race) children	27.5%
• Black children	52.1%
Importance of Grandparents (2012 data):	
• Number of multigenerational households where a grandparent is living with at least one grandchild and possibly their son or daughter	3.726 million[f]
• Percent of multigenerational households that were below 100% of poverty (compared with 12% percent of all family households)	19%[f]

(Continued)

Table 3.1 (Continued)

• Number of children under age 18 living with a grandparent	7.38 million[g]
• Percent of all children living in a household that included a grandparent	10%[g]
• Percent of children living with a grandparent that had no parent present	20%[h]
The Most Vulnerable Families With Children?	
Number of people in poverty in 2012	46.5 million people[i]
Percentage of population living in poverty in 2012	15.1%[i]
National poverty rate for children under the age of 18 years in 2013	21.8%[i]
Real median household income for families with and without children in 2012	$51,017[j]
Number of referrals for possible child abuse or neglect in 2013	3.4 million[k]
Number of children substantiated or indicated as abused or neglected in 2012	678,810[k]
Number of children who died as a result of abuse or neglect in 2012	1,593[k]
Number of children in foster care on September 30, 2012	463,000[l]
Number of children adopted from the public foster care system during the fiscal year ending September 30, 2012	51,229[l]
Number of children waiting to be adopted from the public foster care system as of September 30, 2012	102,000[m]

a. Vespa, J., Lewis, J. M., & Kreider, R.M. (2013). *America's families and living arrangements: 2012 population characteristics.* (Current Population Reports, P20-570). Washington, D.C.: U.S. Department of Commerce Economics and Statistics Administration, U.S. Census Bureau. Retrieved July 1, 2014 from http://www.census.gov/prod/2013pubs/p20-570.pdf.

b. The terms used to describe racial/ethnic groups are those used by the U.S. Census Bureau. See Federal Interagency Forum on Child and Family Statistics (2014). *America's children: Key national indicators of well-being, 2013* (Pop 3 Excel table). Washington, D.C.: Retrieved September 30 , 2014 from: http://www.childstats.gov/americaschildren/glance.asp.

c. Vespa et al. (2013), p. 28.

d. U.S. Census Bureau. (2013). *Father's Day: June 16, 2013.* Part of the Profile America, Facts for Features series. Retrieved July 1, 2014 from http://www.census.gov/newsroom/releases/archives/facts_for_features_special_editions/cb13-ff13.html. Also see: Livingtson, G. (2013). *Growing number of dads home with the kids.* Washington, D.C.: Pew Research Center. Retrieved July 3, 2014. http://www.pewsocialtrends.org/2014/06/05/growing-number-of-dads-home-with-the-kids/. The Pew Foundation survey is based on fathers who are 18 to 69 years of age and have their own (biological, adopted, or step) children less than 18 years of age in the household. Fathers who are living apart from all of their children are not included. "Stay-at-home fathers" were not employed at all in the year prior to the survey, while "working fathers" were considered to be those who worked for pay in the prior year.

e. Vespa et al. (2013). See more at: http://www.childtrends.org/?indicators=family-structure#sthash.m6vTpoKS.dpuf.

f. Grandparents are a major caregiver group. See Vespa et al. (2013), p.8.

g. Source: America's Families and Living Arrangements (2012), Table C4. Retrieved July 7, 2014 from https://www.census .gov/hhes/families/data/cps2012C.html. For a concise factsheet on grandparents as child caregivers, see http:// kidshaverightsblog.org/2013/07/31/us-census-bureau-facts-figures-grandparents-as-caregivers-links/.

h. U.S. Census Bureau. (2013). *About three in four parents living with children are married, Census Bureau reports.* http:// www.census.gov/newsroom/releases/archives/families_households/cb13-199.html. Note that children in nonparental care were 2.7 times as likely as children living with two biological parents to have had at least one of the adverse childhood experiences assessed in National Survey of Child Health. See Bramlett, M. D., & Radel, L F. (2014). *Adverse family experiences among children in nonparental care, 2011–2012.* National Health Statistics Report, 74 (May), p. 4. Retrieved July 7, 2014, from http://www.cdc.gov/nchs/data/nhsr/nhsr074.pdf.

i. U.S. Census Bureau. (2013). *Poverty.* Retrieved July 7, 2014, from http://www.census.gov/hhes/www/poverty/about/ overview/. The data presented here are from the Current Population Survey (CPS), 2013 Annual Social and Economic Supplement (ASEC), the source of official poverty estimates. The CPS ASEC is a sample survey of approximately 100,000 household nationwide. These data reflect conditions in calendar year 2012.

j. DeNavas-Walt, C., Proctor, B.D., & Smith, J.C. (2013). *Income, poverty, and health insurance coverage in the United States: 2012.* Washington, D.C.: U.S. Census Bureau, (P60-245), p. 7. Retrieved July 7, 2014, from http://www.census.gov/ prod/2013pubs/p60-245.pdf. Recently, Diana Pearce has been working to replace the current poverty line measure with an "Index of Economic Self-Sufficiency Standard" that has been used to justify raising the minimum wage and as an outcome indicator for various income assistance programs. See http://www.selfsufficiencystandard.org/standard.html.

k. U.S. Department of Health and Human Services, Administration for Children and Families, Administration on Children, Youth and Families, Children's Bureau. (2013a). *Child maltreatment 2012.* Available from http://www.acf.hhs.gov/programs/ cb/research-data-technology/statistics-research/childmaltreatment.

l. U.S. Department of Health and Human Services, Administration for Children and Families, Children's Bureau (2013b). *The AFCARS report–preliminary FY 2012 estimates as of July 2013 (No.20).* Washington, D.C.: U.S. Department of Health and Human Services. Retrieved May 27, 2014, from http://www.acf.hhs.gov/programs/cb/resource/afcars-report-20.

m. U.S. Department of Health and Human Services, Administration for Children and Families, Children's Bureau. (2013c). *Trends in foster care and adoption—FY 2002-FY 2012.* Washington DC: Author, p. 1. Retrieved May 27, 2014, from http://www.acf.hhs.gov/programs/cb/resource/trends-in-foster-care-and-adoption.

(e.g., Kendall-Tackett, 2013). Thus, child maltreatment is a costly problem, with detrimental consequences that follow the initial trauma of neglect or abuse and continue throughout development to adult emotional and physical adaptation. According to some research, foster care expenditures in the past decade for child maltreatment alone totaled $14.4 billion (Wang & Holton, 2008).

Recently, a somewhat broader framework for child welfare has emerged, and, in the interest of protecting and nurturing of children, greater emphasis is being placed on communities as a whole. Consistent with this expanded frame of reference, child welfare agencies have increased their efforts to form a broader "child welfare system" in which employers as well as mental-health, education, health-care, and other entities form collaborative community strategies aimed at preventing and responding to child abuse and neglect. Child welfare agencies have begun to look beyond the parent–child dyad, considering what is known about the interplay of risk and protective factors at the levels of the child, parent, family, neighborhood, and community. Although children have highly individual needs and characteristics, they are viewed as living in the context of a family structure. In turn, families are viewed as embedded in the context of a culture and a neighborhood. Finally, neighborhoods are seen as clustered in the context of social, economic, cultural, and political environments. Thus, as a field, child welfare has come to embrace a multisystem and ecological perspective.

A child welfare system that fails to incorporate and draw on the richness and strength embodied in this contextual view of what produces family well-being cannot effectively respond to the needs of vulnerable children and troubled families. Although agency mission statements provide the guiding structure for service, it is essential that key goals and outcomes are specified to embrace such functions as establishing strategic plans, using evidence-based programs, securing adequate funding, and implementing practice guidelines within a context that promotes child safety and supports families (American Humane Association, 1998).

A key issue affecting the field is the lack of common procedures for describing and classifying child maltreatment. The definitions of abuse and neglect vary across states. Researchers have tried to address the problem, using data to define maltreatment in terms of severity, incidence, chronicity, extent, type, age of onset, and perpetrator (Barnett, Manly, & Cicchetti, 1993; Hanson, Smith, Saunders, Swenson, & Conrad, 1995; Pecora et al., 2010). Notwithstanding, the field lacks a common definition of child maltreatment. To be sure, there are similarities in state definitions, so that policymakers and others who collect data across states can develop commonalties among the different types of maltreatment (Pecora et al., 2009; U.S. DHHS, 2013a). However, no single, comprehensive, definitive breakdown of maltreatment types and combinations of abuse unifies either research or public policy.

In short, the field of child welfare lacks a common nomenclature for describing and classifying a child's maltreatment experience. A substantial number of children and adolescents entering and exiting foster care placement are known to have emotional, psychological, and cognitive developmental delays as compared with their peers who are in non-foster care placements (Griffin et al., 2012; Haskins, Wulczyn, & Webb, 2007; Stahmer et al., 2005; Webb, Dowd, Jones-Harden, Landsverk, & Testa, 2010). Recently, there has been a growing consensus across states about the fundamental experiences that place children at risk and the procedures that should be used to assess incidents of maltreatment (Chahine, Pecora, & Sanders, 2013).

Key Goals and Outcomes for Child Welfare Services

In spite of foundational disagreements on the definition of maltreatment, the field of child welfare services is gaining clarity and consensus about its primary mission. A primary goal and two secondary goals for child welfare services have emerged with widespread support. First and foremost, the primary goal is to protect children from harm. The second goal, which is focused on child permanency, is to preserve existing family units, including birth, relative, and adoptive families, as appropriate. The third goal is to promote children's development as adults who can live independently and contribute to their communities. This last goal may require a variety of permanency planning alternatives such as family reunification, placement with relatives, different forms of guardianship (depending on local law), adoption, and intentionally planned kinship care with legal safeguards such as guardianship (Pecora et al., 2009; U.S. DHHS, 2003a).

Currently, a challenging and controversial issue facing the child welfare system is the disproportionate number of children of color in foster care placements. Of the 101,719 U.S. children awaiting adoption in 2012, nearly 26% (26,117) were Black and 23% (23,243) were Hispanic (U.S. DHHS, 2013b). In fact, 50% of the foster care population (220,331 children) comprises children of color (i.e., African American/Black, Latino/Hispanic, Asian, and Native American/Indigenous), and some of these children will remain in foster care placements until they are emancipated at age 18 (U.S. DHHS, 2013b; Wulczyn, Hislop, & Chen, 2007). Furthermore, African American children currently represent 26% of the children placed in out-of-home care nationwide (U.S. DHHS, 2013b), which is significantly higher than the percentage of African American children in the general population (14%) (O'Hare, 2011, p. 7).

There is some debate in the field about making child safety a goal superior to family support. Indeed, many family advocates and some researchers have argued that without a simultaneous emphasis on child safety *and* family support, neither goal will be achieved in an equitable manner. Similarly, the capacity of the system to support families and promote positive developmental outcomes for children in custody has been the subject of much criticism and debate (Berrick, Needell, Barth, & Johnson-Reid, 1998; Wulczyn, Barth, Yuan, Jones-Harden, & Landsverk, 2005). The key components of each of these major goals (also called *outcome domains*) are summarized next.

Safety of Children

Maltreatment has a detrimental impact on the cognitive, emotional, and physical development of children. Thus, a core goal for child welfare services is keeping children safe from child abuse and neglect. This goal includes children living with their birth families, children reunited with their families after a maltreatment event, and children placed in out-of-home care when parental custody has been terminated because of maltreatment. In terms of concrete outcomes, the public policies that support child welfare services are intended (a) to prevent children from being maltreated and (b) to keep families safely together, including families that may be functioning at a minimum standard of parenting. Child welfare workers operate on the philosophical basis that all children have a right to live in a safe environment that is free from abuse and neglect. For example, the focus of child protective services should be to deliver services that are preventive, nonpunitive, and geared toward parental rehabilitation through identification and treatment of the factors that underlie maltreatment.

At the most general level, there is consensus regarding the mission of child protection: Services should be designed to protect children from maltreatment committed by their parents or other caretakers. However, in translating this broad mandate into policy and practice, the consensus breaks down in a variety of areas, such as defining what constitutes child abuse or neglect, establishing standards for agency intervention, and specifying what constitutes a minimum standard of parenting (popularized by the question, "What is a good enough parent?"). In the face of this widespread disagreement, child welfare is a policy and practice area that is benefitting from recent research on risk and protective factors in child development.

Permanency: Preserving Families and Creating Permanent Homes for Children

When the state steps in to protect an abused or neglected child, it is not enough to keep the child safe; the state must also consider the child's needs for permanent and stable family ties. In addition to protecting a child, the state should ensure that the child has the opportunity to be brought up by stable and legally secure permanent families, rather than in temporary foster care under the supervision of the state. This principle has been well established in federal law: first by the Adoption Assistance and Child Welfare Act of 1980, and then by the Adoption and Safe Families Act of 1997.

Child and Family Well-Being: Meeting Developmental Needs

Achieving child well-being means not only that a child is safe from child abuse or neglect but also that a child's basic needs are being met and that the child is provided with the opportunity to grow and develop in an environment with consistent nurture, support, and stimulation. In this goal area, we include the need for children to develop a healthy sense of identity; an understanding of their ethnic heritage; and skills for coping with racism, sexism, homophobia, and other forms of discrimination that remain prevalent in our society. Although there are limits to what child welfare services can provide, the system should promote standards of parenting that, at a minimum, will provide a child with the developmental opportunities and emotional nurturance needed to grow into an adult who can live as independently as possible.

Child well-being is related ipso facto to family well-being. Achieving child well-being means that families must have the capacity to care for children and to fulfill children's basic developmental, health, educational, social, cultural, spiritual, and housing needs. Ensuring family well-being also implies that child welfare staff members have responsibility for locating these essential services and supports and for helping to sustain or promote parents in their child-rearing roles.

System Goals Define Outcome Domains

Each of these goals is related to outcome domains, albeit imperfectly, by federal outcome standards as shown in Table 3.2. A report from the U.S. General Accounting Office (2004) proposed the first set of federal outcomes set as benchmarks for the performance of state-level child welfare systems:

> In addition to the on-site review of individual cases, it is against these benchmarks for statewide data indicators that a state is measured. Any state whose performance is found to fall short of substantial conformity (based upon data analysis and an on-site review of individual cases) is given an opportunity to develop and implement a plan to improve performance and avoid the withholding of federal funds. Finally, AFSA [The Adoption and Safe Families Act] also required HHS to prepare and submit to Congress an annual report on the performance of each state on each outcome measure. (McDonald, Salyers, & Shaver, 2004, p. 5)

Using these indicators during a child and family services review, a review team assesses a state's performance by collecting data on (a) seven outcomes in the domains of safety, permanency, and child and family well-being; and (b) seven systemic factors that affect outcomes for children and families. To measure a state's achievement of the outcomes, the review team assesses items (via onsite review) or items and data indicators (via onsite review plus statewide assessment). To measure achievement of the systemic factors, the review team assesses items to determine whether the systemic factors are in place and functioning satisfactorily. The items or data indicators associated with the outcomes and systemic factors are listed in Table 3.2. The numerical performance standards can be found in Appendix H of the federal Child and Family Services Review manual: http://www.acf.hhs.gov/programs/cb/cwmonitoring/tools_guide/.

Across states, these review benchmarks and performance measurement methods have stimulated helpful introspection and discussion. However, many experts have continued to advocate for additional refinement (e.g., National Coalition for Child Protection Reform, 2008; Testa & Poertner, 2010; Wulczyn, Orlebeke, & Haight, 2009). In fact, the U.S. Children's Bureau has issued new standards and in some cases new ways of calculating performance that should be finalized by 2015. (See CFSR federal register announcement at http://www.acf.hhs.gov/programs/cb/resource/cfsr-federal-register-notice.)

Table 3.2 National Child and Family Service Review Standards for Child Welfare: Nonsystemic Standards

Standard	Description
Safety	Safety Outcome 1: Children are protected from abuse and neglect. • Timeliness of initiating investigations of reports of child maltreatment (Item 1) • Repeat maltreatment (Item 2) • Absence of recurrence of maltreatment (data indicator) • Absence of maltreatment of children in foster care (data indicator)
	Safety Outcome 2: Children are safely maintained in their homes whenever possible and appropriate. • Services to family to protect child(ren) in home and prevent removal or re-entry into foster care (Item 3) • Risk assessment and safety management (Item 4)
Permanency	Permanency Outcome 1: Children have permanency and stability in their living situations. • Foster care re-entries (Item 5) • Stability of foster care placement (Item 6) • Permanency goal for child (Item 7) • Reunification, guardianship, or permanent placement with relatives (Item 8) • Adoption (Item 9) • Other planned permanent living arrangement (Item 10) • Timeliness and permanency of reunifications (Permanency Composite 1) • Timeliness of adoptions (Permanency Composite 2) • Achieving permanency for children in foster care (Permanency Composite 3) • Placement stability (Permanency Composite 4)

(Continued)

Table 3.2 (Continued)

	Permanency Outcome 2: The continuity of family relationships and connections is preserved for children. • Proximity of foster care placement (Item 11) • Placement with siblings (Item 12) • Visiting with parents and siblings in foster care (Item 13) • Preserving connections (Item 14) • Relative placement (Item 15) • Relationship of child in care with parents (Item 16)
Child and Family Well-Being	Child and Family Well-Being Outcome 1: Families have enhanced capacity to provide for their children's needs. • Needs and services of child, parents, and foster parents (Item 17) • Child and family involvement in case planning (Item 18) • Caseworker visits with child (Item 19) • Caseworker visits with parent(s) (Item 20)
	Child and Family Well-Being Outcome 2: Children receive appropriate services to meet their educational needs. • Educational needs of the child (Item 21)
	Child and Family Well-Being Outcome 3: Children receive adequate services to meet their physical and mental health needs. • Physical health of the child (Item 22) • Mental/behavioral health of the child (Item 23)

Sources: U.S. Department of Health and Human Services, Administration for Children and Families, Administration on Children, Youth and Families, Children's Bureau. (2006). *Child and Family Services Reviews Procedures Manual.* (Working Draft.) Retrieved from http://www.acf.hhs.gov/programs/cb/cwmonitoring/tools_guide/proce_manual.htm

Appendix B: Index of Outcomes and Systemic Factors, and Associated Items and Data Indicators. Retrieved from http://www.acf.hhs.gov/programs/cb/cwmonitoring/tools_guide/procedures/appendixb.htm

Note that the CFSR assesses: (1) Statewide Information Systems; (2) Case Review Systems; (3) Quality Assurance Systems; (4) Staff and Provider Training; (5) Service Array and Resource Development; (6) Agency Responsiveness to the Community; and (7) Foster and Adoptive Parent Licensing, Recruitment, and Retention. And that the standards will be changing by 2015. See http://www.acf.hhs.gov/programs/cb/resource/cfsr-federal-register-notice.

THEORETICAL FRAMEWORKS UNDERLYING CHILD WELFARE POLICIES AND PROGRAMS

A number of theoretical orientations underpin the design of policies and programs in child welfare, including ecological models, child development theories, social learning and social support theories, and risk and protective factor frameworks.

Ecological Developmental Models

From an ecological and developmental perspective, the life course outcomes of children involved in the child welfare system are perceived as deriving from the complex interaction of life experiences with biological factors (e.g., genetic vulnerability for certain disorders) and a variety of environmental and psychological factors. The conditions that produce developmental outcomes include genetic and epigenetic factors[5] such as experiences of poverty, racism, and dangerous living environments as well as family-of-origin characteristics and functioning. In addition, other factors, such as family characteristics and functioning, child and family supports, and the quality and nature of services provided by various community agencies, interact in various ways with the experiences of child maltreatment to produce outcomes (Cicchetti & Lynch, 1993; Fraser, 2004; O'Connell, Boat, & Warner, 2009).

The ecological perspective delineated by Cicchetti and Lynch (1993) suggested that the family is a powerful microsystem. In typical child development, the family confers protection, whereas in atypical child development—in families in which maltreatment occurs—the family confers risk. The ecological model proposed by Bronfenbrenner (1979, 1986, 2004) posits that individual development occurs and can be understood only within the context of the family and the larger social–environmental context in which the family is embedded. In this model, to understand child developmental outcomes, it is necessary to understand the interplay of factors at the individual, family, and environmental levels. The ecological perspective requires identifying and analyzing risk and protective factors at the level of the child, the level of his or her family, and the level of the broader society: Children's development is conceptualized as arising from the complex interplay of these interwoven circles of influence.

Developmental Theories and Perspectives

Five approaches related to child development theories are especially relevant to child welfare practice. First, attachment theory addresses relationships and traumas occurring prior to the age of 2 years (e.g., Ainsworth, 1989; Weinfield, Ogawa, & Sroufe, 1997). Second, trauma theory (Briere, 1992), as it relates to the effects of abuse and neglect, offers explanations for variations in the influence of abuse and recovery from abuse. Third, as discussed above, the ecological perspective offers useful concepts addressing the relative importance of individual, familial, and societal contexts (e.g., Bronfenbrenner & Morris, 1998; Garbarino, 1992; Pecora et al., 2009). Fourth, risk and protective factor frameworks have descriptive utility for explaining resilience in children and youth who recover from maltreatment and for identifying predictors of life course outcomes. Protective factors can be personal assets (e.g., social competence) and environmental resources (e.g., supportive parents or other relatives) that buffer or suppress risk (Catalano & Hawkins, 1996; Fraser, 2004; Rutter, 1989). Fifth, Erikson's (1985) stages or steps in child development are useful in understanding and predicting child adjustment sequelae, including how children might adjust to foster care (Downs & Pecora, 2004).

Social Learning and Social Support Theories

In addition, social learning theory is widely applied in child welfare practice. This theory emphasizes the reciprocal influences of the environment on the person and the person on the environment. Social learning theory holds that human behavior is learned within an interactive social context and conditioned by relationships with family members, peers, and other close associates. For example, based on social learning theory, Chamberlain (2003) and her colleagues have developed and implemented an evidence-based program called Multidimensional Treatment Foster Care.

Introduced nearly 100 years ago, social support theory is one of the earliest frameworks for understanding social relations and human development. This theory integrates three aspects of human connectedness (the community, social networks, and bonding relationships) and articulates conditions under which children grow to be self-reliant adults (Caplan, 1974; Casey Family Programs, 2003; Maluccio, Pine, & Tracy, 2002). The perspective stresses the value of providing consistent supports to children, birth parents, and foster families. In addition, social support theory postulates that lack of supportive social relationships can negatively affect children's mental health and other developmental outcomes (Caplan, 1974). Social support theory is often applied to placement disruptions and transition from foster care to young adulthood (e.g., Pecora et al., 2010; Ryan & Testa, 2004). On balance, studies suggest that social support reduces stress, buffers risk exposure, and promotes psychological adaptation (DePanfilis, 1996; Mann, 2003; McIntosh, 1991).

RISK, PROTECTION, AND RESILIENCE IN CHILD WELFARE

A variety of biological, psychological, and environmental factors converge to create the conditions in which maltreatment occurs, and a somewhat similar set of factors influences a child's recovery from maltreatment. The application of a risk and resilience perspective to child welfare falls in two areas. The first has to do with factors that elevate the odds for maltreatment, and the second has to do with factors that promote recovery from the experience of maltreatment. As shown in Table 3.3, the factors correlated with maltreatment include poverty, parental substance abuse, parental mental illness, parental history of child maltreatment, social isolation, lack of employment resources in the community, and neighborhood gangs and crime (see Child Welfare Information Gateway, 2010). However, none of these factors alone is sufficient to produce maltreatment. Nevertheless, maltreatment becomes more likely as the number of risk factors increases. At the same time, we now know that a number of factors operate protectively and can reduce the likelihood of maltreatment in the presence of risk. These protective factors are also shown in Table 3.3.

The fourth National Incidence Study (NIS-4) updated the set of risk factors for child maltreatment in key areas:

- *Employment.* Compared to children with employed parents, those with no parent in the labor force had two to three times the rate of maltreatment overall.

- *Family structure and living arrangement.* Compared to children living with married biological parents, those children whose single parent had a live-in partner had more than 8 times the rate of maltreatment overall, over 10 times the rate of abuse, and nearly 8 times the rate of neglect.[6]

Table 3.3   Common Risk and Protective Factors for Child Abuse and Neglect

Risk Factors	Protective Factors
Child Risk Factors	**Child Protective Factors**[a]
• Premature birth, birth abnormalities, low birth weight, exposure to toxins *in utero* • Temperament: difficult or slow to warm up to others • Physical/cognitive/emotional disability, chronic or serious illness • Childhood trauma • Antisocial peer group • Age • Child aggression, behavior problems, attention deficits	• Birth order—first born • Health status—healthy during infancy and childhood • Activity level—multiple interests and hobbies, participation, and competence • Disposition—good-natured, precocious, mature, inquisitive, willing to take risks, optimistic, hopeful, altruistic, personable, independent • Developmental milestones—meets or exceeds age-appropriate expectations • Self-concept—high self-esteem, internal locus of control, ability to give and receive love and affection • Perceptive—quickly assesses dangerous situations and avoids harm • Interpersonal skills—able to create, develop, nurture, and maintain supportive relationships with others; is assertive and articulate; has good social skills and can relate to both children and adults • Cognitive skills—able to focus on positive attributes and ignore negative • Intellectual abilities—high academic achievement
Parental/Family Risk Factors	**Parental/Family Protective Factors**[b]
• External locus of control • Poor impulse control • Depression/anxiety • Low tolerance for frustration • Feelings of insecurity • Lack of trust • Insecure attachment with own parents • Childhood history of abuse • High parental conflict, including domestic violence • Family structure—single parent with lack of support, high number of children in household • Social isolation, lack of support • Parental psychopathology • Substance abuse • Separation/divorce, especially high conflict divorce	• Structure—rules and household responsibilities for all members • Family Relational Factors—coherence and attachment, open exchange and expression of feelings and emotions • Parental Factors—supervision and monitoring of children, a strong bond to at least one parent figure, a warm and supportive relationship, abundant attention during the first year of life, parental agreement on family values and morals, emotional availability (parental accessibility and capacity for reading the emotional cues and meeting the emotional needs of the infant) • Reciprocity—mutually satisfying relationships are built between an infant/young child and a parent • Family size—four or fewer children spaced at least two years apart

(Continued)

Table 3.3 (Continued)

Risk Factors	Protective Factors
• Age • High general stress level • Poor parent–child interaction, negative attitudes and attributions about child's behavior • Inaccurate knowledge and expectations about child development • Mental health problems, including maternal depression • Cultural "mismatch" (i.e., when a parent has a perception of normative development that is incongruent with that of the broader society and its service providers)	• Socioeconomic status (SES)—middle- to upper-level SES • Extended family—nurturing relationships with substitute caregivers such as aunts, uncles, and grandparents • Other positive social network support
Community/Social/Environmental Risk Factors • Low socioeconomic status of the neighborhood • Stressful life events • Lack of access to medical care, health insurance, adequate child care, and social services • Parental unemployment; homelessness • Social isolation/lack of social support • Exposure to racism/discrimination	**Community/Social/Environmental Protective Factors[c]** • Positive peer relationships • Extended family in close proximity • Schools—academic and extracurricular participation and achievements, close relationship with a teacher(s) • Reliance on informal network of family, friends, and community leaders for advice

Source: This table is adapted from Coll and Magnuson (2000); Garbarino and Ganzel (2000); Hodges (1994); Osofsky and Thompson (2000); and U.S. Department of Health and Human Services (2003b).

a. Much of the research on protective factors has focused on individual traits. This category of protective factors refers to factors that are learned (self-care and interpersonal attributes) as well as factors for which the individual has no control (birth order, gender). (Garmezy, 1983, 1985; Rae-Grant, Thomas, Offord, & Boyle, 1989; Rutter, 1979, 1981, 1985, 1987, 1990; Werner, 1989).

b. Family characteristics also act as protective factors (Garmezy, 1983, 1985; Rae-Grant et al., 1989; Rutter, 1979, 1981, 1985, 1987, 1990; Werner, 1989).

c. Community characteristics include individuals and institutions that are external to the family and that provide educational, emotional, and general supportive ties with the family unit as a whole or with individual family members. (Garmezy, 1983, 1985; Rae-Grant et al., 1989; Rutter, 1979, 1981, 1985, 1987, 1990; Werner, 1989).

- *Grandparents as caregivers.* Children cared for by a grandparent had lower rates of physical abuse compared to those with no identified grandparent caregiver.[7]

- *Socioeconomic status.* Children in low socioeconomic status households had significantly higher rates of maltreatment. They experienced some types of maltreatment at more than five times the rate of other children; they were more than three times as likely to be abused and about seven times as likely to be neglected.[8]

- *Family size.* The general pattern was nonlinear: The incidence rates were highest for children in the largest families (those with four or more children), intermediate for singleton children (i.e., "only" children) and those in households with three children, and lowest among children in families with two children. (See the NIS-4 report for more details.)

- *Child's age.* In most cases, 0- to 2-year-old children had significantly lower maltreatment rates than older children.[9]

- *County metropolitan status.* On balance, the incidence of maltreatment was higher in rural counties than in urban counties.

- *Perpetrator's relationship to the child.* Biological parents were the most closely related perpetrators, accounting for 71% of physically abused children and for 73% of emotionally abused children. The pattern was distinctly different for sexual abuse, with 42% of sexually abused children victimized by someone other than a parent (whether biological or nonbiological) or a parent's partner, whereas just over one third (36%) were sexually abused by a biological parent. In addition, the severity of harm from physical abuse varied by the perpetrator's relationship to the child. A physically abused child was more likely to sustain a serious injury when the abuser was not a parent.

- *Perpetrator's alcohol use, drug use, and mental illness.* Alcohol use and drug use contributed approximately equally to maltreatment, each applying to 11% of the countable children, whereas mental illness was a factor in the maltreatment of 7% of the children. All three factors were more often involved in maltreatment when the perpetrator was a biological parent (Sedlak et al., 2010, pp. 14–15).

not as high [handwritten annotation]

In cases involved with child welfare, indeed across all children, the NIS-4 and other research by Putnam-Hornstein (2011), suggest that developmental outcomes are influenced by individual and environmental risk factors as well as by a host of cultural resources and practices that may both buffer against risk and promote recovery from negative life events. One of the most frequently discussed risk factors is poverty. Low-income families are less likely to have adequate food, safe housing, and prenatal or other medical care. Households that are living near or below the poverty line tend to have few social supports and experience more stress in child rearing, all of which can increase the risk of child maltreatment. Generally, poverty has a direct negative influence on maternal behavior and subsequently on the quality of parenting that children receive (Brooks-Gunn, Klebanov, & Liaw, 1995). For children, living in poverty is associated with a host of negative consequences, including poor physical health, diminished cognitive abilities, reduced educational attainment, increased emotional and behavioral problems, and higher risk of maltreatment (Brooks-Gunn & Duncan, 1997; Ridge, 2009; Sedlak et al., 2010).

The relationship of poverty to maltreatment and other negative child developmental outcomes appears mediated in part by stress. Using global data, Wilkinson and Pickett (2009) charted the level of health and social problems against the level of income inequality in 20 of the world's richest nations and in each state of the United States. They found that mental illness, drug and alcohol abuse, obesity, and teenage pregnancy were more common in states and countries with a big gap between the incomes of rich and poor households. Moreover, areas with a large income gap also had higher homicide rates, shorter life expectancies, and lower scores for children's educational performance and literacy. The Scandinavian countries and Japan consistently scored at the positive end of this spectrum, and these countries have the smallest differences between higher and lower incomes and the best record of psychosocial health. The countries with the widest gulf between rich and poor, and the highest incidence of health and social problems, were Britain, the United States, and Portugal.

The Wilkinson and Pickett (2009) data and recent reviews of families living in "deep poverty" (Urban Institute, 2013) suggest that poverty creates not only physical hardship but also a stressful environment that exacerbates social and health problems. Commenting on Wilkinson and Pickett, Carey (2009) argued,

> It is not only the poor who suffer from the effects of inequality, but the majority of the population. For example, rates of mental illness are five times higher across the whole population in the most unequal than in the least unequal societies in their survey. One explanation . . . is that inequality increases stress right across society, not just among the least advantaged. Much research has been done on the stress hormone cortisol, which can be measured in saliva or blood, and it emerges that chronic stress affects the neural system and in turn the immune system. When stressed, we are more prone to depression and anxiety, and more likely to develop a host of bodily ills including heart disease, obesity, drug addiction, liability to infection and rapid ageing. (p. 1)

Although it is far beyond the capacity of service providers to influence national income differentials, these data suggest that health promotion and child safety may be associated with poverty and stress. In seeking to reduce stress, researchers are increasingly looking at protective factors, including cultural rootedness and resources, which buffer against stress related to poverty and other adversities such as racial discrimination.

Consistent with this perspective, the American Psychological Association's Task Force on Resilience and Strength in Black Children and Adolescents (hereafter, APA Task Force) called for reframing research to better conceptualize adaptive and protective processes for African American children. With the intent of providing researchers, policymakers, educators, practitioners, and the public with a useful lens through which to view the design of services for African American youth, the report explored how themes of resilience cut across five widely accepted developmental domains of functioning:

- *Identity development.* A positive racial identity is essential to the well-being of African American youth. Children should be encouraged to develop a positive sense of self in a society that often devalues them through negative stereotypes.

- *Emotional development.* Coping with emotions effectively is directly related to self-esteem and better mental health. African American youth need to be made aware of how their emotional expressions resonate across all situations and circumstances.

- *Social development.* Family and community interaction are crucial to African American youths' social development. This interaction includes having access to high-quality child care, afterschool programs, and faith-based institutions.

- *Cognitive development.* African American youth must believe in their abilities in the classroom. Parents should avoid harsh parenting styles, and schools should continue to look at ways to infuse culturally relevant themes into the classroom as a way to improve academic performance.

- *Physical health and development.* Access to health care must be improved. A wide range of health conditions disproportionately affect African American youth, including obesity, poor oral health, asthma, violent injury, sickle-cell anemia, diabetes, and HIV/AIDS (APA Task Force, 2008).

In addition to African American youth and their families, immigrant families constitute an increasing part of the population served by child welfare. In designing more effective services for these children, data suggest that it is important to understand how the experiences of immigration, immigration stress, and acculturation affect family dynamics, strengths, and risk and protective factors (e.g., Dalla, Defrain, Johnson, & Abbott, 2009; De Anda, 2003).

In child welfare, protection has always been an element of services, but the literature on risk and resilience has given new meaning to protection. For many children, prevailing over the adversity of maltreatment involves strengthening protective processes in the family and community context. These strengthening efforts include building parental competence and teaching positive disciplinary approaches; enhancing the racial and ethnic identities of children; and engaging caregivers, advocates, peer networks, and extended family members in providing culturally anchored social support. Other critical protective characteristics involve inclusion of families in community activities and the availability of medical, educational, and financial resources that allow parents to provide appropriate care for their children.

Although the available research on protective factors associated with child maltreatment is limited, this research has been growing (e.g., Development Services Group, Inc., 2013) and has been informed by the larger body of literature on protective factors. Several studies have outlined factors that differentiate resilient children from children who experience serious adjustment problems. Protective factors appear to fall into three general categories: individual characteristics, family characteristics, and the presence of supportive others (Garmezy, 1985; Rutter, 1990; Werner, 1989). Individual characteristics include attributes such as self-sufficiency, high self-esteem, and altruism. Family characteristics include supportive relationships with adult family members, harmonious family relationships, expressions of warmth between family members, and the ability to mobilize supports in times of stress. Finally, community supports refer to supportive relationships with people or organizations that are external to the family. These external supports provide positive and supportive feedback to the child and act to reinforce and reward the child's positive coping abilities (Hodges, 1994).

Race, Ethnicity, Income, and Maltreatment

Poverty and race/ethnicity are related in the United States, and both are correlated with maltreatment. Indeed, the racial and ethnic distribution of perpetrators in a substantiated case is similar to the race and ethnicity of victims. During 2012, nearly one half (48.9%) of perpetrators were White, 19.9% were African American, and 18.9% were Hispanic. These proportions have changed little in recent years (U.S. DHHS, 2013a, p. 61).

Although the literature is sparse, differences by race and ethnicity should be understood in the context of other known risk factors, especially poverty. The NIS-4 also found significant differences in child abuse rates based on socioeconomic factors. Poor children were three times more likely than other children to experience abuse (Crary, 2010). When income was controlled in analyses, the differences found in maltreatment rates between White and Black children in low-income families were negligible. In fact, larger differences were observed in the "not low income" classification, in which higher rates were observed for African American families as compared to White families. Racial differences in need (Drake, Jolley, Lanier, Fluke, Barth, & Jonson-Reid, 2011) and racial disparities in service provisions and quality (Lorthridge, McCroskey, Pecora, Chambers, & Fatemi, 2011) need to be carefully considered.

The preceding discussion offers a brief overview of the individual, family, and community risk and protective factors related to child abuse and neglect. We have placed emphasis on protective factors because they serve to buffer stress for some children and provide important clues for how to strengthen child welfare services. Given differences in family structure, child-rearing practices, and relationship to community, the degree to which these factors are moderated by race and ethnicity is unclear. This is the subject of much current research. In fact a recent literature review noted that the strength of evidence for protective factors among at-risk children and youth varies considerably by type of factor and specific population. As summarized in Table 3.4, moderate levels of evidence were found for selected factors at the individual, relationship, and community levels of influence for all focus population groups (Development Services Group, Inc., 2013).

Certainly, some of the protective factors associated with, for example, socioeconomic status and academic success are universal. However, other factors may be conditioned on or differentially more important among African American, Latino, and other children with strong racial, ethnic, or religious backgrounds. From Hodges (1994), these protective factors include:

- *Active extended family:* fictive or blood relatives who are active in the child's life; provides material resources, child care, supervision, parenting, and emotional support to the child (Wilson, 1984).

- *Faith-based affiliation:* belongs to and actively participates in a group religious experience (Werner, 1989).

- *Strong racial identity:* exhibits racial pride, strongly identifies with ethnic group through clubs, organizations, political, and social-change movements.

- *Close attachment to the ethnic community:* resides in the ethnic community, easy access to ethnic resources, including social services, merchants, media (newspaper), and demonstrates a commitment to the ethnic community.

Table 3.4   Top 10 Protective Factors that Reduce Risk for Children in Child Welfare Systems

Individual level
Relational skills: Relational skills encompass two main components: (1) a youth's ability to form positive bonds and connections (e.g., social competence, being caring, forming positive attachments and prosocial relationships) and (2) interpersonal skills such as communication skills, conflict resolution skills, and self-efficacy in conflict situations.
Self-regulation skills: Self-regulation skills refer to a youth's ability to manage or control emotions and behaviors. This skill set can include self-mastery, anger management, character, long-term self-control, and emotional intelligence.
Problem-solving skills: Includes general problem-solving skills, self-efficacy in conflict situations, higher daily living scores, decision-making skills, planning skills, adaptive functioning skills and task-oriented coping skills.
Involvement in positive activities: Refers to engagement in and/or achievement in school, extra-curricular activities, employment, training, apprenticeships, or military.
Relationship level
Parenting competencies: Parenting competencies refers to two broad categories of parenting: (1) parenting skills (e.g., parental monitoring and discipline, prenatal care, setting clear standards and developmentally appropriate limits) and (2) positive parent-child interactions (e.g., close relationship between parent and child, sensitive parenting, support, caring).
Positive peers: Refers to friendships with peers, support from friends, or positive peer norms.
Caring adult(s): This factor most often refers to caring adults beyond the nuclear family, such as mentors, home visitors (especially for pregnant and parenting teens), older extended family members, or individuals in the community.
Community level
Positive community environment: Positive community environment refers to neighborhood advantage or quality, religious service attendance, living in a safe and higher-quality environment, a caring community, social cohesion, and positive community norms.
Positive school environment: A positive school environment primarily is defined as the existence of supportive programming in schools.
Economic opportunities: Refers to household income and socioecomic status; a youth's self-perceived resources; employment, apprenticeship, coursework, and/or military involvement; and placement in a foster care setting (from a poor setting).

Source: Development Services Group, Inc. (2013). *Protective factors for populations served by the administration on children, youth, and families. A literature review and theoretical framework: Executive summary.* Washington, D.C.: U.S. Department of Health and Human Services, Administration for Children and Families, Children's Bureau, p. 6. Retrieved May 20, 2014, from http://www.dsgonline.com/acyf/DSG%20Protective%20Factors%20Literature%20Review%202013%20Exec%20Summary.pdf.

- *Dispositional attributes:* activity level, sociability, average intelligence, competence in communication (oral and written), internal locus of control (Werner, 1989).

- *Personal attributes:* high self-esteem, academic achievement, assertiveness, quality of adjustment to single-parent household.

- *Supportive family milieu:* cohesiveness, extensive kinship network, nonconflictual relations.

- *External support system:* involvement of absent fathers, male role models, supportive social environments of various ethnic communities.

RISK, RESILIENCE, AND PROTECTION IN CHILD WELFARE POLICY

Child welfare policy is slowly but steadily being shaped by research related to risk, resilience, protection, neuroscience, and epigenetics. New materials from the Harvard Center on the Developing Child and landmark books such as *Neurons to Neighborhoods* reinforce infant and young child stimulation principles outlined by earlier pioneers and make scientific knowledge accessible to a broad audience (Shonkoff & Phillips, 2000). Other child welfare researchers such as Berrick and colleagues (1998) and Maier (1978) have emphasized the importance of paying attention to child development fundamentals (e.g., attachment theory and social learning) in designing child welfare policy and programs. Advances in the treatment of child abuse and neglect have emphasized how children with varied psychological compositions and differing amounts of social support respond differently to various healing approaches (Briere, 1992; Cohen, Mannarino, Zhitova, & Capone, 2003; Kendall-Tackett, 2013).

Ecological and diversity perspectives underscore the vital roles that broad community networks and environments play in services and healing. In addition, a recent Institute of Medicine report described a growing array of evidence-based programs for preventing emotional, behavioral, and substance abuse disorders in youth and young adults (O'Connell et al., 2009). We are making progress. Policy and program reforms include

- strategically focused family-centered services to strengthen parenting;

- child-centered early intervention and remedial services based on increased understanding of early brain development (Perry & Dobson, 2013; Shonkoff & Phillips, 2000);

- attempts to embed substance abuse treatment services within child welfare and to strengthen linkages across service delivery systems such as mental health, education, and juvenile justice;

- use of least restrictive placement environments, which facilitated the closure of hundreds of residential institutions;

- permanency planning for children to secure a stable family if birth parents are unable to provide care for the child; and

• aggressive permanency planning for older youth in foster care so they do not age out or emancipate from foster care without a legal guardian and a network of supportive relationships.

Three other significant transformations bear mentioning. First, leaders in child protective services, family support, and foster care have identified community collaborations as essential for effective services (Morgan, Spears, & Kaplan, 2003; Pew Foundation, 2008; Schorr & Marchand, 2007). Second, the field has recognized the simultaneous needs of moving all children (i.e., irrespective of background and age) to permanent family situations while also being cognizant of the need to nurture the child development of children who remain involved in the child welfare service system beyond a 3-month protective services intervention (Berrick et al., 1998; Kerman, Maluccio, & Freundlich, 2009). Third, racial and ethnic disproportionality in the provision of services and achievement of permanency outcomes are increasingly acknowledged problems (e.g., Derezotes, Poertner, & Testa, 2005; Fluke, Jones-Harden, Jenkins, & Ruehrdanz, 2011; Hines, Lemon, Wyatt, & Merdinger, 2004; U.S. Government Accountability Office, 2007). A discussion of these and other policy issues follows.

KEY CHILD WELFARE POLICY AND LEGISLATION

A number of public policies influence child welfare programs and affect the families receiving child welfare services. Listed below are some of the key federal policies that are related to child welfare. These policies include adoption, child protection, income support, education, early intervention, family support, and foster care. (For more information, see Appendix A in Pecora et al., 2009.) Medical care, which is also important for child welfare, is discussed more thoroughly in Chapter 6 of this volume.

1970s

• *Child Abuse Prevention and Treatment Act of 1974 (PL 93-247):* Provides some financial assistance for demonstration programs for the prevention, identification, and treatment of child abuse and neglect; mandates that states must provide for the reporting of known or suspected instances of child abuse and neglect (Stein, 1984).

• *Juvenile Justice and Delinquency Prevention Act of 1974 (PL 93-415):* Provides funds to reduce the unnecessary or inappropriate detention of juveniles and to encourage state program initiatives in the prevention and treatment of juvenile delinquency and other status offenses (see http://www.ojjdp.ncjrs .gov/about/ojjjjact.txt).

• *Title XIX of the Social Security Act:* Provides health care to income-eligible persons and families. One of the sections of this act established the Early and Periodic Screening, Diagnosis, and Treatment program, which provides cost-effective health care to pregnant women and young children (see http://www.ssa.gov/OP_Home/ssact/title19/1900.htm).

• *The Education for All Handicapped Children Act of 1975 (PL 94-142):* This law supports education and social services for handicapped children. The act requires states to

(a) offer programs for the full education of handicapped children between the ages of 3 and 18, (b) develop strategies for locating such children, (c) use intelligence testing that does not discriminate against the child racially or culturally, (d) develop an individualized education plan (IEP) for each child, and (e) offer learning opportunities in the *least restrictive educational environment* possible, with an emphasis on mainstreaming: integrating handicapped children into regular classrooms (see http://www .projectidealonline .org/publicPolicy.php).

- *The Individuals with Disabilities Education Act (IDEA):* The Individuals with Disabilities Education Act (IDEA) began as the Education for All Handicapped Children Act of 1975 (PL 94-142) and gave all children with disabilities the right to a free and appropriate public education. This watershed civil rights law resulted from sustained advocacy by parents of children with disabilities. Special education has been shaped by the six core principles that formed the nucleus of the Education for All Handicapped Children Act: (1) zero reject, meaning schools could not opt to exclude any children with disabilities from instruction; (2) nondiscriminatory evaluation, by which every child receives an individualized, culturally and linguistically appropriate evaluation before being placed in special education; (3) IEP, a plan delineating current performance, progress on past objectives, goals, and services for the school year, and evaluation of outcomes; (4) least restrictive environment, which is in settings with nondisabled children; (5) due process, which codifies the legal steps to ensure a school's fairness and accountability in meeting the child's needs and how parents can obtain relief via a hearing or by second opinions; and (6) parental participation, whereby parents have the right to access their child's education records and participate in IEP planning (Kirk, Gallagher, & Anastasiow, 1993, pp. 51–52).

Another part of IDEA that is important for children served by child welfare agencies is early intervention, which has as its purpose the provision of prevention and treatment services to improve cognitive, social, and emotional development of the youngest children (under the age of 3). Children receiving early intervention services either are considered at risk for delayed development or have been identified as having a developmental disability (Ramey & Ramey, 1998).

- *The Indian Child Welfare Act of 1978 (PL 95-608):* Strengthens the standards governing the removal of Native American children from their families. Provides for a variety of requirements and mechanisms for tribal government overseeing and services for children (see http://www.nicwa.org/law/; Plantz, Hubbell, Barrett, & Dobrec, 1989).

1980s

- *The Adoption Assistance and Child Welfare Act of 1980 (PL 96-272):* This is one of the key laws for child welfare reform because it used funding incentives and procedural requirements to implement a wide range of placement prevention and permanency planning (see http://www.ssa.gov/OP_Home/comp2/F096–272.html; Pine, 1986).

- *Independent Living Initiative (PL 99-272):* Provides funding for services to prepare adolescents in foster care for living in the community on an independent basis (Mech, 1988).

1990s

- *Personal Responsibility and Work Opportunity Reconciliation Act (PRWORA):* Funds the Temporary Assistance to Needy Families (TANF), the largest income transfer program for poor families. This is part of the nation's welfare system—administered by the states and funded jointly by state and federal governments. Low-income families of children with disabilities can also receive income transfers through TANF, which is the limited welfare program enacted in 1996 by PRWORA. TANF replaced Aid to Families with Dependent Children (AFDC), which limits program participation (with some exceptions) to 60 months. TANF allows states to exempt up to 20% of their welfare caseload from work requirements, but states have the discretion to establish more strict work participation rules (see http://www.cbpp .org/cms/?fa = view&id = 936).

- *Foster Care Independence Act of 1999 (PL 106-169):* Authorized the Education Training Voucher (ETV) program. Congress provided federal funding of $42 million for the first time in fiscal year (FY) 2003 and increased funding to $45 million for FY 2004. In both years, the president requested $60 million in his budget (see http://www.acf.hhs.gov/programs/cb/laws_policies/cblaws/public_law/p1106_169/p1106_169.htm).

The voucher program is a component of the Chafee Independent Living Program, which helps older youth leaving foster care to get the higher education, vocational training, and other education supports they need to move to self-sufficiency. Up to $5,000 per year is available to a young person for the cost of attending college or vocational school. ETV funds are distributed to the states using the same formula as the Chafee Independent Living Program under the Foster Care Independence Act. If a state does not apply for funds for the ETV program, the funds are reallocated to other states based on their relative need. Although states are generally doing a good job of distributing these funds, more foster youth could take advantage of the vouchers if their availability were more widely known. An additional $60 million is needed for ETVs for youth leaving foster care at age 18 and those adopted from foster care at age 16 or older (Child Welfare League of America, 2004).

- *Keeping Children and Families Safe Act (PL 108-36):* Reauthorizes the Child Abuse Prevention and Treatment Act. Authorizes funds for grants to state child welfare agencies, competitive grants for research and demonstration programs, and grants to states for the establishment of community-based programs and activities designed to strengthen and support families, all of which support services to prevent and treat child abuse and neglect. The act amends the Adoption Reform Act of 1978 (Adoption Opportunities), focusing on the placement of older foster children in adoptive homes with an emphasis on child-specific recruitment strategies and efforts to improve interjurisdictional adoptions. This act also includes amendments to the Abandoned Infants Assistance Act, making aid a priority to infants who are infected with the HIV virus, have a life-threatening disease, or have been exposed perinatally to a dangerous drug. The act also includes an amendment to the Family Violence Prevention and Services Act, extending from FY 2004 through FY 2008 authorization of appropriations for specified family violence prevention programs (see www.naesv .org/Resources/FVPSA.pdf).

2000 to present

- *The Adoption Incentive Program (PL 108-145):* The Adoption Incentive Program was first enacted as part of the Adoption and Safe Families Act in 1997 to promote permanence for children. In 2003, Congress passed the Adoption Promotion Act of 2003 (PL 108-145) to reauthorize the program with modifications. The Adoption Incentive Program is designed to encourage states to finalize adoptions of children from foster care, with additional incentives for the adoption of foster children with special needs. States receive incentive payments for adoptions that exceed an established baseline. The Adoption Promotion Act revises the incentive formula in current law, creating four categories of payment (see http://www.childwelfare.gov/system-wide/laws_ policies/federal/index.cfm?event = federalLegislation.viewLegis&id = 85).

- *Runaway, Homeless, and Missing Children Protection Act (Title III of the 3 Juvenile Justice and Delinquency Prevention Act of 1974), 4 as Amended by the 5 Runaway, Homeless, and Missing Children Protection Act (PL 108-96):* Authorizes funds for the establishment and operation of centers to provide shelter, protection from sexual and other abuse, counseling, and related services to runaway and homeless youth under 18 years of age. The act authorized local groups to open "maternity group homes" for homeless pregnant teens or for those that have been abused. These homes are required to educate runaway youth about parenting skills, child development, family budgeting, health and nutrition, and related skills to promote long-term independence and the health and well-being of youth in their care (see http://www.acf.hhs.gov/programs/fysb/content/aboutfysb/RHYComp.pdf; and http://www.acf.hhs.gov/programs/fbci/progs/fbci_rhyouth.html).

Other landmark pieces of legislation were passed during this time. For example, the Fostering Connections to Success and Increasing Adoptions Act (HR 6893/PL 110-351) of 2008. This law helps children and youth in foster care by ensuring permanent placements for them through kinship and adoption and improving educational and health care outcomes. It will also extend federal support for youth to age 21. The act offers for the first time substantial support to American Indian children residing in child protective custody. Key provisions are listed below:

- Offers federal support to children who leave foster care to live permanently with relative guardians through a federal subsidized guardianship program.

- Helps relatives connect the children with the services and supports they need by using kinship navigator programs.

- Includes separate licensing standards to address non-safety licensing requirements that create barriers to children living with relatives in foster care.

- Provides additional support to older youth and increase their opportunities for success by:

  o Continuing federal support for children in foster care after age 18: The law allows states, at their option, to provide care and support to youth in foster care until the age of 19, 20, or 21.

- o Providing transition support: The act requires child welfare agencies to help youth make this transition to adulthood by requiring, during the 90-day period immediately before a youth exits from care at 18, 19, 20, or 21, the development of a personalized transition plan that identifies options for housing, health insurance, education, local opportunities for mentoring, continuing support services, workforce supports, and employment services.
  - o Granting tribes direct access to Title IV-E: The law ensures that Indian tribes have direct access to IV-E funded programs.
  - o Improving education outcomes for children who live in out-of-home care by improving educational stability by requiring states to ensure that placement of the child in foster care takes into account the appropriateness of the current educational setting and the proximity to the school in which the child is enrolled at the time of placement.
  - o Promoting coordinated health care for children in out-of-home care by requiring that states develop a plan for the oversight and coordination of health, mental health, and dental services for children in foster care.

- Expands and improves adoption assistance programs

- Improves the child welfare workforce: The law allows states to be reimbursed for training provided to an expanded group of individuals and organizations including kinship caregivers, court personnel, court-appointed special advocates, and nonagency workers providing child welfare services.

Second, in 2010, Child Abuse CAPTA Reauthorization Act of 2010 (PL 111-320) amended the Child Abuse Prevention and Treatment Act (CAPTA), the Family Violence Prevention and Services Act, the Child Abuse Prevention and Treatment and Adoption Reform Act of 1978, and the Abandoned Infants Assistance Act of 1988, to reauthorize the Acts and make other changes to them. In addition to many other provisions, this act authorized grants to public or private agencies to develop or expand effective collaborations between child protective service (CPS) entities and domestic violence service entities. It also reauthorized the Child Abuse Prevention and Treatment and Adoption Reform Act of 1978, including appropriations, through FY 2015. Amendments to the act also required efforts to promote the adoption of older children, minority children, and children with special needs. And it renewed through FY 2014 the authority of HHS to authorize States to conduct child welfare program demonstration projects likely to promote the objectives of title IV-B or IV-E.[9]

In 2011, H.R. 2883 amended part B of title IV of the Social Security Act to extend the Child and Family Services Program through FY 2016. It included a wide range of provisions, including:

- Requiring each state plan for oversight and coordination of health care services for any child in foster care to include an outline of the monitoring and treatment of emotional trauma associated with a child's maltreatment and removal from home, and protocols for the appropriate use and monitoring of psychotropic medications.

- Requiring each state plan for child welfare services to describe the activities to reduce the length of time that children under the age of 5 years are without a permanent family and activities to address the developmental needs of such children who receive benefits or services.

In 2013, the Uninterrupted Scholars Act amended the Family Educational Rights and Privacy Act (FERPA) to allow child welfare agencies access to the student records of youth in foster care. When FERPA was written in 1974, lawmakers intended to protect parental control over their children's student records. However, the unintended consequence for children in the custody of the state—like those in foster care—was the creation of time-consuming legal hurdles to access to the school records of children in care. This law should address this problem. (See http://www.gpo.gov/fdsys/pkg/PLAW-112publ278/pdf/PLAW-112publ278.pdf)

Finally, it is likely that some of the provisions of the Affordable Care Act will make it easier for some parents to receive preventive or treatment services as part of a "medical home" and changes in payment structures. The Act should also make it easier for foster care alumni to get and keep some kind of health insurance coverage, even with pre-existing conditions.

Current Policy Challenges

Child welfare faces a number of policy challenges, some of which are exacerbated by the mixed success the United States is having in meeting the basic needs of children; ensuring children's safety, health, relationships, and opportunities; and supporting families as the foundation for positive child development. These challenges include the following 15 issues.

1. **Child maltreatment prevention services are underfunded and lack federal guidance on what would be a coherent approach.** Early intervention services have long been recognized as helping families avoid involvement with the child welfare system. Best practices for early intervention programs involve provision of a range of family-centered services that focus on meeting the needs of the child within the context of the family as well as the larger environment. For example, early intervention might include referring parents to job assistance or adult education and providing parents with assistance in obtaining housing and health care. Child-centered early intervention programs have been linked with improved child development across multiple domains (Karoly, Kilburn, Caulkins, & Cannon, 2000; Kilburn & Karoly, 2008). Given advances in prevention science (Jenson & Bender, 2014), it is quite possible that the design, development, and delivery of improved early intervention services could reduce the incidence of child maltreatment.

However, implementing early intervention programs will require a more unified leadership with a cohesive plan for family support at both the federal and state levels. Communities interested in early intervention will need to invest public resources in evidence-based programs that support parents and strengthen families. Furthermore, those interested in child welfare must work toward increasing the supply of affordable child care, and increasing the awareness among policymakers of the importance of *family economic security.* This need is emphasized by the large proportion of children entering child welfare as a result of parental neglect. As previously mentioned, more effective mental health and substance abuse interventions for parents could also reduce youth entry into foster care.

A risk, resilience, and protective factor perspective undergirds the philosophy supporting early intervention. Early intervention should aim to disrupt risk processes, promote protective mechanisms, and stimulate resilience. Ideally, early intervention services promote well-being and optimal development by providing comprehensive community-based support services to help improve child developmental outcomes. Two examples of such interventions are Point of Engagement (Marts, Lee, McCroy, & McCroskey, 2008) and the Prevention Intervention Development Initiative in Los Angeles (McCroskey et al., 2009). Unfortunately, these types of services are underfunded, and without Title IV-E waivers or more permanent federal fiscal reforms, states often lack the flexibility to reallocate federal funds designated for placement services to fund family support programs. With few exceptions (e.g., Development Services Group, Inc., 2013), the Administration for Children Youth and Families has not issued a practical framework for guiding child maltreatment prevention.

2. **Differential response approaches to child protective services intake need additional testing.** New intake approaches are attempting to refer low-risk families (i.e., those with a low risk for a subsequent maltreatment referral) to supportive programs other than child protective services. Although promising, these approaches need further testing and evaluation to clarify the roles of law enforcement; medical, legal, and social services personnel; and voluntary agencies. If new intake procedures accurately distinguish families in which the likelihood of severe maltreatment is low from those in which it is high, these new protocols could complement family support interventions that have been heavily researched and found to be cost-effective. For example, practice, administrative, policy, and other system-reform strategies exist that can improve well-being for maltreated children and accelerate permanency planning. These strategies can safely reduce the number of children in foster care, and those placement-cost savings can be reinvested in higher quality services for the children for whom out-of-home care is the most appropriate option. (For examples of such programs and their cost-effectiveness, see Pecora, O'Brien & Maher, 2014; Washington State Institute for Public Policy Research, 2013. Also see http://www .wsipp.wa.gov/BenefitCost as this website is periodically updated.)

3. **Family support services are not funded in alignment with desired outcomes.** Family support programs, which include parent hotlines, crisis nursery services, environmental adaptations, personal assistance, and mental health and crisis interventions are often "lifelines." These services allow families to care for their children at home rather than placing a child in out-of-home care, which is expensive and generally publicly financed (Bruns & Burchard, 2000; Schorr & Marchand, 2007). The goals of family support services include enabling families to raise children at home by reducing stress and by strengthening and enhancing caregiving capacities (Pew Foundation, 2008; Walton, Sandau-Beckler, & Mannes, 2001). Family caregivers' acceptance and use of formal support services play a significant role in reducing the burdens and stress associated with caring for a child and in helping families obtain services for unmet needs. Across the United States, family support services are usually jointly financed by the federal and state governments, often using

Medicaid resources, and are typically administered by state or county governments. Not surprisingly, given the differences among the states in the provision of social services, there is variability across states in the funding levels for family support and in the types of services available (Parish, Pomeranz, & Braddock, 2003). Consequently, these services are often not only underfunded but also among the first to be cut during periods of economic downturns.

4. **Changes to key child welfare funding mechanisms require careful consideration.** There appears to be growing agreement among policymakers, advocates, and state child welfare directors that comprehensive child welfare finance reform should align federal funding and policies to incentivize and ensure the safety, permanency, and well-being of children and their families. A number of proposals that would allow states to use federal foster care funds not only to support children in out-of-home care but also to support child abuse prevention and post-adoption services have been presented to Congress. For example, several proposals would change the system for funding key child welfare programs, including foster care entitlement under Title IV-E of the Social Security Act.

These proposals can be seen as efforts to address the family support issue. However, the downside to these proposals is that the overall budget for children's services would decrease if all the areas under proposed legislation are considered. Based on what occurs with the federal block grant process for Medicaid and the Supplemental Nutrition Assistance Program (SNAP, formerly the food stamp program), families would no longer have an entitlement. Therefore, educational efforts are needed to inform the public and policymakers of the importance of policies that preserve the open-ended entitlement for key child welfare programs. In addition, child and family advocates need to raise awareness among policymakers and the public that program funds should be tied to performance. Results should be rewarded, and savings due to lowered rates of foster care should be reinvested to improve the quality of child welfare services (Annie E. Casey Foundation, 2014; Annie E. Casey Foundation and the Jim Casey Youth Opportunities Initiative, 2013; Casey Family Programs, 2010a). The following principles outline what is important to address to achieve this vision:

- Federal funding targeted for child welfare services should be available for any child or his or her family on the basis of risk rather than an income standard but also should be available for a limited time period and for a specific set of services.

- Federal funding for child welfare should be flexible enough to allow states to address their unique challenges and issues.

- Federal funding should incentivize and encourage better outcomes for children and their families (Casey Family Programs and the Brookings Institution, 2013)

5. **Policies and funding to treat mental health and substance abuse problems must be coordinated with child welfare services.** Fragmented funding streams and policies for mental health, substance abuse, developmental disabilities, and child welfare services unduly complicate the treatment of parents and children with co-morbid conditions (Kessler & Magee, 1993). Depending upon the community, over 30% of the families with children who have been placed in out-of-home care also have substance abuse problems

(Barth, Gibbons, & Guo, 2006; Besinger, Garland, Litrownik, & Landsverk, 1999). To serve the dual needs of these families, many agency administrators are diverted from other activities while trying to "braid" or cobble together sources of funding to cover the costs of drug treatment and other programs. Such efforts highlight the need for increased program coordination at the federal and state levels to maximize the effectiveness of existing resources (Johnson, Knitzer, & Kaufmann, 2003). This type of increased coordination requires a system of care approach. (For a discussion of systems of care in mental health, see Chapter 5 in this volume.)

6. **All youth in high school should receive the tutoring and employment experiences that build work-related skills.** Youth preparing to emancipate must have greater access to experiential life skills and classroom-based training. However, systems change is essential to accomplish this goal. Among others, the MacArthur Foundation transition scholars have documented the failure of major American institutions to keep pace with societal changes that require new ways of working (Carnegie Council on Adolescent Development, 1989; First Focus, 2008).

7. **Policies should provide fiscal incentives to improve high-school graduation rates and to support postsecondary education and training for children and youth in foster care.** Recent changes in the federal Higher Education Act, reauthorized in 2008 as the Higher Education Opportunity Act (HEOA; PL 110-315), provide more consideration of the special needs of children and youth in foster care. Further policy innovations are needed to strengthen elementary and secondary education programs, including special education initiatives. In addition, federal and state policies must maintain the financial viability and array of services within the Medicaid and State Children's Health Insurance Program (SCHIP) programs for youth in foster care and ensure that no young person leaves foster care without access to appropriate health care.

8. **Policies should increase the likelihood that youths will achieve and maintain permanency in a reasonable period through foster care, reunification, relative placement, guardianship, or adoption.** In many states, a substantial number of children have a case goal of *alternative planned living arrangement* (APLA), such as emancipation from foster care at age 18 or exit before age 18 via independent living. APLA is not a legal form of permanence, and it does not provide children with a long-term supportive relationship with an adult. Reforms that are needed include crafting policies to ensure that kinship care families have access to resources that allow them to raise healthy children in stable home environments (Casey Family Programs, 2010b). Adoption policy must more thoroughly address how to better respond to the legal concerns expressed in the Multi-Ethnic Placement Act and Inter-Ethnic Adoption Provisions Act.

9. **Policymakers need to recognize the seriousness of, and make changes to reduce, racial and ethnic disproportionality and disparity.** Although the disproportionate numbers of children of color in the child welfare system, and the disparities in the outcomes of those children have been recognized as ethical, policy, and program issues, much needs to be done to fully address them. First, we need to promote the investment of public resources into gathering accurate data about African American, Native American, Asian

American, and Hispanic children who are involved in the child welfare system. This information ranges from the level of access to services of birth parents for children of color in the child welfare system to data concerning use of substance abuse and mental health services both before entering and during their contact with the system (Fluke et al., 2011; Hill, 2007; Hines et al., 2004). Second, using this information, officials must enhance national awareness of the disproportionate number of children of color in the foster care system and pinpoint the reasons for this disproportionality. Finally, communities should launch efforts to reduce disparities as was recently accomplished in Sacramento County (Ellis, Eskenazi, Bonnell & Pecora, 2013). The goal of these efforts should be to remove race and ethnicity as a predictor of outcome in child welfare services. Table 3.5 provides an example of a Point of Engagement strategy used in Los Angeles to reduce racial and ethnic disparities in child welfare.

10. **Kinship care funding, licensing, and practice policies need to be aligned.** More than 6.7 million children—about 1 out of every 12 U.S. children—are living in households headed by grandparents or other relatives. The number of children raised in relative-headed households has increased significantly. U.S. Census data show that 2.4 million grandparents are taking primary responsibility for the basic needs of their grandchildren. Kinship caregivers often lack the information and range of supports they need to fulfill their parenting role. In an effort to remedy this situation, a group of advocates from child welfare, aging, and research organizations prepared a set of revised kinship care fact sheets (Children's Defense Fund, 2008). These sheets provide state-specific data and information directing grandparents or other kinship caregivers to support services that can help make their jobs easier. The Fostering Connections legislation (PL 110-351) authorizes federal support for *kinship navigators* to advise these parents. However, more work needs to be done to help resolve the policy inconsistencies in licensing and support of these families.

11. **Tribal access to federal child welfare services funding should be increased and existing infrastructure should be improved.** Consistent with their cultures, Native American tribes have exercised jurisdiction over their children, but most tribes have seriously underdeveloped services. Tribal entities need to build a variety of service infrastructures such as management information systems and quality improvement programs. The Fostering Connections legislation enables American tribes to access Federal Title IV-E funds directly.

12. **Agency policies should promote better assessment and support of gay, lesbian, bisexual, and transgendered youth in out-of-home care.** Few child welfare systems have encouraged staff members and foster parents to protect and nurture gay, lesbian, bisexual, and transgendered (GLBT) youth. Such youth are vulnerable to victimization, depression, and suicide. Because of their sexual orientations, GLBT youth have a higher risk of placement disruption. Special efforts are needed both to assess the needs of these youths and to devise supportive services for them (Mallon, 1999; Wornoff & Mallon, 2006).

13. **Cross-systems collaboration should be strengthened.** The risk and protective factors related to child maltreatment bear remarkable resemblance to risk and protective factors for other social and health problems. This suggests that a more integrated and coordinated approach to family support and children's services could be designed

to address common risk factors. Income assistance, education, mental health, public health, intimate-partner violence, law enforcement, juvenile justice, and child welfare agencies need to work more toward a common purpose and minimize operating in isolation from each other. (See for example, Chahine, Pecora & Sanders, 2013.) Cross-systems collaboration—sometimes called a system of care—is needed to strengthen provision of services to families with concurrent occurrences of child maltreatment, depression, drug abuse, and partner violence.

14. **Transition policies and support for emancipating youth must be overhauled.** Too many graduates of the foster care system are undertrained and underemployed. Many youth and young adults are part of a large group of marginalized youth who age out of the system without adequate skills for independent living and without a support system. Children placed in foster care vary widely in their level of preparation for emancipation from foster care in terms of education and income (Courtney et al., 2007; Goerge et al., 2002).

Programmatically, child welfare systems should promote investment in culturally relevant services, support, and opportunities to ensure that every youth in foster care makes a safe, successful transition to adulthood. Preparation for independent living must be redesigned to start at the age of 10 years, rather in late adolescence. A comprehensive transition plan should be developed for every child. It should include planning for supportive relationships, community connections, education, life skills assessment and development, identity formation, housing, employment, physical health, and mental health (Casey Family Programs, 2001; Los Angeles County Departments of Children and Family Services/Probation, Youth Development Service, 2013; Wald & Martinez, 2003). Employment training and work experience should be expanded for many youth while they are in care. Policies and incentives should ensure that no young person leaves foster care without housing, access to health care, employment skills, and permanent connections to at least one adult.

15. **Performance-based contracting should be fully implemented.** Attempts to implement state and county policies to promote performance-based contracting have been hampered by a lack of knowledge of baseline conditions, concrete target goals, and infrastructure funding gaps. Clear performance criteria, cohort-based and longitudinal data analyses, and quality improvement systems must be in place to enable agencies to improve performance-based contracting and the implementation of evidence-based practice models (Mordock, 2002; Wulczyn et al., 2009).

USING KNOWLEDGE OF RISK, PROTECTION, AND RESILIENCE TO ACHIEVE SERVICE INTEGRATION

We have described the major policies that influence the well-being of children and families involved with the child welfare system. The lack of service and funding integration were noted as well as many policy developments that illustrate how risk-reduction strategies could improve child welfare services. To disrupt the risk mechanisms that lead

Table 3.5   Point of Engagement and Up-Front Assessment Services in Los Angeles

The process works as follows:

- An upfront assessment is recommended when an emergency response worker suspects a problem connected with mental health, substance abuse or domestic violence and needs additional expertise about the degree of involvement.
- An assessment is not made if a safety issue indicates immediate removal or if the hotline allegation is unfounded.
- The assessment is voluntary. If the parent agrees to the assessment, a trained clinician from a community-service organization goes to the home no later than 48 hours after the referral.
- The assessment is an expanded bio/psycho/social analysis that looks at seven major areas of functioning: physical health, mental health, substance use, educational and occupational functioning, social relationships, domestic violence/domestic relationships and criminal activity. The assessor uses a computer-based, online tool called a Behavioral Severity Assessment Program (BSAP) and interviews caregivers separately. The assessment is comprehensive, looking at strengths as well as needs, and often taking two hours to complete. ..... Trevor Daniels explained: "You have to get a full understanding about the dynamics of a family's world. You have to understand people's functional level, and whether there's a risk to the kids because of their parents' problems."
- The assessors do not make recommendations about child placement. Removal—or not—is the responsibility of the Department of Child and Family Services (DCFS). Rather the assessor talks to the family and to DCFS about the results of the assessment and makes recommendations to DCFS for services.
- DCFS makes the decision about removal and services. Because the agency conducting the assessments is a community provider with expertise in domestic violence, mental health and substance abuse and because it has information on what the caregivers really need, it can start services right away.
- Ideally a Team Decision Meeting takes place soon after the assessment, and the community agency participates with family members, DCFS, and others in determining a plan of action.

Source: Casey Family Programs. (2009). *Stories of practice change: What flexible funding means to the children and families of Los Angeles County.* Seattle, WA: Casey Family Programs, pp. 7–8.

to child maltreatment and that complicate recovery from victimization, child welfare agencies need adequate funding, as well as new and more effective ways to link funding to effective programs.

Child welfare policy, performance incentives, and practices lack alignment (e.g., Wulczyn et al., 2009). Critics argue that the child welfare system needs to be overhauled to better address risk factors leading to child abuse and neglect (Edna McConnell Clark Foundation, 2004; Lindsey, 2004; Whittaker & Maluccio, 2002). In addition, the emerging literature on protective processes, which buffer children from risk and promote recovery from victimization, holds potential to influence policy and practice.

To underscore the complexity of the challenges incumbent in reform, a case study is presented in the accompanying box. The case describes a family in which multiple forms of child neglect are present. This family situation illustrates how child neglect can have serious consequences for child development. The complexity of this family situation is evident; it is the too-frequent situation in which genuine love for children is interwoven with mental health problems, partner violence, poverty, and deficits in parenting skills. In this scenario, the concepts of risk, resiliency, and protective factors have utility for guiding case decision making and the choice of interventions.

Children Who Are Not Headliners

This case example involves multiple forms of child neglect. An intergenerational cycle may be at work here: a "passing on of infantilism, mother to daughter, through processes of deprivation leading to detachment (the deprivation-detachment hypotheses), failure to provide stimulation, and the child's identification with an inadequate role model. Hence the cycle of neglect might be said to derive from a cycle of infantilism" (Polansky, Chalmers, Buttenweiser, & Williams, 1981, p. 43). Although it must be emphasized that generalizing these families is not wise because of their diversity, some of the research data depict a group of neglectful caregivers who are generally (a) less able to love; (b) less capable of working productively; (c) less open about feelings; (d) more prone to living planlessly and impulsively; (e) susceptible to psychological symptoms and to phases of passive inactivity and numb fatalism; (f) more likely to live in a situation of family conflict, to be less organized and more chaotic; (g) less verbally expressive; and (h) less positive and more negative in affect (Gaudin, Polansky, Kilpatrick, & Shilton, 1996; Polansky et al., 1981; Polansky, Gaudin, & Kilpatrick, 1992). Although many families involved with substance abuse never come to the attention of child welfare agencies, when they do they very often are identified as having problems related to child neglect (U.S. Department of Health and Human Services, 1999).

In a sense, the parenting/nurturing instinct has been weakened or distorted in its aim, or overwhelmed by the parent's struggle in personal survival. This stunting or crippling of parenting or nurturing is not often an emergent response to current stress but is predictable from the social history of the parent and the lack of nurturance in his or her childhood (Polansky et al., 1981, pp. 147–157). Some of those risk factors (and family strengths and resources) are illustrated by the following case example.

The family consists of Mona Stay, twenty-three, and her common-law husband Frank Brown, aged twenty-six. There are three children: Frank Stay, three and a half, Sylvia Stay, eighteen months, and Wilma, seven months. The Stay-Browns have been together over five years. Although they quarrel and separate periodically, they seem very mutually dependent and likely to remain a couple.

Their original referral was from a nurse who had become aware of the eldest child's condition. He was difficult to discipline, was eating dirt and paint chips, and seemed hyperactive. Although over two, he was not speaking. His father reacted to him with impatience. He was often slapped, and hardly ever spoken to with fondness. The caseworker got Mona to cooperate in taking young Frank in for a test for lead poisoning, and for a full developmental evaluation. This child had had several bouts with

(Continued)

(Continued)

impetigo, had been bitten through the eyelid by a stray dog, and had a series of ear infections resulting in a slight hearing loss. Although physically normal, he appeared already nearly a year delayed.

Often this child was found outside the house alone when the caseworker came to see the family. On one occasion he was seen hanging from a broken fire escape on the second floor. The worker was unable to rouse his mother, or to enter the house until she got help from the nearby landlord, after which she ran upstairs and rescued the child. Only then did the sleeping Mona awaken!

With much effort having been expended on his behalf, this child had been attending a therapeutic nursery. His speech is already improved after four or five months, and his hyperactivity has calmed. He comes through as a lovable little boy.

Sylvia is surprisingly pale . . . and indeed, suffers from severe anemia. This child has had recurrent eye infections, and had a bout with spinal meningitis at age three months which, fortunately, seems to have left no residual effects. Much effort has gone into working with Mona concerning Sylvia's need for proper diet and iron supplement. After a year of contact this is still a problem.

The baby was born after the family had become known to the agency. Despite the agency's urging, Mona refused to go for prenatal care until she was in her second trimester, but she did maintain a fairly good diet, helped by small "loans" from the agency when her money for food ran out. When Wilma was born, she had to remain for a time at the hospital for treatment of jaundice. After she went home, she was left to lie most of the time in her bassinet, receiving very little attention from either parent. At four months of age, Wilma weighed only five pounds and was tentatively diagnosed as exhibiting "failure to thrive" by the hospital. Thereafter the mother avoided going to the clinic, and the caseworker spent much effort concerning the feeding and sheer survival of Wilma. The baby is now slowly gaining weight but is still limp and inactive.

In addition to an active caseworker, a homemaker was assigned to this family for months. Much more was involved than trying to help Mona learn to organize her day: she had almost no motivation to get started. Rather than learning how to manage, she tried to manipulate the homemaker into doing her housework for her. However, with time and patience, Mona has been persuaded to go with the caseworker on shopping trips, is learning how to buy groceries to best advantage, and from time to time manages to get the laundry into and out of the laundromat. So far as her plans for herself, Mona has talked of seeking training as a beauty operator, but has never followed through on this or on other positive plans.

The family's sole support is public assistance. Frank Brown, the father, was on drugs earlier in their relationship, but managed to get off them. Now, however, he drinks heavily, and although he manages to work, he never contributes to the household.

Mona, apparently, was herself a neglected child, and was removed from her parents in infancy. Placed with an adoptive family, there was constant friction during her growing up, and she ran away from home several times. During her teens, she was placed in an institution for incorrigible girls. Later she spent a period in a mental hospital during which she was withdrawn from heroin addiction. It is a commentary on her life that she regards this period in the adolescent ward as one of her happiest ever. Her adoptive mother is now dead, and her father wants nothing more to do with her, so she was more or less living on the streets when she met with Frank and set up their present establishment.

Frank and Mona, despite his obvious exploitativeness, seem to love each other and their children, and to want to keep the family together. They are able to relate to those who try to help them, so at least one is not operating constantly against hostile resistance. Mona is an intelligent woman and now shows adequate ability to handle the children. She can be an excellent cook—when there is food. Yet this remains a disorganized household. Bills are never paid, clothes are thrown around, the children never sleep on clean sheets, trash is piled around the house so that flies and maggots abound. Mona still leaves the youngsters quite alone for brief periods. There is no heat in the house, and the family will soon have to move, with neither any idea where to go nor funds for rent deposits and the like. Mona, at least, is currently wearing an IUD.

The Stay-Brown menage was not invented, although of course we have altered names and some facts to protect all concerned. These are real people, and they are clearly involved in child neglect. The failures center on poor feeding, uncleanliness, extremely bad housing, filthy circumstances which make the children prone to infections, lack of medical care, inadequate supervision and protections from danger, lack of intellectual stimulation, inattentiveness to the children bordering on rejection—one could go on. The fine staff trying to help Mona improve her child care finally gave up and closed her case after about fifteen months of effort. The care was improving slowly, if at all, and there were recurrent instances of regression.

Frank proved superficially amenable to suggestions when he could be seen, but in fact evaded any real responsibility for the household. The time, money, and—more importantly—motivation for hard work with such families are chronically in short supply. So the decision was made to try to help someone else who might be more treatable.

Meanwhile these children are with their parents. Since they have not literally been abandoned, it is uncertain whether a local judge would decide the home is so bad that the children must be removed. If a catastrophe were to occur, if one were to read that these three children had burned to death in a fire, one would be saddened but not greatly surprised. If one of the three were to die of an infectious disease or an undiagnosed appendicitis, one would not be surprised either. For the present, however, they are among the group child-protection workers know well, but that the public does not, because they do not make headlines—or at least not yet.

Source: Polansky, Chalmers, Buttenweiser, & Williams, *Damaged Parents: An Anatomy of Child Neglect,* pp. 5–7. Copyright © 1981. Reprinted with permission of the University of Chicago Press.

SUMMARY

In this chapter, we have reviewed policies and legislation in American child welfare, and discussed a number of critical issues and potential reforms. A risk and resilience perspective was explored. From the concepts of protection and resilience, models of service that consider child and family development in the context of community and culture may be useful in future child welfare initiatives. In many states, private child welfare programs play a major role in protecting and nourishing maltreated children who were placed in foster care. Policy experts would be wise to consider the roles of public and voluntary agencies when considering ways to improve child welfare services and increase funding.

On balance, our review suggests that child welfare needs to adopt a broader framework to protect children from maltreatment. The growing knowledge base regarding risk and resilience, combined with the growing number of studies showing that child maltreatment can be prevented (Pew Foundation, 2008; Schorr and Marchand, 2007), present a clear challenge to design more "upstream" prevention-focused services while concurrently improving services for maltreated children. Meeting this challenge will demand a measure of leadership, funding, cross-systems collaboration, and accountability that is visionary.

QUESTIONS FOR DISCUSSION

1. What are the implications of the literature on risk and protective factors for the design of policies and programs for family support, foster care, and permanency planning?

2. What policy changes would you recommend to better integrate service delivery and to provide an evidence-based system of child welfare services for families with children at risk of child maltreatment?

3. In what ways might the increasing federal and state emphasis on measurable outcomes promote service delivery approaches that are culturally appropriate and oriented to child well-being?

4. How will some of the provisions of the Affordable Care Act help some of the parents who are coming to the attention of child welfare agencies?

NOTES

1. There were 3 million reports involving the welfare of about 5 million children in 2001 and 1.8 million in 2002. For the most recent federal child maltreatment statistics, see U.S. DHHS (2013a). In 1990, there were an estimated 611,924 victims, based on projections using data from 35 states. See U.S. DHHS (1999, pp. 4–2); for the 2002 statistics, see http://www.acf.hhs.gov/programs/cb/publications/cm02/summary.htm.

2. These data are from the federal Adoption and Foster Care Analysis and Reporting System (AFCARS), which derived these estimates using data from nearly all 50 states and other jurisdictions (e.g., Washington, D.C., and Puerto Rico; U.S. DHHS, 2013b). For total children served in 2012, see U.S. DHHS (2013c). Note that AFCARS data are periodically updated; therefore, the data cited in this chapter may not match the data on the current website.

3. Section 1130 of the federal Social Security Act, enacted in 1994, gave the Secretary of Health and Human Services (HHS) the authority to approve waivers to Title IV-E rules for the

purpose of funding demonstration projects in state or county child welfare systems. This authority provides an opportunity for states and tribes that administer Title IV-E funding to use the funds more flexibly in order to test innovative approaches for child welfare service delivery and financing. Across the country, Title IV-E Child Welfare Demonstration Projects are expected to document the benefits of a more balanced array of child welfare services.

4. Permanency roundtables (PRTs) were designed to expedite the permanency planning process by identifying realistic solutions to permanency barriers for youth. A team of professionals, including a facilitator, the youth's case manager, the case manager's supervisor, a master practitioner (a local permanency expert), a permanency consultant (an external permanency expert), and others who may be able to contribute to a permanency plan meet for two hours to discuss the youth's case. The primary desired youth outcome is the achievement of legal permanency (through reunification, adoption, or guardianship). The desired organizational outcomes include increasing staff expertise around permanency and "busting" systemic barriers to permanency. (See http://www.casey.org/georgia-permanency-roundtables/.)

5. The concept of *epigenetic change*—alterations in gene expression that are due to environmental or other reasons not related to DNA—is an important idea in child development. There is ample evidence that subtle changes in the early environment influence adulthood disease appearance; this early environment is not restricted to the fetal period but is expanded to encompass the plastic phase of early child development. Moreover, evidence supports that our genetic background, which is the result of our evolution, is an important contributor to susceptibility to perinatal imprinting. However, rapid adjustment and optimization, which are necessary at times for survival, require a type of plasticity that the genome sequence alone cannot achieve. Without changing the genomic backbone, epigenetic modulation, in reaction to a given environment, results in functional adaptation of the genomic response. Thus, evolutionally acquired genomic susceptibilities and environmentally induced epigenomic modulations occurring early in life impact on later development of human diseases (Tremblay & Harnet, 2008).

6. Family structure reflects the number of parents in the household and their relationship to the child; living arrangement reflects their marital or cohabitation status. Considering both factors, the NIS-4 classified children into six categories: living with two married biological parents, living with other married parents (e.g., stepparent, adoptive parent), living with two unmarried parents, living with one parent who had an unmarried partner in the household, living with one parent who had no partner in the household, and living with no parent.

7. The NIS-4 could identify a grandparent as a child's caregiver under three conditions: when the grandparent was the child's primary caregiver, when the primary caregiver did not have a spouse or partner and the grandparent was the secondary caregiver, and when the grandparent was a caregiver and maltreated the child.

8. To contend with missing data on individual items, the NIS-4 analyses combined three indicators into a general measure of socioeconomic status: household income, household participation in any poverty program, and parents' education. Low socioeconomic status households were those in the bottom tier on any indicator: household income below $15,000 a year, parents' highest education level less than high school, or any member of the household a participant in a poverty program, such as TANF, food stamps, public housing, energy assistance, or subsidized school meals.

9. It is possible that the lower rates at these younger ages reflect some undercoverage of these age groups. That is, prior to attaining school age, children are less observable to community professionals.

REFERENCES

Ainsworth, M. D. S. (1989). Attachments beyond infancy. *American Psychologist, 44,* 709–716. doi:10.1037/0003–066X.44.4.709

American Humane Association, Children's Division; American Bar Association, Center on Children and the Law; Annie E. Casey Foundation; The Casey Family Program; Casey Family Services; and Institute for Human Services Management. (1998). *Assessing outcomes in child welfare services: Principles, concepts, and a framework of core indicators.* Englewood, CO: The Casey Outcomes and Decision-Making Project. Retrieved from http://www.aecf.org/upload/publicationfiles/assessing%20 framework.pdf

American Psychological Association Task Force on Resilience and Strength in Black Children and Adolescents. (2008). *Resilience in African American children and adolescents: A vision for optimal development.* Washington, DC: Author. Retrieved from http://www.apa.org/pi/families/resources/ resiliencerpt.pdf

Annie E. Casey Foundation. (2014). *The cost of doing nothing.* Retrieved May 24, 2014 from http://www .aecf.org/ ~ /media/Pubs/Topics/Child%20Welfare%20Permanence/Other/CostofDoingNothingInfo/ CostOfDoingNothingInfo.pdf

Annie E. Casey Foundation and the Jim Casey Youth Opportunities Initiative. (2013). *When child welfare works: A working paper.* Baltimore, MD: Author. Retrieved May 27, 2014, from http://www.aecf.org/ KnowledgeCenter/Publications.aspx?pubguid = {2437146B-7A85-4E9F-9524-94114F185106}

Avery, R. (1998). *Public agency adoption in New York State: Phase I report. Foster care histories of children freed for adoption in New York State: 1980–1993.* Ithaca, NY: Cornell University Press.

Barnett, D., Manly, J. T., & Cicchetti, D. (1993). Defining child maltreatment: The interface between policy and research. In D. Cicchetti & S. Toth (Eds.), *Child abuse, child development and social policy* (pp. 7–74). Norwood, NJ: Ablex.

Barth, R. P., Gibbons, C., & Guo, S. (2006). Substance abuse treatment and the recurrence of maltreatment among caregivers with children living at home: A propensity score analysis. *Journal of Substance Abuse Treatment, 30,* 93–104. doi:10.1016/j.jsat.2005.10.008

Berrick, J. D., Needell, B., Barth, R. B., & Johnson-Reid, M. (1998). *The tender years: Toward developmentally sensitive child welfare services for very young children.* New York: Oxford University Press.

Besinger, B. A., Garland, A. F., Litrownik, A. J., & Landsverk, J. A. (1999). Caregiver substance abuse among maltreated children placed in out-of-home care. *Child Welfare, 78*(2), 221–239.

Biglan, A., Flay, B. R., Embry, D. D., & Sandler, I. N. (2012). The critical role of nurturing environments for promoting human well-being. *American Psychologist, 67*(4), 257–271. doi: 10.1037/a0026796

Briere, J. (1992). *Child abuse trauma theory and treatment of the lasting effects.* Newbury Park, CA: Sage.

Bronfenbrenner, U. (1979). *The ecology of human development.* Cambridge, MA: Harvard University Press.

Bronfenbrenner, U. (1986). Ecology of the family as a context to human development: Research perspectives. *Developmental Psychology, 22,* 723–742. doi:10.1037/0012–1649.22.6.723

Bronfenbrenner, U. (2004). *Making human beings human: Bioecological perspectives on human development.* Thousand Oaks, CA: Sage.

Bronfenbrenner, U., & Morris, P. A. (1998). The ecology of developmental processes. In W. Damon (Ed.), *Handbook of child psychology* (5th ed., pp. 993–1028). New York: John Wiley.

Brooks-Gunn, J., & Duncan, G. J. (1997). The effects of poverty on children. *Future of Children, 7,* 55–71. doi:10.2307/1602387

Brooks-Gunn, J., Klebanov, P. K., & Liaw, F. (1995). The learning, physical, and emotional environment of the home in the context of poverty: The Infant Health and Development program. *Children and Youth Services Review, 17,* 251–276. doi:10.1016/0190–7409(95)00011-Z

Bruns, E. J., & Burchard, J. D. (2000). Impact of respite care services for families with children experiencing emotional and behavioral problems. *Children's Services: Social Policy, Research, and Practice, 3,* 39–61. doi:10.1207/S15326918CS0301_3

Caplan, G. (1974). *Support systems and community mental health: Lectures on concept development.* New York: Behavioral Publications.

Carey, J. (2009, March 9). The spirit level: Why more equal societies almost always do better by Richard Wilkinson and Kate Pickett [Book review]. *London Sunday Times.* Retrieved from http://entertainment.timesonline.co.uk/tol/arts_and_entertainment/books/non-fiction/article5859108.ece

Carnegie Council on Adolescent Development. (1989). *Turning points: Preparing youth for the 21st century.* Washington, DC: Author.

Casey Family Programs. (2001). *It's my life—A framework for youth transitioning from foster care to successful adulthood.* Seattle, WA: Author. Retrieved from http://www .casey.org/Resources/Publications/pdf/ItsMyLife_Framework.pdf

Casey Family Programs. (2003). *Family, community, culture: Roots of permanency—A conceptual framework on permanency from Casey Family Programs.* Seattle, WA: Author.

Casey Family Programs. (2009). *Stories of practice change: What flexible funding means to the children and families of Los Angeles County.* Seattle, WA: Casey Family Programs, pp. 7–8.

Casey Family Programs. (2010a). *Public policy agenda: A comprehensive finance reform package framework.* Seattle, WA: Author.

Casey Family Programs. (2010b). *No time to lose: An ecological practice model for adolescent and young adult permanency* (Preliminary title). Seattle, WA: Author.

Casey Family Programs and the Brookings Institution. (2013). *Working paper: Child protection reform principles to achieve improved outcomes.* (Mimeograph). Seattle, WA: Casey Family Programs.

Catalano, R. F., & Hawkins, J. D. (1996). The social developmental model: A theory of antisocial behavior. In J. D. Hawkins (Ed.), *Delinquency and crime: Current theories* (pp. 149–197). New York: Cambridge University Press.

Chahine, Z., Pecora, P.J. & Sanders, D. (2013). Special foreword: Preventing severe maltreatment-related injuries and fatalities: Applying a public health framework and innovative approaches to child protection. *Child Welfare, 92(2), 13–18.*

Chamberlain, P. (2003). *Treating chronic juvenile offenders: Advances made through the Oregon multidimensional treatment foster care model.* Washington, DC: American Psychological Association. doi:10.1037/10596–000

Child Welfare Information Gateway, Children's Bureau, FRIENDS National Resource Center For Community-Based Child Abuse Prevention. (2010). *Strengthening families and communities: 2010 resource guide.* Washington, DC: Author. Retrieved from http://www.childwelfare.gov/pubs/res_guide_2010/

Child Welfare League of America. (2004). *Making children a national priority: A framework for community action.* Washington, DC: Author.

Children's Defense Fund. (2008). *State factsheets for grandparents or other relatives raising children.* Retrieved from http://www.childrensdefense.org/child-research-data-publications/data/state-data-repository/grandparents-other-relatives-raising-children-state-factsheets.html

Cicchetti, D., & Lynch, M. (1993). Toward an ecological/transactional model of community violence and child maltreatment: Consequences for children's development. *Psychiatry, 56,* 96–118.

Cohen, J. A., Mannarino, A. P., Zhitova, A. C., & Capone, M. E. (2003). Treating child abuse-related post-traumatic stress and comorbid substance abuse in adolescents. *Child Abuse & Neglect, 27,* 1345–1365. doi:10.1016/j.chiabu.2003.08.001

Coll, C. G., & Magnuson, K. (2000). Cultural differences as sources of developmental vulnerabilities and resources. In J. P. Shonkoff & S. J. Meisels (Eds.), *Handbook of early childhood intervention* (2nd ed., pp. 94–114). Cambridge, UK: Cambridge University Press.

Courtney, M. E., Dworsky, A., Cusick, G. R., Keller, T., Havlicek, J. , Perez, A., Terao, S., & Bost, N. (2007). *Midwest evaluation of adult functioning of former foster youth: Outcomes at age 21.* Chicago: University of Chicago, Chapin Hall Center for Children.

Crary, D. (2010, February 2). *U.S. study shows drop in child abuse* (Associated Press). Retrieved from http://www.thefreelibrary.com/APNewsBreak % 3a + US + study +   shows + drop + in + child + abuse-a01612134912

Dalla, R. L., Defrain, J., Johnson, J., & Abbott, D. A. (2009). *Strengths and challenges of new immigrant families: Implications for research, education, policy, and service.* Lanham, MD: Lexington Books.

De Anda, D. (2003). *Social work with multicultural youth.* New York: Haworth Press.

DePanfilis, D. (1996). Social isolation of neglectful families: A review of social support assessment and intervention. *Child Maltreatment, 1*(1), 37–52. doi:10.1177/1077559596001001005

Derezotes, D., Poertner, J., & Testa, M. (Eds.). (2005). *Race matters in child welfare: The overrepresentation of African American children in the system.* Washington, DC: Child Welfare League of America Press.

Development Services Group, Inc. (2013). *Protective factors for populations served by the administration on children, youth, and families. A literature review and theoretical framework: Executive summary.* Washington, D.C.: U.S. Department of Health and Human Services, Administration for Children and Families, Children's Bureau, p. 6. Retrieved May 20, 2014, from http://www.dsgonline.com/acyf/DSG % 20Protective % 20Factors % 20Literature % 20Review % 202013 % 20Exec % 20Summary.pdf

Downs, A. C., & Pecora, P. J. (2004). *Application of Erikson's psychosocial theory to the effects of child abuse and ameliorative foster care* (Working Paper No. 2). Seattle, WA: Casey Family Programs.

Drake, B., Jolley, J. M., Lanier, P., Fluke, J., Barth, R. P., & Jonson-Reid, M. (2011). Using national data racial bias in child protection? A comparison of competing explanations, *Pediatrics.* doi:10.1542/peds.2010-1710, http://www.pediatrics.org

Edna McConnell Clark Foundation. (2004). *Theory of change behind the program for children.* New York: Author. Retrieved from http:// www.emcf.org/programs/children/indepth/theory.htm

Ellis, M. L., Eskenazi, S., Bonnell, R. & Pecora, P. J. (2013). *Taking a closer look at the reduction in entry rates for children in Sacramento County with an emphasis on African American children: A spotlight on practice.* Seattle, WA: Casey Family Programs, www.Casey.org

Erikson, E. H. (1985). *The life cycle completed.* New York: Norton.

Finkelhor, D., & Jones, L. (2006). Why have child maltreatment and child victimization declined? *Journal of Social Issues, 62*(4), pp. 685–716.

First Focus. (2008). *Big ideas for children: Investing in our nation's future.* Washington, DC: Author.

Fluke, J., Jones-Harden, B., Jenkins, M., & Ruehrdanz, A. (2011). *Research synthesis on child welfare disproportionality and disparities.* Denver, CO: American Humane Association and the Annie E. Casey Foundation.

Fraser, M. W. (Ed.). (2004). *Risk and resilience in childhood: An ecological perspective* (2nd ed.). Washington, DC: NASW Press.

Garbarino, J. (1992). *Children and families in the social environment.* New York: Aldine de Gruyter.

Garbarino, J., & Ganzel, B. (2000). The human ecology of early risk. In J. P. Shonkoff & S. J. Meisels (Eds.), *Handbook of early childhood intervention* (2nd ed., pp. 76–93). Cambridge, UK: Cambridge University Press.

Garmezy, N. (1983). Stressors of childhood. In N. Garmezy & M. Rutter (Eds.), *Stress, coping and development in children* (pp. 43–84). New York: McGraw-Hill.

Garmezy, N. (1985). Stress resistant children: The search for protective factors. In J. E. Stevenson (Ed.), *Recent research in developmental psychopathology* (pp. 76–93). Oxford, UK: Pergamon Press.

Gaudin, J. M., Polanksy, N. A., Kilpatrick, A. C., & Shilton, P. (1996). Family functioning in neglectful families. *Child Abuse & Neglect, 20,* 363–377. doi:10.1016/0145-2134(96)00005-1

Griffin, G., McClelland, G., Holzberg, M., Stolbach, B., Maj, N., & Kisiel, C. (2012). Addressing the impact of trauma before diagnosing mental illness in child welfare. *Child Welfare, 90*(6), 69–89.

Goerge, R., Bilaver, L., Lee, B. L., Needell, B., Brookhart, A., & Jackman, W. (2002). *Employment outcomes for youth aging out of foster care. Final report.* Chicago: University of Chicago, Chapin Hall Center for Children. Retrieved from http://aspe.hhs.gov/hsp/fostercare-agingout02/

Hanson, R. F., Smith, D. W., Saunders, B. E., Swenson, C. C., & Conrad, L. (1995). Measurement in child abuse research: A survey of researchers. *The APSAC Advisor, 8,* 7–10.

Haskins, R., Wulczyn, F., & Webb, M.B. (Eds.). (2007). *Child protection: Using research to improve policy and practice.* Washington, DC: Brookings Press.

Hill, R. B. (2007). *Analysis of racial/ethnic disproportionality and disparity at the national, state and county levels.* Washington, DC: The Casey-CSSP Alliance for Racial Equity and the Center for the Study of Social Policy.

Hines, A. M., Lemon, K., Wyatt, P., & Merdinger, J. (2004). Factors related to the disproportionate involvement of children of color in the child welfare system: A review and emerging themes. *Children and Youth Services Review, 26,* 507–527. doi:10.1016/j.childyouth.2004.01.007

Hodges, V. (1994). Assessing for strengths and protective factors in child abuse and neglect: Risk assessment with families of color. In P. J. Pecora, & D. J. English (Eds.), *Multi-cultural guidelines for assessing family strengths and risk factors in child protective services* (pp. II–1–11). Seattle: University of Washington School of Social Work, and Washington State Department of Social Services.

Jenson, J. M., & Bender, K. A. (2014). *Preventing child and adolescent problem behavior: Evidence-based strategies in schools, families and communities.* New York, NY: Oxford.

Johnson, K., Knitzer, J., & Kaufmann, R. (2003). *Making dollars follow sense: Financing early childhood mental health services to promote healthy social and emotional development in young children.* New York: Columbia University, National Center on Children in Poverty.

Karoly, L. M., Kilburn, R. M., Caulkins, J. P., & Cannon, J. S. (2000). *Assessing costs and benefits of early childhood intervention programs: Overview and application.* Santa Monica, CA: RAND Corporation.

Kendall-Tackett, K. (2013). *Treating the lifetime health effects of childhood victimization.* (2nd ed.) Kingston, NJ: Civic Research Institute.

Kerman, B., Maluccio, A. N., & Freundlich, M. (2009). *Achieving permanence for older children and youth in foster care.* New York: Columbia University Press.

Kessler, R. C., & Magee, W. J. (1993). Childhood adversities and adult depression: Basic patterns of association in a US national survey. *Psychological Medicine, 23,* 679–690. doi:10.1017/S0033291700025460

Kilburn, M. R., & Karoly, L. A. (2008). *The economics of early childhood policy: What the dismal science has to say about investing in children* (RAND Doc. No. OP-227-CFP). Santa Monica, CA: RAND Corporation.

Kirk, S., Gallagher, J., & Anastasiow, N. (1993). *Educating exceptional children* (7th ed). Boston: Houghton Mifflin.

Los Angeles County Departments of Children and Family Services/Probation. (2013). *Los Angeles County Departments of Children and Family Services/Probation, Youth Development Service (YDS) Individualized Transition Skills Program (ITSP) fact sheet.* Retrieved July 2, 2014, from http://dcf-silp.co.la.ca.us/documents/ITSPPromotionalFACTSHEET2013.pdf.

Lindsey, D. (2004). *The welfare of children* (2nd ed.). New York: Oxford University Press.

Lorthridge, J., McCroskey, J., Pecora, P. J., Chambers, R., & Fatemi, M. (2011). Strategies for improving child welfare services for families of color: First findings of a community-based initiative in Los Angeles. *Children and Youth Services Review.* 34, 281–288.

Maier, H. W. (1978). *Three theories of child development* (3rd ed.). New York: Harper & Row.

Mallon, G. P. (1999). *Let's get this straight: A gay- and lesbian-affirming approach to child welfare.* New York: Columbia University Press.

Maluccio, A. N., Pine, B. A., & Tracy, E. M. (2002). *Social work practice with families and children.* New York: Columbia University Press.

Mann, A. (2003). Relationships matter: Impact of parental, peer factors on teen, young adult substance abuse. *NIDA Notes, 18*(2), 11–13. doi:10.1151/v18i2RMIPPFTYASA

Marts, E. J., Lee, R., McCroy, R., & McCroskey, J. (2008). Point of engagement: Reducing disproportionality and improving child and family outcomes. *Child Welfare, 87*(2), 335–358.

McCroskey, J., Christie, T., Lorthridge, J., Chambers, R., Pecora, P. J., Azzam, T. , Fleischer, D., Rosenthal, E., Weisbart, A., Custodio, C., Franke, T., Nunn, P., Carter, S., Yoo, J., Bowie, P., & Wold, C. (2009). *Prevention Initiative Demonstration Project (PIDP): Year one evaluation summary report.* Los Angeles: Casey Family Programs. Retrieved from http://www.casey.org/Resources/Publications/pdf/pidp_fr.pdf

McDonald, J., Salyers, N., & Shaver, M. (2004). *The foster care straitjacket: Innovation, federal financing & accountability in state foster care reform.* Urbana-Champaign: University of Illinois at Urbana-Champaign, Fostering Results Project. Retrieved from http://www.pewtrusts.org/our_work_report_detail.aspx?id=17842

McIntosh, N. (1991). Identification and investigation of properties of social support. *Journal of Organizational Behavior Management, 12,* 201–217. doi:10.1002/job.4030120304

Mech, E. V. (Ed.). (1988). Independent-living services for at-risk adolescents. *Child Welfare, 67,* 483–634.

Mordock, J. B. (2002). *Managing for outcomes: A basic guide to the evaluation of best practices in the human services.* Washington, DC: Child Welfare League of America Press.

Morgan, L. J., Spears, L. S., & Kaplan, C. (2003). *A framework for community action: Making children a national priority.* Washington, DC: Child Welfare League of America Press.

National Coalition for Child Protection Reform. (2008). *The trouble with child and family services reviews: The federal government's failed attempt to measure child welfare system performance.* Alexandria, VA: Author. Retrieved from http://www.nccpr .org/reports/cfsr.doc

O'Connell, M. E., Boat, T., & Warner, K. E. (Eds.). (2009). *Preventing mental, emotional and behavioral disorders among young people: Progress and possibilities.* Washington, DC: National Academies Press. Retrieved from http://www .nap.edu/catalog.php?record_id=12480

O'Hare, W. (2011). *The changing child population of the United States: Analysis of data from the 2010 census.* Baltimore, MD: The Annie E. Casey Foundation, p. 7. Retrieved July 7, 2014, from http://www.aecf.org/m/resourcedoc/AECF-ChangingChildPopulation-2011-Full.pdf. Note that the 2010 data are derived from U.S. Census Bureau, News Release, "U.S. Census Bureau Delivers Final State Census. Population Totals for Legislative Redistricting," CB 11-CN.123, March 24, 2011. Retrieved July 7, 2014, from https://www.census.gov/2010census/news/releases/operations/cb11-cn123.html

Osofsky, J. D., & Thompson, D. (2000). Adaptive and maladaptive parenting: Perspectives on risk and protective factors. In J. P. Shonkoff & S. J. Meisels (Eds.), *Handbook of early childhood intervention* (2nd ed., pp. 54–75). Cambridge, UK: Cambridge University Press.

Parish, S. L., Pomeranz, A. E., & Braddock, D. (2003). Family support in the United States: Financing trends and emerging initiatives. *Mental Retardation, 41,* 174–187. doi:10.1352/0047-6765(2003)41 < 174:FSI TUS > 2.0.CO;2

Pecora, P. J., Kessler, R. C., Williams, J., Downs, A. C., English, D.J., White, J., & O'Brien, K. (2010). *What works in family foster care? Key components of success from the Northwest foster care alumni study.* New York and Oxford: Oxford University Press.

Pecora, P.J., O'Brien, K. & Maher, E. (2014). *Levels of research evidence and benefit-cost data for Title IV-E waiver interventions: A Casey research brief.* Seattle, WA: Casey Family Programs.

Pecora, P. J., Whittaker, J. K., Maluccio, A. N., Barth, R. P., & Depanfilis, D. (with R. Plotnick). (2009). *The child welfare challenge: Policy, practice, and research* (3rd ed.). Piscataway, NJ: Aldine-Transaction.

Perry, B.D. & Dobson, C. (2013). Application of the neurosequential nodel (NMT) in maltreated children. In J. Ford & C. Courtois (Eds.) *Treating complex traumatic stress disorders in children and adolescents,* pp. 249–260. New York: Guilford Press.

Pew Foundation. (2008). *Time for reform: Investing in prevention: Keeping children safe at home.* Philadelphia: Author. Retrieved from http://kidsarewaiting.org/tools/reports/files/0011.pdf

Pine, B. A. (1986). Child welfare reform and the political process. *Social Service Review, 60,* 339–359. doi:10.1086/644381

Plantz, M. C., Hubbell, R., Barrett, B. J., & Dobrec, A. (1989). Indian Child Welfare Act: A status report. *Children Today, 18,* 24–29.

Polansky, N. A., Chalmers, M. A., Buttenweiser, E., & Williams, D. P. (1981). *Damaged parents: An anatomy of child neglect.* Chicago: University of Chicago Press.

Polansky, N. A., Gaudin, J. M., Jr., & Kilpatrick, A. C. (1992). Family radicals. *Children and Youth Services Review, 14,* 19–26. doi:10.1016/0190-7409(92)90010-S

Putnam-Hornstein, E. (2011). Report of maltreatment as a risk factor for injury death: A prospective birth cohort study. *Child Maltreatment, 16*(3), 163–174.

Rae-Grant, N., Thomas, B. H., Offord, D. R., & Boyle, M. H. (1989). Risk, protective factors, and the prevalence of behavioral and emotional disorders in children and adolescents. *Journal of American Academy Child and Adolescent Psychiatry, 28,* 262–268. doi:10.1097/00004583-198903000-00019

Ramey, C. T., & Ramey, S. L. (1998). Early intervention and early experience. *American Psychologist, 53,* 109–120. doi:10.1037/0003-066X.53.2.109

Ridge, T. (2009). *Living with poverty: A review of the literature on children's and families' experiences of poverty* (Research Report No. 594). Colegate, Norwich: United Kingdom Department for Work and Pensions. Retrieved from http://research.dwp.gov.uk/asd/asd5/rports2009-2010/rrep594.pdf

Rutter, M. (1979). Protective factors in children's responses to stress and disadvantage. In M. W. Kent & J. E. Rolf (Eds.), *Primary prevention of psychopathology: Vol. 3. Social competence in children* (pp. 49–74). Hanover, NH: University Press of New England.

Rutter, M. (1981). Stress, coping and development: Some issues and some questions. *Journal of Child Psychology & Psychiatry, 22,* 323–356. doi:10.1111/j.1469 7610.1981.tb00560.x

Rutter, M. (1985). Resilience in the face of adversity: Protective factors and resistance to psychiatric disorder. *British Journal of Psychiatry, 147,* 598–611. doi:10.1192/bjp.147.6.598

Rutter, M. (1987). Psychosocial resilience and protective mechanisms. *American Journal of Orthopsychiatry, 57,* 316–331.

Rutter, M. (1989). Intergenerational continuities and discontinuities in serious parenting difficulties. In D. Cicchetti & V. Carlson (Eds.), *Child maltreatment: Theory and research on the causes and consequences of child abuse and neglect* (pp. 317–348). Cambridge, UK: Cambridge University Press.

Rutter, M. (1990). Psychosocial resilience and protective mechanisms. In J. Rolf (Ed.), *Risk and protective factors in the development of psychopathology* (pp. 42–73). New York: Cambridge University Press.

Ryan, J., & Testa, M. (2004). *Child maltreatment and juvenile delinquency: Investigating the role of placement and placement instability.* Champaign-Urbana: University of Illinois at Urbana-Champaign, School of Social Work, Children and Family Research Center.

Schorr, E., & Marchand, V. (2007). *Pathway to the prevention of child abuse and neglect.* Washington, DC: Project on Effective Interventions, Pathways Mapping Initiative Retrieved from http://www.cssp.org/uploadFiles/PCANPDFFI NAL11–14–07.pdf

Sedlak, A. J., Mettenburg, J., Basena, M., Petta, I., McPherson, K., Greene, A., & Li, S. (2010). *Fourth National Incidence Study of Child Abuse and Neglect (NIS-4): Report to Congress.* Washington, DC: U.S. Department of Health and Human Services, Administration for Children and Families. Retrieved from http://www.acf.hhs.gov/programs/opre/abuse_neglect/natl_incid/nis4_ report_congress_full_pdf_jan2010.pdf

Shonkoff, J., & Phillips, D. (Eds.). (2000). *From neurons to neighborhoods: The science of early childhood development.* Washington, DC: National Academies Press. Retrieved from http://books.nap.edu/openbook.php?record_id = 9824&page = R1

Stahmer, A. C., Leslie, L. K., Hurlburt, M. S., Barth, R., Webb, M. B., Landsverk, J., & Zhang, J. (2005). Developmental and behavioral needs as predictors of service use for young children in child welfare. *Pediatrics, 116,* 891–900. doi:10.1542/peds.2004–2135

Stein, T. (1984). The Child Abuse Prevention and Treatment Act. *Social Service Review, 58,* 302–314. doi:10.1086/644194

Testa, M. F., & Poertner, J. (2010). *Fostering accountability: Using evidence to guide and improve child welfare policy.* New York: Oxford University Press.

Tremblay, J., & Harnet, P. (2008). Impact of genetic and epigenetic factors from early life to later disease. *Metabolism, 57*(Suppl.), S27-S31.

Urban Institute. (2013). *Addressing deep and persistent poverty. A framework for philanthropic planning and investment.* Washington, D.C.: Author. Retrieved from: http://www.urban.org/UploadedPDF/412983-addressing-deep-poverty.pdf

U.S. Department of Health and Human Services, Administration on Children, Youth and Families. (1999). *Child maltreatment 1997: Reports from the states to the National Child Abuse and Neglect Data Systems.* Washington, DC: Government Printing Office. Retrieved from http://www.acf.hhs.gov/programs/cb/pubs/ncands97/index.htm

U.S. Department of Health and Human Services, Administration on Children, Youth and Families, Children's Bureau. (2003a). *Safety, permanency and well-being: Child welfare outcomes 1998, 1999, & 2000.* Washington, DC: Government Printing Office.

U.S. Department of Health and Human Services, Administration for Children, Youth, and Families, Children's Bureau. (2003b). *AQ1 Emerging practices in the prevention of child abuse and neglect.* Washington, DC: Author.

U.S. Department of Health and Human Services, Administration for Children and Families, Administration on Children, Youth and Families, Children's Bureau. (2013a). *Child maltreatment 2012.* Retrieved from http://www.acf.hhs.gov/programs/cb/research-data-technology/statistics-research/childmaltreatment

U.S. Department of Health and Human Services, Administration for Children and Families, Children's Bureau (2013b). *The AFCARS report—preliminary FY 2012 estimates as of July 2012 (No.20).* Washington, D.C.: U.S. Department of Health and Human Services. Retrieved May 27, 2014, from http://www.acf.hhs.gov/programs/cb/resource/afcars-report-20

U.S. Department of Health and Human Services, Administration for Children and Families, Children's Bureau. (2013c). *Trends in foster care and adoption—FFY 2002–FFY 2012.* Washington DC: Author. Retrieved May 27, 2014, from http://www.acf.hhs.gov/programs/cb/resource/trends-in-foster-care-and-adoption

U.S. General Accounting Office. (2004). *Child and family services reviews: Better use of data and improved guidance could enhance HHS's oversight of state performance* (GAO-04–333). Washington, DC: Government Printing Office. Retrieved from http://www.gao.gov/cgi-bin/getrpt?GAO-04–333

U.S. Government Accountability Office. (2007). *African American children in foster care: Additional HHS assistance needed to help states reduce the proportion in care* (GAO 07–816; Report to the Chairman, Committee on Ways and Means, House of Representatives). Washington, DC: Author. Retrieved from http://www .gao.gov/new.items/d07816.pdf

Wald, M., & Martinez, T. (2003). *Connected by 25: Improving the life chances of the country's most vulnerable 14–24 year olds* (Working Paper). Menlo Park, CA: William and Flora Hewlett Foundation. Retrieved from http://betterfutures .fcny.org/betterfutures/connected_by_25.pdf

Walton, E., Sandau-Beckler, P., & Mannes, M. (Eds.). (2001). *Balancing family- centered services and child well-being: Exploring issues in policy, practice, and research.* New York: Columbia University Press.

Wang, C-T., & Holton, J. (2008). *Total estimated cost of child abuse and neglect in the United States.* Chicago: Prevent Child Abuse America.

Washington State Institute for Public Policy. (2013). *Benefit-cost results.* Olympia, WA: Author. Retrieved from http://www.wsipp.wa.gov/BenefitCost. (Retrieved February 14, 2014, as this website is periodically updated.)

Webb, M. B., Dowd, K., Jones-Harden, B., Landsverk, J., & Testa, M. (Eds.). (2010). *Child welfare and child well-being: New perspectives from the National Survey of Child and Adolescent Well-Being.* New York: Oxford University Press.

Weinfield, N. S., Ogawa, J. R., & Sroufe, L. A. (1997). Early attachment as a pathway to adolescent peer competence. *Journal of Research on Adolescence, 7,* 241–265.

Werner, E. E. (1989). High-risk children in young adulthood: A longitudinal study from birth to 32 years. *American Journal of Orthopsychiatry, 59,* 72–81.

Whittaker, J. K., & Maluccio, A. N. (2002). Rethinking "child welfare": A reflective essay. *Social Service Review, 76,* 107–134. doi:10.1086/324610

Wilkinson, R., & Pickett, K. (2009). *The spirit level: Why more equal societies almost always do better.* New York: Penguin.

Wilson, M. (1984). Mothers' and grandmothers' perceptions of parental behavior in three-generational Black families. *Child Development, 55,* 1333–1339. doi:10.2307/1130003

Wornoff, R., & Mallon, G.P. (Eds.). (2006). *Lesbian, gay, bisexual, and transgender issues in child welfare.* Washington, DC: Child Welfare League of America Press.

Wulczyn, F., Barth, R.P., Yuan, Y.Y., Jones-Harden, B., & Landsverk, J. (2005). *Beyond common sense: Child welfare, child well-being, and the evidence for policy reform.* Somerset, NJ: Transaction Aldine.

Wulczyn, F. H., Hislop, K. B., & Chen, L. (2007). *Foster care dynamics: 2003–2005: A report from the multistate foster care data archive.* Chicago: Chapin Hall at the University of Chicago.

Wulczyn, F. H., Orlebeke, B., & Haight, J. (2009). *Finding the return on investment: A framework for monitoring local child welfare agencies.* Chicago: Chapin Hall at the University of Chicago. Retrieved from http://www.chapinhall.org/sites/default/files/Finding_Return_On_Investment_07_20_09.pdf

ADDITIONAL READING

Chibnall, S., Dutch, N., Jones-Harden, B., Brown, A., Gourgine, R., Smith, J., Boone, A., & Snyder, S. (2003). *Children of color in the child welfare system: Perspectives from the child welfare community.* Washington, DC: U.S. Department of Health and Human Services Administration for Children and

Families Children's Bureau, Administration for Children and Families. Retrieved from http://www .childwelfare.gov/pubs/otherpubs/children/

Child Welfare League of America. (2003). *Making children a national priority: A framework for community action*. Washington, DC: Author. Retrieved from http://www.cwla.org/membersonly/ cig021009b.pdf

Shonkoff, J. P., & Meisels, S. J. (Eds.). (2000). *Handbook of early childhood intervention* (2nd ed.). New York: Cambridge University Press.

Wulczyn, F., Barth, R. P., Yuan, Y. Y., Jones Harden, B., & Landsverk, J. (2005). *Beyond common sense: Evidence for child welfare policy reform*. Somerset, NJ: Transaction Aldine.

Wulczyn, F. H., Orlebeke, B., & Mitchell-Herzfeld, S. (2005). *Improving public child welfare agency performance in the context of the federal child and family services reviews*. Chicago: Chapin Hall at the University of Chicago. Retrieved from http://www.chapinhall.org/research/report/improving-public-child-welfare-agency-performance-context-federal-child-and-family-s

WEB-BASED RESOURCES

American Psychological Association, Task Force on Resilience and Strength in Black Children and Adolescents. (2008). *Resilience in African American children and adolescents: A vision for optimal development*. Retrieved from http://www.apa .org/pi/families/resources/resiliencerpt.pdf

Child Trends for key statistical summaries, child and family trend data and issue summaries, http:// www.childtrends.org

Resilience and strength in Black children and adolescents, http://psychcentral.com/news/2008/08/21/ resiliency-among-black-youth/279

U.S. Children's Bureau for state outcomes and foster care statistics, http://www.acf.hhs.gov/programs/ cb/publications

CHAPTER 4

Education Policy for Children, Youth, and Families

Andy J. Frey

Myrna R. Mandlawitz

Armon R. Perry

Hill M. Walker

Public education in the United States occurs in the context of a complex and often contentious system composed of diverse interest groups. Several competing viewpoints about the primary purpose of education lie at the heart of debates on education policy. These competing interests include preparing students for the workforce, teaching basic academic skills, developing social and cognitive skills, and preparing youth to be productive future citizens (Fuhrman & Lazerson, 2005). The purpose of this chapter is to identify and describe significant education policies of the past century in the context of a risk, protection, and resilience framework. Herein, we discuss the prevalence and trends for school dropout and failure; identify and describe the primary risk and protective factors associated with school adjustment and academic achievement; summarize past and present education policies; and consider and discuss ways in which principles of risk, protection, and resilience might be used to develop or enhance education policy.

TRENDS IN SCHOOL FAILURE AND ACADEMIC ACHIEVEMENT

Public education is often referred to as the great equalizer. This label suggests that access to education plays a prominent role in the acquisition of economic and social benefits associated with gainful employment. Unfortunately, evidence from years of research indicates that access to quality public education is far from equal. In 2010, nearly 3.1 million children dropped out of school before earning a high school diploma

(National Center for Education Statistics, 2013). Historically, marginalized groups have faced severe challenges and discrimination in their attempts to take advantage of educational opportunities. Despite progress on many fronts, recent reports have indicated that the American education system is still struggling to reach all students effectively. Although it is widely known that a lack of educational attainment has a deleterious impact on future economic status, many children begin school without the necessary readiness skills and begin a pattern of failure that leads to dropout and poor prospects for employment.

Studies have shown that student-specific factors are associated with dropout and academic failure (Fall & Roberts, 2012; Wang & Fredricks, 2014). These student-specific risk factors include low academic achievement, student misbehavior, suspensions and expulsions, negative narrative comments in school records, frequent referrals for in- and out-of-school problems (Arcia, 2006; Finn, Fish, & Scott, 2008), number of elementary schools attended, and early involvement in the juvenile justice system (Sweeten, 2006). In addition to these individual risk factors, larger environmental influences also affect school failure and dropout rates. The notion of school engagement is central to the influence of environmental factors. Students perform better and achieve at higher levels when they feel a sense of attachment to school, which is characterized by bonding or connection that occurs through a process of school engagement (Fredricks, 2011). Conversely, students who are unable to establish a connection to school and thus cannot fully engage in the schooling process are at increased risk for dropout (Kemp, 2006). Lack of engagement may occur among students whose families move frequently (South, Haynie, & Bose, 2007) and those who have negative interactions with school personnel or who are minimally involved in extracurricular activities (Kemp, 2006).

For other students, particularly for youth of color, structure and culture in school are often quite different from those in the home. This disparity often alienates students and contributes to disengagement and subsequent dropout (Patterson, Hale, & Stessman, 2007). Youth of color are at greatest risk for school adjustment problems during the elementary grades, and they are more likely than other students to become school dropouts (Patterson et al., 2007; Substance Abuse and Mental Health Services Administration, 2008). This pattern also contributes to higher dropout rates in urban areas that are heavily populated by racial and ethnic minorities (Patterson et al., 2007). As shown in Table 4.1, overall graduation rates increased slightly from the 2010–2011 to the 2011–2012 academic year. However, female graduation rates were higher than male graduation rates over this period of time, and both African American and Hispanic students had lower graduation rates than their White counterparts. In a recent study, Carpenter and Ramirez (2007) examined reasons for school dropout and found that being retained in a grade, or held back, predicted school dropout for all races, whereas family composition and time spent on homework were factors related to school dropout only for White and Hispanic students. Among African American students, the number of suspensions and level of parental involvement in school predicted dropout (Carpenter & Ramirez, 2007). Most important, these findings suggest that many racial and ethnic differences in academic achievement and dropout rates may stem from key differences in risk status at the family, school, and neighborhood levels.

Table 4.1   Public High School Four-Year Adjusted Cohort Graduation Rates

	2010–2011	2011–2012
	%	%
Gender		
Male	77	78
Female	84	85
Race/ethnicity		
White	84	86
African American	67	69
Hispanic	71	73
Total	79	80

Source: Stester & Stillwell (2014).

RISK AND PROTECTIVE FACTORS FOR SCHOOL ADJUSTMENT AND ACHIEVEMENT PROBLEMS

The term *risk factor* was defined by Fraser and Terzian (2005) as "any event, condition, or experience that increases the probability that a problem will be formed, maintained, or exacerbated" (p. 5). Risk factors for school-related problems may be either specific or general in nature. Within the context of education, nonspecific risk factors such as poverty are not directly related to school adjustment and achievement problems. Nevertheless, such factors have the potential to create maladaptive emotional and behavioral contexts and outcomes, which in turn, can have an adverse effect on academic performance (Greenberg, Domitrovich, & Bumbarger, 1999). Nonspecific risk factors may set into motion what Fraser and colleagues have called a chain of risk (Fraser, Kirby, & Smokowski, 2004), which can culminate in negative outcomes such as academic failure.

Other risk factors directly affect the likelihood of school adjustment and academic failure. For example, factors such as low commitment to schooling contributes to truancy, poor grades, and poor overall academic performance (Carnahan, 1994). As shown in Table 4.2, risk factors occur at the individual, family, school, and neighborhood levels of influence.

Protective factors are characteristics or traits that buffer and moderate exposure to risk. In high-risk situations, protective factors like attachment to teachers or other adults at school have the potential to reduce risk and decrease the likelihood of school-related problems. In the absence of risk, protective factors have a neutral effect. The concept of promotion is closely related to protection. *Promotive factors* are defined as forces that exert positive influences on behavior, irrespective of the presence or absence of risk (Sameroff

Table 4.2   Risk Factors for Academic Failure by Level of Influence

Level of Influence	Risk Factors
Individual	• Learning-related social skills (listening, participating in groups, staying on task, organizational skills) • Substance use • Pregnancy • Social behavior • Limited intelligence • Disability • Minority status • Special education status • Inability to read by the fourth grade
Family	• Residential mobility • Early exposure to familial antisocial behavior • Parent–child conflict • Lack of connectedness with peers, family, school, and community
School	• Large school size • Limited school resources • High staff turnover • Inconsistent classroom-management practices • Percentage of low socioeconomic status students • Negative school and classroom climate • School violence • Overcrowding • High student–to–teacher ratios • Insufficient curricular and course relevance • Weak, inconsistent adult leadership • Poor building design • Overreliance on physical security measures
Neighborhood	• Poverty • Low percentage of affluent neighbors

& Gutman, 2004). Examples of promotive factors include high intelligence and strong social skills, which can promote positive behavioral outcomes regardless of risk exposure. Table 4.3 summarizes protective and promotive factors that affect academic performance.

EDUCATION POLICY: PAST AND PRESENT

American educational policies and practices are profoundly influenced by political ideology, which is most frequently viewed in terms of a conservative or liberal stance. Historically,

Table 4.3   Promotive and Protective Factors for Academic Failure by Level of Influence

Level of Influence	Promotive Factors	Protective Factors
Individual	• Cognitive skills (e.g., intelligence, ability to work collaboratively with others, and capacity to focus in the face of distraction) • High socioemotional functioning • Ability to adapt to changes in school or work schedule • Effective and efficient communication skills • Ability to use humor to de-escalate negative situations • Social skills • Understanding and accepting capabilities and limitations • Maintaining a positive outlook • Involvement in extracurricular activities	
School	• Positive and safe environment • Setting high academic and social expectations • Positive relationships with teachers • School bonding • Positive and open school climate • Positive ratings for overall educational performance	• School climate • Classroom-management strategies that reduce classroom disruption and increase learning • School bonding • Consistent and firm rules for students
Peer		• Acceptance by pro-social peers • Involvement in positive peer groups

a conservative view of education has promoted the idea that individual students have the capacity to earn—or fail to earn—their place among the academic elite. Policy approaches based on conservative views tend to emphasize knowledge-centered education, traditional forms of learning and curricula, respect for authority and discipline, and the adoption of rigorous academic standards. In contrast, educational approaches based on liberal perspectives have tended to support curricula that are responsive to the individual as well as to social and environmental contexts (Apollonia & Abrami, 1997). Educational policies and programs in the past 100 years are reviewed and summarized in Table 4.4. The impact of policies that have been subjected to evaluation is also discussed.

Early Public Policy

From its inception, public education was thought of as a social vehicle for minimizing the importance of class and wealth and for determining who might excel economically.

Table 4.4 Major American Education Policies, Court Cases, and Public Reports, 1852–2010

Policy, Court Case, or Public Report	Date	Summary	Influence on Education
Compulsory School Attendance Act	1852	Required public school attendance for all able-bodied children of a certain age, unless the parent of the child could establish that the child was obtaining equivalent instruction outside of the public schools.	Resulted in programs designed to have all children attend school and graduate. Existing programs would need to change to accommodate a very different student population that had not previously attended school.
Plessy v. Ferguson	1896	Commonly referred to as "separate but equal," this decision supported separate transportation systems for Blacks and Whites.	Validated the belief that separate schools for Blacks and Whites was a constitutionally sound practice.
National School Lunch Act	1946	The purpose of the act was to provide for the health and well-being of the nation's children by assisting states to provide a school lunch program.	The program recognized that external factors, such as hunger and inadequate nutrition, played a part in children's ability to attend and learn in school.
Brown v. Board of Education	1954	The U.S. Supreme Court ruled that laws assigning students to schools based on race were unconstitutional. The court ruled unanimously that such laws violated the 14th Amendment's guarantee that the rights of all Americans deserved equal protection. The rationale for the verdict was that being separated from White students could result in feelings of inferiority in students of color and compromise their futures.	Desegregation gained momentum and competed for attention in the national spotlight and attempted to force school districts to desegregate.
Numerous Public Reports	Late 1960s and early 1970s	Highlighted the structural inequalities in the educational system (particularly for African American children and those from disadvantaged backgrounds) and the relationship between socioeconomic status and unequal educational outcomes.	Justified busing students between schools and between school districts, suggesting that reassigning poor students to schools with middle-class students would improve poor students' academic achievement.

Policy, Court Case, or Public Report	Date	Summary	Influence on Education
Head Start Act	1965	Head Start was designed to address a host of factors that affect poor children and their families, with the ultimate goal of increasing early school readiness by providing health, educational, nutritional, family support, social, and other services for 3- and 4-year-old children from low-income households.	The first primary prevention program of its kind, designed to prepare disadvantaged children on a universal level for kindergarten.
Elementary and Secondary Education Act (ESEA)	1965	The ESEA of 1965 provided funds for compensatory education in schools that had high percentages of disadvantaged students (Title I).	Title I has had the greatest impact on high-risk youth. Title I has been the largest source of federal funding for poor children in schools, serving 10 million children in more than 50,000 schools.
Milliken v. Bradley	1974	The courts declared that if segregation was the result of an individual's choice, school districts could not be forced to remedy the situation.	Released a district from desegregation orders after it demonstrated it had done everything possible to desegregate schools. This ruling set a precedent for similar rulings that resulted in an end to racially balanced schools in many American cities.
Education of All Handicapped Children Act, PL 94-142	1975	Provided screening and identification for children with a wide range of disabilities and required schools to provide a variety of services for children based on an individualized education program developed by school district personnel, including teachers, parents, and the child, as appropriate. Not until 1997 did the law mention having, at parents' or school district's discretion, participation of specialized instructional support personnel, including school social workers, as team members.	Altered the education of those with disabilities for many years to come.

(Continued)

Table 4.4 (Continued)

Policy, Court Case, or Public Report	Date	Summary	Influence on Education
A Nation at Risk	1983	Cited high rates of adult illiteracy and low achievement test scores as indicators of declining literacy and educational standards. The report recommended that educational policies strive to improve education for all students and develop more rigorous and measurable standards to assess academic performance. It highlighted the failure of education to ameliorate social problems and blamed these policies for producing mass mediocrity in education that resulted in the decline of authority and standards in schools.	Federal, state, and local policy switched to the improvement of curriculum, school-based management, the tightening of standards, the importance of discipline, and the establishment of academic goals and assessment.
Individuals with Disabilities Education Act (PL 94-142 Reauthorized)	1990	The Education for All Handicapped Act was renamed the Individuals with Disabilities Education Act. This new iteration of PL 94-142 added social work services to the list of "related services." The Act also required transition planning for students moving to post-school training and/or employment. In addition, the categories of autism and traumatic brain injury were added to the list of disabilities qualifying children for services.	Marked a broader look at disability and the services that might be necessary for children to be successful in school and beyond.
America 2000	1992	President George H. Bush called for voluntary testing in Grades 4, 8, and 12 and proposed six goals for education, called America 2000.	Began what would become a major movement toward standards- and accountability-based education policy.
Goals 2000	1994	President Bill Clinton proposed this initiative, which enacted the six national education goals proposed by President George H. Bush.	Continued the trend toward standards and accountability testing.
Improving America's Schools Act (IASA; reauthorization of ESEA)	1994	IASA was much more comprehensive than the previous version of ESEA, promoting alignment of curriculum and instruction, professional development, school leadership, accountability, and school improvement to help students meet challenging state standards.	IASA codified much of the earlier discussion about school improvement and continued a focus on what conditions are important for students to be able to learn.

Policy, Court Case, or Public Report	Date	Summary	Influence on Education
		IASA included several new programs: (a) the Safe and Drug-Free Schools and Communities Act to encourage safe learning environments; (b) the Gun-Free Schools Act, conditioning States' receipt of ESEA funds on having in place zero-tolerance policies for students bringing weapons to school; and (c) provisions promoting gender equity in education.	
Individuals with Disabilities Education Act (reauthorized)	1997	Recommended that behavior intervention plans based on a functional behavior assessment should be developed for children suspected of having severe emotional disturbance. Behavior intervention plans were mandated for children with disabilities who had been suspended for 10 days or more before a change of placement could be initiated.	Marked the beginning of a trend in educational policy to promote positive, proactive strategies for children with challenging behavior.
No Child Left Behind (NCLB)	2001	NCLB is the most recent reauthorization of the ESEA. It is designed to create a stronger, more accountable education system; seeks to change the culture of education; and purports to use evidence-based strategies found to be effective through rigorous research. NCLB holds students accountable to high educational outcomes and standards. NCLB requires each state to set clear and high standards and to put an assessment system in place to measure student progress toward those standards.	Initiated focus on evidence-based strategies in regular education and provided a much stronger emphasis on accountability testing than previous policies.
Individuals with Disabilities Education Improvement Act (PL 94-142 Reauthorized)	2004	Mandated the use of interventions known to be effective and placed a premium on primary prevention by substantially altering the screening and identification procedures for children with learning disabilities. Added "early intervening services" for struggling students not yet identified as needing special education services.	Continued the trend to promote positive, proactive interventions and to adopt interventions supported by the scientific literature.

(Continued)

Table 4.4 (Continued)

Policy, Court Case, or Public Report	Date	Summary	Influence on Education
Parents Involved in Community Schools v. Seattle School District No. 1 (2007)	2007	The U.S. Supreme Court struck down voluntary student assignment plans in Louisville, Kentucky, and Seattle, Washington, thereby continuing and extending the trend toward resegregation in the public schools.	Extended the trend toward resegregation in public schools and illustrated the deep divisions between the liberal and conservative factions of the newly configured Supreme Court. The ruling applied pressure on school districts that rely on race-conscious criteria to assign students to schools to revisit their plan so it fits within the context of this precedent.
American Recovery and Reinvestment Act	2009	This large economic stimulation package included emergency funds for education programs, including the creation of several new programs, to offset the effects of the country's economic recession.	Several states received significant funds from competitive grant programs including Race to the Top and Investing in Innovation, and large one-time investments were made in key formula grant programs, including Title I of the ESEA and the IDEA State grant program. Also, the State Fiscal Stabilization Fund provided funds to states to save over 300,000 education jobs, including school social workers.

Social policy in the late 19th and early 20th centuries was based on the liberal ideas of Horace Mann and John Dewey. In the mid-19th century, Mann proclaimed that education, more than any other process, was the great equalizer of people from various walks of life (Cremin, 1957). Similarly, Dewey's (1916) philosophy of education held the role of education as the "leveler" of the socially advantaged and disadvantaged. Education policy also stemmed from the conservative notion that mass education was necessary to ensure that the citizenry could obey the law, vote, pay taxes, serve on juries, and participate in the armed forces (Derezinski, 2004). The Massachusetts Compulsory School Attendance Act of 1852 required public school attendance for all able-bodied children of a certain age unless a child's parent could establish that the child was obtaining equivalent instruction outside the public schools. By 1918, 48 states had adopted similar attendance policies (Derezinski, 2004). This change resulted in programs based on the idea that all children must attend school and graduate; these assertions were nonexistent before compulsory attendance laws. At this point, segregated education was determined to be constitutional, as evidenced by the separate but equal clause in *Plessy v. Ferguson* (1896), which supported separate transportation systems for African American and White people; the ruling was later applied to children in the context of public school integration.

Education Policy From 1930 to 1970

In the post-World War I era, education policy was dominated by debates about the academic and social goals of education and by discussions about whether all children should receive the same quality education. Although the focus on curriculum and teaching methods remained, a values-based debate ensued that was associated with the issues of equity and excellence. By 1930, the direction of education policy shifted toward equality in education. During the 1930s, the National Association for the Advancement of Colored People initiated a campaign to overthrow the *Plessy v. Ferguson* (1896) decision, with school desegregation as a major goal. As the achievement gap between advantaged and disadvantaged students became increasingly evident, efforts at desegregation in public education gained momentum and competed for policy attention in the national spotlight.

The achievement gap between White and African American students as well as the achievement gap between economically advantaged and disadvantaged children became the most important educational issues of the century in the 1940s. The debate that ensued served as a catalyst for efforts to close the achievement gap and to maximize educational opportunities for people of color. The integration movement scored a significant victory in 1954, when the U.S. Supreme Court ruling in *Brown v. Board of Education of Topeka* (1954) established that laws assigning students to schools based on race were unconstitutional. The Supreme Court ruled unanimously that such laws violated the 14th Amendment's guarantee that the rights of all Americans deserved equal protection. The rationale for the verdict was that separating African American students from White students could result in feelings of inferiority in students of color and serve to compromise the quality of their education. It took nearly two decades for all states to comply with the court's order to desegregate schools, and many of the initial advancements achieved by integration have since given way.

During this same period, conservatives attacked progressive directions in education, suggesting that the American education system was sacrificing intellectual goals for social ends. The discussion between the progressives, who saw the educational arena as the most legitimate vehicle for leveling the playing field, and the critics, who demanded more academic rigor in education, became known as "The Great Debate" (Ravitch, 1983). This debate was fueled by the launching of the Soviet space satellite Sputnik, an event that suggested the United States was no longer the world's leader in scientific research and development. From the mid-1950s to the mid-1960s, the pursuit of excellence, standards-based education, curriculum reform, assessment, and accountability gained momentum. However, standards-based education would not take center stage in education policy until the 1980s.

The 1960s witnessed great divisiveness in education policy as illustrated by the tension evident in the eventual move toward a more liberal reform orientation. This change mirrored larger societal issues, predominantly the emphasis on equity issues raised by the Civil Rights Movement. In the 1960s and early 1970s, several influential books highlighted the structural inequalities in the educational system, particularly for African American children and children from disadvantaged backgrounds (Clark, 1965; Kohl, 1967; Kozol, 1967; Rosenfeld, 1971). These books, along with a report by Coleman (1966) entitled *Equality of Educational Opportunity,* highlighted the relationship between socioeconomic status and disparity in educational outcomes. The Coleman report suggested that the composition of the student body within schools was highly correlated with student achievement (Sadovnik, Cookson, & Semel, 2001). The implications of the report were shocking, primarily because Coleman set out to demonstrate that the achievement gap between African American and White students could be attributed to the organizational structure of American schools. The Coleman report justified busing students between schools and between school districts, suggesting that reassigning poor students to schools with middle-class students would equalize educational opportunities. Many researchers, who questioned the premise, method, and findings, challenged the report.

Other progressive policies also emerged in the 1960s. In 1965, the Head Start Act funded an innovative preschool program for disadvantaged children. Head Start was designed to address a host of factors that affected poor children and their families, and specifically school readiness. The goal of the program was to increase early school readiness by providing health, educational, nutritional, family support, social, and other services to preschool children from low-income households.

Congress also passed the Elementary and Secondary Education Act (ESEA) in 1965. Similar to the Head Start Act, the ESEA was passed on the assumption that inequities in educational opportunities were largely responsible for the achievement gap between advantaged and disadvantaged children. ESEA provided funds for schools that had high percentages of disadvantaged students to compensate for many years of unequal education under segregation. ESEA has been revised and reauthorized several times since 1965. Provisions of the act are currently responsible for funding bilingual education; education for homeless, migrant, and neglected children; drug education; and teacher training (Nelson, Palonsky, & McCarthy, 2004).

Title I of ESEA has had the greatest impact on vulnerable and high-risk youth. Title I has been the largest source of federal funding for poor children in schools for 40 years (Cook,

2005), serving more than 33.4 million students in more than 66,000 schools in the 2011–2012 school year (Institute of Education Sciences, 2014). In addition, the Safe and Drug-Free Schools and Communities (SDFSC) program provides early screening; remedial academic support; and prevention programming that addresses issues of violence, substance abuse, sexual abuse, and teenage pregnancy. Funds support transition programs for youth coming to public schools from residential and juvenile justice settings as well.

Education Policy From 1970 to 2000

The 1970s brought new attempts to integrate schools through complex busing plans and magnet schools designed to attract White students to neighborhood schools that they would not ordinarily attend (Cecelski, 1994). However, desegregation became increasingly difficult to maintain as a host of court cases gradually began to undo the *Brown* mandate. In the 1974 case of *Milliken v. Bradley,* the U.S. Supreme Court declared that if segregation was the result of an individual's choice, school districts could not be forced to remedy the situation. Put simply, once a district had done all it could to desegregate its schools, the district was released from further desegregation orders. Similar rulings led to renewed efforts to achieve a racial balance in schools in many American cities (Nelson et al., 2004).

In 1975, Congress passed the Education of All Handicapped Children Act (EHA; PL 94-142), which altered educational patterns for students with disabilities. EHA provided screening and identification services for children with a wide range of disabilities and required schools to offer a variety of services for them based on an individualized education program developed by a school district representative, teachers, parents, and the student, as appropriate. The EHA was designed to ensure (a) screening and identification of children with disabilities, (b) provision of a free appropriate public education (FAPE) for children with disabilities, including special education and related services, (c) inclusion of students in the least restrictive environment with nondisabled students to the greatest extent possible, and (d) procedural safeguards to ensure students' right to a FAPE was protected.

In the late 1970s, many proponents of conservative policy pointed to the government's inability to solve social problems in the schools. Some spoke critically of the way in which EHA interfered with individual freedoms. Many experts argued that progressive reforms had not only failed to narrow the achievement gap between advantaged and disadvantaged children but also had exacerbated problems in the schools related to discipline and other behavioral issues. Anyon (1997) suggested that this belief was fueled by the publication of *A Nation at Risk*, a report on the state of U.S. education issued by the National Commission on Excellence (1983). The report was issued in 1983 under Terrel Bell, President Ronald Reagan's Secretary of Education; it discussed the ongoing problems of declining literacy and education standards, leading to high rates of adult illiteracy and low achievement test scores. The report recommended that educational policies should strive to improve educational experiences for all students and to develop more rigorous and measurable standards to assess academic performance. *A Nation at Risk* paved the way for educational reform efforts focused on excellence for all students, rather than concentrating on subgroups of children such as high-risk youth or children with disabilities. The report highlighted the failure of education to ameliorate social problems and blamed past policies for producing mass mediocrity in education, which supposedly resulted in the decline of authority and standards in schools.

Subsequently, the focus of most federal, state, and local policy switched to the improvement of curriculum, school-based management, tightening of standards and discipline, and the establishment of academic goals and assessments. School-based management emphasized a structural shift away from bureaucratic boards of education to local forms of control. New policies were developed to engage parents, teachers, and administrators in decision-making processes. Teacher empowerment, a concept closely related to school-based management, was emphasized as a way to give teachers more decision-making power within schools. In addition, school choice options, such as vouchers, charter schools, and magnet schools, were created to provide parents with alternatives to the traditional public school offerings.

The EHA was renamed the Individuals with Disabilities in Education Act (IDEA) in 1990, and "social work services" were added for the first time in the list of possible related services. The ESEA was reauthorized again in 1994 as the Improving America's Schools Act. That reauthorization included the Safe and Drug-Free Schools and Communities Act to promote safe and drug-free learning environments. The Act also supported linguistically diverse children and promoted the inclusion and participation of women in all aspects of education. These funds were used for whole school reform, compensatory education, remediation for the country's most disadvantaged children, and free and reduced-price lunches for children in need. Partially because the discipline provisions in IDEA made expelling a student with a severe emotional disturbance nearly impossible, the Gun-Free Schools Act of 1994 was passed, which allowed ESEA funds to be given only to those states that adopted zero-tolerance policies for weapons on school grounds. Public and political concern over discipline-related policies also heightened in the mid-1990s with the outbreak of mass shootings in schools (Jenson & Howard, 1999). This heightened awareness of the safety risk in the school environment resulted in the expansion of zero-tolerance policies for less severe infractions. Alternative schools and increased school security strategies were also implemented to address school safety issues. However, a substantial body of evidence suggests that exclusionary discipline measures such as office referrals, suspension and expulsion, additional security, and other punitive alternatives exacerbate the very problems they are intended to address (Skiba, 2002). Furthermore, the evidence supports that children of color, particularly African Americans, are disproportionately represented among the students receiving such discipline, which is also evidence of institutional biases inherent in the use of exclusionary discipline (Skiba, Michael, Nardo, & Peterson, 2000). The overreliance on punishment and exclusionary practices in the presence of convincing evidence to suggest the practices are ineffective has resulted in the development of policies during the past decade that mandate the use of evidence-based, or empirically supported, practices.

Head Start, which has served as a laboratory for a variety of prevention, early intervention, and program evaluation research since its inception in 1965, was expanded in 1995 (Love, Tarullo, Raikes, & Chazen-Cohen, 2006). Specifically, Early Head Start was launched to expand Head Start services to pregnant women and to children during the birth-to-3-year period, thereby providing earlier opportunities for preventive interventions. Federal appropriations for Head Start tripled during the 1990s, both to increase the number of children served and to improve the quality of programs, but funding has remained level since the early 2000s. In fiscal year (FY) 2013, the Head Start and Early Head Start programs served nearly 1 million children and pregnant mothers (Administration for Children and Families, 2013).

Finally, in 1997, the IDEA was again reauthorized, focusing on ensuring that children with disabilities were exposed to positive, proactive interventions. Specifically, IDEA recommended certain measures for any student whose behavior challenges impeded his or her ability to learn. The first step was for qualified professionals to conduct a functional behavioral assessment of the student and then construct a behavior intervention plan based on that assessment. In addition, a new or revised behavior plan was mandated after a child with a disability had been suspended for more than 10 days or before a change of placement to a more restrictive setting (i.e., alternative classroom or school). IDEA was also noteworthy for mandating the inclusion of parents in the planning process for their child.

Education Policy From 2001 to 2010

The momentum of educational reforms in the 1990s culminated in the passage of the 2001 No Child Left Behind Act (NCLB). NCLB is the most sweeping federal reform in education since ESEA was passed in 1965. Technically, NCLB was the most recent reauthorization of ESEA. However, NCLB added many new initiatives. For example, NCLB was designed to create a stronger, more accountable education system, to change the culture of education, and to use evidence-based strategies that have been determined effective through rigorous research. Rather than providing specific resources for at-risk youth, NCLB proposed assisting children and youth by holding them accountable to high educational outcomes and standards. NCLB required each state to set clear and high standards and to put an assessment system in place to measure student progress toward those standards (Paige, 2002). Specifically, NCLB required states to test all students annually in Grades 3 through 8 and once in Grades 10 through 12 in reading and math. Scores reported by states must be disaggregated by poverty, race and ethnicity, disability, and English-language proficiency so that potential achievement gaps can be identified. Schools that fail to make adequate yearly progress toward identifiable goals are identified for improvement and are subject to corrective action (Paige, 2002). NCLB mandates that teachers use strategies that have been shown to be effective. In addition to its emphasis on early reading programs, NCLB is noteworthy for its attention to the critical role that parents play in children's educational experiences. NCLB has dramatically affected educational practices, which now place a premium on students meeting standards of learning and assessment and on school-based management, teacher empowerment, and school choice (e.g., vouchers, magnet schools, charter schools, and privatization options).

The Individuals with Disabilities Education Improvement Act of 2004, a reauthorization of PL 94-142, continued the trend of promoting the adoption of effective interventions and placed a premium on primary prevention by altering substantially the screening and identification procedures for children with learning disabilities. Specifically, the Act permits school districts to use a process that determines if the child responds to scientific, research-based intervention as a part of the evaluation procedures used to assess functional capacity. This modified method can replace assessment using the discrepancy between ability and achievement to identify students with learning difficulties, but data from this process must be only one component of a comprehensive evaluation. This approach, referred to as Response to Intervention, has been applied to academic and behavioral supports in special and routine education. Batsche et al. (2005) defined Response to Intervention as the practice of (a) providing effective instruction and interventions based on students' needs and (b) regularly monitoring students' progress to guide decisions about changes in instruction or goals. The model suggests that more intensive interventions should be considered for individual students based on their response (or lack thereof) to less intensive, high-quality interventions.

In 2007, the U.S. Supreme Court struck down voluntary student assignment plans in Louisville, Kentucky, and Seattle, Washington, thereby continuing and extending the trend toward resegregation in public schools. In the 2007 case, *Parents Involved in Community Schools v. Seattle School District No. 1,* the petitioners contended that assigning students to schools solely to achieve racial balance in the schools was a violation of individuals' rights guaranteed under the 14th Amendment (e.g., Equal Protection Clause) as well as the Civil Rights Act of 1964. The Louisville and Seattle districts argued unsuccessfully that educational and social benefits such as socialization and good citizenship are derived from an educationally diverse learning environment and that because racial diversity was their primary interest, promoting that interest using race-conscious criteria alone was necessary and justified. Although the justices were sharply divided in a 5–4 vote, the Court's opinion allows districts to use race-conscious measures so long as such measures do not use race to treat individual students differently "solely on the basis of a systematic individual typing by race" (*Parents Involved in Community Schools v. Seattle School District No. 1,* 2007, p. 7). Even though the decision appears likely to result in increased educational resegregation, it does not overtly forbid school districts seeking diversity to pursue that goal by using race-conscious means.

Educational Policy From 2011 to 2014

Education policy has been significantly affected by the deepening divide in the appropriate role of government that has occurred between conservatives and liberals in the past several years. The advent and influence of the Tea Party within the Republican Party has further fueled an already highly charged political climate. Republicans generally support leaving education decisions to states and local school districts, including choices about how federal dollars will be spent. They assert that local communities and school administrators are in the best position to know the demographics and needs of their students and thus fewer federal mandates should be attached to how funds are used. On the other hand, Democrats support stronger oversight by the federal government on the basis of past inequities in access to quality education and disparities in outcomes across student populations. They believe a strong federal presence, including investment in education, is critical to ensuring success for all students.

Those differences in philosophy have affected discussions on a number of key education issues. Policy themes emerging in the last few years focus on early childhood education, school choice, college- and career-readiness, and standards and high-stakes assessments. The importance of evidence-based practice, professional preparation and evaluation, and school improvement and reform has been at the forefront in many of these discussions. The long delay in reauthorizing the ESEA (known as the NCLB in its current form) has compromised many policy discussions and decisions. While Congress has not come to consensus on what changes to the law are needed, there is general agreement the law as enacted in 2002 has not been successful in reducing the achievement gap for the four subgroups named in the law (i.e., disadvantaged students, racial and ethnic minorities, students with disabilities, and English language learners).[1]

Early Childhood Education. Congress has begun to take a much closer look at the impact of early education in recent years. The political aspect of the debate focuses on whether current programs are adequate, and perhaps in some cases even duplicative, or whether a more expansive approach and investment in early childhood education is necessary. President Obama proposed the *Preschool for All* program in his FY 2014 and FY 2015 budgets. The FY 2014 budget proposal included a request of $75 billion over 10 years ($1.3 billion for FY 2014) to support state efforts to provide access to high-quality preschool for all 4-year-old children from low- and moderate-income families. Preschools would be required to hire teachers with bachelor's degrees; provide ongoing professional development; have low staff–child ratios and class sizes; provide a full-day program; and offer developmentally appropriate, evidence-based instructional programs as well as comprehensive support services for children. In FY 2014, Congress approved $250 million

under the *Race t*   to create or expand
high-quality pres   ew Early Head Start-
Child Care Partne   rtment of Education
and the U.S. Dep   igh-quality learning
to infants and toc   Head Start programs
with center-base   eet Early Head Start
program standar

School Choice. T   n leadership, passed
the Student Succ   ough several current
ESEA programs a   equirements for state
standards and h   ontinued, while any
requirements rel   n October 2013, the
Senate Health, F   1 the Strengthening
America's School   demic standards and
continuation of t   ch to education. The
proposed legisla   ories of schools for
interventions. Th   ngress.

College and Career Readiness. Federal guidelines require states to adopt college- and career-ready standards in mathematics and reading/language arts and to conduct assessments to measure growth for students in Grades 3 through 8 and at least once in high school. In addition, rather than the federally imposed accountability provisions of the law, states must develop their own differentiated recognition, accountability, and support in all school districts. Receipt of a waiver from these guidelines also requires adoption of new teacher and principal-evaluation systems, allowing states to adopt one system to be used in all its districts or flexibility for school districts to adopt their own evaluation plans. States with waivers may apply for an extension of the waiver for the 2014–2015 school year as a full reexamination of the ESEA seems unlikely in the immediate future.

Standards and High-Stakes Assessments. In recent years, the education debate in Grades K through 12 has centered on *Common Core State Standards* (CCSS). CCSS is a bottom-up effort, rather than a federal program, initiated by the Council of Chief State School Officers. Federal involvement in CCSS began when the U.S. Department of Education tied *Race to the Top* funding to the adoption of rigorous state standards, which many people viewed as an endorsement of CCSS. However, CCSS remains a state-driven process with more than 40 states having adopted these standards, despite critics who label CCSS as national standards or a national curriculum. Adoption of these standards remains voluntary. As the political cycle moves toward the next presidential election, the debate about whether CCSS should be a required federal program is likely to continue.

Next Steps. The Obama administration, under the leadership of the U.S. Department of Education, has taken an activist role in education policy. This activism has drawn criticism at times from both sides of the political aisle. In addition to the ESEA waivers, the Administration established several competitive grant programs first funded under the *American Recovery and Reinvestment Act* in FY 2009, including *Race to the Top* (RTTT) and *Investing in Innovation* (i3). Several states have received significant federal funding under RTTT for which they promised to adopt rigorous academic standards and use results on aligned high-stakes tests in evaluating teacher and principal performance. States also agreed to allow expansion of charter schools and use of alternative certification for teachers. The Obama administration has proposed different foci for RTTT grants in subsequent fiscal years, including a school district rather than state competition for funds and another iteration targeting early childhood programs. A proposal to develop an RTTT for higher education was not funded by Congress. A proposal called *Race to the Top—Equity and Opportunity* has yet to be debated by the full Congress. Critics of this initiative say that states have not been able to deliver on past promises, citing little improvement in student outcomes. Advocates believe investing funds in foundational programs such as ESEA and the IDEA will provide states with the resources necessary to improve academic achievement.

SUMMARY OF FEDERAL POLICY

Public education in the United States has witnessed a number of reform movements in the past century. From the end of World War I until the mid-1940s, education policy focused on equity and attempted to narrow or eliminate the achievement gap between advantaged and disadvantaged youth. From the 1950s to the 1970s, issues of equity dominated federal education policy. However, policies favoring equity in education were not without criticism during these years; many critics of equity policies believed intellectual and academic goals were being sacrificed for social ends. These attacks created fertile ground for alternative strategies to spring forth, such as the adoption of standards, curriculum reform, and accountability systems. Since the mid-1970s, most education policies and programs have been more closely aligned with the standards-based education movement, which has focused more heavily on the use of standardized assessment as a measure of improvement, possibly to the detriment of addressing non-academic barriers to learning.

PRINCIPLES OF RISK, PROTECTION, AND RESILIENCE IN EDUCATION POLICY

Evidence exists to both support and criticize the effectiveness of the policies and programs discussed in the prior section. Next, we briefly evaluate the extent to which historic and current educational policies and programs have been based on principles of risk and resilience. We begin with those that are clearly within this framework.

Several policies illustrate the relationship between risk, protection, and educational approaches to change and reform. For example, Head Start, IDEA, and NCLB emphasize principles that are consistent with the models of risk and resilience discussed earlier in this chapter. Head Start targets youth who are at highest risk for academic failure because of low socioeconomic status. The program attempts to bolster school readiness skills, and this approach is consistent with evidence suggesting that the preschool years represent a critical developmental phase for prevention and early intervention services (Reid, 1993). Although IDEA permits intervention with children before they enter school and targets children at risk of developing disabilities and school failure, most IDEA funding is intended for children who are already identified as having a disability. In addition, NCLB attempts to raise awareness of the achievement gap and encourages school districts to address the gap by requiring states to report standard test scores disaggregated by poverty, race/ethnicity, disability, and English-language proficiency. The recent NCLB emphasis on standards-based education sets high academic expectations for all students, and such expectations are an identified protective factor against school failure and dropout (Furlong & Morrison, 2000).

The emphasis on evidence-based prevention efforts highlighted in IDEA is compatible with risk and protective factors. This emphasis should result in improvements to the learning environment, such as school connectedness, school climate, teacher expectations, family involvement, and community services to support students and families. Many of these improved environmental conditions have been highlighted previously as key protective influences for children (Haberman, 2000; Hawkins, Catalano, Kosterman, Abbott, & Hill, 1999).

Other policies appear to ignore principles of risk and resilience at best and to undermine or contradict such principles at worst. Specifically, standards such as those promoted in NCLB and CCSS have the potential to be counterproductive to children and youth who are not able to compete academically. Standards-based policies may actually be contrary to principles of risk and resilience because those policies may lower teachers' expectations of students and subsequently have a negative impact on achievement. In addition, zero-tolerance policies, particularly those that apply to minor infractions, have been shown to increase the risk of poor outcomes among high-risk children in general and among youth of color specifically (Skiba & Peterson, 1999).

In sum, the application of risk and protective factors to the design of educational policy is inconsistent. Some policies (e.g., the Compulsory School Attendance Act, the Head Start Act, EHA, and IDEA), court cases (e.g., *Brown v. Board of Education*), and programs (e.g., Head Start and special education) support the constructs of risk and resilience. Other policies (e.g., NCLB and Gun-Free Schools Act) and court cases (e.g., *Plessy v. Ferguson* and *Milliken v. Bradley*) ignore or may even reject the constructs of risk and resilience. New and sustained efforts are needed to implement a risk-and-resilience framework in education policy.

USING PRINCIPLES OF RISK, PROTECTION, AND RESILIENCE TO ACHIEVE INTEGRATED EDUCATION POLICY

Principles of risk, protection, and resilience can be applied to education policy in two fundamental ways. One option requires policymakers to focus efforts on youth who are most likely to experience school adjustment and achievement problems. Such a strategy tends to concentrate program and policy efforts on youth from disadvantaged backgrounds because socioeconomic status is a key risk factor for educational failure (Brooks-Gunn & Duncan, 1997). A second approach uses knowledge of risk, protection, and resilience to design promotive educational policies and programs that are beneficial for all children, regardless of risk exposure. We begin our discussion with policy recommendations for programs that promote healthy outcomes for all children and youth.

PROMOTIVE INTERVENTIONS AND STRATEGIES

We recommend educational policies and programs that promote social competence, develop caring relationships, and create high expectations for all students. Policies that promote participation in positive academic and social groups, enhance school bonding or connectedness, and create positive and safe learning environments should receive priority in national policy and program debates. Simply adopting effective promotion interventions and strategies is not sufficient to produce sustainable change. Specific promotion strategies include the following:

- Establishing positive behavioral and rigorous academic expectations for all students

- Making environmental arrangements and providing active supervision

- Applying consequences to encourage desired behavior and discourage undesirable behavior

- Developing school and community linkages

- Developing school and home linkages (Frey, Lingo, & Nelson, 2010)

Other programs designed to positively affect school culture, such as conflict resolution, peer mediation, and antibullying strategies, illustrate the growing emphasis on changing peer and institutional culture and are likely to have protective value. Recent research has demonstrated that many strategies and programs work for a short time but that effects quickly fade; thus, there is a need to learn more about the specific conditions and settings in which intervention effects can be sustained over time (Duncan, 2009). A report by the Center for Mental Health in Schools (2002) indicated that school-based reform efforts have been unsuccessful because projects and services designed to remove barriers to learning are usually viewed as supplementary services. The result may be seen in the fragmentation of services, marginalization of professionals, and overall inadequacies in policy reform. Specialized instructional support personnel (SISP), including school social workers, school psychologists, speech language pathologists, school nurses, and school counselors, must be trained to support the primary mission of schools. Furthermore, policies are needed to enhance standards while promoting reasonable professional-to-student ratios for all schools and students.

A critically important element in affecting positive change in schools is the process of *enculturation,* or "the manner in which a school embeds a systems change process into its own unique culture, assumes 'ownership' of the process, and has the process become a part of business as usual at the school" (Sailor, Wolf, Choi, & Roger, 2009, p. 664). Policies and programs should strive to increase service cohesion by addressing the need for multiple interventions within schools in an integrated fashion. Walker and colleagues (1996) suggested that prevention efforts have generally lacked coordination and integration because no comprehensive strategic plan for coordinating and linking behavioral supports existed at the school or district level. Evidence from efficacious school-based practices also supports the need to attend to interactions among key individual and environmental factors. Over the past several decades, our knowledge of "what works" in school-based prevention programs has increased dramatically (Jenson & Bender, 2014). For example, it is widely believed that interventions are more effective if they are integrated and coordinated with other interventions along a continuum of support representing primary, secondary, and tertiary levels of intervention (Dunlap, Sailor, Horner, & Sugai, 2009). Within this continuum, the promise of primary prevention is increasingly emphasized because it not only is efficient and effective but also increases the likelihood that the needs of students with elevated risk status will be targeted for intervention. We believe that targeted educational policies and programs should focus on schools that have high percentages of students living in poverty and that identification of and intervention with high-risk students should occur as early as possible. Examples of targeted policies and programs are reviewed next.

THE ROLE OF TARGETED INTERVENTIONS AND STRATEGIES

Redistribution of Tax Dollars to Support Schools in Low-Income Neighborhoods

The most obvious recommendation for using principles of risk and protection in targeted educational policy may involve school financing. Nearly 50% of school funding comes from local property taxes (Nelson et al., 2004). Therefore, adequately funding schools in low-income neighborhoods is an ongoing and persistent challenge to policy officials and school administrators. To address this problem, a larger percentage of school financing may need to come from state and federal taxes rather than from local tax bases. Equalizing the funding base between advantaged and disadvantaged communities is not likely to produce equal educational outcomes, given variations in individual, family, neighborhood, and community risk factors across schools and communities. Furthermore, providing more money to disadvantaged schools would require people in wealthy districts to partially fund poor districts, which is a practice that runs counter to the beliefs of many Americans. However, such a strategy may well be necessary to create positive change and promote effective policies based on principles of risk and protection.

Early Identification and Intervention at the Point of School Entry

Between 9.5% and 14.2% of children up to 5 years old experience social or emotional problems that adversely affect their functioning and development (e.g., school readiness skills), with children living in poverty being more likely to experience these problems (Brauner & Stephens, 2006; Duncan, Brooks-Gunn, & Klebanov, 1994). Whether in preschool or early elementary school, the importance of early screening for risk factors that lead to poor educational outcomes cannot be overstated. Given the proper tools, it requires minimal effort for educators to predict—with great accuracy—which children will require extensive academic or behavioral supports. Systemwide screening, particularly for emotional and behavioral indicators leading to school failure, may be a cost-effective strategy to improve educational outcomes. We believe that school readiness skills should be the primary focus of policy reforms and recommend increased funding for intervention programs that target these skills.

As noted, several federal programs, such as those promoted through Title IV and Title V funds, provide nonspecific funding to address a wide range of educational issues. Title I is consistent with the risk-and-protection framework because the primary criteria to access these funds are linked to students' socioeconomic status. However, there is no mandate requiring that interventions created with these funds address known risk and protective factors. In addition, there are no mandates requiring the funds, or a portion of the funds, to be used for evidence-based practices. Policymakers should address these gaps in funding mandates to ensure that funds are used for effective early intervention programs that have sustained effects. For example, early intervention programs that focus on family-risk factors are particularly promising; Duncan and Brooks-Gunn (2000) reported that interventions targeting parenting practices can mediate up to half of the impact of poverty on child development.

The presence of high-quality primary prevention programs is increasingly being recognized as a necessary prerequisite for more intensive interventions (Greenberg, 2004; Scott, Anderson, Mancil, & Alter, 2009). In sum, a series of policy and system reforms is needed to improve the condition of the country's schools. Principles of risk, protection, and resilience promotion offer a framework for thinking more systematically about a continuum of education policy defined by levels of service. Moreover, integration of policy and programs across other systems of care should be a part of such a continuum.

Targeted and Intensive Strategies to Integrate Education Policy

It is both important and challenging to envision integrating educational policies and programs across service domains such as child welfare, substance abuse, mental health, juvenile justice, developmental disabilities, and health. In many respects, the compartmentalized approach used to channel federal and state funding as well as the isolated educational training of professionals in each problem area runs counter to the vision of cohesive integrated services. Given the number of children involved in the educational system, the number of hours children spend in school, and the numbers of families and communities that can be linked by mobilized schools, we believe that the education system is an ideal context in which to identify children in need of services across many domains. The following case study demonstrates how services can lack integration and coordination.

A Case for Integrated Service Delivery

Jeremy is a 14-year-old male who was physically and sexually abused as a young child. His mother was incarcerated when he was 6 years old, and her parental rights were terminated when Jeremy was 8 years old. He experienced six out-of-home placements before age 10, when he was finally placed in a stable foster care home with loving and supportive parents.

Jeremy has struggled socially and emotionally in school since kindergarten, but he was not identified for special education services under the severe emotionally disturbed (SED) category until his current foster parents advocated for an evaluation at age 11 years. He has done well in some settings, but he was suspended 13 times last year during his first year of middle school. Jeremy has been convicted twice for misdemeanor charges and is currently on probation.

He receives a variety of support services from a learning specialist and a school social worker at his middle school, a counselor at the local mental health agency, and a child protection caseworker. Jeremy reports to a probation officer regularly and sees a psychiatrist yearly for medication monitoring. These individuals have never met together, and many of the services provided to Jeremy are duplicated across settings.

Cross-system funding for education, health, and social services may be one means for achieving integrated policy. Cross-system funds could be used to

- provide early screening to identify children most at risk;
- promote school readiness skills for high-risk youth;
- deliver comprehensive services and case management to children who display signs of adjustment problems before the second grade;
- provide seamless access to and provision of educational, health, and social services through support service providers and family resource or youth service centers; and
- implement primary prevention programs at key developmental stages.

An integrated approach to service delivery would be very beneficial to youth such as Jeremy and his foster parents in several ways. First, if the services provided by his teacher, learning specialist, school social worker, counselor, caseworker, probation officer, and psychiatrist were monitored and coordinated, each provider would know what other services Jeremy was receiving and how he was functioning in other aspects of his life. Such an approach could reduce redundancy in service provision and likely would be more cost-effective. An integrated service-delivery system would facilitate communication between professionals and allow each provider easy access to the information the other providers possess. Furthermore, an integrated approach would also produce one set of goals, one treatment plan, and one system to evaluate progress. In addition, an integrated strategy would likely make it easier for his foster parents to attend the requisite meetings associated with each service. Last, it is exciting to imagine the range and quality of services that could be put in place if the requisite departments of education, juvenile justice, and child welfare shared costs, problem ownership, and approaches for all the services directed toward complex cases such as Jeremy's. Most important, if an integrated approach had been in place to offer assessment and service delivery early in Jeremy's life, it is possible his early antisocial behavior and school failure would have raised warning flags that might have altered Jeremy's path to later destructive outcomes.

CONCLUDING REMARKS

Education policy in the past century has vacillated among liberal, progressive, and conservative ideologies, which has led to inconsistent and constantly changing priorities and practices in schools. According to Anyon (1997), education policy continues to revolve "around the tensions between equity and excellence, between the social and intellectual functions of schooling, and over such questions as, 'Education for whom and support for whose interests?'" (p. 87). Policy directed at the nation's schools has lacked a guiding set of consistent values and principles. Principles of risk, protection, and resilience offer real promise as a systematic method of designing and enhancing education policy and programs based upon such policy. Policymakers at all levels would do well to incorporate these principles into the nation's struggling educational system.

QUESTIONS FOR DISCUSSION

1. What are the major risk factors for school failure? Which of these risk factors should receive the most attention in educational policy and why?

2. What educational policies and programs over the past 100 years have best served the concept of risk and resilience? Why?

3. What have been the major trends in policy and practice reform since 2000?

4. What factors inhibit the integration of policies and programs across problem domains?

5. What are some possible solutions to the barriers to the integration of policies and programs across problem domains?

NOTE

1. To address this concern, the U.S. Department of Education offered states the option of applying for waivers of certain provisions of NCLB, including loosening requirements for determining adequate yearly progress and student proficiency, identification of schools for improvement or specific corrective actions, and highly qualified teacher plans. Certain provisions of the law specifically cannot be waived, including civil rights requirements. Forty-three states, the District of Columbia, and Puerto Rico have received flexibility waivers.

REFERENCES

Administration for Children and Families. (2013). *Head Start fact sheet.* Washington, DC: U.S. Department of Health and Human Services. Retrieved from http://eclkc.ohs.acf.hhs.gov/hslc/mr/factsheets/2013-hs-program-factsheet.html

Anyon, J. (1997). *Ghetto schooling: A political economy of urban reform.* New York: Teachers College Press.

Apollonia, S., & Abrami, P. C. (1997). Student ratings: The validity of use. *American Psychologist, 52,* 1199–1208.

Arcia, E. (2006). Achievement and enrollment status of suspended students: Outcomes in a large, multicultural school district. *Education & Urban Society, 38,* 359–369.

Batsche, G. M., Elliott, J., Graden, J. L., Grimes, J., Kovaleski, J. F., & Prasse, D. (2005). *Response to intervention: Policy considerations and implementation.* Alexandria, VA: National Association of State Directors of Special Education.

Brauner, C. B., & Stephens, B. C (2006). Estimating the prevalence of early childhood serious emotional/behavioral disorder: Challenges and recommendations. *Public Health Reports, 121,* 303–310.

Brooks-Gunn, J., & Duncan, G. J. (1997). The effects of poverty on children. *Future of Children, 7,* 55–71.

Brown v. Board of Education of Topeka, 347 U.S. 483 (1954).

Carnahan, S. (1994). Preventing school failure and dropout. In R. J. Simeonsson (Ed.), *Risk, resilience, and prevention: Promoting the well-being of all children* (pp. 103–124). Baltimore: Paul H. Brooks.

Carpenter, D. M., & Ramirez, A. (2007). More than one gap: Dropout rate gaps between and among Black, Hispanic, and White students. *Journal of Advanced Academics, 19,* 32–64.

Cecelski, D. (1994). *Along freedom road.* Chapel Hill: University of North Carolina Press.

Center for Mental Health in Schools. (2002). *An introductory packet: About mental health in schools* (ERIC Document No. 463509).Los Angeles: University of California at Los Angeles. Retrieved from http://www.eric.ed.gov/ERICDocs/data/ericdocs2sql/content_storage_01/0000019b/80/19/f2/3a.pdf

Clark, K. (1965). *Dark ghetto: Dilemmas of social power.* New York: Harper & Row.

Coleman, J. S. (1966). *Equality of educational opportunity* (No. OE-38001). Washington, DC: National Center for Education Statistics.

Cook, G. (2005). Title I at 40. *American School Board Journal, 192,* 24–26.

Cremin, L. A. (1957). *The republic and the school: Horace Mann on the education of free men.* New York: Teachers College Press.

Derezinski, T. (2004). School attendance. In P. Allen-Meares (Ed.), *Social work services in schools* (4th ed., pp. 95–118). Boston: Allyn & Bacon.

Dewey, J. (1916). *Democracy and education.* New York: Macmillan.

Duncan, A. (2009, June 8). Plenary address. Paper presented at the Annual Institute of Education Sciences conference, Washington, DC.

Duncan, G. J., & Brooks-Gunn, J. (2000). Family poverty, welfare reform, and child development. *Child Development, 71,* 188–161. doi:10.1111/1467-8624.00133

Duncan, G. J., Brooks-Gunn, J., & Klebanov, P. K. (1994). Economic deprivation and early childhood development. *Child Development, 65,* 296–318. doi:10.2307/1131385

Dunlap, G., Sailor, W., Horner, H. F., & Sugai, G. (2009). Overview and history of positive behavior support. In W. Sailor, G. Dunlap, G. Sugai, & H. F. Horner (Eds.), *Handbook of positive behavior support: issues in clinical child psychology* (pp. 3–16). New York: Springer. doi:10.1007/978-0-387-09632-2_1

Fall, A., & Roberts, G. (2012). High school dropouts: Interactions between social context, self perceptions, school engagement, and student dropout. *Journal of Adolescence, 35*(4), 787–798.

Finn, J. D., Fish, R. M., & Scott, L. A. (2008). Educational sequelae of high school misbehavior. *Journal of Educational Research, 101,* 259–274. doi:10.3200/JOER.101.5.259-274

Fraser, M. W., Kirby, L. D., & Smokowski, P. R. (2004). Risk and resilience in childhood. In M. W. Fraser (Ed.), *Risk and resiliency in childhood: An ecological perspective* (2nd ed., pp. 13–66). Washington, DC: NASW Press.

Fraser, M. W., & Terzian, M. A. (2005). Risk and resilience in child development: Practice principles and strategies. In G. P. Mallon & P. M. Hess (Eds.), *Handbook of children, youth, and family services: Practices, policies, and programs* (pp. 55–71). New York: Columbia University Press.

Fredricks, J. (2011). Engagement in school and out of school contexts: A multidimensional view of engagement. *Theory into Practice, 50*(4), 327–335.

Frey, A. J., Lingo, A., & Nelson, C. M. (2010). Implementing positive behavior support in elementary schools. In M. R. Shinn & H. M. Walker (Eds.), *Interventions for achievement and behavior problems in a three-tier model including RTI* (pp. 397–434). Bethesda, MD: National Association of School Psychologists.

Fuhrman, S., & Lazerson, M. (2005). *The public schools.* New York: Oxford University Press.

Furlong, M., & Morrison, G. (2000). The school in school violence. *Journal of Emotional & Behavioral Disorders, 8,* 71–82. doi:10.1177/106342660000800203

Greenberg, M. T. (2004).Current and future challenges in school-based prevention: The researcher perspective. *Prevention Science, 5,* 5–13. doi:10.1023/B:PREV.0000013976.84939.55

Greenberg, M. T., Domitrovich, C., & Bumbarger, B. (1999). *Preventing mental disorders in school-age children: A review of the effectiveness of prevention programs.* University Park: Pennsylvania State University, Prevention Research Center for the Promotion of Human Development.

Haberman, M. (2000). Urban schools: Day camps or custodial centers? *Phi Delta Kappan, 82*(3), 203–208.

Hawkins, J. D., Catalano, R. F., Kosterman, R., Abbott, R. D., & Hill, K. G. (1999). Preventing adolescent health-risk behaviors by strengthening protection during childhood. *Archives of Pediatrics & Adolescent Medicine, 153,* 226–234.

Institute of Education Sciences. (2014). *Common core of data.* Retrieved from National Center for Education Statistics website: http://nces.ed.gov/ccd/

Jenson, J.M., & Bender, K.A. (2014). *Preventing child and adolescent problem behavior. Evidence-based strategies in schools, families, and communities.* New York: Oxford University Press.

Jenson, J. M., & Howard, M. O. (1999). *Youth violence: Current research and recent practice innovations.* Washington, DC: NASW Press.

Kemp, S. (2006). Dropout policies and trends for students with and without disabilities. *Adolescence, 41,* 235–250.

Kohl, H. (1967). *36 children.* New York: New American Library.

Kozol, J. (1967). *Death at an early age: The deconstruction of the hearts and minds of Negro children in the Boston public schools.* Boston: Houghton Mifflin.

Love, J. M., Tarullo, L. B., Raikes, H., & Chazen-Cohen, R. (2006). Head Start: What do we know about its effectiveness? What do we need to know? In K. McCartney & D. Phillips (Eds.), *Blackwell handbook on early childhood development* (pp. 550–575). Malden, MA: Blackwell. doi:10.1002/9780470757703.ch27

Milliken v. Bradley, 418 U.S. 717 (1974).

National Center for Education Statistics. (2013). *Digest of Education Statistics: 2012.* Washington, DC: U.S. Department of Education.

National Commission on Excellence. (1983). *A nation at risk. The imperative for educational reform.* Washington, DC: Author. Retrieved from http://www2.ed.gov/pubs/NatAtRisk/index.html

Nelson, J. L., Palonsky, S. B., & McCarthy, M. R. (2004). *Critical issues in education: Dialogues and dialectics* (5th ed.). Boston: McGraw-Hill.

Paige, R. (2002). An overview of America's education agenda. *Phi Delta Kappan, 83*(9), 708–713.

Parents Involved in Community Schools v. Seattle School District No. 1, 127 U.S. 2738 (2007).

Patterson, J. A., Hale, D., & Stessman, M. (2007). Cultural contradictions and school leaving: A case study of an urban high school. *High School Journal, 91,* 1–15. doi:10.1353/hsj.2008.0001

Plessy v. Ferguson, 163 U.S. 537 (1896).

Ravitch, D. (1983). *The troubled crusade: An American education, 1945–1980.* New York: Basic Books.

Reid, J. B. (1993). Prevention of conduct disorder before and after school entry: Relating interventions to developmental findings. *Development and Psychopathology, 5,* 243–262. doi:10.1017/S0954579400004375

Rosenfeld, G. (1971). *"Shut those thick lips!" A study of slum school failure.* New York: Holt, Rinehart, & Winston.

Sadovnik, A. R., Cookson, P. W., & Semel, S. F. (2001). *Exploring education: Introduction to the foundations to education.* Needham Heights, MA: Allyn & Bacon.

Sailor, W., Wolf, N., Choi, H., & Roger, B., (2009). Sustaining positive behavior support in a context of comprehensive school reform. In W. Sailor, G. Dunlap, G. Sugai, & R. Horner (Eds.), *Handbook of positive behavior support: Issues in clinical child psychology* (pp. 633–670). New York: Springer. doi:10.1007/978-0-387-09632-2_26

Sameroff, A. J., & Gutman, L. M. (2004). Contributions of risk research to the design of successful interventions. In P. Allen-Meares & M. W. Fraser (Eds.), *Intervention with children and adolescents: An interdisciplinary perspective* (pp. 9–26). Boston: Allyn & Bacon.

Scott, T. M., Anderson, C. M., Mancil, R., & Alter, P. (2009). Function-based supports for individual students in school settings. In W. Sailor, G. Dunlap, G. Sugai & H. F. Horner (Eds.), *Handbook of positive behavior support: Issues in clinical child psychology* (pp. 421–441). New York: Springer. doi:10.1007/978-0-387-09632-2_18

Skiba, R. (2002). Special education and school discipline: A precarious balance. *Behavioral Disorders, 27,* 81–97.

Skiba, R., Michael, R. S., Nardo, A.C., & Peterson, R. (2000). *The color of discipline: sources of racial and gender disproportionality in school punishment.* Retrieved December 13, 2009, from http://www.indiana.edu/ ~ safeschl/cod.pdf

Skiba, R., & Peterson, R. (1999). The dark side of zero tolerance: Can punishment lead to safe schools? (ERIC Document No.ED 456 546). *Phi Delta Kappan, 80,* 381–382.

South, S. J., Haynie, D.L., & Bose, S. (2007). Student mobility and school drop out. *Social Science Research, 36,* 68–94. doi:10.1016/j.ssresearch.2005.10.001

Stester, M.C. & Stillwell, R. (2014). *Public high school four-year on time graduation rates and event dropout rates: School years 2010–2011 and 2011–2012.* Washington, DC: U.S. Department of Education, National Center for Education Statistics.

Substance Abuse and Mental Health Services Administration. (2008). *National household survey on drug abuse: Main findings.* Washington, DC: U.S. Department of Health and Human Services.

Sweeten, G. (2006). Who will graduate? Disruption of high school education by arrest and court involvement. *Justice Quarterly, 23,* 462–480.

Walker, H., Horner, R. H., Sugai, G., Bullis, M., Sprague, J. R., Bricker, D., & Kaufman, M. J. (1996). Integrated approaches to preventing antisocial behavior patterns among school-age children and youth. *Journal of Emotional & Behavioral Disorders, 4,* 193–256. doi:10.1177/106342669600400401

Wang, M., & Fredricks, J. (2014). The reciprocal links between school engagement, youth problem behaviors, and school dropout during adolescence. *Child Development, 85*(2), 722–737.

ADDITIONAL READING

Fraser, M. W., Kirby, L. D., & Smokowski, P. R. (2004). Risk and resilience in childhood. In M. W. Fraser (Ed.), *Risk and resiliency in childhood: An ecological perspective* (2nd ed., pp. 13–66.). Washington, DC: NASW Press.

Nelson, J. L., Palonsky, S. B., & McCarthy, M. R. (2004). *Critical issues in education: Dialogues and dialectics* (5th ed.). Boston: McGraw-Hill.

Sailor, W., Dunlap, G., Sugai, G, & Horner, R. (2009). *Handbook of positive behavior support.* New York: Springer. doi:10.1007/978-0-387-09632-2

Sprague, J. R., & Walker, H. (2000). Early identification and intervention for youth with antisocial and violent behavior. *Exceptional Children, 66,* 367–379.

Walker, H., & Shinn, M. K. (2010). *Interventions for achievement and behavior problems: Preventive and remedial approaches* (Vol. 3). Bethesda, MD: National Association of School Psychologists.

WEB-BASED RESOURCES

Center on Education Policy, http://www.cep-dc.org/
Education Commission of the States, http://www.ecs.org/
Education Policy Institute, http://www.educationalpolicy.org/
Education Policy and Leadership Center, http://www.eplc.org/about_description.html

CHAPTER 5

Child Mental Health Policy

Promise Without Fulfillment?

Mary E. Fraser

Paul Lanier

Children and their families are our nation's most valuable and perhaps most endangered resource. Today's children and families face unprecedented challenges, including exposure to persistent poverty, alcohol and other drugs, and violence. It is no wonder that one of every five children and adolescents in the United States has a diagnosable emotional or behavioral disorder that can lead to school failure, alcohol or other drug use, violent conduct, or suicide (Burns et al., 1995; Costello, Mustillo, Erkanli, Keeler, & Angold, 2003). The prevalence and impact of mental, emotional, and behavioral disorders makes children's mental health a major public health concern in this country (Perou et al., 2013).

According to the Surgeon General's (1999) report on mental health, at least 1 in 10 young people, or as many as 6 million youth, meet the criteria for serious emotional disturbances (SED). Prior prevalence estimates have ranged from 9% to 26% (Brauner & Stevens, 2006); the most recent research indicates a 22.2% lifetime prevalence of SED among adolescents (Merikangas et al., 2010) and a 5.7% prevalence in school populations (Li, Green, Kessler, & Zaslavsky, 2010). Children and adolescents with SED have symptoms that substantially disrupt their social, academic, and emotional functioning. Many children are in out-of-home placements or are at risk for such placement. Although many youth with SED have multiple social and health problems that lead to referral or involvement in the mental health, special education, child welfare, and juvenile justice systems (Brauner & Stephens, 2006; Brendenberg, Freidman, & Silver, 1990), only 59% of children with mental health needs receive any type of formal mental health care (Commonwealth Fund, 2006).

Studies indicate that the prevalence of SED is higher among certain groups of children. Children suffering from SED are more likely to be male, low-income, and from a racial/ethnic minority group (Mark & Buck, 2006; Wagner, Kutash, Duchnowski, Epstein, &

Sumi, 2005). Among special education students, those identified as having an emotional disturbance have poorer social skills, communication skills, cognitive and academic functioning, and are more likely to change schools and be suspended or expelled (Wagner et al., 2005).

The 7-year National Adolescent and Child Treatment Study (NACTS) identified a number of risk factors that are common among youth with SED. Researchers leading the investigation found that youth with SED had poorer social skills, lower academic achievement, less financial independence, and more limited interpersonal relationships than youth without SED (Greenbaum et al., 1996). In addition, the study showed that youth with SED were more involved in substance abuse and illegal activity than youth with no SED symptoms.

Without comprehensive policies and interventions that diminish risk and strengthen protection for youth with SED, the adult outcomes for these at-risk youth can be expected to be poor. This forecast is supported by a body of literature on risk factors associated with emotional and behavioral problems in childhood as well as a growing body of evidence on protective factors that mitigate the effects of these problems. Because children with SED are found in all public child-serving agencies, public policies that promote cross-agency, integrated approaches to providing effective risk and protection interventions are needed.

This chapter reviews the literature on risk and protective factors related to emotional and behavioral disorders in children and adolescents and summarizes the complex evolution of child mental health policy in the United States. Two case examples of state policies that were designed to improve and integrate services for youth with SED are described. Finally, suggestions are made for future policies that combine the risk and resilience perspective with integrated service structures.

PREVALENCE OF CHILD MENTAL HEALTH DISORDERS

A defining feature of the mental health field is the use of a system of classification that relies on diagnostic categories linked to service strategies, both psychosocial and pharmacological. One of the primary classification sources used in the United States is the *Diagnostic and Statistical Manual of Mental Disorders (DSM)*, published by the American Psychiatric Association (2000). This manual was recently updated with publication of its fifth edition (*DSM-5*) but most recent studies are based on the fourth edition (*DSM-IV-TR*). Table 5.1 displays the most common *DSM-IV-TR* diagnoses found in children and youth. The first column shows the diagnostic prevalence rates for each disorder within the subgroup of youth who have SED based on findings from the NACTS study. Public health surveillance of mental disorders among children has improved in recent years, providing valuable updates to previous general population prevalence estimates. The second column includes lifetime prevalence estimates of disorders for children aged 3 to 17 years from the 2007 National Survey of Children's Health (NSCH) and the 2011 National Health Interview Survey (NHIS). The third column includes lifetime prevalence estimates for adolescents aged 13 to 18 years from another nationally representative survey using a diagnostic interview, the National Comorbidity Study-Adolescent Supplement (NCS-A) (Merikangas et al., 2010).

Table 5.1 Diagnostic Prevalence Rates for Children

Diagnosis	SED Population (8 to 18 years)[a]	General Child Population (3 to 17 years)[b]	General Adolescent Population (13 to 18 years)[c]
Anxiety	41.0%	4.7%	31.9%
Phobias, separation anxiety disorder, generalized anxiety disorder, obsessive-compulsive disorder, posttraumatic stress disorder			
Depression Major depressive disorder, dysthymia	18.5%	3.9%	11.7%
Disruptive disorders		4.6%	
Conduct disorder	66.9%		6.8%
Oppositional defiant disorder			12.6%
Attention deficit hyperactivity disorder (ADHD)	11.7%	8.9%	8.7%
Childhood schizophrenia	4.7%	0.01%	
Eating disorders		0.1%	2.7%

a. Greenbaum et al. (1996)

b. Perou et al. (2013)

c. Merikangas et al. (2010)

Anxiety is the most common mental health problem found in childhood and adolescence (Merikangas et al., 2010). Anxiety manifests in a variety of forms, including phobias, separation anxiety disorders, generalized anxiety disorders, and obsessive-compulsive disorders. *Phobias* are unreasonable fears. One of the most common phobias among children and adolescents is *social anxiety disorder*, which is characterized by an unremitting fear of embarrassment in social and performance situations that sometimes leads to full-blown panic attacks. Children and adolescents with this disorder tend to avoid social situations and try to avoid going to school.

Separation anxiety disorder occurs in about 8% of adolescents (Merikangas et al., 2010) and is characterized by irrational fears that parents will be killed or taken away, which may lead to clinging behavior, difficulty falling asleep at night, and inability to participate in school and social events away from home. The disorder can last for many years and can be a precursor to panic disorder and agoraphobia experienced as an adult.

Generalized anxiety disorder is characterized by excessive and persistent worry. Children and adolescents with this anxiety disorder tend to be perfectionists and insecure.

Obsessive-compulsive disorder is characterized by recurrent, time-consuming, obsessive, or compulsive behaviors that cause distress or impairment. The obsessions may be intrusive images, thoughts, or impulses. Compulsive behaviors, such as hand washing and other cleaning rituals, are considered to be attempts to displace obsessive thoughts. Prevalence estimates range from 1% to 2.3% for children and adolescents (Perou et al. 2013; APA 2000).

Posttraumatic stress disorder (PTSD) is a prolonged, pathologic anxiety that occurs in both adults and adolescents following a severe trauma. The onset of PTSD in adolescence is common and may impair the acquisition of life skills needed for independent, self-sufficient living. PTSD is common among youth who have been victims of physical or sexual abuse and who have witnessed violence in their homes or neighborhoods. An estimated 5% of adolescents suffer from PTSD in their lifetime (Merikangas et al., 2010).

Depression in children and adolescents usually presents in two different forms. A diagnosis of *major depressive disorder* requires either a depressed, irritable mood or a diminished interest or pleasure in activities. Accompanying symptoms must include some combination of significant weight change, either gain or loss; sleep disturbance; loss of energy or feelings of extreme fatigue; psychomotor agitation or retardation; feelings of worthlessness or inappropriate guilt; diminished ability to think or concentrate; and recurrent thoughts of death. These symptoms must be present for at least 2 weeks and produce significant functional impairment. Diagnostic criteria for *dysthymia* also require a depressed or irritable mood that has continued for a period longer than 1 year and requires many of the same accompanying symptoms as major depression. Although the description of dysthymia appears similar to that of major depressive disorder, the symptoms of major depressive disorder are more debilitating than those of dysthymia. However, dysthymia tends to be chronic, more persistent, and longer lasting than major depressive disorder.

A disruptive behavior disorder, *conduct disorder,* is based on a repetitive and persistent pattern of behavior in which the basic rights of others or the major age-appropriate social norms or rules are violated. Characteristic behaviors of conduct disorder include aggression toward persons or animals, destruction of property, deceitfulness, and theft. Girls with a conduct disorder are prone to early sexual activity and homelessness. About 40% of youth with a conduct disorder develop an antisocial personality disorder and become involved in the criminal justice system. Those with an early onset of conduct disorder have a worse prognosis and are at higher risk for adult antisocial disorder. Conduct disorder frequently co-occurs with attention deficit and hyperactivity disorder.

Oppositional defiant disorder (ODD) is typically characterized by problem behaviors such as persistent arguing, habitual fighting, and frequent loss of temper. Children and adolescents with this disorder frequently test limits, deliberately refuse to comply with adult requests, and intentionally annoy others. These behaviors lead to difficulties with family members, peers, and teachers. ODD is sometimes a precursor of conduct disorder.

As implied by the name, *attention deficit and hyperactivity disorder* (ADHD) is made up of two distinct sets of symptoms. Although these two problems often co-occur, one set of symptoms can be present without the other. Children with attention deficit disorder have difficulty paying attention and are easily distracted. These children are often disorganized, and they have difficulty following through with tasks. The symptoms of hyperactivity include the compulsion to move that may be expressed as fidgeting, squirming, or wriggling around when seated or getting up and moving around the room. Children with ADHD often perform poorly at school and have difficulties with peer relationships. Hyperactive behavior is often associated with the development of conduct and oppositional defiant disorders.

Eating disorders, such as anorexia nervosa and bulimia nervosa, are the most fatal mental disorders, with 10% of cases ending in death (Steiner & Lock, 1998; Arcelus, Mitchell, Wales, & Nielsen, 2011). The prevalence of eating disorders is a particular concern because these disorders are among the most common chronic illnesses of adolescent girls, following obesity and asthma (Lucas, Beard, O'Fallon, & Kurland, 1991; Stice & Agras, 1998). Anorexia nervosa is characterized by a distorted body image that triggers an intense fear of gaining weight. The symptoms of bulimia nervosa include recurrent episodes of binge eating and purging.

Although rare, *childhood schizophrenia* is a serious illness. Children with schizophrenia may experience auditory and visual hallucinations and feel detached from the real world. It is sometimes difficult to distinguish between childhood schizophrenia and autism. Onset of adult schizophrenia usually occurs between puberty and young adulthood. Children with an earlier onset of schizophrenia generally experience symptoms that are longer lasting and more severe (American Psychiatric Association, 2000).

In this chapter, the terms *serious emotional and behavioral disorders* and *SED* are used interchangeably. Although not diagnostically specific, either term may include any or several of the diagnostic categories described above. However, readers should note that simply having a diagnosis of one of these disorders does not mean that a child is seriously emotionally disturbed or impaired. Moreover, it is important to recognize that the different diagnostic categories relate to different risks and intervention strategies. For example, children with eating disorders differ markedly from those with conduct disorders. Thus, child mental health policies must address a wide range of behaviors and conditions that are differentially categorized by diagnostic labels and terms such as SED.

A RISK, PROTECTION, AND RESILIENCE PERSPECTIVE ON MENTAL HEALTH DISORDERS

Allen-Meares and Fraser (2004) outlined a set of empirically supported principles to describe the concepts of risk, protection, and resilience. These principles inform our discussion of mental health disorders and child mental health policy. Allen-Meares and Fraser argued that (a) identifiable risk and protective factors exist for social and mental health problems in childhood, (b) cumulative risk is generally more predictive of developmental outcomes than any single risk factor, (c) some risk factors are more responsive than others to change strategies, (d) reduction of risk can produce improved outcomes, and (e) more salutary outcomes occur when risk factors are reduced and protective factors are increased. In addition, Allen-Meares and Fraser noted important differences between protective and promotive factors. Protective factors reduce, suppress, and buffer risk but are neutral (i.e., have no effect) in the absence of risk. In contrast, promotive factors, which are the opposite of risk factors, operate actively to promote positive developmental outcomes for all youths. Universal prevention strategies focus on promotive factors, whereas targeted interventions strengthen protective factors to reduce known risks. We apply these definitions to the discussion that follows.

Most serious childhood emotional disorders are considered to be biosocial in nature. Although children endure countless negative life experiences, most children are naturally resilient. That is, when faced with adversity, children tend to make self-righting adaptations. However, such adaptations do not happen in isolation. Resilience results from the nexus of individual effort and environmental conditions that facilitate adaptations. Most people share the viewpoint that mental health problems emerge in children and adolescents when there is a biological vulnerability combined with exposure to adverse environmental factors (Surgeon General, 1999). The principles of risk and resilience can be used to better understand not only which biological and environmental factors might predict serious emotional and behavioral disorders in children and adolescents but also which children should be targeted for prevention and early intervention efforts. A touch point for this chapter, these principles can also be used to determine which protective factors should be bolstered to promote resilience.

RISK FACTORS

Biological Risk

Shown in Table 5.2, biological risk factors can occur at either the individual or family level. Common examples of biological risk factors include genetics, chemical imbalances, and damage to the central nervous system through trauma or prenatal exposure to alcohol and drugs. Researchers have established clear genetic links to some conditions, including ADHD, mood and anxiety disorders, and childhood schizophrenia (R. Goodman & Stevenson, 1989; Jellinek & Synder, 1998; Maziade & Raymond, 1995; Rutter, Silberg, O'Conner, & Simonoff, 1999). Although the genetic mechanism of many disorders remains unclear, having a parent, sibling, or even a grandparent with a mental health problem increases a person's odds for developing a mental disorder.

Gender is correlated with the diagnosis of certain emotional and behavioral disorders in children. For instance, girls are at greater risk than boys for internalizing mental health problems such as depression, anxiety, and suicide (Spirito et al., 1993). Adolescent girls are about twice as likely as boys to be diagnosed with mood, anxiety, and eating disorders, whereas boys are twice as likely as girls to be diagnosed with a conduct disorder and ADHD (Merikangas et al., 2010; Nolen-Hoeksema & Girgus, 1994; Perou et al., 2013; Piquero & Chung, 2001; Robins, 1991; Rogers, Resnick, Mitchel, & Blum, 1997; Ross & Ross, 1982).

Once a child is diagnosed with one disorder, the risk of having additional mental problems and co-morbid disorders is increased. Children and youth with a history of psychiatric disorder have been found to be three times more likely to have a subsequent diagnosis of psychiatric disorder. It is not unusual to see a progression from one diagnosis to another, such as from a diagnosis of depression to a diagnosis of anxiety and from a diagnosis of anxiety back to a diagnosis of depression. Similarly, a common diagnosis pattern might start with ADHD and move to ODD or start with a diagnosis of anxiety and conduct disorder and expand to include a diagnosis of substance abuse. Sequential diagnosis may be more common among girls (Costello et al., 2003).

Evidence supports that a child's difficult early temperament is related to emotional and behavioral problems later in life. Agitated and tearful infants have been found to show symptoms of anxiety by the age of 4 years (Kagan, Snidman, & Arcus, 1998). Connections between difficult infant temperaments and conduct disorder have also been observed (Olds et al., 1998).

Table 5.2   Risk Factors for Child and Adolescent Mental Health Disorders

Individual Level	Familial Level	Extrafamilial Level
Genetic vulnerability to a mental health disorder	Low socioeconomic status	Frequent violence
Victim of physical or sexual abuse	Multiple moves	High stress
Poor self-esteem	Parental substance abuse	Rejection by peers
Difficult temperament	Parental mental illness	Social isolation
Chronic childhood illness or developmental delay	Poor maternal bonding and attachment	
Race/ethnicity	Poor parenting skills	
Previous diagnosis of a mental health disorder	Four or more siblings in the home	
Gender Girls: depression, anxiety, eating disorders Boys: conduct disorder	Parental criminality	

Environmental Risk

A child's social environment is an equal—or possibly more important—determinant of later mental health problems than constitutionally based factors (Sameroff & Gutman, 2004). Bronfenbrenner's (1979) ecological model of child and adolescent development stressed the importance of contextual factors, including families, communities, and social institutions. Children and youth at high risk for serious emotional disorders are more likely to be raised in environments that heighten the effects of biological vulnerability (Caspi, Taylor, Moffitt, & Plomin, 2000; Resnick & Burt, 1996). Some of the more common environmental risks that exacerbate vulnerability include poverty, dysfunctional family, exposure to violence, and parental psychopathology or criminality.

Poverty is often associated with mental health problems in children and adolescents. Children with SED have been found to be overrepresented in low-income families (Mark & Buck, 2006). Werner and Smith (1992) found that low parental income was the single greatest predictor of emotional disturbances in youth under 18 years of age. Although African American and Latino youth have also been found to be overrepresented in SED samples

(Mark & Buck, 2006), the factor of race/ethnicity, once thought to be a strong predictor of certain emotional and behavioral problems, loses its strength when adjusted for income (Neal, Lilly, & Zakis, 1993; Peeples & Loeber, 1994; Robins, 1991; Siegel, Aneshensel, Taub, Cantwell, & Driscoll, 1998). Moreover, early childhood poverty has been shown to have an association with depression, antisocial behavior, adolescent anxiety, and adolescent hyperactivity (McLeod & Shanahan, 1996; Pagani, Boulerice, Tremblay, & Vitaro, 1997).

Poverty is also associated with increased violence and substance abuse (Rutter, 1985; Spearly & Lauderdale, 1983). The Children's Defense Fund (1995) has estimated that, each year, between 3 million and 10 million children are witnesses to domestic violence. On the basis of a nationally-representative survey, Finkelhor and colleagues estimated that 20.3% of children witness family assaults in their lifetime (Finkelhor, Turner, Ormrod, & Hamby, 2009). Witnessing violent acts can have long-term deleterious effects on children (Jenkins & Bell, 1997).

Exposure to substantial incidents of violence can impair a child's capacity for emotional regulation (Gerrity & Folcarelli, 2008). In turn, a child's problems with controlling his or her anger and modulating mood can seriously complicate the child's ability to perform in school and to develop healthy peer relations (Fairbank, Putnam, & Harris, 2007). Child abuse and neglect can negatively affect both neurological and psychosocial development, including the formation of personal morals and values, the capacity for relationships, the development of respect for social institutions and mores, and the ability to comply with rules of social conduct (Putnam, 2006). Although the risk process is not well understood, the experience of physical and sexual abuse increases a child's risk for major depressive and anxiety disorders (Dykman et al., 1997; Flisher et al., 1997; Silverman, Reinherz, & Giaconia, 1996), conduct disorders (Livingston, Lawson, & Jones, 1993), ADHD (Wolfe, Sas, & Wekerle, 1994), and eating disorders (Douzinas, Fornari, Goodman, Sitnick, & Packman, 1994).

Trauma exposure is widespread. For example, a longitudinal study of children living in a primarily rural area in North Carolina found that, by the age of 16 years, more than 67% of the children reported exposure to at least one traumatic event (Copeland, Keeler, Angold, & Costello, 2007). Those events included child maltreatment or domestic violence, a major medical trauma, traffic injury, traumatic loss of a significant other, or sexual assault (Copeland et al., 2007). Although the role that trauma exposure plays in the development of various disorders is not clear, experiencing trauma appears to affect emotional regulation and the processing of social information.

Similarly, poor social and economic conditions have been correlated with family pathology, child abuse, and poor parental supervision. However, the causal pathway is uncertain. It may be that poverty itself does not cause poor mental health outcomes in children and adolescents. Instead, living in poverty may produce poor child mental health outcomes because the parental experience of financial strain and economic loss diminishes some parents' capacity to provide involved and supportive parenting (Linver, Fuligni, Hernandez, & Brooks-Gunn, 2004; Oyserman, 2004). Another environmental pathway of poverty may be related to nutrition. Even after controlling for poverty status, food insecurity has been found to increase the risk for adolescent mental health disorder (McLaughlin et al., 2012).

Dysfunctional parenting—rejection, neglect, maltreatment, and inability to provide appropriate structure and supervision—is associated with increased risk of emotional and behavioral disorders in children and adolescents (Johnson, Cohen, Kasen, Smailes, & Brook, 2001; Resnick & Burt, 1996). In one review, Loeber and Stouthamer-Loeber (1996) noted that poor parental supervision and lack of parental involvement were among the strongest correlates of conduct disorder in children. Other research has linked harsh, abusive, and inconsistent discipline patterns to serious conduct problems in children (Lahey et al., 1995; Robins, 1991; Shaw, Gillion, Ingoldsby, & Nagin, 2003). In stressed or large families, parental attention can be in short supply and may be unduly focused on negative behaviors. Because such behaviors garner much-desired parental attention, the negative and aggressive behaviors are reinforced, which may lead to patterns of antisocial behaviors (Surgeon General, 1999).

In addition, a number of studies have linked poor family management and emotional climate to depression in children. As compared with families raising children who are not depressed, families of children with depression tend to be less emotionally expressive, more hostile, more critical, and less accepting. Families with depressed children also have family structures that are less cohesive, more disorganized, and more conflictual in nature than families without depressed children (Gilbert, 2004).

Parents who are depressed themselves find it hard to provide consistent discipline, supervision, and emotionally positive interactions with their children (Wilson & Durbin, 2010). Children and adolescents of parents with depression have been found to be at increased risk for internalizing and externalizing disorders (S. H. Goodman, et al., 2011; Wickramaratne & Weissman, 1998). Not surprisingly, parental mental illness itself is associated with poor parenting ability (Oyserman, Mowbray, Allen-Meares, & Firminger, 2000).

Negative life events have also been associated with poor emotional and behavioral outcomes in children and adolescents (Gerrity & Folcarelli, 2008; Goodyer, 1990; Kessler, 1997; Tiet et al., 2001). Examples of negative life events include multiple moves; loss of a parent through death, divorce, or out-of-home placement; physical assault; exposure to violent acts; and injury. A longitudinal study found that suicidal ideation in 16-year-olds was strongly predicted by early adversities such as childhood maltreatment, residential instability, and community violence (Thompson et al., 2012).

In a 1999 review of the mental health research literature, the U.S. Surgeon General noted that exposure to emotional abuse and physical violence disrupted the normal development of children and adolescents and had profound effects on mental, physical, and emotional health. The review found that children's exposure to abuse and violence was associated with characteristics such as insecure attachment; impaired social functioning with peers; and psychiatric disorders such as PTSD, ADHD, conduct disorder, and depression (Surgeon General, 1999). When compared with peers who did not experience adverse events in childhood, adults who experienced four or more categories of childhood adverse events (e.g., having witnessed violence, having a parent who abused alcohol or drugs, or having lived in poverty) had a 4- to 12-fold increased risk for alcoholism, drug abuse, depression, and suicide attempts (Felitti et al., 1998).

Certain groups of disorders are more closely associated with negative life events than are others. In addition, the effect of negative life events also appears to differ by gender. For example, depression is associated with loss and grief, particularly in girls (Breier et al., 1988; Goodyer, 2001; Moore, Rohde, Seeley, & Lewinsohn, 1999). The earlier a child experiences the loss of a parent or caretaker, the more severe the outcome. Being a victim of a crime, a violent act, or an assault is strongly associated with PTSD and conduct disorder in both girls and boys (Famularo, Kinscherff, & Fenton, 1992); however, the association between being a victim of crime, violence, or assault and the occurrence of ODD is particularly strong among girls (Tiet et al., 2001). Among boys, a parent being arrested and jailed is strongly associated with conduct disorder and dysthymia, whereas among girls, parental arrest is more often associated with conduct disorder and overanxious disorder.

In sum, a number of risk factors are associated with emotional and behavioral disorders in children and adolescents. These risk factors can be grouped at the individual, familial, and extrafamilial levels. The level of individual risk appears to be related to the number of risk factors a child has in various domains (Fergusson, Horwood, & Lynsky, 1994; Rutter, 1979). Moreover, cumulative risk appears to be more important than any single risk factor (Sameroff & Gutman, 2004).

Indeed, it is estimated that nearly half of children entering kindergarten have at least one risk factor (Zill & West, 2001). Similarly, the Adverse Childhood Experiences Study, which was conducted in a primary-care setting, found that more than 50% of respondents had experienced at least one type of adverse experience in childhood and that 25% reported more than two types (Felitti et al., 1998). Moreover, increased exposure to adverse experiences in childhood is related to a greater likelihood of developing a variety of behavioral, health, and mental health problems, including smoking, multiple sexual partners, heart disease, cancer, lung disease, liver disease, sexually transmitted diseases, substance abuse, depression, and suicide attempts (Lu, Mueser, Rosenberg, & Jankowski, 2008). Table 5.2 summarizes risk factors for mental health disorders at the individual, familial, and extrafamilial levels.

PROTECTIVE FACTORS

Protective factors reduce risk. Indeed, the impact of risk factors on children's outcomes can be moderated by protective factors. Furthermore, just as a greater number of risk factors are associated with increased risk, resilience can be a function of the number of protective and promotive factors present in a child or adolescent's life (Sameroff, Bartko, Baldwin, Baldwin, & Seifer, 1999). Garmezy (1993) identified three broad sets of variables that have potential to operate as protective factors. These variables include (a) child characteristics, such as easy temperament, cognitive skills, and social skills; (b) family characteristics, such as families that are marked by warmth, cohesion, and structure; and (c) the social characteristic of having a support system available. As shown in Table 5.3, social-adaptive behavior is an important protective factor that is related to most emotional and behavioral disorders.

According to the NACT longitudinal study of youth with SED, risk can be mitigated with adaptive social behavior, such as interpersonal relationship skills or coping skills (Armstrong, Dedrick, & Greenbaum, 2003). Good communication skills have also been found to be protective against hospital readmissions among children with SED (Greenbaum et al., 1996).

Life history reports of adolescents treated for mental health problems indicate that young people who had positive life outcomes tended to have had more stable living situations, better family relationships, and more positive relationships with peers. In addition, children who seemed to prevail over adversities were more goal-oriented and experienced more successes and fewer stresses (McConaughy & Wadsworth, 2000). Findings from studies sponsored by the World Health Organization have suggested that adversities such as the long-term disability associated with childhood schizophrenia can be minimized through supportive relationships with family or community members (Hopper & Wanderling, 2000). Thus, just as poor parenting practices are risk factors for many antisocial behaviors (Loeber, Farrington, Stouthamer-Loeber, & Van Kammen, 1998), warm, supportive family relationships and parental monitoring appear to function as protective factors for both boys and girls (Fraser, 2004; Green, 1995; Santilli & Beilenson, 1992). Table 5.3 shows protective factors for mental health disorders summarized at the individual, familial, and extrafamilial levels.

Table 5.3   Protective Factors Against Child and Adolescent Mental Health Disorders

Individual Level	Familial Level	Extrafamilial Level
Good social skills	Parental monitoring	Presence of nurturing/caring adults
Academic achievement	Good communication and cohesion	Opportunities and support for achievement
Easy-going temperament; good problem-solving skills		

HISTORY OF CHILD MENTAL HEALTH POLICY IN THE UNITED STATES

Whereas risk and protection are relatively new concepts, the concept of childhood mental illness has a history dating to the late 19th century. The first discussion in a textbook of psychological problems in children was Maudsley's chapter on "The Insanity of Early Life" in 1867 (Hergenhahn, 2001; Parry-Jones, 1989). However, the prevailing thought was that people could not "go mad" until they had reached adulthood. Children and adolescents who exhibited serious emotional or behavioral symptoms were hospitalized or imprisoned alongside adults. A public system devoted solely to child mental health did not emerge for another 100 years.

Precursors of Mental Health Policy

The earliest public mental health efforts on behalf of children were a result of changes that came about at the turn of the 20th century in approaches to handling "wayward" youth. Public policy in juvenile justice was changing from an approach that focused on punitive measures to an approach that sought corrective measures. The nation's first juvenile court was established in Chicago in 1899. In 1909, several members of the Hull House Association board became impressed with the new juvenile courts and created the Juvenile Psychopathic Institute to study the problems of juvenile offenders. The institute's first director, William Healy, MD, was a pioneer in the field and applied emerging psychiatric theory related to children and adolescents to individualize treatment of juvenile offenders. Growing from Healy's influence, juvenile court clinics developed across the country, providing the first publicly funded community mental health services to troubled youth. Even though mental health theory and practice provided a foundation for much of the evolving juvenile justice and child welfare policies, no formal child mental health policy had yet been developed (Jones, 1999).

During the 1920s, juvenile court clinics began serving more than just children with antisocial problems, and they became attached to a variety of new structures such as charities, universities, and teaching hospitals. Referred to as child guidance clinics, their major areas of concentration became school and home problems. Child guidance clinics primarily served children and adolescents with internalizing problems, and the clinicians used Freudian and Ericksonian developmental theories in addressing those problems.

The federal government first became involved in child mental health policy in the 1930s through the advocacy of the federal Children's Bureau, which supported the development of a child mental health field and advocated for the expansion of child guidance clinics. Child guidance clinics became the major source of mental health care for children and youth until the 1970s.

World War II brought an unexpected focus to the mental health needs of children. Because of the huge military draft, life histories were available for hundreds of thousands of young soldiers from varied backgrounds and socioeconomic levels. By the end of the war, it was apparent that soldiers who had had behavior problems as children were much more likely to be prematurely discharged, disciplined, wounded, or killed (Schowalter, 2003). The country learned that mental illness is blind to both color and income and that the outcomes of mental health problems are costly to both individuals and society.

Community Mental Health Centers

In 1963, President John F. Kennedy signed the Mental Retardation Facilities and Community Mental Health Center Act, which changed the face of mental health care nationally. Focused primarily on adults with mental illness, the law established funding for community mental health centers. These centers were designed to provide mental health services in community rather than in hospital settings. Similar to the child guidance movement that had preceded it, the Community Mental Health Center Act provided mental health services to only a small percentage of children with SED. The act did not mandate that affordable mental health services be provided to all children in need (Lourie & Hernandez, 2003), and little, if any attention was afforded to prevention or early intervention.

However, advocacy efforts on behalf of children and youth with emotional problems continued to grow, which eventually led Congress to establish the Joint Commission on Mental Health of Children. In its 1969 report, the commission found that millions of children and youth were not receiving the mental health services they needed. Moreover, many of those receiving care were served in inappropriately restrictive settings such as state psychiatric hospitals. In 1975, Congress acted to require community mental health centers to serve children and adolescents.

Despite the congressional mandate to provide mental health services to children and adolescents, community mental health centers were slow to respond. A report issued by the President's Commission on Mental Health (1978) strongly criticized community mental health centers for their failure to address the needs of children and youth with serious emotional and behavioral problems. President Jimmy Carter's Mental Health Commission also noted that few communities were providing either the number or the continuum of services needed. Therefore, the commission recommended that a community-based network of integrated services be developed to meet the needs of seriously emotionally disturbed children and adolescents.

Although similar recommendations had been voiced throughout the 1970s, it was not until the 1982 publication of Jane Knitzer's widely read book, *Unclaimed Children,* that Congress mobilized to take action. Knitzer boldly stated that of 3 million children and adolescents with SED in the United States, 2 million did not receive the services they needed. Furthermore, Knitzer reported that at least 40% of hospital placements for children were in inappropriately restrictive settings, including facilities for people with mental retardation and adult psychiatric hospital wards. She observed that most states had no specific policies for children with SED and noted that millions of "unclaimed" children were adrift in the public health, mental health, education, juvenile justice, and child welfare systems, and these children were not receiving appropriate mental health services (Knitzer, 1982).

Systems of Care

Knitzer (1982) documented a lack of services; poor coordination among service agencies; overuse of residential and institutional care; and failure of the federal, state, and local governments to respond to the crisis. In suggesting ways to improve these conditions, she coined the term *system of care* to describe a new approach to mental health. In 1984, Congress appropriated funds to the National Institute of Mental Health (NIMH) to establish a national agenda to deal with the problems outlined by Knitzer. In response, NIMH created the Child and Adolescent Service System Program (CASSP).

Following the example of the innovative Community Support Program for adults with serious and persistent mental illness, CASSP focused on the needs of children with SED by providing financial incentives to states to develop systems of care to serve these children. The CASSP initiative was the first federal mental health program to clearly identify youth with SED as its target population. CASSP created a movement and momentum for change. It became the vehicle for the development and articulation of federal and state child mental health policy.

The CASSP program was based on the following four assumptions:

1. Children and adolescents with serious emotional disorders are found in all of the nation's public health, mental health, education, juvenile justice, and child welfare systems.

2. Most children and adolescents with serious problems are served in more than one of these agencies at the same time.

3. Regardless of the agencies with which children are affiliated, the mental health needs of children have been overlooked and have not been addressed appropriately.

4. Few states have planning mechanisms to identify children and adolescents who are served across multiple systems.

The policy imperative in the CASSP initiative was to develop a multi-agency approach to the delivery of mental health services.

In a widely circulated monograph, Stroul and Friedman (1986) defined Knitzer's concept of a system of care (SOC) as "a comprehensive spectrum of mental health and other necessary services, which are organized into a coordinated network to meet the multiple and changing needs of children and adolescents with severe emotional disturbances and their families" (p. iv). These authors stated that an SOC should be a community-based, child-centered, family-focused, and culturally competent approach to integrating services. The multiple needs of each child and family should be met by providing a full range of services, including mental health, substance abuse, health, social, educational, and vocational services, with case management providing the mechanism to guide the family toward the appropriate mix and timing of services. Figure 5.1 illustrates a model SOC for mental health service delivery.

The ideal SOC includes enough flexibility to allow services to be tailored to the specific needs of the child and family involved, regardless of which agency has overall responsibility for the child or which system provided the services. For example, a child or adolescent with an SED might have psychological needs that require intervention by a mental health center, special education needs filled by the school system, and residential needs for a structured living environment provided by a social services agency.

Stroul and Friedman's (1986) outline of an SOC was used as the blueprint by the CASSP program for organizing child mental health services across the country. To receive federal funding, states were expected to create a protocol for interagency cooperation that would effectively coordinate all child-serving agencies and services. Coordination and cooperative development were to start at the state level and then be replicated at the local level. States were urged to develop strategies and methods for pooling financial resources among agencies so that all needed services could be provided, regardless of the child's service eligibility or insurance coverage. By the fall of 1990, all 50 states and the District of Columbia had received CASSP grants. By 1995, all states had at least one state-level, full-time, child mental health specialist working to develop a statewide system of care (Davis, Yelton, Katz-Leavy, & Lourie, 1995).

SYSTEMS OF CARE AND MENTAL HEALTH POLICY

The policy of creating SOCs to serve the mental health needs of the nation's youth was formally endorsed in 1992 when Congress passed the Children's and Community Mental Health Services Improvement Act, also referred to as the Children's Mental Health Initiative (CMHI). (See Table 5.4 for a listing of federal mental health policy initiatives.) This act created a program called the Comprehensive Community Mental Health Services for Children and Their Families. Administered by the Center for Mental Health Services in the Substance

Figure 5.1 A System of Care Framework for Children and Adolescents

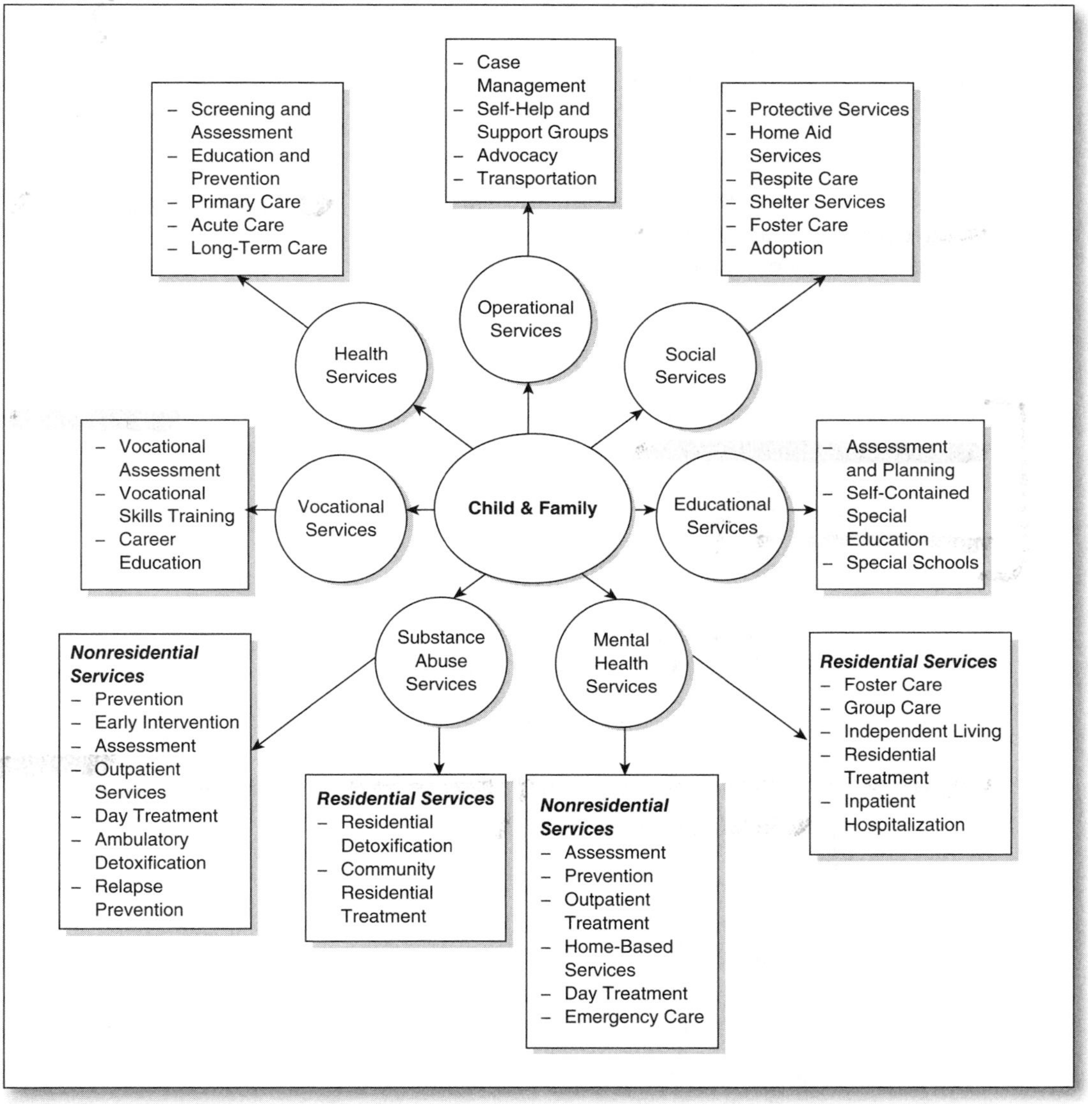

Abuse and Mental Health Administration (SAMHSA), this program provided grants to states to expand the SOC concept. To date, this program is the largest federal initiative supporting the development of children's mental health services.

By the close of the 20th century, at least half of the states had enacted laws requiring some sort of SOC (Davis, Yelton, & Katz-Leavy, 1995). The Children's and Community

Mental Health Services Improvement Act provided nearly $460 million in federal funding to 67 local SOCs that served more than 40,000 children across the country (Center for Mental Health Services, 1999). Now, many years after their initial authorization, SOCs continue to be the primary policy approach to governing public mental health systems. Experts in this area now propose that "some elements of the system of care philosophy and approach can be found in nearly all communities across the nation" (Stroul & Friedman, 2011, p. 2). Congress continues to provide annual funding through a competitive grant structure to states wishing to enhance their SOCs. The CMHI has invested over $1.6 billion in grants to all 50 states and many territories and American Indian/Alaska Native communities to develop sustainable SOCs (Stroul & Friedman, 2011). The major principles underlying this approach remain intact.

Ongoing issues related to the implementation of SOCs are apparent particularly when one looks at *where* children receive mental health services. The SOC approach demands that services be family-driven, child-centered, and delivered in a least-restrictive community-based setting. However, many children have symptoms that require a higher level of care and need longer-term services at facilities where they can receive constant professional supervision. Children with SED commonly require placement in a psychiatric residential treatment facility (PRTF). These placements are extremely costly, and advocates have questioned the legal and ethical acceptability of their use. There is also concern that the lack of community-based mental health services is driving the use of these services more than child need.

Given the major expense of PRTFs to the Medicaid system, the federal government initiated a waiver demonstration program in ten states to serve children with SED in their homes and communities. The evaluation of this program was completed in 2013 and concluded that children in the waiver program maintained and often improved their clinical functional status (Urdapilleta et al., 2013). On average, state Medicaid costs were never more than a third of the PRTF costs, saving about $40,000 per child. While there will likely always be children with SED that may require care in a PRTF or other institutional setting, this evaluation demonstrated that most children can be served in their home or community. This has the advantage of maintaining natural supports with the child's family, peers, and school. The major challenge is ensuring that services are available and accessible in every community. From a policy and cost-effectiveness standpoint, it makes sense to invest in developing community-based program infrastructure, adequately reimbursing providers, and supporting workforce development to avoid these more expensive and restrictive care settings.

Service Integration Within a System of Care

A growing body of literature has described the overall characteristics of children with SED and their families (Epstein, Cullinan, Quinn, & Cumblad, 1995; Quinn & Epstein, 1998; Wagner et al., 2005). Most of these studies indicated that children with SED have a number of common risk factors, including inadequate social skills, poor academic performance, family violence, alcohol and drug use, and mental illness. Despite these commonalities, there is no single system of mental health care for these youth. In fact, more youth with SED are found in other service systems than are treated within the child mental health system. For example, up to 80% of all children entering the juvenile justice system have mental health disorders

Table 5.4   Major Federal Mental Health Policy Initiatives

Policy	Date	Impact
Mental Retardation Facilities and Community Mental Health Center Construction Act (PL 88-164)	1963	Established funding to build and staff community mental health centers
Community Mental Health Center Act Amendments of 1965 (PL 91-211)	1965	Grants provided to support the development of mental health services in low-income areas. Included a new program of grants to support further development of children's services. Extended grant eligibility to centers serving those with alcohol and substance abuse problems.
Social Security Amendments of 1965	1965	Provided funding for medically necessary services to low-income families, pregnant women, and persons who are aged, blind, and disabled. Coverage of most mental health services was optional to states.
Education of All Handicapped Children Act (P L 94-162)	1974	Required that schools provide mental health services to children with serious emotional disturbances (SED) as part of their Individual Education Plan (IEP)
Community Mental Health Center Act Amendment (PL 94-63)	1975	Required community mental health centers to provide mental health services to children and adolescents
Mental Health Systems Act (PL 96-398)	1980	Based on recommendations of President's Commission on Mental Health and designed to improve services for people with severe, persistent mental disorders
Omnibus Budget Reconciliation Act (OBRA; PL 97-35)	1981	Repealed the Mental Health Systems Act and consolidated social services funding into a single block grant that allows each state to determine spending of its funds. Act required that 10% of mental health block grant funds be spent on children and adolescents. Federal role becomes providing technical assistance to improve state and local providers of mental health services.
Alcohol, Drug, and Mental Health Administration (ADAMHA) Appropriations Act	1984	Directed the National Institute of Mental Health (NIMH) to provide incentive grants to states to develop state and local-level child mental health structures to coordinate care to children with SED and their families. NIMH created the Child and Adolescent Service System Program (CASSP).

(Continued)

Table 5.4 (Continued)

Children's and Community Mental Health Services Improvement Act	1992	Created the Comprehensive Community Mental Health Services for Children and Their Families Program within the Center for Mental Health Services, which provided funding to states to develop systems of care for children with SED
Surgeon General's Reports	2000	Called for increased research on and use of evidence-based mental health practices
President's New Freedom Commission Report on Mental Health and the Federal Action Agenda	2003–2005	Called for a transformation of the mental health system, recommending a public health approach that emphasizes mental health promotion, early identification, and treatment
The Home- and Community-Based Alternatives to Psychiatric Residential Treatment Facilities Medicaid Demonstration Waiver (Deficit Reduction Act of 2005 PL 109-171)	2005	Allowed ten states grantees to use Medicaid reimbursement to serve children/youth with SED in their homes and communities versus care in psychiatric residential treatment facilities
Project LAUNCH (SAMHSA)	2008	Provided grants to states to address unmet mental health needs for children 0 to 8 years of age by funding community-based strategies to integrate and enhance services
Maternal, Infant, and Early Childhood Home Visiting (MIECHV)	2010	Provided funding for states to expand evidence-based home visiting program for low-income families
Patient Protection and Affordable Care Act (ACA; PL 111-148)	2010–2014	Reformed the U.S. health-care system. Several aspects of the ACA will impact children's mental health, including coverage of mental health conditions as part of the essential benefits package, funding for prevention, expansion of Medicaid/CHIP, improved care coordination, and no coverage denial for pre-existing mental health conditions.

(President's New Freedom Commission on Mental Health, 2003), and researchers have estimated that 20% of incarcerated youth have SED, which is double the rate of SED found in the general population (Mears & Aron, 2003). Nearly 20% of children with SED are involved in the child welfare system; a staggering 70% of youth with SED receive mental health services from local school systems (Burns et al., 1995).

It is clear that children in these separate systems need appropriate mental health care that is tailored to meet their individual needs. Over the past 20 years, mental health leaders, policymakers, and service providers have been struggling with how to best integrate mental health services into these systems. The most common state-level integration approaches involve coordinating mental health, child welfare, and juvenile justice services using one of the following three structures:

1. Separate agencies are maintained as individual departments. In this model, coordination of services is accomplished through formal interagency planning structures.

2. A part or all of the three agencies (mental health, child welfare, and juvenile justice) are housed within a single umbrella department, such as a department of human services. Each division maintains its own staff, policy development process, and budget. Coordination is facilitated because each agency reports to a single department director, and departmental rules and procedures that might inhibit service integration can be changed without legislative intervention.

3. The three agencies are combined into a single departmental agency, with a single agency budget and policy-making body.

A quick review of these three options might lead a person to conclude that combining all child services into a single agency would be the most advantageous option. However, such an arrangement has costs as well as benefits. Single, integrated agencies tend to be quite large, making management time-consuming, cumbersome, and often inefficient. Turf issues remain problematic. In addition, many child advocates object to the fact that the allocation of funds across different child populations would occur within a single budget process that might not be open to the public for review and comment.

States have found that restructuring alone does not overcome turf issues, policy conflicts, leadership challenges, and inadequate or disproportionate funding. Arguably the most important elements of successful service integration are agreeing on a common target population and blending funding streams so that an appropriate set of individually tailored services can be provided. Which agency provides the actual services may not be as important as having an arrangement in place so that services are provided to children who need them, regardless of the child's custody status or the family's financial ability to pay for services.

Systems of Care Implementation Evaluations

On the clinical level, integrated SOCs appear to produce positive developmental outcomes for children and adolescents involved in them. The Comprehensive Community Mental Health Services for Children and Their Families program is evaluated annually by SAMHSA. Findings from these evaluations have been detailed in "short reports," provided on the SAMHSA website (SAMHSA, 2009). These evaluations have used parent and teacher reports of youth behavior as well as youth self-reports from model SOCs. The findings have indicated that youth served in these SOCs demonstrate positive benefits as compared with their pre-enrollment behavior, including fewer emotional and behavioral problems, improved school performance, and less likelihood of engaging in harmful behaviors.

Despite the positive outcomes of model SOCs, and notwithstanding the large level of federal and private foundation support allocated to states, SOCs have proven difficult to implement.

The model requires many systems-level alterations, including developing links among child-serving agencies, creating a continuum of community-based services, blending funding streams, developing interagency policy, and organizing treatment teams to coordinate care.

The Center for Mental Health Services conducted reviews of SOC implementation in 1995 and 2002. Researchers from both reviews found substantial changes had occurred in each funded site. Indeed, changes in policies and procedures had been made that facilitated cross-agency training, programming, and co-location of services. The researchers also found changes that enhanced interagency communication and collaboration. Even so, no site had implemented all the aspects required of a comprehensive SOC model (Stroul, 2006; Vinson, Brannan, Baughman, Wilce, & Gawron, 2001).

A number of interagency coordination issues emerged as significant barriers in the SOC approach. Sometimes called "turf problems," these issues revolved around poor inter-agency collaboration, which was attributable to factors such as a lack of trust, a sense of competition, a fear of sharing resources, and a lack of understanding regarding the partner agencies' mandates and capacities. In addition to these turf problems, the greatest barrier to full-scale change was likely the sheer amount of time required to develop meaningful collaborations (Behar, 2003).

At the state level, many states have also struggled to sustain and expand their SOC approach after the federal funding period (Stroul & Manteuffel, 2007). Few states are able to support child mental health services with state dollars that are not also attached to federal Medicaid funds. The Medicaid program was created in 1965 as a health-care financing program; it is governed by federal rules and is jointly managed by federal and state authorities. Medicaid pays for about 50% of all mental health services provided to poor children and adolescents (Kenny, Oliver, & Poppe, 2002). Thus, policies flowing from federal and state Medicaid offices are as influential on state child mental health delivery systems as the federal policy initiatives that come through NIMH or the Center for Mental Health Services.

Unfortunately, state spending limits for Medicaid and expansion initiatives for mental health services are frequently in conflict. Although federal Medicaid policies have become more flexible over the past years, most state policies on Medicaid spending have become increasingly restrictive. Because Medicaid spending has been the highest growth factor in most states' budgets, state-level Medicaid policies are frequently focused on cost containment, especially in times of economic downturn or recession. In turn, the state mental health departments try to stretch their limited funds by matching state appropriations to federal Medicaid funds. In addition, the Medicaid program has inherent limitations and barriers related to supporting SOC structures.

THE FORT BRAGG STUDY

During the early 1990s, the Department of Defense and NIMH funded a major research study to test the impact of developing comprehensive and coordinated continuums of care for youth with SED at Fort Bragg, North Carolina. The demonstration program sought to fill the service gap between outpatient therapy and inpatient hospitalization by providing non-clinic-based services such as in-home crisis stabilization, afterschool group treatment, therapeutic foster care, and crisis management.

The Fort Bragg study demonstrated substantial system improvements, including increased service capacity, enhanced collaboration among service agencies, and reduced use of hospitals and residential treatment facilities. However, the demonstration program did not produce significant clinical outcomes with regard to alleviation of symptoms, increased functioning, or reduction of impairments (Bickman et al., 1995). The findings of the Fort Bragg project were in line with the evaluation results of the Robert Wood Johnson Foundation Mental Health Services Program for Youth program, which examined the development of SOCs in eight communities over a 10-year period (Cross & Saxe, 1997; Johnsen, Morrissey, & Calloway, 1996).

These disappointing findings caused ongoing debate in the child mental health field. Some researchers have advocated for a change in policy emphasis from system development to service effectiveness (Salzer & Bickman, 1997), whereas others continued to support large systems reforms (Hernandez & Hodges, 2003). Recent policy discourse has suggested requiring simultaneous system reform and the delivery of evidence-based interventions (Burns, 2001; Rosenblatt & Woodbridge, 2003). Although the risk-and-resilience framework for targeting interventions is not yet widely used within the mental health field, many policy leaders and advocates are focusing attention on identifying and using evidence-based practices that will provide cost-effective client-level improvements.

Evidence-Based Care and Mental Health Policy

In 1998, the American Psychological Association (APA) convened a special task force to systematically evaluate the evidence base (i.e., the available evidence from empirical research using rigorous scientific methods) for treating individual disorders in children and adolescents (Chambless & Ollendick, 2001). In its report, the APA Task Force determined two levels of criteria against which to evaluate the evidence base of particular interventions. The first, more rigorous criterion was "well established," and the other, less rigorous, was "probably efficacious." The major distinction between the two criteria is the strength of the supporting evidence. A *well-established treatment* is one that has been shown to be superior to either a placebo or another treatment, whereas a *probably efficacious treatment* needs to be shown only as superior to the outcomes of either a waiting list condition or a no-treatment control group. Evidence of the effectiveness of well-established treatments must be supported by at least two separate research teams. Using these criteria, Lonigan, Elbert, and Johnson (1998) conducted a review of psychosocial interventions for children and adolescents and found that most did not meet the first level of empirical support. In the years since the Lonigan et al. review, several more well-established treatments have been shown to be effective for children and adolescents with diagnoses of anxiety, ADHD, autism, bipolar disorder, conduct disorder/ODD, phobia, or depression. These treatments include behavioral parent training and classroom behavior modification for ADHD and parent training, functional family therapy, and multisystemic therapy for conduct disorder and ODD. In addition, graduated exposure, participant modeling, and reinforced practice were found to be well-established interventions for children and adolescents with phobias.

A number of other treatments, including those based on cognitive-behavioral therapy, have been identified. Cognitive-behavioral techniques have been shown to be effective for children with ADHD; depression; anxiety disorders, including PTSD; conduct disorders; and phobias. In addition, several skills-training interventions appear to be effective for children with major depression and conduct disorders. Other promising interventions include (a) school-based contingency management for children with ADHD and conduct disorders (Brestan & Eyberg, 1998); Pelham, Wheeler, & Chronis, 1998); (b) classroom-based social skills training for conduct problems, which is delivered in combination with parent training and systematic communication with teachers (Fraser, Day, Galinsky, Hodges, & Smokowski, 2004; Reid, Eddy, Fetrow, & Stoolmiller, 1999); (c) classroom-based social skills training for elementary school-aged children with depression (Gillam, Reivick, Joaycox, & Seligman, 1995); (d) parent-mediated behavioral interventions for child disruptive behavior problems (Comer et al., 2013; McMahon & Kotler, 2008); and (e) home visiting and early interventions for child socioemotional development (Avellar & Supplee, 2013; Heckman, 2006).

Many of the interventions commonly used in the child mental health system either have not been tested in controlled research investigations or have not met the scientific rigor necessary for inclusion in the APA Task Force Report. Examples of this lack of scientific rigor include studies assessing the effects of partial hospitalization, day treatment, case management, and home-based services (Surgeon General, 1999).

Unfortunately, no single resource exists for the increasingly long list of evidence-based interventions. SAMHSA developed the National Registry of Evidenced-Based Programs and Practices (available at http://nrepp.samhsa.gov). Over 200 behavioral health interventions for children and adolescents are reviewed on this database. Several professional and advocacy organizations have also created listings of evidence-based services for children and youth. Several of these resources are listed at the end of this chapter.

Given all of the policy rhetoric, it is surprising that no national legislation has yet been drafted to support evidence-based practices. However, many states are beginning to enact legislative language that requires the use of empirically supported interventions in child mental health SOCs. In this context, state mental health statutes often include the requirement to create interagency SOCs, within which evidence-based services are provided to children with SED and their families.

RISK, PROTECTION, AND RESILIENCE FRAMEWORK AND MENTAL HEALTH POLICY

The risk, protection, and resilience perspective provides a promising new framework in which to develop new mental health policies as it offers a valuable cross-problem, multidisciplinary approach for individually tailored interventions within an integrated SOC. Although it is not yet used widely within the mental health field, there are several good examples of its potential benefit. The Ventura County System of Care and the Willie M. Program will be described here as case examples. The Willie M. Program, which grew out of a class action lawsuit, provides a good example of using the risk and resilience framework to individualize care. The Ventura County System of Care was enacted by state statute and required its county agencies to work together. Ventura County's success in providing integrated services to SED youth led to statewide legislation supporting SOCs and has opened the door for multi-agency prevention and early intervention approaches targeted at children and youth at risk for mental health problems.

PROGRAM AND CASE EXAMPLE

The Willie M. Program

The Willie M. Program grew out of a class action lawsuit (*Willie M. et al. v. James B. Hunt, Jr. et al.,* 1980) filed against the State of North Carolina on behalf of children with serious emotional disorders (SED) and aggressive behavior who were institutionalized because of inadequate community-based care. Seeing the negotiations to settle the lawsuit as an opportunity to improve the service structure, administrators in the North Carolina Division of Mental Health, Developmental Disabilities, and Substance Abuse Services (MH/DD/SAS) created a comprehensive continuum of community-based care for high-risk and hard-to-manage children and adolescents with SED.

To be represented and served under the class action suit, youths had to meet criteria as a class member: be younger than 18 years old; have a serious emotional, mental, or neurological disorder; have a history of violent or chronically aggressive behavior; have been placed in public custody, such as institutions, or be at risk of such placement; or have been denied access to needed treatment or educational services. Although many youths met the criteria, four youths were ultimately named as plaintiffs in the litigation. Willie M., the first of four plaintiffs, was an 11-year-old boy diagnosed as emotionally disturbed with unsocialized aggression.

The North Carolina Department of Human Services avoided a trial by agreeing to the court's complaints and demands. Each member of the class was guaranteed individualized treatment in the least restrictive setting possible. The treatment was to be based on the child's needs rather than the availability of service providers to provide a service or set of services. If needed services did not exist, such services were to be created.

Leaders within the Division of MH/DD/SAS welcomed the challenge and advocated for the development of local systems of care (SOCs) within which they could create and provide services to class members. The Willie M. Program became among the first model SOCs in the country, serving as many as 1,500 severely aggressive youth with SED a year; two thirds of them lived in specialized foster care or group homes. The SOC required cooperative arrangements among the multiple agencies serving these youth. Court officers monitored the interagency relationships, making sure that public education, child welfare, and juvenile justice personnel worked in concert with the Division of MH/DD/SAS on behalf of these children. Comprehensive case management, also called *wraparound case management,* was the primary tool used to tailor services to the individual needs of members of the class action lawsuit. Each class member was required to have an individual habilitation plan. Beginning in 1995, the individual habilitation plan was based on an assessment process that reviewed both risk and protective factors.

An Assessment and Outcomes Instrument (AOI) was created to assess and to measure the progress of children in the Willie M. Program. The instrument used a risk and protective factor perspective

(Continued)

(Continued)

and measured both fixed characteristics (i.e., factors that could not be changed through intervention, such as the loss of a parent) and dynamic characteristics (i.e., factors that were malleable in treatment, such as school performance). Risk factors included family-level characteristics (e.g., living in poverty; parental loss; parental mental health and substance abuse problems, parental criminality, and large family size) and individual-level characteristics (e.g., fetal substance exposure, neurologic or developmental disorders, poor mother-infant attachment, difficult or shy early temperament, witness to violent acts, and history of physical and sexual abuse, school failure, and delinquent behavior). Of the possible 30 risk factors assessed by the AOI, each of the *Willie M.* class members had experienced an average of 13 risk factors—a number that far exceeds most definitions of a high-risk youth (e.g., Rutter, 1979). Consistent with the literature on risk and conduct disorders, most *Willie M.* class members with poor behavioral outcomes had histories of negative parent–child interactions and poor academic performance. Better behavioral outcomes were predicted by protective factors such as having good skills in areas such as problem solving, interpersonal relationships, and reading; having social support networks available, including involvement with family members and prosocial peers; and having a parent who was consistently employed (Vance, Bowen, Fernandez, & Thompson, 2002).

Each member's individual rehabilitation plan specified interventions that were likely to result in positive behavioral changes. Because most risk factors associated with *Willie M.* class members were fixed historical experiences and family features that were not amenable to change, few options were available that would reduce the impact of those risk factors on current behaviors. However, evaluations of the Willie M. Program found that strengthening protective factors was directly associated with improved behavioral outcomes (Bowen & Flora, 2002; Vance et al., 2002). Depending on individual needs, protective factors such as reading skills, relationships with adults, social skills, positive beliefs and attitudes, and involvement in community activities were strengthened through a variety of targeted interventions. In addition, parental and caretaker positive discipline skills were strengthened. The protective factors that were found to be strongly associated with behavioral improvement included increased levels of home and school social skills. Interventions targeting these factors included teaching skills in anger management, empathy development, and making and keeping friends (Bowen & Flora, 2002). Because of these positive behavioral changes, youth served in the Willie M. Program attended school more often and had fewer arrests. Class member and family satisfaction with services was high. As an individualized SOC was successfully developed, the *Willie M.* class action lawsuit was resolved in 2000.

The Willie M. Program in North Carolina was both successful and expensive. The court demanded the provision of needed services, regardless of cost. Many state legislators resented this open-checkbook approach. As costs went up for class members' services, appropriations to other parts of the mental health system declined or were not increased accordingly. Once the class action lawsuit was resolved and its mandates removed, funding for the Willie M. Program was reduced and realigned within the Division of MH/DD/SAS.

Ventura County System of Care

In 1985, the California State Legislature passed a landmark bill (AB 3920) authorizing a demonstration program to integrate mental health services across a core group of service systems, including child welfare, public education, and juvenile justice. The legislation provided for creation of a comprehensive, coordinated system of care (SOC) and facilitated interagency cooperation by integrating numerous federal and state statutes that addressed public mental health services for children and by amending various statutes and regulations. Ventura County was selected as one of three demonstration sites under Assembly Bill 3920. As part of the demonstration program, all child-serving agencies in Ventura County were required to engage in interagency planning and to develop interagency protocols and agreements that emphasized providing services to children in their homes or in the least-restrictive setting.

The Ventura County System of Care had five interdependent components as outlined in the enabling legislation: (a) a clearly defined target population, (b) a systemwide goal to preserve family unity and locally based treatment, (c) a commitment to developing collaborative programs of services and standards tailored to individual needs of children and their families, (d) a continuum of service options and settings that cross agency boundaries, and (e) a mechanism for system evaluation.

Client outcomes for the Ventura County System of Care reflected a cross-agency perspective. The overarching goal was for children with serious emotional disturbances to remain or to be reunified with their families, to attend and progress in public schools, and—as appropriate—to desist from problem behavior such as delinquency and drug use. A cross-agency target population experiencing serious emotional disturbance (SED) was identified, including populations within each agency that had been mandated for services. The target population included emotionally or behaviorally disordered youth, such as (a) court dependents whose histories included neglect, physical or sexual abuse, multiple foster home placements, residential treatment, and psychiatric hospitalization; (b) court wards for whom the public sector had legal responsibility because of delinquent behavior and who were at risk of out-of-home placement; (c) special education pupils who required mental health services to benefit from their Individual Education Plans; and (d) children who were not part of a formal agency other than mental health and who were at risk of out-of-home placement to state hospitals or residential treatment.

Mental health treatment was integrated into the service systems of the other major child-serving public agencies. The county mental health department was given responsibility for serving the mental health needs of the targeted children involved in the public school, child welfare, and juvenile justice systems. Mental health staff located their services in places where targeted children lived and went to school, a step that required reorganization of the Department of Mental Health. Most of the mental health staff was deployed to agency and school settings to provide or supervise mental health services in those settings. Depending on the needs of the agency, mental health staff provided consultation, assessments, case management, counseling, day treatment, special day classes, in-home care, family therapy, enriched foster-home care services, or crisis intervention.

(Continued)

(Continued)

The state legislation that created the demonstration project also facilitated the blending of categorical funds so that each agency domain was enabled to determine the array of mental health services it needed. Specific roles and relationships between agencies were delineated in interagency agreements and facilitated by a number of interagency coordinating mechanisms. An interagency juvenile justice council became the policy-making body of the county system. This policy-making body was created to serve as a vehicle for identifying problems, developing interagency solutions, and working through agency conflicts. The council's permanent members included the county counselor, public defender, district attorney, sheriff, chief administrative officer of the juvenile court, director of probation, a member of the board of supervisors, the superintendent of schools, the director of the Department of Child Welfare, and the director of the Department of Mental Health. Still in operation today, the council reviews all agency budgets and looks for ways to mingle and coordinate funding streams.

The Ventura County demonstration project met the system-level performance outcomes required by the statute. By integrating mental health services into each system, more children were served—especially children from ethnic minority backgrounds—and fewer youth required placement in restrictive and costly state hospitals or residential treatment centers. The project netted a substantial savings to the state. The demonstration program was expanded to more counties in 1989. In 1992, the California State Legislature enacted the Children's Mental Health Services Act, which expanded the SOC model to all counties. In 2001, the legislature enacted a law requiring an agency-integrated SOC statewide (Stortz, 2003).

California can be a beacon for other states. Its formal adoption of SOC principles and policies in statute has provided fiscal incentives for many local county collaborations. The state's shift to the rehabilitative option for federal Medicaid billing has allowed clinical staff to work outside of their offices and support field-based, in-home, and wraparound service delivery models. A state match to the federal EPSDT (Early and Periodic Screening, Detection, and Treatment) program has provided an important fiscal engine to expand and sustain services and supports to children and youth 0 to 21 years old. Most recently, the California Mental Health Services Act (Proposition 63), enacted in 2007, has provided additional and ongoing state funds to further transform the mental health system in California with increased funding for mental health promotion, prevention, and early intervention services to children and adolescents statewide (Hodges, Ferreira, Israel, & Mazza, 2007).

Criticisms of Child Mental Health Policies

Child mental health policies in the United States have been widely criticized over the past 50 years. The mental health services and programs resulting from these policies have been described as fragmented, spotty, nontargeted, and generally ineffective (Joint Commission on the Mental Health of Children, 1969; Knitzer, 1982; Lourie & Hernandez, 2003; President's Commission on Mental Health, 1978). In response to this criticism,

Congress supported the creation of SOCs to coordinate and enhance mental health care to youth with SED. Private funding sources, such as the Robert Wood Johnson and Annie E. Casey foundations, also contributed millions of dollars to develop model SOCs across the country. Unfortunately, the evaluations of many of these model programs have produced only mixed results.

Although supportive of the SOC concept, child mental health advocacy groups such as the Federation of Families for Children's Mental Health and the Child and Adolescent Network (a branch of the National Alliance for the Mentally Ill) remain frustrated by and critical of the slow process of implementation. These advocacy groups have not seen policy rhetoric translated into significant changes at the child or family level. These criticisms were echoed in both the Surgeon General's (2000) *National Action Agenda* and the report of the President's New Freedom Commission on Mental Health (2003). The Surgeon General (2000) stated that despite the existence of mental health programs in many communities, the nation lacked a basic infrastructure for adequate mental health care, and that "unmet need for services remains as high today as it was 20 years ago" (p. 13).

Two years after the Surgeon General's report, President Bush signed Executive Order 13263 establishing the President's New Freedom Commission on Mental Health. The executive order charged the commission with the responsibility of conducting a comprehensive study of the problems and gaps in the nation's mental health service system. In his cover letter to the President's New Freedom Commission on Mental Health (2003) final report, Michael Hogan, chair of the Commission, wrote,

> Today's mental health care system is a patchwork relic—the result of disjointed reforms and policies. Instead of ready access to quality care, the system presents barriers that all too often add to the burden of mental illnesses for individuals, their families, and our communities. (p. 1)

TRANSFORMATION OF THE MENTAL HEALTH SYSTEM

As a way to address these gaps and fundamentally transform how mental health care is delivered in America, the New Freedom Commission on Mental Health's report recommended a public health model of mental health care that would support mental health promotion and early intervention efforts as well as direct treatment services. SAMHSA followed up on the commission's report by creating a Federal Mental Health Action Agenda and inviting key federal agencies to help propose a set of action steps to address the commission's vision and to move its agenda forward (SAMHSA, 2005). The key federal agencies contributing to this agenda of action steps included the departments of Education, Housing and Urban Development, Justice, Labor, and Veterans' Affairs, all the divisions within the Department of Health and Human Services, and the Social Security Administration.

In 2009, Kathryn Power, director of the Center for Mental Health Services, reported that the federal government was committed to the transformation of the mental health system. It appears that "transformation of the mental health system" is fast becoming the 21st century's de facto policy on child mental health. However, it remains unclear how this policy will evolve under the Patient Protection and Affordable Care Act (ACA), judicial decisions, and other legislation.

Transforming Mental Health in Early Childhood

Clearly, part of the transformation will involve placing greater emphasis on early childhood. A child's early experience lays the foundation for lifelong mental health. A key element of the country's emerging mental health system will be an acknowledgement of the importance of promoting mental health in early childhood. The parent–child relationship is perhaps the most important area on which to focus. Because of what we know about the importance of healthy attachment for brain development and also because we know that parenting behavior can be improved with evidence-based interventions, socioemotional development will be emphasized. Although genetic liability and environmental risk may be challenging to change, we can help parents learn about child development and the importance of providing a nurturing environment. Many parents did not have positive examples from their own caregivers and may lack a role model or source of support to help raise their own child. Many researchers in diverse fields of economics and child development are bringing a message to policymakers that the best investment we can make is in our youngest citizens. There are several examples of ways to develop and expand federal policy based on compelling evidence from rigorous longitudinal research.

To help pregnant women and new parents in their roles as caregivers, home visiting has been a successful public health strategy for over a century. Many countries have universal home visiting programs in which every family receives at least one visit in the home environment to check in, answer questions, and provide referrals. Although the United States does not offer universal home visiting, the most rigorous research demonstrating the impact of home visiting on a broad range of outcomes, including child development, was generated from programs implemented in the United States.

The Nurse-Family Partnership (NFP) is one home-visiting model that has led the field. Work by David Olds and his colleagues across three randomized-controlled trials have tracked outcomes for mothers and their infants for well over a decade (Olds, 2013). NFP is provided to first-time at-risk mothers, beginning prenatally with visits by nurses and continuing until the child's second birthday. Findings indicate sustained improvements for the mother and child including decreased child abuse and neglect and improved outcomes in child development. Another promising home-visiting model, Attachment and Biobehavioral Catch-up (ABC), has demonstrated impacts on stress neurobiology and behavior regulation in young foster children (Dozier et al., 2008).

Building on these research findings and the growing literature demonstrating the need for primary prevention strategies beginning at birth, advocates successfully pushed for a federal investment in home visiting. The Maternal, Infant, and Early Child Home Visiting (MIECHV) program authorized by the Patient Protection and Affordable Care Act in 2008 provided five years of funding for state grants to expand home visiting services. The program was recently re-authorized for an additional six months.

Notwithstanding, home visiting alone is not sufficient to promote healthy child development. A comprehensive set of services and support for all parents is needed. The challenge of the early childhood system will be to develop strategies to ensure that the right program reaches the right family at the right time. The Centers for Disease Control and Prevention (CDC) is currently developing a strategy known as Essentials for Childhood. The program provides a roadmap for states and communities to cultivate "safe, stable, and nurturing relationships and environments" for children. While a major focus is on the prevention of child abuse and neglect, both of which are risk factors for child mental health disorders, promoting positive relationships and environments is a shared strategy for enhancing protective factors for child mental health. The Essentials for Childhood strategies focus on changing social norms and public policies to reflect the importance of healthy child development using the best available information.

Early childhood systems could also benefit from improved integration across agencies to remove service silos. For example, the child welfare system is mandated by law to ensure the well-being of children in care. Outcomes for children in foster care consistently fall well behind those for other children, particularly in areas of mental health. However, children under the care of the state should be those receiving the best services. This issue has recently received attention from policymakers and has sparked an explicit focus on promoting child socioemotional well-being for child welfare systems. One obvious strategy is to ensure that maltreated children have access to trauma-informed mental health interventions. This will require improved coordination of child welfare and mental health services.

The child care setting is another sector of early childhood policy that can have an impact on child emotional development. Some of the strongest research demonstrating the return on investment for early childhood comes from enhanced child care programs such as the Chicago Child–Parent Centers and the Perry Preschool Project (Temple & Reynolds, 2007). While child care programs focus primarily on school readiness, research is demonstrating that socioemotional skill development, and not just the traditional academic focus on building intellectual knowledge, may be the key to improving later outcomes for disadvantaged populations. Federal child care settings such as those provided by Head Start are critical to the development of the social skills and emotional regulation needed to succeed in school. President Obama recently proposed a plan that would provide universal high-quality preschool, including socioemotional skills training, for every 4-year-old child in America.

Transforming Mental Health Through the Affordable Care Act

The transformation of the mental health system will be driven largely by the implementation of the ACA. The ACA is a complicated policy that is being implemented in several phases over many years. States also have a great deal of discretion in reforming their health-care systems, so there will be significant variation in how the law is interpreted. At this point, the full impact of the ACA is unclear. However, we highlight three themes that may improve the accessibility and quality of services for children: parity of physical and mental health, the focus on prevention and early intervention, and the integration of physical and behavioral health care. Behavioral health care includes a range of prevention and treatment services related to mental health and substance abuse.

Under the ACA, all benchmark insurance plans must provide a set of "essential health benefits." Pediatric care and behavioral health services are examples of this class of services that must be covered in all plans. Furthermore, the ACA mandates full parity for mental health and substance abuse services. These services cannot have higher copays or different coverage limits compared with physical health services in the same plan. This aspect of the law attempts to lower barriers to mental health services related to out-of-pocket costs or limitations in certain insurance plans. Advocates have been fighting for mental health parity for years, and prior successes laid the groundwork for guaranteeing its inclusion in the ACA.

An overarching theme of the ACA is prevention. Although much of the focus is targeted at costly preventable physical health outcomes, there is also a clear emphasis on early detection of mental health problems in children and expansion of evidence-based preventive interventions. The National Prevention Council was formed as part of the ACA and is beginning to set recommendations to prioritize prevention efforts. Mental and emotional well-being is listed as one of seven priority areas in the first National Prevention Strategy. The first recommendation in this priority area is to "promote positive early childhood development, including positive parenting and violence-free homes." Also outlined in the ACA, appropriations for mental health screening have been directed to support the expansion of behavioral health services in federally qualified health centers. Screening for child depression in primary care centers is one of a fairly short list of federally endorsed preventive services. Many preventive services that will now be offered to parents may also have an indirect impact on preventing child mental health problems by targeting the risk factors discussed earlier. For example, women's preventive services, including domestic violence screening, are provided with no copay.

The details of how service-integration strategies will be implemented are still evolving. However, the basic idea is that the delivery system for health services, including mental health services, should be easier to access for patients with less duplication and complexity in the system. This benefits patients but also should make the health-care system more efficient and reduce unnecessary cost. One strategy will be to shift the financing structure away from a fee-for-service, volume-driven algorithm to an outcomes-driven algorithm. Providers delivering different types of services to the same pool of patients will have an incentive to work together through some arrangement such as an accountable care organization or health home. It makes sense to have clinical social workers, pediatricians, school nurses, and others on the same page regarding the care plans of children and, administratively, to have a shared incentive to produce better child-centered outcomes.

Integration of behavioral health into primary care is also a core strategy of another major federal program. Project LAUNCH (Linking Actions for Unmet Needs in Children's Health), funded by SAMHSA focuses on children (up to 8 years of age) and provides five-year grants to communities to improve service delivery for children's mental health. There are many exciting and innovative examples of communities bringing child mental health into the primary-care office. This program also supports mental health consultation in child care settings and enhanced home visiting services that target child socioemotional development. Service coordination for child mental health has been attempted in prior SOC efforts with mixed success. It remains to be seen how integration with primary-care systems will affect access to high-quality mental health care and service coordination for all children.

SUMMARY

In 2008, the National Center for Children in Poverty published a study as a 25-year follow-up to Jane Knitzer's heralded report, *Unclaimed Children: The Failure of Public Responsibility to Children in Need of Mental Health Services.* In the intervening years, although there has been an explosion of knowledge about the biological and social determinants of mental disorders in childhood and about ways of providing preventive and treatment services, the report found that state policies and the SOCs in place for most troubled children and youth appear all too similar to those criticized 25 years earlier (Cooper et al., 2008).

This is not to say that there has been no change. The vast majority of states were found to have taken tangible steps to improve their mental health delivery systems for children. However, a closer analysis revealed that those changes, while promising, were often limited in scope and depth. Although all 50 states reported that they had incorporated SOC values and principles into their delivery systems, only 18 states had taken steps to sustain these efforts through legislation and regulation, practice standards, and strategic planning. Too few resources were expended for states to develop a workable, comprehensive policy framework for addressing the needs of children and youth with serious mental health conditions. Even fewer resources had been committed by states to implement service systems and approaches grounded in the public health framework of mental health prevention, promotion, and early intervention (Cooper et al., 2008).

Much can be learned, however, from the Ventura County System of Care and the Willie M. Program case examples provided in this chapter. In addition, lessons about the effectiveness of mental health policies and programs can be derived from many other state and local efforts on behalf of children and adolescents with mental health problems. Based these examples and a growing base of evidence-supported program, at least four core strategies for policy reform in child mental health should be considered:

1. Structures should be developed to integrate mental health services into key child-serving agencies, such as public education, child welfare, and juvenile justice.

2. Systematic assessment should identify malleable risk and protective factors.

3. Evidence-based interventions should be selected and provided to reduce risk and strengthen protective factors.

4. Services should be developmentally and culturally appropriate and sequenced sufficiently early in childhood to disrupt negative developmental trajectories.

Mental health disorders can often be identified in young children and adolescents (Kenny et al., 2002). It is unfortunate that these disorders are not usually diagnosed and treated until youth are older. State legislatures spend millions of dollars annually treating older youth with serious emotional and behavioral disorders. Too often, these funds are expended in the juvenile justice and child welfare systems, which begs the question, "Are these efforts too little, too late?" Increasingly, many experts think this is the case.

In many communities, mental health services are now being integrated into public schools through programs such as school-based health clinics. These clinics improve access to primary health care and provide a less stigmatized entry into mental health services for many youth (Wu, Katic, Liu, Fan, & Fuller, 2010). School-based health clinics provide preventive and early intervention screenings for many health conditions that inhibit learning. Regular screenings for emotional and behavioral problems can also be incorporated into clinic services.

For these reasons, schools may be the best public setting in which to identify troubled children and to link them with appropriate services. More than 52 million youth attend U.S. public schools (President's New Freedom Commission on Mental Health, 2003). The integration of mental health and public school policies has the potential to save public money and private heartache by positioning resources to detect and treat mental health problems before they become florid disorders.

The good news is that some federal policymakers are taking notice and have proposed legislation that emphasizes mental health promotion and risk prevention in school settings. For instance, in 2007, Senators Christopher J. Dodd, Pete Domenici, and Edward M. Kennedy proposed legislation that would fund local education agencies to expand school mental health efforts through community–family–school partnerships. Two other recent Senate bills reflect growing federal support for school-based mental health services: House of Representatives Bill 3003, the School-Based Health Clinic Establishment Act of 2009; and Senate Bill 1034, the Healthy Schools Act of 2009. Although these measures did not pass into law, prevention-, promotion-, and treatment-oriented school-based mental health initiatives continued to gain resonance with policymakers, culminating in the inclusion of school-based health centers (SBHCs) in the ACA.

Becoming a federally authorized program is a historic victory for SBHCs, as it recognizes them as part of the federally supported health-care system. This historic health reform legislation allows eligible SBHCs to receive funds supporting management and operation of programs, salaries for health-care professionals and other personnel, purchase or lease of equipment, construction projects, and training. However, the SBHC authorization will be a hollow victory unless it is followed by appropriations. Currently, only capital improvements have been funded, with no federal financial support for the actual provision of mental health services in SBHCs. Until funds are appropriated, only limited federal support exists for SBHC operations, leaving little hope for the expansion that has been called for by many, including U.S. Department of Health and Human Services' Secretary, Kathleen Sebelius (2010): "We are thrilled that part of the [health reform] legislation calls for an expanded footprint of school-based health clinics. . . . I can't think of a better way to deliver primary and preventive care to not only students, but their families, than through school-based clinics."

 Although there is still much work to do, this is an exciting time for child mental health policy. The coming years may yield a massive improvement in the availability of mental health services as federal policies and programs such as the ACA and Project LAUNCH are implemented in states. The focus on prevention, screening, and early detection coupled with the broad dissemination of evidence-based interventions holds promise to make a dramatic impact on the course of mental illness and the public health burden at a population level. As with any policy, the details of how these policies are implemented and strategies for continued sustainability when federal funding and oversight is removed are absolutely critical to maintaining any progress that is made. Ensuring adequate funding and the availability of a well-trained workforce are key challenges to overcome at the federal and state policy levels.

We now know a great deal about risk and protective factors for childhood mental health disorders. Arguably the most important is that identifying, diagnosing, and treating high-risk children early may interrupt developmental trajectories that lead to poor outcomes in adolescence and adulthood. Improving our abilities to prevent or minimize these poor outcomes should become the goal to which mental health, child welfare, public education, and juvenile justice policymakers and leaders direct their concerted efforts.

QUESTIONS FOR DISCUSSION

1. What child mental health policies and practices have inhibited the integration of mental health services into other child-serving systems such as juvenile justice and child welfare?

2. Are there reasons to keep child-serving agencies organizationally separate at the state level? Local level?

3. Given what we know about risk factors for a variety of emotional and behavioral disorders, how can we combine mental health and public education resources to support prevention and early intervention strategies?

REFERENCES

Allen-Meares, P., & Fraser, M. W. (2004). *Intervention with children and adolescents: An interdisciplinary perspective.* Boston: Allyn & Bacon.

American Psychiatric Association. (2000). *Diagnostic and statistical manual of mental disorders* (4th ed., Text revision). Washington, DC: Author.

Armstrong, K. H., Dedrick, R. F., & Greenbaum, P. E. (2003). Factors associated with community adjustment in young adults with serious emotional disturbance: A longitudinal analysis. *Journal of Emotional and Behavioral Disorders, 1,* 66–76. doi:10.1177/106342660301100201

Arcelus, J., Mitchell, A.J., Wales, J., & Nielsen, S. (2011). Mortality rates in patients with anorexia nervosa and other eating disorders: A meta-analysis of 36 studies. *Archives of General Psychiatry, 68*(7), 724–731.

Avellar, S. A., & Supplee, L. H. (2013). Effectiveness of home visiting in improving child health and reducing child maltreatment. *Pediatrics, 132*(Supplement 2), S90–S99.

Behar, L. B. (2003). Mental health management environments: Children's mental health services—The challenge of changing policy and practice. In W. R. Reid & S. B. Silver (Eds.), *Handbook of mental health administration and management* (pp. 149–162). New York: Brunner-Routledge.

Bickman, L., Guthrie, P. R., Foster, E. M., Lamber, E. W., Summerfelt, W. T., Breda, C. S., & Heflinger, C. A. (1995). *Evaluating managed mental health services: The Fort Bragg experiment.* New York: Plenum.

Bowen, N. K., & Flora, D. B. (2002). When is it appropriate to focus on protection in interventions for adolescents? *American Journal of Orthopsychiatry, 72,* 526–538. doi:10.1037/0002-9432.72.4.526

Brauner, C.B., & Stephens, C.B. (2006). Estimating the prevalence of early childhood serious emotional/behavioral disorders: Challenges and recommendations. *Public Health Reports, 121*(3), 303–310.

Breier, A., Kelsoe, J. R., Kirwin, P. D., Bellar, S. A., Wolkowitz, O. M., & Pickar, D. (1988). Early parental loss and development of adult psychopathology. *Archives of General Psychiatry, 45,* 987–993.

Brendenberg, N., Freidman, R., & Silver, S. (1990). The epidemiology of childhood psychiatric disorders: Prevalence findings from recent studies. *Journal of the American Academy of Child and Adolescent Psychiatry, 29,* 76–83.

Brestan, E. V., & Eyberg, S. M. (1998). Effective psychosocial treatments of conduct-disordered children and adolescents: 29 years, 82 studies, and 5,272 kids. *Journal of Child Clinical Psychology, 27,* 180–189. doi:10.1207/s15374424jccp2702_5

Bronfenbrenner, U. (1979). *The ecology of human development: Experiments by nature and design.* Cambridge, MA: Harvard University Press.

Burns, B. J. (2001). Commentary on the special issue on the National Evaluation of the Comprehensive Community Mental Health Services for Children and Their Families Program. *Journal of Emotional and Behavioral Disorders, 9,* 71–76. doi:10.1177/106342660100900108

Burns, B. J., Costello, E. J., Angold, A., Tweed, D., Stangl, D., Farmer, E. M., & Erkanli, A. (1995). Children's mental health service use across service sectors. *Health Affairs, 14,* 147–159. doi:10.1377/hlthaff.14.3.147

Caspi, A., Taylor, A., Moffitt, T. E., & Plomin, R. (2000). Neighborhood deprivation affects children's mental health: Environmental risks identified in a genetic design. *Psychological Science, 11*(4), 338–342.

Center for Mental Health Services. (1999). *Annual report to Congress on the evaluation of the Comprehensive Community Mental Health Services for Children and Their Families Program.* Atlanta, GA: ORC Macro.

Chambless, D. L., & Ollendick, T. H. (2001). Empirically supported psychological interventions: Controversies and evidence. *Annual Review of Psychology, 52,* 685–716.

Children's Defense Fund. (1995). *The state of America's children yearbook: 1995.* Washington, DC: Author.

Comer, J. S., Chow, C., Chan, P. T., Cooper-Vince, C., & Wilson, L. A. (2013). Psychosocial treatment efficacy for disruptive behavior problems in very young children: a meta-analytic examination. *Journal of the American Academy of Child & Adolescent Psychiatry, 52*(1), 26–36.

Commonwealth Fund, Commission on a High Performance Health System. (2006). *Why not the best? Results from a National Scorecard on U.S. Health System Performance.* Retrieved from http://www .commonwealthfund.org/Content/Publications/Fund-Reports/2006/Sep/Why-Not-the-Best-Results-from-a-National-Scorecard-on-U-S-Health-System-Performance.aspx

Cooper, J. L., Aratani, Y., Knitzer, J., Douglas-Hall A, Masi, R., Banghard, P., & Dababnah, S. (2008). *Unclaimed children revisited: The status of children's mental health policy in the United States.* New York: The National Center for Children in Poverty.

Copeland, W. E., Keeler, G., Angold, A., & Costello, E. J. (2007). Traumatic events and posttraumatic stress in childhood. *Archives of General Psychiatry, 64,* 577–584. doi:10.1001/archpsyc.64.5.577

Costello, E. J., Mustillo, S, Erkanli, A, Keeler, G. & Angold, A. (2003). Prevalence and Development of Psychiatric Disorders in Childhood and Adolescence. *Archives of General Psychiatry, 60,* 837–844. doi:10.1001/archpsyc.60.8.837

Cross, T. P., & Saxe, L. (1997). Many hands make mental health systems a reality: Lessons from the mental health services program for youth. In C. T. Nixon & D. A. Northrup (Eds.), *Children's mental health services: Research, policy, and evaluation* (pp. 45–72). Thousand Oaks, CA: Sage.

Davis, M., Yelton, S., & Katz-Leavy, J. (1995). *State child and adolescent mental health: Administration, policies, and laws.* Tampa: University of South Florida, Florida Mental Health Institute.

Davis, M., Yelton, S., Katz-Leavy, J., & Lourie, I. (1995). Unclaimed children revisited. *Journal of Mental Health Administration, 22,* 142–166.

Douzinas, N., Fornari, V., Goodman, B., Sitnick, T., & Packman, L. (1994). Eating disorders and abuse. *Child Psychiatric Clinics of North America, 3,* 777–796.

Dozier, M., Peloso, E., Lewis, E., Laurenceau, J. P., & Levine, S. (2008). Effects of an attachment-based intervention on the cortisol production of infants and toddlers in foster care. *Development and Psychopathology, 20*(3), 845–859.

Dykman, R. A., McPherson, B., Ackerman, P. T., Newton, J. E., Mooney, D. M., Wherry, J., & Chaffin, M. (1997). Internalizing and externalizing characteristics of sexually and/or physically abused children. *Integrative Physiological & Behavioral Science, 32,* 62–74. doi:10.1007/BF02688614

Epstein, M. H., Cullinan, D., Quinn, K. P., & Cumblad, C. (1995). Personal, family, and service use characteristics of young people served by an interagency community-based system of care. *Journal of Emotional and Behavioral Disorders, 3,* 55–64. doi:10.1177/106342669500300107

Fairbank, J. A., Putnam, F. W., & Harris, W. W. (2007). The prevalence and impact of child traumatic stress. In M. J. Friedman, T. M Keane, & P. A. Resick (Eds.), *A handbook of PTSD: Science and practice* (pp. 229–251). New York: Guilford Press.

Famularo, R., Kinscherff, R., & Fenton, T. (1992). Psychiatric diagnoses of maltreated children: Preliminary findings. *Journal of American Academy of Child and Adolescent Psychiatry, 31,* 863–867.

Felitti, V. J., Anda, R. F., Nordenberg, D., Williamson, D. F., Spitz, A. M., Edwards, V.,.Koss, M. & Marks, J. S. (1998). Relationship of childhood abuse and household dysfunction to many of the leading causes of death in adults: The Adverse Childhood Experiences (ACE) Study. *American Journal of Preventive Medicine, 14,* 245–258. doi:10.1016/S0749-3797(98)00017-8

Fergusson, D. M., Horwood, L. J., & Lynsky, M. T. (1994). The childhoods of multiple problem adolescents: A 15-year longitudinal study. *Journal of Child Psychology and Psychiatry, 35,* 1123–1140. doi:10.1111/j.1469-7610.1994.tb01813.x

Finkelhor, D., Turner, H., Ormrod, R., & Hamby, S. L. (2009). Violence, abuse, and crime exposure in a national sample of children and youth. *Pediatrics, 124*(5), 1411–1423.

Flisher, A. J., Kramer, R. A., Hoven, C. W., Greenwald, S., Alegria, M., Bird, H. R., Canino, G., Connell, R., & Moore, R. E. (1997). Psychosocial characteristics of physically abused children and adolescents. *Journal of the American Academy of Child and Adolescent Psychiatry, 36,* 123–131. doi:10.1097/00004583-199701000-00026

Fraser, M. W. (Ed.). (2004). *Risk and resilience in childhood: An ecological perspective* (2nd ed.). Washington, DC: NASW Press.

Fraser, M. W., Day, S. H., Galinsky, M. J., Hodges, V. G., & Smokowski, P. R. (2004). Conduct problems and peer rejection in childhood: A randomized trial of the Making Choices and Strong Families programs. *Research on Social Work Practice, 14,* 313–324. doi:10.1177/1049731503257884

Garmezy, N. (1993). Children in poverty: Resilience despite risk. *Psychiatry, 56,* 127–136.

Gerrity, E., & Folcarelli, C. (2008). *Child traumatic stress: What every policymaker should know.* Durham, NC: National Center for Child Trauma Stress.

Gilbert, C. (2004). Childhood depression: A risk factor perspective. In M. W. Fraser (Ed.), *Risk and resilience in childhood: An ecological perspective* (2nd ed., pp. 315–346). Washington, DC: NASW Press.

Gillam, F., Reivick, K., Joaycox, L., & Seligman, M.E.P. (1995). Prevention of depressive symptoms in school children: Two-year follow-up. *Psychological Science, 6,* 343–351. doi:10.1111/j.1467-9280.1995.tb00524.x

Goodman, R., & Stevenson, J. (1989). A twin study of hyperactivity. II. The etiological role of genes, family relationships and perinatal adversity. *Journal of Child Psychology and Psychiatry, 30,* 691–709. doi:10.1111/j.1469-7610.1989.tb00782.x

Goodman, S. H., Rouse, M. H., Connell, A. M., Broth, M. R., Hall, C. M., & Heyward, D. (2011). Maternal depression and child psychopathology: a meta-analytic review. *Clinical Child and Family Psychology Review, 14*(1), 1–27.

Goodyer, I. (1990). *Life experiences, development, and childhood psychiatry.* New York: John Wiley.

Goodyer, I. (2001). Life events: Their nature and effects. In I. M. Goodyer (Ed.), *The depressed child and adolescent* (2nd ed., pp. 204–232). New York: Cambridge University Press.

Green, W. (1995). Family, peer, and self factors as predictors of male and female adolescent substance abuse at 9th and 12th grade. *Dissertation Abstracts International: Section B: Sciences and Engineering, 55,* 2771.

Greenbaum, P. E., Dedrick, R. F., Friedman, R., Kutash, K., Brown, E., Lardieri, S., & Pugh, A. (1996). National adolescent and child treatment study (NACTS): Outcomes for individuals with serious emotional and behavioral disturbance. *Journal of Emotional and Behavioral Disorders, 4,* 130–146. doi:10.1177/106342669600400301

Heckman, J. J. (2006). Skill formation and the economics of investing in disadvantaged children. *Science, 312*(5782), 1900–1902.

Hergenhahn, B. R. (2001). *An introduction to the history of psychology* (4th ed.). Belmont, CA: Wadsworth.

Hernandez, M., & Hodges, S. (2003). Building upon the theory of change for systems of care. *Journal of Emotional and Behavioral Disorders, 11,* 19–26. doi:10.1177/106342660301100104

Hodges, S., Ferreira, K., Israel, N., & Mazza, J. (2007). *Strategies for system of care development: Locally identified factors for system implementation* (Supplement to issue brief 2, Lessons from successful systems: Critical factors in system of care implementation). Tampa: University of South Florida, Louis de la Parte Florida Mental Health Institute, Research and Training Center for Children's Mental Health.

Hopper, K., & Wanderling, J. (2000). Revisiting the developed versus developing country distinction in course and outcome in schizophrenia: Results from IsoS, the WHO collaborative followup project. International study of schizophrenia. *Schizophrenia Bulletin, 26,* 835–846.

Jellinek, M., & Synder, J. (1998). Depression and suicide in children and adolescents. *Pediatrics in Review, 19,* 255–265.

Jenkins, E., & Bell, C. (1997). Exposure and response to community violence among children and adolescents. In J. Osofsky (Ed.), *Children in a violent society* (pp. 9–31). New York: Guilford Press.

Johnsen, M. C., Morrissey, J. P., & Calloway, M. O. (1996). Structure and change in child mental health service delivery networks. *Journal of Community Psychology, 24,* 275–289. qqdoi:10.1002/(SICI)1520–6629(199607)24:3<275::AID-JCOP7>3.0.CO;2-W

Johnson, J. G., Cohen, P., Kasen, S., Smailes, E., & Brook, J. S. (2001). Association of maladaptive parental behavior with psychiatric disorder among parents and their offspring. *Archives of General Psychiatry, 58,* 453–460. doi:10.1001/archpsyc.58.5.453

Joint Commission on the Mental Health of Children. (1969). *Crisis in child mental health: Challenges for the 1970s.* New York: Harper & Row.

Jones, K. (1999). *Taming the troublesome child: American families, child guidance, and the limits of psychiatric authority.* Cambridge, MA: Harvard University Press.

Kagan, J., Snidman, N., & Arcus, D. (1998). Childhood derivatives of high and low reactivity in infancy. *Child Development, 69,* 1483–1493.

Kenny, H., Oliver, L., & Poppe, J. (2002). *Mental health services for children: An overview.* Washington, DC: National Conference of State Legislatures.

Kessler, R. C. (1997). The effects of stressful life events on depression. *Annual Review of Psychology, 48,* 191–214. doi:10.1146/annurev.psych.48.1.191

Knitzer, J. (1982). *Unclaimed children.* Washington, DC: Children's Defense Fund.

Lahey, B. B., Loeber, R., Hart, E. L., Frick, P. J., Applegate, B., Zhang, Q., Green, S. M., & Russo, M. F. (1995). Four-year longitudinal study of conduct disorder in boys: Patterns and predictors of persistence. *Journal of Abnormal Psychology, 104,* 83–93. doi:10.1037/0021–843X.104.1.83

Li, F., Green, J. G., Kessler, R. C., & Zaslavsky, A. M. (2010). Estimating prevalence of serious emotional disturbance in schools using a brief screening scale. *International Journal of Methods in Psychiatric Research, 19*(S1), 88–98.

Linver, M., Fuligni, A., Hernandez, M., & Brooks-Gunn, J. (2004). Poverty and child development: Promising interventions. In P. Allen-Meares & M. W. Fraser (Eds.), *Intervention with children and adolescents: An interdisciplinary perspective* (pp. 106–129). Boston: Allyn & Bacon.

Livingston, R., Lawson, L., & Jones, J. G. (1993). Predictors of self-reported psychopathology in children abused repeatedly by a parent. *Journal of the American Academy of Child and Adolescent Psychiatry, 32,* 948–953. doi:10.1097/00004583-199309000-00009

Loeber, R., Farrington, D. P., Stouthamer-Loeber, M., & Van Kammen, W. B. (1998). Multiple risk factors for multi-problem boys: Co-occurrence of delinquency, substance use, attention deficit, conduct problems, physical aggression, covert behavior, depressed mood, and shy/withdrawn behavior. In R. Jessor (Ed.), *New perspectives on adolescent risk behavior* (pp. 90–149). Cambridge, UK: Cambridge University Press.

Loeber, R., & Stouthamer-Loeber, M. (1996). The development of offending. *Criminal Justice and Behaviour, 23,* 12–24. doi:10.1177/0093854896023001003

Lonigan, C. J., Elbert, J. C., & Johnson, S. B. (1998). Empirically supported psychosocial interventions for children: An overview. *Journal of Clinical Child Psychology, 27,* 138–145. doi:10.1207/s15374424jccp2702_1

Lourie, I. S., & Hernandez, M. (2003). A historical perspective on national child mental health policy. *Journal of Emotional and Behavioral Disorders, 2,* 5–9. doi:10.1177/106342660301100102

Lu, W., Mueser, K. T., Rosenberg, S. D., & Jankowski, M. K. (2008). Correlates of adverse childhood experiences among adults with severe mood disorders. *Psychiatric Services, 59,* 1018–1026. doi:10.1176/appi.ps.59.9.1018

Lucas, A. R., Beard, C. M., O'Fallon, W. M., & Kurland, L. T. (1991). 50-year trends in the incidence of anorexia nervosa in Rochester, MN: A population-based study. *American Journal of Psychiatry, 148,* 917–922.

Mark, T. L., & Buck, J. A. (2006). Characteristic of U.S. youth with Serious Mental disturbances: Data from the National Health Interview Study. *Psychiatric Services, 57,* 1573–1578. doi:10.1176/appi.ps.57.11.1573

Maziade, M., & Raymond, V. (1995). The new genetics of schizophrenia. In C. L. Shriqui & H. A. Nasrallah (Eds.), *Contemporary issues in the treatment of schizophrenia* (pp. 61–79). Washington, DC: American Psychiatric Press.

McConaughy, S. H., & Wadsworth, M. E. (2000). Life history reports of young adults previously referred for mental health services. *Journal of Emotional and Behavioral Disorders, 8,* 202–215. doi:10.1177/106342660000800401

McLaughlin, K. A., Green, J. G., Alegría, M., Jane Costello, E., Gruber, M. J., Sampson, N. A., & Kessler, R. C. (2012). Food insecurity and mental disorders in a national sample of US adolescents. *Journal of the American Academy of Child & Adolescent Psychiatry, 51*(12), 1293–1303.

McLeod, J. D., & Shanahan, M. J. (1996). Poverty, parenting and children's mental health. *American Sociological Review, 58,* 351–366. doi:10.2307/2095905

McMahon, R. J., & Kotler, J. S. (2008). Evidence-based therapies for oppositional behavior in young children. In *Handbook of Evidence-based Therapies for Children and Adolescents* (pp. 221–240). New York, NY: Springer US.

Mears, D. P., & Aron, L. Y. (2003). *Addressing the needs of youth with disabilities in the juvenile justice system: The current state of knowledge* (The Urban Institute). Retrieved from http://www. urban. org/UploadedPDF/410885_youth_with_ disabilities.pdf

Merikangas, K.R., He, J., Burstein, M., Swanson, S.A., Avenevoli, S., Cui, L., . . . Swendsen, J. (2010). Lifetime prevalence of mental disorders in US adolescents: Results from the National Comorbidity

Study-Adolescent Supplement (NCS-A). *Journal of the American Academy of Child and Adolescent Psychiatry, 49*(10), 980–989.

Moore, S. M., Rohde, P. L., Seeley, J. R., & Lewinsohn, P. M. (1999). Life events and depression in adolescence: Relationship loss as a prospective risk factor for first onset of major depressive disorder. *Journal of Abnormal Psychology, 108,* 606–614. doi:10.1037/0021-843X.108.4.606

Neal, A. M., Lilly, R. S., & Zakis, S. (1993). What are African American children afraid of? *Journal of Anxiety Disorders, 7,* 129–139. doi:10.1016/0887-6185(93)90011-9

Nolen-Hoeksema, S., & Girgus, J. S. (1994). The emergence of gender differences in depression during adolescence. *Psychological Bulletin, 115,* 424–443. doi:10.1037/0033-2909.115.3.424

Olds, D. (2013). Moving toward evidence-based preventive interventions for children and families. In *C. Henry Kempe: A 50 Year Legacy to the Field of Child Abuse and Neglect* (pp. 165–173). Springer Netherlands.

Olds, D., Henderson, C. R., Jr., Cole, R., Eckenrode, J., Kitzman, H., Luckey, D., Pettitt, L., Sidora, K., Morris, P., & Powers, J. (1998). Long-term effects of nurse home visitation on children's criminal and antisocial behavior. *Journal of the American Medical Association, 280,* 1238–1244. doi:10.1001/jama.280.14.1238

Oyserman, D. (2004). Depression during the school-aged years. In P. Allen-Meares & M. W. Fraser (Eds.), *Intervention with children and adolescents: An interdisciplinary perspective* (pp. 264–281). Boston: Allyn & Bacon.

Oyserman, D., Mowbray, C. T., Allen-Meares, P. A., & Firminger, K. B. (2000). Parenting among mothers with a serious mental illness. *American Journal of Orthopsychiatry, 70,* 296–315. doi:10.1037/h0087733

Pagani, L., Boulerice, B., Tremblay, R. E., & Vitaro, F. (1997). Behavioral development in children of divorce and remarriage. *Journal of Child Psychology and Psychiatry, 38,* 769–781. doi:10.1111/j.1469-7610.1997.tb01595.x

Parry-Jones, W. L. (1989). Annotation: The history of child and adolescent psychiatry: Its present day relevance. *Journal of Child Psychology and Psychiatry, 30,* 3–11. doi:10.1111/j.1469-7610.1989.tb00766.x

Peeples, F., & Loeber, R. (1994). Do individual factors and neighborhood context explain ethnic differences in juvenile delinquency? *Journal of Quantitative Criminology, 10,* 141–158. doi:10.1007/BF02221156

Pelham, W. E., Jr., Wheeler, T., & Chronis, A. (1998). Empirically supported psychosocial treatments for attention deficit hyperactivity disorder. *Journal of Clinical Child Psychology, 27,* 190–205. doi:10.1207/s15374424jccp2702_6

Perou, R., Bitsko, R.H., Blumberg, S.J., Pastor, P., Ghandour, R.M., Gfroerer, J.C., . . . Huang, L.N. (2013). Mental health surveillance among children–United States, 2005–2011. *Morbidity and Mortality Weekly Report, 62*(02), 1–35.

Piquero, A. R., & Chung, H. L. (2001). On the relationships between gender, early onset, and the seriousness of offending. *Journal of Criminal Justice, 29,* 189–206. doi:10.1016/S0047-2352(01)00084-8

Power, A. K. (2009). Focus on transformation: A public health model of mental health for the 21st century. *Psychiatric Services, 60,* 580–584. doi:10.1176/appi.ps.60.5.580

President's Commission on Mental Health. (1978). *Report of the sub-task panel on infants, children and adolescents.* Washington, DC: Government Printing Office.

President's New Freedom Commission on Mental Health. (2003). *Achieving the promise: Transforming mental health care in America* (Final report, DHHS Pub. No. SMA-03-3832). Rockville, MD: U.S. Department of Health and Human Services.

Putnam, F. W. (2006). The impact of trauma on child development. *Juvenile and Family Court Journal, 57*(1), 1–11. doi:10.1111/j.1755-6988.2006.tb00110.x

Quinn, K. P., & Epstein, M. H. (1998). Characteristics of children, youth, and families serviced by local interagency systems of care. In M. H. Epstein, K. Kutash, & A. Duchowski (Eds.), *Outcomes for children and youth with emotional and behavioral disorders and their families: Programs and evaluation best practices* (pp. 81–114). Austin, TX: PRO-ED.

Reid, J. B., Eddy, M. J., Fetrow, R. A., & Stoolmiller, M. (1999). Description and immediate impacts of preventive intervention for conduct problems. *American Journal of Community Psychology, 27,* 483–517. doi:10.1023/A:1022181111368

Resnick, G., & Burt, M. R. (1996). Youth at risk: Definitions and implications for service delivery. *American Journal of Orthopsychiatry, 66,* 172–188. doi:10.1037/h0080169

Robins, L. N. (1991). Conduct disorder. *Journal of Child Psychology and Psychiatry and Allied Disciplines, 32,* 193–212. doi:10.1111/j.1469–7610.1991.tb00008.x

Rogers, L., Resnick, M. D., Mitchel, J. E., & Blum, R. W. (1997). The relationship between socioeconomic status and eating disorders in a community sample of adolescent girls. *International Journal of Eating Disorders, 22,* 15–23. doi:10.1002/(SICI)1098–108X(199707)22:1 < 15::AID-EAT2 > 3.0.CO;2-5

Rosenblatt, A., & Woodbridge, M. W. (2003). Deconstructing research on systems of care for youth with EBD: Frameworks for policy research. *Journal of Emotional and Behavior Disorders, 11,* 27–37. doi:10.1177/106342660301100105

Ross, D. M., & Ross, S. A. (1982). *Hyperactivity: Current issues, research, and theory.* New York: John Wiley.

Rutter, M. (1979). Protective factors in children's responses to stress and disadvantage. In M. W. Kent & J. E. Rolf (Eds.), *Primary prevention of psychopathology: Vol. 3. Social competence in children* (pp. 49–74) Hanover, NH: University Press of New England.

Rutter, M. (1985). Resilience in the face of adversity: Protective factors and resistance to psychiatric disorders. *British Journal of Psychiatry, 147,* 598–611. doi:10.1192/bjp.147.6.598

Rutter, M., Silberg, J., O'Conner, T., & Simonoff, E. (1999). Genetics and child psychiatry: I. Advances in quantitative and molecular genetics. *Journal of Child Psychology and Psychiatry and Allied Disciplines, 40,* 3–18. doi:10.1111/1469–7610.00422

Salzer, M., & Bickman, L. (1997). Delivering effective children's services in the community: Reconsidering the benefits of system interventions. *Applied & Preventive Psychology, 6,* 1–13. doi:10.1016/S0962–1849(05)80062–9

Sameroff, A. J., Bartko, W. T., Baldwin, A., Baldwin, C., & Seifer, R. (1999). Family and social influences on the development of child competence. In M. Lewis & C. Feiring (Eds.), *Families, risk, and competence* (pp. 167–185). Mahwah, NJ: Lawrence Erlbaum.

Sameroff, A. J., & Gutman, L. M. (2004). Contributions of risk research to the design of successful interventions. In P. Allen-Meares & M. W. Fraser (Eds.), *Intervention with children and adolescents: An interdisciplinary perspective* (pp. 9–26). Boston: Allyn & Bacon.

Santilli, J. S., & Beilenson, P. (1992). Risk factors for adolescent sexual behavior, fertility and sexually transmitted diseases. *Journal of School Health, 62,* 271–279. doi:10.1111/j.1746–1561.1992.tb01243.x

Schowalter, J. E. (2003, September 1). A history of child and adolescent psychiatry in the United States. *Psychiatric Times, 20*(9). Retrieved from http://www.psychia trictimes.com/display/article/10168/48051?pageNumber = 1

Sebelius K. (2010, April 7). Opening plenary remarks. Presented at Coalition for Community Schools National Forum, Philadelphia.

Shaw, D. S., Gillion, M., Ingoldsby, E. M., & Nagin, D. (2003). Trajectories learning to school-age conduct problems. *Developmental Psychology, 39,* 189–200. doi:10.1037/0012–1649.39.2.189

Siegel, J. M., Aneshensel, C. S., Taub, B., Cantwell, D. P., & Driscoll, A. K. (1998). Adolescent depressed mood in a multiethnic sample. *Journal of Youth and Adolescence, 27,* 413–427. doi:10.1023/A:1022873601030

Silverman, A. B., Reinherz, H. Z., & Giaconia, R. M. (1996). The long-term sequelae of child and adolescent abuse: A longitudinal community study. *Child Abuse and Neglect, 20,* 709–723. doi:10.1016/0145-2134(96)00059-2

Spearly, J., & Lauderdale, M. (1983). Community characteristics and ethnicity in the prediction of child maltreatment rates. *Child Abuse and Neglect, 7,* 91–105. doi:10.1016/0145-2134(83)90036-4

Spirito, A., Bond. A., Kurkjian, J., Devost, L., Bosworth, T., & Brown, L. K. (1993). Gender differences among adolescent suicide attempters. *Crisis, 14,* 178–184.

Steiner, H., & Lock, L. (1998). Anorexia nervosa and bulimia nervosa in children and adolescents: A review of the past 10 years. *Journal of the American Academy of Child and Adolescent Psychiatry, 37,* 352–359.

Stice, E., & Agras, W. S. (1998). Predicting onset and cessation of bulimic behaviors during adolescence: A longitudinal grouping analysis. *Behavior Therapy, 29,* 257–276. doi:10.1016/S0005-7894(98)80006-3

Stortz, M. (2003). *The tale of two settings: Institutional and community-based mental health services in California since realignment in 1991.* Oakland: California Protection and Advocacy. Retrieved from http://www.disabilityrightsca.org/pubs/540301.pdf

Stroul B. A. (2006). *The sustainability of systems of care: Lessons learned. A report on the special study on the sustainability of systems of care.* Atlanta, GA: ORC Macro.

Stroul, B.A., & Friedman, R.M. (1986). *A system of care for severely emotionally disturbed children and youth.* Washington, DC: Georgetown University Center for Child and Human Development.

Stroul, B.A., & Friedman, R.M. (2011). *Issue brief: Strategies for expanding the system of care approach.* Washington, DC: Technical Assistance Partnership for Child and Family Mental Health.

Stroul, B. A., & Manteuffel, B.A. (2007). The sustainability of systems of care for children's mental health: Lessons learned. *Journal of Behavioral Health Services and Research, 34,* 237–259. doi: 10.1007/s11414-007-9065-3

Substance Abuse and Mental Health Services Administration. (2005). *Transforming mental health care in America: The federal action agenda: First steps.* Rockville, MD: Author.

Substance Abuse and Mental Health Services Administration. (2009). *Working together to help youth thrive in schools and communities.* Retrieved January 11, 2010 from http://www.samhsa.gov/children/docs/shortreport.pdf

Surgeon General. (1999). *Mental health: A report from the Surgeon General.* Washington, DC: Department of Health and Human Services.

Surgeon General. (2000). *Report of the surgeon general's conference on children's mental health: A national action agenda.* Washington, DC: Department of Health and Human Services.

Temple, J. A., & Reynolds, A. J. (2007). Benefits and costs of investments in preschool education: Evidence from the Child–Parent Centers and related programs. *Economics of Education Review, 26*(1), 126–144.

Thompson, R., Litrownik, A. J., Isbell, P., Everson, M. D., English, D. J., Dubowitz, H., . . . Flaherty, E. G. (2012). Adverse experiences and suicidal ideation in adolescence: Exploring the link using the LONGSCAN samples. *Psychology of Violence, 2*(2), 211.

Tiet, Q. Q., Bird, H. R., Hoven, C. W., Moore, R., Wu, P., Wicks, J., Jensen P., Goodman S., & Cohen, P. (2001). Relationship between specific adverse life events and psychiatric disorders. *Journal of Abnormal Child Psychology, 29,* 153–164. doi:10.1023/A:1005288130494

Urdapilleta, O., Kim, G., Wang, Y., Howard, J., Varghese, R., Waterman, G., Busam, S., & Palmisano, C. (2013). *National evaluation of the Medicaid demonstration waiver home- and community-based alternatives to psychiatric residential treatment facilities: Final report.* Columbia, MD: IMPAQ International.

Vance, J. E., Bowen, N. K., Fernandez, G., & Thompson, S. (2002). Risk and protective factors as predictors of outcome in adolescents with psychiatric disorder and aggression. *Journal of the American Academy of Child & Adolescent Psychiatry, 41,* 36–43. doi:10.1097/00004583-200201000-00009

Vinson, N. B., Brannan, A. M., Baughman, L. N., Wilce, M., & Gawron, T. (2001). The system-of-care model: Implementation in twenty-seven communities. *Journal of Emotional and Behavioral Disorders, 9,* 30–42. doi:10.1177/106342660100900104

Wagner, M., Kutash, K., Duchnowski, A. J., Epstein, M. H., & Sumi, W. C. (2005). The children and youth we serve: A national picture of the characteristics of students with emotional disturbances receiving special education. *Journal of Emotional and Behavioral Disorders, 13,* 79–96. doi:10.1177/106 34266050130020201

Werner, E. E., & Smith, R. S. (1992). *Overcoming the odds: High risk children from birth to adulthood.* Ithaca, NY: Cornell University Press.

Wickramaratne, P. J., & Weissman, M. M. (1998). Onset of psychopathology in offspring by developmental phase and parental depression. *Journal of the American Academy of Child and Adolescent Psychiatry, 37,* 933–942. doi:10.1097/00004583–199809000–00013

Willie, M. v. James B. Hunt, Jr., et al., Civil No. C-C-79-294-M (W.D. N.C. 1980).

Wilson, S., & Durbin, C. E. (2010). Effects of paternal depression on fathers' parenting behaviors: A meta-analytic review. *Clinical Psychology Review, 30*(2), 167–180.

Wolfe, D. A., Sas, L., & Wekerle, C. (1994). Factors associated with the development of posttraumatic stress disorder among child victims of sexual abuse. *Child Abuse and Neglect, 18,* 37–50. doi:10.1016/0145–2134(94)90094–9

Wu, P, Katic, B. J., Liu, X, Fan, B., & Fuller, C. J. (2010). Mental health service use among suicidal adolescents: Findings from a U.S. national community survey. *Psychiatric Services, 61,* 17–24. doi:10.1176/appi.ps.61.1.17

Zill, N., & West, J. (2001). *Entering kindergarten: A portrait of American children when they begin school: Findings from The Condition of Education 2000* (NCES 2001–035). Washington, DC: Department of Education, Government Printing Office. Retrieved from http://files.eric.ed.gov/fulltext/ED448899.pdf

ADDITIONAL READING

Allen-Meares, P., & Fraser, M. W. (2004). *Intervention with children and adolescents: An interdisciplinary perspective.* Boston: Allyn & Bacon.

Burns, B. J., Phillips, S. D., Wagner, H. R., Barth, R. P., Kolko, D. J., Campbell, Y., & Landsverk, J. (2004). Mental health need and access to mental health services by youths involved with child welfare: A national survey. *Journal of the American Academy of Child & Adolescent Psychiatry, 43*(8), 960–970.

Center for Mental Health Services. (1999). *Annual report to Congress on the evaluation of the Comprehensive Community Mental Health Services for Children and Their Families Program.* Atlanta, GA: ORC Macro. Retrieved from http://mentalhealth.samhsa.gov/publications/allpubs/ CB-E199/default.asp

Costello, E. J., Angold, A., Burns, B. J., Stangl, D. K., Tweed, D. L., Erkanli, A., & Worthman, C. M. (1996). The Great Smoky Mountains Study of youth: Goals, design, methods, and the prevalence of *DSM-III-R* disorders. *Archives of General Psychiatry, 53,* 1129–1136. PMID: 8956679

Gerrity, E., & Folcarelli, C. (2008). *Child traumatic stress: What every policymaker should know.* Durham, NC: National Center for Child Trauma Stress. Retrieved from http://www.nctsnet.org/nctsn_assets/ pdfs/PolicyGuide_CTS2008.pdf

Mark, T. L., & Buck, J. A. (2006). Characteristics of U.S. youth with serious mental disturbances: Data from the National Health Interview Study. *Psychiatric Services, 57,* 1573–1578.

Merikangas, K.R., He, J., Burstein, M., Swanson, S.A., Avenevoli, S., Cui, L., . . . Swendsen, J. (2010). Lifetime prevalence of mental disorders in US adolescents: Results from the National Comorbidity

Study-Adolescent Supplement (NCS-A). *Journal of the American Academy of Child and Adolescent Psychiatry, 49*(10), 980–989.

National Alliance for the Mentally Ill. (2001). *Families on the brink: The impact of ignoring children with serious mental illness.* Arlington, VA: Author.

President's New Freedom Commission on Mental Health. (2003). *Achieving the promise: Transforming mental health care in America.* Rockville, MD: U.S. Department of Health and Human Services. Retrieved from http://www.mentalhealth commission.gov/reports/FinalReport/toc.html

Substance Abuse and Mental Health Services Administration. (2005). *Transforming mental health care in America: The federal action agenda: First steps.* Rockville, MD: Author.

Surgeon General. (1999). *Mental health: A report from the Surgeon General.* Washington, DC: Department of Health and Human Services. Retrieved from http://mental health.samhsa.gov/cmhs/surgeongeneral/surgeongeneralrpt.asp

Surgeon General. (2000). *Report of the surgeon general's conference on children's mental health: A national action agenda.* Washington, DC: Office of the Surgeon General. Retrieved from http://www.surgeongeneral.gov/topics/cmh/childreport.html

WEB-BASED RESOURCES (GENERAL)

Bazelon Center for Mental Health and Law, http://www.bazelon.org/

Federation of Families for Children's Mental Health, http:/www.ffcmh.org

Mental Health America, http://www.nmha.org/

National Alliance for the Mentally Ill, http://www.nami.org/Hometemplate.cfm

National Institute of Mental Health, http://www.nimh.nih.gov/

Substance Abuse and Mental Health Services Administration, http://www.mental health.samhsa.gov/

WEB-BASED RESOURCES (EVIDENCE-BASED PRACTICES)

Association for Cognitive and Behavioral Therapies & Society of Clinical Child and Adolescent Psychology. (n.d.). Evidence-based mental health treatment for children and adolescents. *Retrieved from http://www.effectivechildtherapy.com/*

National Child Traumatic Stress Network. (2010). *Empirically supported treatments and promising practices.* Retrieved from http://www.nctsnet.org/nccts/nav.do? pid = ctr_top_trmnt_prom

Substance Abuse and Mental Health Services Administration. (2007). *A guide to evidence-based practices on the web.* Retrieved from www.samhsa.gov/ebpWebGuide/index.asp

Substance Abuse and Mental Health Services Administration. (2010). *National registry of evidence-based practices: NREPP.* Retrieved from www.nrepp.samhsa.gov/

CHAPTER 6

Health Policy for Children and Youth

Kathleen A. Rounds

William J. Hall

Guadalupe V. Huitron

PURPOSE AND OVERVIEW OF HEALTH POLICIES FOR CHILDREN AND YOUTH

The primary purpose of health policies aimed at children and youth is to provide access to preventive and medical care. Access is defined as the ability to obtain needed care, and lack of access is an indication of unmet health care needs (Shi & Singh, 2001). Access to health care encompasses a number of dimensions, including

- *Availability:* Does the service exist?

- *Cultural acceptability:* Is there a fit between the cultural belief systems and languages of the client and the provider?

- *Convenience:* Does the client have transportation to the service, and can the client access the service at a convenient time?

- *Affordability:* Can the client pay for the service, or does the client have private or public insurance to cover the cost? (Anderson, 1995; Donabedian, 1973)

The U.S. health-care environment is distinguished from health-care systems in other industrialized nations by three critical features. First, the United States is the only country in the Western world that does not have universal health-care coverage for its children and adolescents (Stein, 1997). The full implementation of the Patient Protection and Affordable Care Act (ACA) will increase coverage considerably, but universal coverage will still not be a reality in the United States (Nardin, Zallman, McCormick, Woolhandler, & Himelssem, 2013). Second, the U.S. health care system is a heavily privatized delivery system financed by public dollars. In 2011, federal, state, and local dollars constituted about 52% of all health-care expenditures (National Center for Health Statistics, 2014). The current system is an amalgam of private and government sources that operates in a market-oriented, commodity-driven economy in which many of the key players are motivated by profit margins (Halfon & Hochstein, 1997; Shi & Singh, 2001). Third, in large part, U.S. health care is a poorly coordinated, fragmented system (Institute of Medicine of the National Academies, 2012).

Halfon and Hochstein (1997) posed two major policy questions regarding the delivery of health care for children and youth. The first question is referred to as the "insurance question." It focuses on expanding access to health insurance for children and youth in addition to the elimination of nonfinancial barriers to access (e.g., outreach and transportation). Halfon and Hochstein labeled the second question the "systems question." It asks how health-care services might be organized and integrated with other systems to meet the needs of children and youth more effectively.

Federal health-care policies affect all children, youth, and their families. However, these policies have a more dramatic effect on low-income households, which are disproportionately African American, Latino, or other racial/ethnic minorities. The public insurance programs Medicaid and Children's Health Insurance (CHIP) have made a significant positive difference in coverage for minority children who are more likely to have health problems and be uninsured than White children (Kaiser Commission on Medicaid and the Uninsured, 2013). Even with these federal programs, gaps in eligibility for Medicaid and CHIP have left large numbers of minority children without insurance. Researchers have found that children who lack insurance coverage or experience insurance instability (i.e., disruptions in coverage) are significantly more likely to lack a usual source of care, to delay care, or to have unmet medical needs than children with insurance (Cassedy, Fairbrother, & Newacheck, 2008). Starfield (2008) noted that having both insurance and a usual source of care are critical; the insurance is the pathway to a usual source of care, which then leads to children receiving needed services. The ACA addresses insurance gaps through provisions aimed at expanding and stabilizing insurance coverage and through promoting "patient-centered medical homes" (PCMH). These increase the likelihood that all children and youth will have a usual source of care.

Because of special vulnerabilities, some federal health-care policies specifically target infants, very young children, or adolescents. For example, eligibility for public health-insurance programs (e.g., Medicaid) has been expanded to provide access to greater numbers of infants and young children, who otherwise would likely have unmet health needs. This policy change was based on the recognition that a child's early years are important not only for preventive care (i.e., well-baby checkups and immunizations) but also for screenings to detect developmental and health problems. Adolescents are another developmentally vulnerable group because they have a high likelihood of engaging in high-risk behaviors (e.g., unprotected sex, substance use, smoking) that have long-term health consequences. During early adolescence, most youths develop health behaviors that persist into adulthood (Greydanus, Patel, & Greydanus, 2003).

Federal health policy also targets children who meet the definition of "children with special health care needs." However, uncertainty over which children made up this population prompted the Maternal and Child Health Bureau [MCHB] of the U.S. Department of Health and Human Services [DHHS] to form a work group expressly to establish a clear definition. This definition has been adopted by the DHHS as well as the American Academy of Pediatrics: "Children who have, or are at increased risk for, chronic physical, developmental, behavioral, or emotional conditions and who also require health and related services of a type or amount beyond that required by children generally" (McPherson et al., 1998, p. 138). Based on this definition, and according to the *2011/12 National Survey of Children with Special Health Care Needs,* 19.8% of U.S. children between the ages of 0 and 17 years have special health-care needs. The prevalence of special health-care needs has been estimated at 23% of U.S. households with children (Child and Adolescent Health Measurement Initiative, 2013). However, these rates do not include children in the at-risk category that is encompassed in the definition used by the MCHB (Bethell, Read, Blumberg, & Newacheck, 2008).

In this chapter, we review the prevalence of four health problems experienced by children and youth: low birth weight, asthma, overweight and obesity, and sexually transmitted infections. We identify the risk and protective factors associated with these health problems. We summarize the historical development of child health policy and examine ways in which child health policy has been based on risk and protective factors. Using a case example, we discuss strategies for integrating health care with other service systems that serve children and youth.

RISK AND PROTECTIVE FACTORS FOR HEALTH PROBLEMS IN CHILDHOOD AND ADOLESCENCE

Infants, children, and adolescents in the United States experience a range of health problems, with the most frequent being low birth weight, asthma, overweight or obesity, and sexually transmitted infections. In this chapter, we focus on the prevalence of these health problems; health disparities associated with race, ethnicity, and socioeconomic status; and risk factors across multiple system levels. (See Table 6.1 for prevalence data on low birth weight, asthma, overweight, and obesity.) This section concludes with a discussion of protective factors related to access to health-care services.

Low Birth Weight

Infants with low birth weight (LBW) are defined as those weighing less than 2,500 grams (about 5.5 pounds). The incidence of LBW in the United States increased nearly 20% between 1990 and 2006 and is a serious public-health concern because it can lead to adverse health outcomes throughout life. In 2012, the rate was 7.99%, a 3% dip from the 2006 high of 8.26%. The rate of infants born in 2012 with *very low birth weight* (VLBW), that is, weighing less than 1,500 grams, also edged downward to 1.42% from a 2006 high of 1.49% (Martin, Hamilton, Osterman, Curtin, & Mathews, 2013). LBW and VLBW infants are at increased risk for a host of health and developmental problems, including neonatal mortality, neurodevelopmental disorders, respiratory distress syndrome, cardiac problems (March of Dimes Foundation, 2014), and delayed cognitive functioning (Reuner, Hassenpflug, Pietz, & Philippi, 2009). Compared with infants of normal birth weight, LBW infants face a greater than fivefold increase in risk of death during their first year and VLBW infants incur a 100-fold increase risk of death in their first year (Martin et al., 2013).

Racial and ethnic disparities in the incidence of LBW and VLBW infants present a serious public-health issue in the United States. The rate of LBW live births among non-Hispanic African American mothers in 2012 (13.18%) was about 2 times the rate reported for either non-Hispanic White mothers (6.97%) or Hispanic mothers (6.96%; Martin et al., 2013). In addition, non-Hispanic African American mothers were nearly 2 times more likely to have a VLBW live birth than non-Hispanic White mothers or Hispanic mothers (2.94%, 1.13%, and 1.2%, respectively; Martin et al., 2013). Researchers are increasingly examining the impact of maternal stress, particularly stress caused by maternal perceived racism (Dominguez, 2008; Holland, Kitzman, & Veazie, 2009; Rosenthal & Lobel, 2011) and the role of living in hypersegregated residential areas (Love, David, Rankin, & Collins, 2010; Osypuk & Acevedo-Garcia, 2008) and their contribution to low birth weight. Using a life-course approach to explain birth outcome disparities, Lu et al. (2010) developed a model that accounts for the life-long cumulative effect of experiencing racism and social inequality and the resulting allostatic load and its impact on birth outcomes.

A variety of factors, including genetics, lifestyle, and environmental conditions, can substantially affect birth weight. Maternal characteristics that are risk factors for LBW include smoking or drug use during pregnancy, limited or late prenatal care, and the number of previous pregnancies (Institute of Medicine of the National Academies, 2006). In the decades since Simpson's 1957 report on the prenatal effects of maternal smoking, smoking during pregnancy has become well established as one of the most preventable risk factors for LBW (Bailey, McCook, Hodge, McGrady, 2012; Rogers, 2008). According to the CDC Pregnancy Risk Assessment Monitoring System (PRAMS) in 2010, 12.3% of pregnant women smoked during their pregnancy and 10.7% smoked during the last trimester of their pregnancy (Tong et al., 2013). Researchers analyzing 2002 birth data estimated that 5% to 8% of very and moderately preterm births and 13% to 19% of term LBW deliveries could be attributed to maternal smoking during pregnancy (Dietz et al., 2010).

Early childbearing (i.e., maternal age 15 years or younger) has been noted as a significant risk factor for preterm delivery and low birth weight. In a systematic review of 20 studies, Gibbs, Wendt, Peters, and Hogue (2012) found a relationship between maternal age and LBW; as maternal age increased, this association decreased. Their review provides evidence that very young maternal age (15 years or younger) has a negative, biological impact on preterm delivery and birth weight. Most likely, biological as well as social factors contribute to this relationship. Although early childbearing occurs across the socioeconomic spectrum, researchers investigating maternal age trends have argued that the incidence of early childbearing is disproportionately high among ethnic minority and impoverished young women (Chen, Wen, Fleming, Yang, & Walker, 2008). Chen and colleagues noted that the poverty faced by many young women also contributes to their delayed entry into prenatal care, to their inadequate weight gain during pregnancy, and to their increased incidence of perinatal medical complications. The nutritional demands of normal physiological development during adolescence may be one factor contributing to the increased prevalence of LBW among newborns of adolescent mothers because these demands create a maternal–fetal competition for nutrients (Kramer & Lancaster, 2010). This competition may be exacerbated in low-income families, which often experience food insecurity because they cannot afford food and live in communities where nutritional foods may be less available or cost-prohibitive.

Table 6.1   Estimated Prevalence of Health Conditions Among Children and Adolescents in the United States

	U.S. Population (all races)	African American (not Hispanic or Latino)	Hispanic or Latino	White (not Hispanic or Latino)
Low Birth Weight				
Percent of live births <2,500 grams	7.99	13.18	6.0	6.97
Percent of live births <1,500 grams	1.42	2.94	1.13	1.2
Overweight and Obesity				
Percent overweight or obese (ages 2–5)	23	22	30	21
Percent overweight or obese (ages 6–11)	34	38	46	29
Percent overweight or obese (ages 12–19)	35	40	38	31
Percent obese (ages 2–5)	8	11	16	4
Percent obese (ages 6–11)	18	24	26	13
Percent obese (ages 12–19)	21	22	23	20
Asthma (<age 18)				
Percent ever told had asthma	14	22	14	12
Percent who still have asthma	9	16	9	8
Percent with current asthma who had an asthma attack in past 12 months	55	56	51	58

Note. Overweight is defined as Body Mass Index (BMI) at or above the 85th percentile and lower than the 95th percentile; obesity is defined as a BMI at or above the 95th percentile (Centers for Disease Control and Prevention [CDC], 2014a,b,c; Ogden, Carroll, Kit, & Flegal, 2014).

In the last three decades, the United States experienced a significant increase in the rate of multiple births, which—in part—was the result of delayed childbearing and increased use of fertility drugs and procedures. These increases in multiple births, particularly twin births, had a significant impact on the increased incidence of LBW, preterm delivery, and prenatal mortality in the United States (Boulet et al., 2008). However, the rising incidence seems to have peeked. Between 1980 and 2009, the number of twin births doubled in the United States. In 2012, the twin birth rate was 33.1 per 1,000 total births, unchanged from 2009 to 2011 (Martin et al., 2013). Similarly, between 1980 and 1998, the rate of higher-order multiple births increased from 37 to 193.5 births per 100,000 live births. The rate in 2012 was 124.4 per 100,000 births, which is more than a one-third reduction from the 1998 high (Martin et al., 2013).

Asthma

Asthma, a long-term lung disease that is characterized by recurrent periods of inflammation in the airways, shortness of breath, coughing, and wheezing, is the most common chronic illness and the most prevalent cause of disability among children in the United States (Williams, Sternthal, & Wright, 2009; Wu, Smith, Bokhour, Hohman, & Lieu, 2008). Indeed, the prevalence of childhood asthma has more than doubled since 1980 (Akinbami, Moorman, Garbe, & Sondik, 2009). Approximately 10 million U.S. children and adolescents have been diagnosed with asthma at some point in their lives, representing 14% of the U.S. population younger than 18 years (CDC, 2013a). Over half of children with asthma reported at least one attack in the past year (CDC, 2014a). During an asthma attack or episode, a child's airways narrow, making it difficult to breathe, often resulting in wheezing. Asthma is the third leading cause of hospitalization among children under the age of 15 years, and each year asthma accounts for more than 14 million missed school days (American Lung Association, 2012). Asthma is the second most costly health problem among children in the United States (Soni, 2014).

Racial and ethnic minority children have higher rates of asthma. Lifetime and current prevalence rates of asthma were higher for both African American children (22% and 16%, respectively) and Hispanic children (14% and 9%, respectively) as compared with White children (12% and 8%, respectively) (CDC, 2013a). In addition, compared with White children, African American children are 4 times more likely to be hospitalized because of asthma and 5 times more likely to die from asthma (Wu et al., 2008).

Although the exact causes of asthma are not fully understood, an array of risk factors increases children's risk of developing asthma; many of these risk factors are related to poverty. Low socioeconomic status and family income are associated with both previous asthma diagnosis and incidence of asthma attacks (Williams et al., 2009). Children living below the federal poverty level (FPL) are more likely to have been diagnosed with asthma (19%) than those living between 100% and 200% of federal poverty guidelines (14%) and those living at or above 200% of the FPL (12%) (CDC, 2013a). Children receiving Medicaid are much more likely to have been diagnosed with asthma (18%) at some point in their lives than children with private insurance (12%) (CDC, 2013a).

Social and environmental factors are associated with increased risk for the development of asthma during childhood and adolescence. Exposure to tobacco smoke, most commonly from parental smoking in the household, increases the likelihood of developing childhood asthma as well as exacerbating existing asthma (Baena-Cagnani, Gomez, Baena-Cagnani, & Canonica, 2009; Gerald et al., 2009; Lawson, Janssen, Bruner, Hossain, & Pickett, 2014). Research also indicates that prenatal exposure to tobacco smoke increases the risk that a child will subsequently develop childhood asthma (Baena-Cagnani et al., 2009; Midodzi, Rowe, Majaesic, Saunders, & Senthilselvan, 2010). Other environmental risks include dust mite, cat, and cockroach allergens (Subbarao, Mandhane, & Sears, 2009; Wang et al., 2009). One study showed that exposure to cockroaches at some point in childhood significantly increased the risk for developing childhood asthma, and exposure to cockroach allergens during infancy was associated with a twofold increase in the risk of developing asthma (Salam, Li, Langholz, & Gilliland, 2004). Research suggests that poverty at the individual, household, and community levels is directly associated with both increased risk of developing asthma and increased risk of experiencing greater severity of asthma attacks (Midodzi et al., 2010; Subbarao et al., 2009; Thakur et al., 2013; Williams et al., 2009).

Other health-related factors also affect children's risk of asthma. There is evidence of an association between LBW and childhood asthma (Ahmad et al., 2009; Midodzi et al., 2010). In addition, overweight and obese children and adolescents not only are more likely to develop asthma but also are more likely to develop severe asthma, which is associated with more frequent hospital and clinic visits for asthma-related issues (Black, Zhou, Takayanagi, Jacobsen, & Koebnick, 2013; Liu, Kieckhefer, & Gau, 2013).

Overweight and Obesity

Since the 1960s, the prevalence of overweight and obese children and adolescents in the United States has tripled (Ogden & Carroll, 2010). Overweight and obesity are terms that refer to ranges of body weight that exceed what is considered healthy for a given height. Overweight is defined as a body mass index (BMI) at or above the 85th percentile and lower than the 95th percentile, and obesity is defined as a BMI at or above the 95th percentile for youth of the same age and sex (Barlow & Expert Committee, 2007).

Almost one-third (32%) of children and adolescents in the United States are overweight or obese (15% and 17%, respectively) (Ogden et al., 2014). Prevalence rates of obesity increase with age: 8% of children between the ages of 2 and 5 years are obese, 18% of children between the ages of 6 and 11 years are obese, and 21% of adolescents between the ages of 12 and 19 years are obese. Rates of overweight and obesity do not differ markedly by gender. On the other hand, there are significant differences by race/ethnicity. Rates of overweight and obesity are highest among Hispanic (39%) and Black (35%) children, with White (29%) and Asian (20%) children showing lower prevalence rates (Ogden et al., 2014). Childhood and adolescent obesity is associated with a number of health problems, including high blood pressure, high cholesterol, impaired glucose tolerance, insulin resistance, type-2 diabetes, sleep apnea, asthma, bone and joint problems, fatty liver disease, gallstones, heartburn, and low self-esteem (Freedman, Mei, Srinivasan, Berenson, & Dietz, 2007; Han, Lawlor, & Kimm, 2010; Sutherland, 2008; Swartz & Puhl, 2003; Taylor, Theim, & Mirch, 2006).

Various risk factors predispose children and adolescents to become overweight and obese. Emerging research suggests that maternal obesity during pregnancy may be associated with childhood obesity (Catalano et al., 2009; Dabelea, 2007; Kral et al., 2006; Lawlor et al., 2008). Children's dietary behaviors also influence their weight. Strong evidence supports the relationship between the consumption of sugar-sweetened beverages and child obesity (Moreno & Rodriguez, 2007). Children's food and beverage intake is highly dependent on what is available at home, which is highly dependent on the availability and cost of foods and beverages in local food outlets (Powell & Bao, 2009). Researchers found that higher prices for fresh fruits and vegetables in neighborhood food outlets were significantly associated with higher BMIs among children (Powell & Bao, 2009). In addition, lower-income children and adolescents are more likely to be obese than their higher-income peers (Ogden, Lamb, Carroll, & Flegal, 2010). Other dietary risk factors for child obesity include buying lunch at school, eating dinner without parental supervision, missing breakfast, and consuming fewer calories at breakfast and more at dinner (Moreno & Rodriguez, 2007). In terms of health education for children and adolescents, 18% of U.S. school districts do not require that elementary, middle, and high schools teach students about nutrition and dietary behavior. In addition, 31% of U.S. school districts do not require that elementary, middle, and high schools teach students about physical activity and fitness (CDC, 2013b).

Low levels of physical activity are associated with childhood obesity (Jimenez-Pavon, Kelly, & Reilly, 2010). Approximately 40% of U.S. school districts do not require that elementary schools provide students with regularly scheduled recess. In addition, 8% of districts do not have a policy requiring physical education for middle and high school students (CDC, 2013b). Engagement in sedentary activities, such as watching television, playing video games, using a computer, and using the telephone, is associated with child obesity (Marshall, Biddle, Gorely, Cameron, & Murdey, 2004). Higher levels of screen time are associated with lower family income and the presence of a television in a child's bedroom (He, Harris, Piché, & Beynon, 2009). On the other hand, protective factors include participating in sports and after-school programs (He et al., 2009).

Sexually Transmitted Infections

Sexually transmitted infections (STIs) are a significant health problem facing adolescents in the United States. Compared with older adults, adolescents and young adults are at increased risk for acquiring STIs (CDC, 2014b). Although those between the ages of 15 and 24 years represent only 25% of the sexually experienced population in the United States, this age group accounts for almost half of the estimated 20 million new STI cases each year (CDC, 2014b).

Unprotected sexual intercourse can lead not only to STIs but also to unwanted pregnancy; therefore, teen pregnancy rates are considered to be an indicator of rates of high-risk sexual behavior. The most recent data show that 57 out of 1,000 women between the ages of 15 and 19 years became pregnant in 2010 (Kost & Henshaw, 2014). In other words, approximately 6% of teens became pregnant in 2010. This rate represents a 30-year low in the teen pregnancy rate due to significant drops between 2008 and 2010. Nonetheless, 82% of teen pregnancies are unplanned (Finer & Zolna, 2011). The connection between unintended teen pregnancies and STI risk is crucial because risky sexual behaviors that may result in pregnancy also place teens at high risk for STIs.

It is difficult to estimate national STI rates because states have different reporting requirements. Currently, chancroid, chlamydia, gonorrhea, syphilis, HIV, and hepatitis B are the only STIs reported by every state to the CDC (Workowski & Berman, 2010). The accurate collection of incidence and prevalence data is profoundly inhibited by the wide variation in the quality of surveillance data at local and state levels as well as the lack of standardized state reporting mechanisms for many common STIs, including genital herpes (herpes simplex viruses type 1 and type 2) and human papillomavirus. Disparities in reporting between public and private health-care providers further challenge accurate STI data collection, resulting in the potential underestimation of STIs diagnosed in the private health sector (Rounds, 2004). In addition, many STIs can be asymptomatic and remain undetected, which further contributes to the underestimation of STI rates among adolescents (Rounds, 2004). Lack of access to health care—a significant issue among many adolescents—may also add to the underestimation of STI rates.

Chlamydia and gonorrhea are the most prevalent among the STIs that states are required to report to the CDC, and each can cause serious health consequences if undetected or left untreated, particularly in young women (CDC, 2014b). In 2012, nearly 69% of all reported chlamydia infections (for which data on age were available) were among young people between the ages of 15 and 24 years (CDC, 2014b). Among women in 2012, the highest age-specific reported prevalence rates of chlamydia were in young women between the ages of 15 and 19 years and those between the ages of 20 and 24 years, with 3,291 and 3,695 cases per 100,000 females, respectively. These rates were significantly higher than those among males in the same age groups (CDC, 2014b). Compared with many other STIs, syphilis is relatively rare among U.S. adolescents and young adults. The prevalence rates of syphilis for 2012 are based on estimates of reported cases and indicate about four reported cases per 100,000 persons 15 to 19 years old and 15 reported cases per 100,000 persons 20 to 24 years old (CDC, 2014b).

Approximately 58% of gonorrhea infections reported in 2012 were among those 15 to 24 years old (CDC, 2014b). In 2012, the incidence was highest among women between the ages of 15 and 24 years old and among men between 20 and 24 years old (CDC, 2014b). For young women (15 to 19 years old) in 2012, there were 521 cases of gonorrhea per 100,000 (CDC, 2014b). Among young men (15 to 19 years old) in 2012, the gonorrhea incidence rate was significantly lower, at 239 cases per 100,000 (CDC, 2014b).

As previously noted, states are not required to report cases of herpes simplex virus and human papillomavirus to the CDC (Workowski & Berman, 2010). Both of these viral infections can be asymptomatic and, therefore, are frequently transmitted to others by those unaware of their infection. There is little precise information about the prevalence or incidence of either STI among adolescents in the United States, although both are widely prevalent among young people. However, the prevalence of these STIs is an important public health concern because prior exposure to STIs has been linked to predisposition for contracting the HIV virus (CDC, 2014c).

The overall U.S. STI rates do not reflect the disproportionate impact of STIs on certain high-risk adolescent populations such as youth involved with the juvenile justice system. Youth in the juvenile justice system have elevated rates of engaging in sexual risky behavior and have higher rates of STIs than their peers. These rates may be attributable to three factors: Youth involved in the juvenile justice system report onset of sexual activity at younger ages and with more partners than their peers; youth involved in the juvenile justice system are disproportionately African American, and African Americans are disproportionately affected by STIs; and youth involved in the juvenile justice system have higher rates of psychiatric disorders, which are associated with engaging in high-risk sexual behaviors, than the general population (Elkington et al., 2008). The prevalence rates of chlamydia and gonorrhea in juvenile detention settings are consistently higher than in any other subpopulation group (CDC, 2012). In 2011, the overall chlamydia prevalence rate was 16% among adolescent females entering juvenile correction facilities and 6% among young men entering juvenile correctional facilities (CDC, 2012). The median site-specific gonorrhea rate among adolescent females entering juvenile correctional facilities in 2011 was 3%, compared with 1% among males (CDC, 2012).

Human immunodeficiency virus (HIV), the virus that over time leads to acquired immunodeficiency syndrome (AIDS), disproportionately affects adolescents in the United States. In 2010, 26% of all new HIV infections in the United States occurred among young people 13 to 24 years old, the majority of whom acquired the virus through sexual transmission (CDC, 2014c). Within this age group, gay, bisexual, and other men who have sex with men are particularly affected by HIV/AIDS (CDC, 2014c). The large majority of new HIV/AIDS cases among male adolescents 13 to 19 years old were attributed to male-to-male sexual contact (CDC, 2014c). In addition, there is a racial disparity in the HIV/AIDS epidemic in the United States, with African American adolescents disproportionately affected. The link between HIV and other STIs is important because the presence of an STI places an individual at greater risk for contracting HIV when exposed to the virus through sexual contact (CDC, 2014c).

As compared with older adults, many biological, developmental, and social factors place sexually active adolescents at higher risk for contracting STIs. Table 6.2 presents a summary of risk factors associated with adolescents' risky sexual behaviors. Adolescents are more likely than are older adults to have unprotected sex and multiple sex partners (either concurrent or sequential), which increases the risk of exposure to an STI-infected partner (Monasterio, Hwang, & Shafer, 2007). According to the Youth Risk Behavior Survey, 41% of all sexually active adolescents reported not using a condom during their last sexual intercourse and 22% of sexually active youth reported having used alcohol or other drugs before their last sexual intercourse (Kann et al., 2014). As compared with young men, the higher rates of STIs among young women appear to be based in both behavior and physiology. Behaviorally, young women have a greater likelihood of choosing older, experienced sexual partners, which increases their potential exposure to STIs (Manlove, Terry-Humen, & Ikramullah, 2006). The higher rates of STIs among young women are also accounted for, in part, by anatomy, which makes females physiologically more susceptible to many STIs than males (Manlove et al., 2006).

Research has shown that there is a link between childhood sexual abuse and re-victimization and high-risk sexual behaviors (Lalor & McElvaney, 2010). Adolescent females who self-report a history of childhood and adolescent sexual abuse are more likely to have had consensual intercourse at a younger age, to have not used birth control, to have had multiple sex partners, and to have used alcohol or drugs during their most recent sexual experience

Table 6.2   Common Risk Factors for Risky Adolescent Sexual Behaviors

System Level		
Individual Characteristics	**Family Conditions**	**Environmental Conditions**
• Inadequate communication skills • Substance abuse • Depression • Sense of invulnerability • Negative attitudes, beliefs, and intentions about safer sex practices • Inadequate perception of risk • Lack of knowledge about sexuality and safer sex practices • Having been sexually abused • Early puberty • Early initiation of sexual activity • Incomplete cognitive development • Intention to initiate intercourse • Inability to use condoms properly	• Poor parental supervision • Family sexual abuse • Older siblings who are sexually active • Chaotic family life • Family norms that accept early initiation of sexual intercourse and multiple partners • Poor parent–adolescent relationship and communication	• Limited sexuality education (e.g., abstinence-only) • Lack of easy/free condom availability in community • Peer pressure • Community norms that accept early initiation of sexual intercourse and multiple partners • Media that sexualize women and promote risky sexual practices • Lack of emphasis on prevention • Environments or activities where alcohol and drugs are used • High-risk environment

(Senn, Carey, & Vanable, 2008). Morrison-Beedy, Carey, Feng, and Tu (2008) found that adolescent females with a history of psychological distress were at increased risk for multiple adverse sexual and reproductive health outcomes. Lee, O'Riordan, and Lazebnik (2009) posited that depressed individuals may engage in risky sexual behaviors as a way of coping with depressive symptoms. In a study of African American adolescent females, a history of depressive symptoms was associated with a greater number of lifetime sexual partners, history of STIs, and previous or current pregnancy (Lee et al., 2009). Adolescents may face numerous barriers to accessing high-quality STI prevention and treatment services. Lack of insurance or alternative payment source, lack of youth-friendly services, lack of transportation, and confidentiality concerns can all inhibit adolescents from accessing quality services that address sexual health needs (Monasterio et al., 2007).

ACCESS TO CARE AS A PROTECTIVE FACTOR

Although research has clearly identified biological, developmental, lifestyle, and environmental risk factors associated with health problems, research on protective factors has been more limited. In the case of children and youth at risk for poor health outcomes, access to health care is a protective factor. A host of factors that facilitate access to health care may also be seen as providing a protective effect. Health insurance and health-care-delivery models that make health care accessible (e.g., community-based care, school-based care, convenient hours, support services, perceived confidentiality among adolescents, and culturally competent services) have a major impact on whether services are accessible and used. Access to health care (i.e., an acceptable provider is available, the individual can get to the provider, and the individual has health insurance to pay for medical care) serves as a protective factor when a child needs medical care (Fraser & Terzian, 2005). That is, access to medical treatment may reduce or buffer the effect of the health condition. For example, ongoing medical treatment for asthma reduces the likelihood that a child will experience an acute episode requiring treatment in the emergency room. Access to health care can also serve as a protective factor by interrupting a chain of risk (Fraser & Terzian, 2005). For instance, early medical treatment for chlamydia, combined with counseling and education on safe sexual practices, may reduce the likelihood that an adolescent girl will develop long-term reproductive-health problems. As a protective factor, access to care can also prevent or block the onset of a risk factor (Fraser & Terzian, 2005). One example is the case of a mother whose access to ongoing preventive health services may prevent her young child from becoming at risk for obesity.

Access to health services, or the lack thereof, is closely related to the discussion of poverty-related risk factors identified for each of the previously discussed childhood and adolescent health problems. According to U.S. national data, older adolescents, racial/ethnic minorities, sexually active youth, and uninsured youth are more likely to have neglected health care—a significant risk factor for a wide array of health problems (Kaiser Commission on Medicaid and the Uninsured, 2013).

The availability of health insurance as one component of access to care is a critical protective factor to increase the likelihood that children and adolescents will have a usual source of care, which increases their likelihood to receive health care. Children and adolescents without health insurance, either public or private, are more likely to lack a usual health care provider, to have unmet health needs, and to miss at least annual contact with a health-care provider (DeVoe, Petering, & Krois, 2008). It is estimated that 10.9% of children in the United States had no form of health insurance in 2007; this percentage dropped to 6.6% in 2012 (Kaiser Commission on Medicaid and the Uninsured, 2013). Between 2002 and 2012, among children in families with income just above the poverty level (100% to 199% of poverty guidelines), the percentage of uninsured children under the age of 18 years dropped from 17.0% to 10.4%, while the percentage with coverage through Medicaid or the Children's Health Insurance Program (CHIP) increased from 38.6% to 57.3%. In 2011 to 2012, 28.4% of uninsured children did not have a usual source of health care, compared with 1.7% of children who were covered by private insurance and 3.1% of those who were covered by Medicaid (National Center for Health Statistics, 2014).

Although the absence of insurance coverage is a major factor related to access to health care, health insurance alone may not be enough to ensure that children and adolescents receive needed health-care services, particularly among those who are low income (DeVoe et al., 2007). As previously noted, having a usual source of care may reduce many barriers to accessing health-care services, although it does not ensure that such services will be used or received when needed (Szilagyi, Schuster, & Cheng, 2009). Many nonfinancial factors also appear to affect health-care accessibility and utilization. These factors include delivery system structure, provider availability and cultural competence, preventive care education, enabling services (e.g., transportation and translation), child care, and appointment reminders (Newacheck, Hung, Park, Brindis, & Irwin, 2003).

RISK, RESILIENCE, AND PROTECTION IN HEALTH POLICY FOR CHILDREN AND YOUTH

In this section, we present a brief overview of the development of child health policy from the beginning of the 20th century to the present. We also examine the effectiveness of health policies in meeting the health- care needs of children and youth. We conclude by discussing the extent to which policy has been based on risk and protective factors.

Historical Development of Child Health Policy

Child health policy has developed in a piecemeal way, with policy initiatives often having been episodic responses to the failure of the private marketplace (Barr, Lee, & Benjamin, 2003). Although the federal government was involved to some extent in responding to children's health and mental health needs through the establishment of the Children's Bureau in 1912 and then later through the establishment of the Maternal and Child Health service system, it did not become heavily involved in financing health care for children and youth until the establishment of the Medicaid program in 1965. Table 6.3 provides a chronological listing of major policy initiatives and their primary purposes.

At the turn of the 20th century, living conditions were so poor for many American families that the average state infant mortality rate was 150 per 1,000. In some industrial cities, it was as high as 180 per 1,000 (Margolis & Kotch, 2013). In response to this high infant mortality rate, social workers joined forces with public health workers and advocates from the fields of education, medicine, and labor to lobby for the passage of legislation to establish the Children's Bureau in 1912 (Margolis & Kotch, 2013). The Children's Bureau was initially created with a mandate to study the problem of infant mortality and address the problem by disseminating information on promising interventions to the states. Based on the success of the Children's Bureau, Congress passed the Sheppard-Towner Maternity and Infancy Act in 1921, creating the first national maternal and child health program that provided grants-in-aid to states. The Sheppard-Towner Act represented the first federal effort to establish a maternal and child health infrastructure within the states, and it laid the groundwork for future collaboration between state and federal governments to address maternal and child health (Kessel, Jaros, & Harker, 2003; Margolis & Kotch, 2013). During the 8 years for which the act was in effect, the number of permanent maternal and child health centers and state child hygiene and welfare programs increased.

The Sheppard-Towner Act was not renewed in 1929, and the Great Depression had a major impact on the ability of states to provide maternal and child health services. These events contributed to an increase in infant mortality across the nation. In response to rising infant mortality rates and the widespread poverty among women and children, Title V of the Social Security Act was passed in 1935. Title V had three parts that were administered under the Children's Bureau: (1) Maternal and Child Health Services (MCH) enabled states to expand services that had been provided by the Sheppard-Towner Act; (2) the Services for Crippled Children's Program enabled states to locate and provide medical and other services for children who had "crippling conditions"; and (3) Child Welfare Services enabled

Table 6.3   Chronology of Key Child Health Policy Legislation 1900 to Present

Year	Legislation	Purpose
1912	Children's Bureau established	Studied and began to address the high rates of infant mortality
1921	Sheppard-Towner Maternity and Infancy Act	Established the first national Maternal and Child Health program, provided grants-in-aid to states to develop local and state maternal and child health infrastructures
1935	Social Security Act, including Title V Maternal and Child Health Program	Title V—Created a coordinated Maternal and Child Health service system based on a federal–state partnership
1965	Title XIX amended the Social Security Act to establish the Medicaid program	Provided health insurance to children and families in poverty
1981	Omnibus Budget Reconciliation Act of 1981 (OBRA '81) Maternal and Child Health Services Block Grant Amendments to Title V	Shifted program planning, control, and accountability for Maternal and Child Health programs from federal to state and local governments
1989	Omnibus Budget Reconciliation Act (OBRA '89)	Established stricter reporting requirements for Title V and supported development of systems of care for Children with Special Health Care Needs (CSHCN); expanded the Early and Periodic, Screening, Diagnosis, and Treatment (EPSDT) program; mandated Medicaid coverage of children younger than 6 years with family income up to 133% of FPL
1996	Personal Responsibility Work and Opportunity Reconciliation Act (PRWORA)	Delinked Medicaid eligibility and public assistance
1997	Title XXI (SSA), State Child Health Insurance Program (SCHIP) established	Expanded the health insurance safety net to cover more low-income children who were not eligible for Medicaid and whose families could not afford private insurance
2003	Jobs and Growth Tax Relief Reconciliation Act	Raised all state Medicaid matching rates by 2.95 percentage points for the period of April 2003 through June 2004 as a temporary federal fiscal relief for the states due to the downturn of the economy, provided that the state maintains its Medicaid eligibility levels
2006	Deficit Reduction Act of 2005 (DRA)	Allowed states to impose cost-sharing for most services on children eligible for Medicaid on an "optional" basis (generally those with family incomes above 100% of the FPL); required all children and parents who apply for Medicaid and who claim to be U.S. citizens to document their citizenship and identity; Medicare beneficiaries and most individuals with disabilities are exempt from this requirement; allowed states to offer disabled children under 19 with family incomes below 300% of FPL to purchase Medicaid coverage by paying income-related premiums

Year	Legislation	Purpose
2009	Children's Health Insurance Program Reauthorization Act (CHIRPA)	Expanded Child Health Insurance Program (CHIP) to an additional 4 million children; gave states the option to eliminate a 5-year waiting period for legal immigrant children and pregnant women to be eligible for Medicaid and CHIP; rescinded the August 17 Directive, which had restricted states' ability to cover children in families with income above 250% of the FPL
2009	American Recovery and Reinvestment Act (ARRA)	Provided enhanced Medicaid matching funds to states from October 1, 2008, through December 31, 2010, to help states maintain Medicaid eligibility levels and enrollment
2010	Patient Protection and Affordable Care Act (ACA)	Expands health insurance coverage to 32 million people by 2019; prevents states from reducing income eligibility threshold for CHIP and maintains current income eligibility for children's Medicaid until 2019; regulates insurance companies to prevent insurers from dropping individuals when they become sick and denying coverage for pre-existing conditions

states to provide services to homeless, dependent, and neglected children (Kessel et al., 2003). Title V funding through the Services for Crippled Children's Program was the only source of federal funding for children with special health-care needs (the majority of whom needed orthopedic treatment as a result of the polio epidemic) until 1965, when the Medicaid program was established.

Title V has been amended numerous times over the past decades. The Omnibus Budget Reconciliation Act of 1981, PL 97-35, consolidated seven Title V categorical programs into a block grant program. The Omnibus Budget Reconciliation Act of 1989 (OBRA '89), PL 101-239, introduced stricter requirements for state planning and reporting regarding use of Title V funds. OBRA '89 gave authority to the Maternal and Child Health Bureau to help develop systems of care for children with special health-care needs and their families and expanded the mission of related programs to promote the development of community-based systems of services (McPherson et al., 1998). State health departments administer the Title V MCH Services Block Grant Program (Maternal and Child Health Bureau, n.d.). The federal government requires states to conduct a statewide needs assessment every 5 years and to submit a plan for meeting those needs. Title V block grant funds are used primarily for service system development to reduce infant mortality and the incidence of disabilities and to provide and ensure access to health care for women of reproductive age, access to preventive and primary care services for children, and access to family-centered, community-based, coordinated care for children with special health-care needs.

The Medicaid program was enacted in 1965 as a joint state and federally funded health insurance program for women who were on public assistance and their children and other persons who were elderly, blind, or disabled. Each state administers its own Medicaid program according to federal guidelines. The federal government provides matching funds for some of the state Medicaid costs (on average about 57% of costs are matched). In 1967, the

Early and Periodic Screening, Diagnosis, and Treatment Program (EPSDT) was created as a unique prevention component of the Medicaid program to ensure that children receiving Medicaid would receive preventive health services in addition to acute and chronic medical care (Sardell & Johnson, 1998). The EPSDT program requires states to offer age-appropriate screenings and immunizations, follow-up diagnostic services, and medical treatment. Because many states never fully implemented their EPSDT program, and to increase the number of children receiving preventive care, Congress included provisions in OBRA '89 that expanded the EPSDT program. The expanded provisions required states to conduct aggressive outreach and case-finding efforts as well as to provide enabling services such as case management, transportation, and translation services (Rosenbach & Gavin, 1998).

During the 1980s and 1990s, the rates of children and youth covered by private health insurance substantially declined. This decline was the result of several factors, including the loss of manufacturing jobs, which often offered employees and their families affordable health insurance, and the concomitant rise in lower-paying service jobs, which often did not offer employees health insurance. The proportion of workers who were hired to fill contract or part-time positions, which typically do not carry health insurance benefits for the worker or his or her family, also increased. In addition, during this period, the cost of health insurance for employers rose significantly, and many employers changed policies to cover only the employee and not the family (Moniz & Gorin, 2014).

To deal with the loss of private health insurance coverage and the resulting increase in uninsured children and youth, Congress passed a series of Medicaid expansions beginning in the mid-1980s. For example, the Omnibus Budget Reconciliation Act of 1989 (OBRA '89) required states to cover pregnant women and children up to the age of 6 years with family incomes that were up to 133% of federal poverty guidelines. The early expansions focused solely on infants and young children. Later, the Omnibus Budget Reconciliation Act of 1990 (OBRA '90) mandated coverage of adolescents up to 16 years of age with family incomes of as much as 100% of the federal poverty guidelines (Newacheck, Brindis, Cart, Marchi, & Irwin, 1999).

These Medicaid expansions began the "delinking" of Medicaid and public assistance status. This delinking process was finally completed in 1996 with the passage of the Personal Responsibility Work and Opportunity Reconciliation Act (PRWORA) (Moniz & Gorin, 2014). PRWORA separated the determination of eligibility for Medicaid from receipt of public assistance, which was called Temporary Assistance for Needy Families (TANF). The federal government required states to provide Medicaid coverage for children up to the age of 5 years in families with incomes of as much as 133% of the poverty guidelines and to cover children from the ages of 6 to 19 years old in families with incomes at or below the FPL.

The Balanced Budget Act of 1997 created the State Children's Health Insurance Program (SCHIP) to address the large number of uninsured children of low-income working families who were not eligible for Medicaid because their family income exceeded the eligibility criteria. Unlike Medicaid, SCHIP is not an entitlement program. Under federal legislation, states have been given tremendous flexibility to use SCHIP allocations to create separate SCHIP programs, expand their Medicaid programs, or develop a combination of both. States are also allowed to determine SCHIP eligibility; among the states, eligibility ranges from less than 200% to 400% of the federal poverty guidelines. State dollars are matched by federal dollars. States with lower per capita income receive a higher federal match rate. States are also allowed to require monthly premiums or copayments for participation in their SCHIP programs. In 2009, premiums were required by 35 states, with some premiums as high as $100 or more per month (Henry J. Kaiser Family Foundation, 2009). The success of SCHIP has been highly variable and largely dependent on each state conducting aggressive and effective outreach, enrollment, and renewal efforts. Because of barriers to enrollment and renewal, many eligible children are currently not enrolled. In addition, because of constraints on state budgets, outreach efforts have been reduced in many states, and some states have enacted measures to restrict coverage in their SCHIP programs (Henry J. Kaiser Family Foundation, 2009).

In 2009, Congress passed the Children's Health Insurance Program Reauthorization Act (CHIPRA) and increased the funding by $33 billion with the expectation that 4.1 million additional children would be covered by 2013 (Moniz & Gorin, 2014). The Children's Health Insurance Program (now called CHIP) is currently authorized through 2019; however, funding is only guaranteed through 2015.

Landmark health-care-reform legislation, The Patient Protection and Affordable Care Act (ACA), was signed into law by President Barack Obama in March 2010. The overall goals of the ACA are to (1) expand health insurance coverage, (2) increase focus on prevention, and (3) improve health-care efficiency and reduce costs (Hellerstedt, 2013). Key provisions of the act that affect children and youth include (1) eliminating lifetime caps on insurance coverage; (2) preventing states from reducing the income eligibility threshold for CHIP, extending CHIP through 2019 with funding through 2015, and providing funding for increased outreach efforts to enroll eligible children; (3) requiring insurers to cover comprehensive screenings and preventative care at no cost to the patient; (4) mandating Medicaid coverage for children aging out of the foster care system up to the age of 26 years; (5) barring insurance companies from denying coverage for pre-existing conditions; (6) allowing families to purchase child-only insurance packages from the Exchanges; (7) allowing young adults to remain on their parents' insurance until they reach 26 years of age; (8) establishing a $200 million federal authorization program to expand school-based health centers; and (9) including $1.5 billion for the Home Visitation Grant Program to implement evidence-based maternal, infant, and early childhood visitation models (First Focus, 2012). Under the ACA, individuals are required to have minimal health insurance coverage or pay a penalty; federal subsidies or tax credits may be used to help offset costs for low- and middle-income people who must purchase individual plans.

Since the enactment of the ACA, numerous cases have been filed against specific provisions of the Act. In June 2012, the U.S. Supreme Court upheld the constitutionality of the ACA but ruled that the ACA mandated expansion of Medicaid coverage would not be required for states. This expansion would have covered adults under the age of 65 years, including many low-income parents with incomes up to 133% of the FPL. Also, at the time of this writing, the *Halbig v. Burwell* case is working its way through the federal court system; this case challenges the health-care insurance subsidies used by close to 5 million Americans who bought insurance through the Exchange established by the federal government (Perkins & Singh, 2014).

THE DEGREE TO WHICH POLICY HAS BEEN BASED ON RISK AND PROTECTIVE FACTORS

As stated earlier in this chapter, for many children and youth, access to care serves as a protective factor in the face of health risk. Federal health policy has primarily attempted to address risk factors associated with poor health outcomes by increasing access to preventive and medical care services. It has been addressed in two ways: (1) through the creation of public health insurance programs for low-income children (e.g., Medicaid and CHIP, and provisions of the ACA) and (2) through supporting infrastructure development to ensure that services are delivered in a coordinated and accessible manner (primarily through Title V of the Social Security Act and, most recently, the ACA).

Protective Role of Health Insurance

Numerous studies have demonstrated the key role that health insurance plays in increasing access to health care for children and youth (Newacheck et al., 1999; Newacheck, Pearl, Hughes, & Halfon, 1998). Beginning in the 1980s, with the expansion of eligibility for Medicaid, and extending through the implementation of the CHIP program, and provisions of the ACA, the federal insurance safety net has covered an increasing percentage of low-income children. A study of the New York state SCHIP program demonstrated that enrollment in SCHIP reduced preexisting racial/ethnic disparities in unmet need and access to and continuity of care among 2,290 children (Shone, Dick, Klein, Zwanziger, & Szilagyi, 2005). Kempe and associates (2005), in a study of Colorado's SCHIP program, found that one year after enrollment, families ($N = 480$) reported improved access to care, a decrease in unmet medical needs, an increase in routine-care visits, and a higher perception of quality care. Experts argue that the most effective way to ensure that children have health insurance coverage and receive needed care is to approach insurance coverage at the family level as opposed to the individual level. DeVoe, Tillotson, and Wallace (2008) found that, compared with insured children who had at least one insured parent, children with uninsured parents were more likely to have never received preventive counseling services, to have insurance coverage gaps, and to have unmet health-care needs. Research findings such as these undergird the ACA's goal of expanding health insurance coverage to low-income adults, many of whom are parents.

Concept of a "Medical Home"

Although public insurance programs such as Medicaid, CHIP, and provisions of the ACA provide an important health insurance safety net for children and youth, insurance coverage alone is not sufficient for ensuring access to health services (Newacheck et al., 2003). A usual source of care and coordinated systems of care (Starfield, 2008) also need to be in place to respond to the health-care needs of children and youth. Federal policymakers have addressed systems issues primarily through programs funded by Title V of the Social Security Act. For example, one of the hallmarks of coordinated care is to ensure that children have continuous access to routine health care and that medical services are integrated with other child and youth services. The American Academy of Pediatrics and other advocacy groups have worked closely with the MCHB to implement the "medical home" concept for all children, especially children with special health care needs (American Academy of Pediatrics, 2012).

Although the term *medical home* was originally defined as a physical location, it has evolved to define a partnership with families to ensure that children and youth are receiving care that is "accessible, family centered, coordinated, comprehensive, continuous, compassionate, and culturally effective" (Sia, Tonniges, Osterhus, & Taba, 2004, p. 1473). Examining data from the National Survey of Children with Special Health Care Needs, investigators found that when children have a medical home, they experience significantly less delay in seeking care and have fewer unmet health-care needs and fewer unmet needs for family support services (Strickland et al., 2004). One of the child health objectives in *Healthy People 2020* is to "increase the proportion of children with special health care needs who have access to a medical home" (U.S. DHHS, n.d.). The Head Start program and the Maternal and Child Health Bureau Services V Block Grant program require that states report on how and to what extent they are achieving this objective.

One of the goals of the ACA is to improve the quality and efficiency of health-care delivery. To meet this goal, the ACA has incorporated the medical home concept as one of its initiatives; the ACA uses the term *patient-centered medical home (PCMH)*. The Agency for Healthcare Research and Quality (AHRQ) defines PCMH as a "model for organizing primary care that is comprehensive, patient-centered, coordinated, accessible, and high quality and safe" (AHRQ, n.d.).

Another systems-change approach to increasing access to health care for children and youth is to deliver health care in settings where the majority of children spend a large portion of their day. This approach is reflected in policy initiatives to support the development and ongoing operation of school-based and school-linked health centers. Delivering integrated services through school-based health centers will be discussed in the next section on service integration.

The Case of "Abstinence Only" Versus More Comprehensive Programs

One area of controversy regarding how well federal health policy has been informed by risk and protective factors is that of adolescent sexual health. Comprehensive sexual health education can serve as a protective factor by providing youth with the knowledge and skills necessary to make healthy decisions about sexual behavior (Chin et al., 2012). In fiscal year 2008, the federal government allocated $176 million for abstinence-only education. At that time, there was no federal program that supported comprehensive sex education to teach young people about both abstinence and contraception (Boonstra, 2009). Federal law required that abstinence-only sexuality education teach that sexual activity outside of marriage is wrong and harmful for everyone, irrespective of age (Boonstra, 2009). This mandate prohibited educators from providing information on contraceptive methods, with the exception of emphasizing their ineffectiveness (Boonstra, 2009). Perhaps most disturbing is that, after years of evaluation of abstinence-only programs, no credible evidence has shown that such restrictive education delays adolescent sexual activity (Boonstra, 2009).

However, empirical evidence did suggest that abstinence-only models may reduce contraceptive use among sexually active young people, thereby increasing their risk for STIs and unplanned pregnancies (Boonstra, 2009; Rosenbaum, 2009).

Furthermore, research has demonstrated that the most effective sexuality education programs are comprehensive in nature, incorporating both abstinence promotion and discussion of safer sex options (Kohler, Manhart, & Lafferty, 2008). In 2009, the Obama administration created the Office of Adolescent Health (OAH) and introduced a new initiative that replaced the Community Based Abstinence Program. This initiative, called the Teen Pregnancy Prevention Initiative, focused on replicating programs that have proven effectiveness, allocated funds to develop and test innovative models and new strategies for preventing teen pregnancy, and developed a collaboration with the CDC to develop community-wide, multicomponent interventions (National Campaign to Prevent Teen and Unplanned Pregnancy, 2010; Sexuality Information and Education Council of the United States [SIECUS], 2012). More recently, the Affordable Care Act of 2010 created the Personal Responsibility Education Program (PREP), which is administered by the Administration for Children & Families. This program provides grants to states to fund evidence-based programs to educate adolescents about abstinence and contraception to prevent HIV, STIs, and pregnancy (SIECUS, 2012). PREP specifically targets adolescents who are in foster care or homeless, live in rural areas or areas with a high teen birth rate, or are from a racial or ethnic minority group. During the Obama administration, there has been a clear move toward funding evidence-based interventions that target risk and protective factors related to adolescent sexual health.

USING KNOWLEDGE OF RISK, PROTECTION, AND RESILIENCE TO ACHIEVE SERVICE INTEGRATION IN HEALTH POLICY

Service Integration in Health Policy: School-Based Health Centers

Meeting the health and social needs of children and adolescents, especially those involved in multiple service systems, requires policies that promote integration and collaboration among service systems. School-based health centers (SBHCs) are a prime example of effective service integration in the area of health and social policy. We will provide an overview of the history and funding of SBHCs, followed by a discussion of the services provided and evidence regarding their impact. This section is followed by a case study of an adolescent with multiple problems to illustrate how integrated service systems can best meet the needs of children and youth.

Historical Overview

In the United States, the first school-based health initiative began in New York City in 1894 to assess and contain children with contagious diseases, such as measles, scarlet fever, whooping cough, and tuberculosis (Keeton, Soleimanpour, & Brindis, 2012). In 1902, the first school nurse began providing treatment and care to students and also making home visits to provide health education to families regarding hygiene and other methods of disease control. The first SBHCs were opened in the late 1960s and early 1970s in

Cambridge, Massachusetts, Dallas, Texas, and Saint Paul, Minnesota, to provide accessible and affordable health care to poor children. In 1978, the Robert Wood Johnson Foundation sponsored the expansion of SBHCs throughout the United States in an effort to increase access to community-based health care for children and adolescents in underserved communities. Through these efforts, policymakers became more aware of SBHCs and their value. In 1995, the Health Resource and Service Administration began providing grant funding for SBHCs (Gustafson, 2005). Since the 1990s, the number of SBHCs has increased with the help of multiple funding streams. As part of the Affordable Care Act, $200 million was appropriated to SBHCs between 2010 and 2013 to improve and expand services to an estimated 875,000 youth per year, a 50% increase compared with youth served in 2009 (U.S. Department of Health and Human Services, 2011). A national SBHC advocacy organization, the School-Based Health Alliance, in a position statement, noted that the SBHC model has the components of a Patient Centered Medical Home (PCMH) as outlined in the ACA and that SBHCs across the country should strive to meet PCMH goals and standards (School-Based Health Alliance, n.d.).

There are nearly 2,000 school-based health centers located on elementary, middle, and high school campuses across the country (Keeton et al., 2012). These centers provide a range of services, including primary medical care, mental and behavioral health care, reproductive health services, dental/oral health care, and health education and promotion. Once primarily located in inner cities, SBHCs have expanded to rural, suburban, and urban areas (Lofink et al., 2013). SBHCs typically operate via a partnership between a school district and a local health organization such as a community health center, hospital, or health department. Most SBHCs are open five days a week before, during, and after school. SBHC staff include a mix of professionals: physicians, nurse practitioners, physician assistants, nurses, dieticians, dental hygienists, psychologists, counselors, social workers, and health educators (Brown & Bolen, 2012).

SBHCs rely on various funding and billing sources. Over 80% of SBHCs bill a state Medicaid agency, 71% bill Medicaid managed care organizations, 64% bill private insurance, and 40% bill Tri-Care (i.e., the health insurance program for military families). In addition to billing, SBHCs receive funds from state governments (75%), the federal government (53%), private foundations (40%), school districts (33%), hospitals (33%), local governments (32%), private health insurance organizations (27%), businesses (18%), and professional associations (7%) (Lofink et al., 2013).

Primary Care

SBHCs provide a range of primary care services including physical exams, immunizations, treatment for acute illnesses and injuries, treatment for common chronic diseases (e.g., asthma and diabetes), and routine health screening (Brown & Bolen, 2012). Researchers found overall significantly higher completion rates for immunization series among adolescents at SBHCs compared to those at community health centers despite serving an adolescent population with lower health insurance coverage (Federico, Abrams, Everhart, Melinkovich, & Hambidge, 2010). In a study of children with asthma, those with SBHCs showed less activity restriction due to asthma and fewer emergency department visits compared with the non-SBHC group (Mansour, Rose, Toole, Luzader, & Atherton, 2008).

Mental and Behavioral Health Care

In order to meet both the physical and mental health needs of youth, 78% of SBHCs provide some form of mental/behavioral health care (Lofink et al., 2013). These services include crisis intervention (78%), individual psychosocial assessment and treatment (73%), case management (69%), classroom behavior support (62%), substance abuse counseling (53%), assessment and treatment of learning problems (50%), peer mediation (43%), and prescription and management of psychoactive medication (39%). A longitudinal study showed that adolescents who were enrolled in a school with a SBHC were more likely to access mental health services (Guo, Wade, & Keller, 2008). The authors of another study concluded that "on-site mental health services and their immediate availability for crisis intervention allow teenagers to engage in individual, family, and group treatment before problems become so severe that they interfere with their education" (Pastore & Techow, 2004, p. 194).

Health Education and Prevention

Most SBHCs are also involved in health education and prevention activities in the areas of violence, substance use, nutrition, and physical activity. SBHC engagement in prevention activities varies by the type of preventive intervention (i.e., individual, small group, classroom, and school-wide interventions). Depending on the intervention format, 35% to 83% of SBHCs were involved in bullying and violence prevention, 30% to 76% were involved in school safety planning, 20% to 76% were involved in sexual assault and rape prevention and counseling, and 23% to 76% were involved in intimate partner and dating violence prevention and counseling. In terms of substance use, 36% to 82% of SBHCs were involved in some form of tobacco preventive intervention, 34% to 78% were involved in alcohol preventive interventions, and 33% to 78% were involved in drug preventive interventions. Finally, 37% to 90% of SBHCs were involved in health promotion activities regarding healthy eating, active living, and weight management (Lofink et al., 2013).

Reproductive Health Care

Many SBHCs in middle and high schools provide reproductive health services in the form of abstinence counseling (82%), pregnancy testing (81%), STD diagnosis and treatment (69%), testicular examinations (69%), contraceptive counseling (65%), and gynecological examinations (59%) (Lofink et al., 2013). Half of SBHCs were prohibited from dispensing contraceptives, most often due to school, district, and state policies. In centers that were allowed to provide contraceptive services, SBHCs were more likely to provide condoms as opposed to other methods of birth control such as the pill (Fothergill & Feijoo, 2000). Although prenatal care is not available in most SBHCs, a study comparing adolescents receiving prenatal care in SBHCs had babies with higher birth weight compared with those receiving prenatal care in hospitals (Barnet, Duggan, & Devoe, 2003). Further, studies show that receiving prenatal care in SBHCs is associated with lower rates of absenteeism and dropout (Barnet, Arroyo, Devoe, & Duggan, 2004; Barnet et al., 2003).

Oral and Dental Health Care

Dental and oral health services are becoming more available at SBHCs and are provided on-site and through mobile units. Over 70% of SBHCs reported conducting dental screenings, which may be conducted by a dental/oral health or primary care provider. In addition, almost 40% of SBHCs provide dental examinations by either a dentist or dental hygienist and over 30% of SBHCs provide dental cleanings. Barriers to providing these services include cost, equipment needs, provider availability, space, and reimbursement (Lofink et al., 2013).

Evaluations of School-Based Health Centers: Acceptability and Accessibility

Evaluation findings of the acceptability of SBHCs among students have been promising. One study found that 86% of students rated the quality of care from their SBHC as satisfactory to excellent and 79% rated privacy in their SBHC as satisfactory to excellent (Santelli, Kouzis, & Newcomer, 1996). Similarly, another study found that 92% of students were satisfied with the services received at their SBHC, 79% felt comfortable receiving care at their SBHC, and 74% felt that their visits were confidential (Pastore, Juszczak, Fisher, & Friedman, 1998).

SBHCs provide developmentally appropriate and comprehensive care to children and adolescents in a familiar and accessible setting. The SBHC model links schools, communities, and health systems to provide an array of primary and preventive health-care services. SBHCs were designed to address barriers in access to care and help meet the needs of underserved children. The convenient location allows youth to access care in a timely manner, which might otherwise be delayed. Parents do not have to take time off from work to take their child to a provider, which may be particularly challenging for low-income and single-parent families. Furthermore, children do not have to miss school to receive care (Gustafson, 2005). In addition, despite recent improvements to expand health insurance coverage among children, millions of children remain uninsured or underinsured. Low-income and racial/ethnic minority children are less likely to have a regular source of health care and therefore may benefit from the SBHC model (Brown & Bolen, 2012). In some rural areas, SBHCs are the only source of primary care for children and youth (Hossain, Coughlin, & Zickafoose, 2014). SBHCs are also beneficial for youth with multiple health needs as well as high-risk youth, who benefit from immediate access to care (Jepson, Juszczak, & Fisher, 1998). Youth are more likely to use health-care services on a "spontaneous basis" (Pastore & Techow, 2004, p. 195); therefore, SBHCs offer location, convenience, confidentiality, and trust—all factors associated with the utilization of health and psychosocial services by youth (Brindis et al., 2003).

The following case study illustrates how a school-based health center serves as a protective factor by providing access to care to a youth with several risk factors for poor health and mental health outcomes. Because of their location in school settings and the collaborative philosophy and interdisciplinary approach to providing services, school-based health centers are well positioned to integrate services for children and youth.

Case Study

James, a 14-year-old African American male, lives with his 31-year-old single mother and 8-year-old sister in a public housing project on the outskirts of town. James's mother works in a local fast-food restaurant and has no health insurance. As a freshman in high school, James is experiencing a great deal of anxiety about fitting in with his classmates, often feels sad, is not sleeping well, and is falling behind in his course work because of his lack of motivation and problems concentrating. Like many of his friends, James is experimenting with alcohol, marijuana, and other drugs and has recently become sexually active. He had unprotected vaginal sex at a party the previous week, and for the past 2 days, he has been experiencing a fire-like burning during urination. James is worried that he might have gonorrhea, but he has no idea of where to go for help. He is very uncomfortable and does not want to go to school, yet he feels that there is no way he can let his mom find out about his condition.

James is fortunate in that he attends a school with a school-based health center that offers comprehensive services. On the urging of his best friend, who has had several good experiences at the center, James drops by the center for a visit during lunch. Because his mother signed an enrollment form for the health center when James entered high school, he is able to receive confidential services without the center contacting her. A nurse practitioner sees him initially for assessment and medical treatment of his STI. The social worker also conducts an initial psychosocial assessment and schedules a time to meet with James the next day. She plans to follow-up with his concerns about school and his feelings of sadness and to learn more about his recent drug and alcohol use and sexual behavior. James has given the social worker permission to access his school records and talk with his teachers and school counselor. The social worker will be able to contact other staff at the health center for assistance in evaluating James and providing him with needed services. A psychiatrist provides consultation services to the school-based health center staff. The psychiatrist also conducts psychiatric evaluations and prescribes and monitors psychiatric medications. In addition, the health center staff provides counseling and conducts groups on a number of health and mental health topics, such as substance abuse, sexual health, and coping with relationships. The health center has recently begun participating in an innovative CHIP outreach initiative to increase the enrollment of eligible youth. The social worker thinks that James probably meets the eligibility criteria and, with James's permission, she will contact his mother to assist her in enrolling both of her children. James's enrollment in the CHIP program will allow the center to be reimbursed for services and will help the social worker access additional health and mental health services for James if he needs them.

Case Study Questions for Discussion

- What would most likely happen to James if a school-based health center did not exist in his school?
- How would he find out how to get care?
- Where would he receive care and when?
- Who would pay for his care?
- How comprehensive would his care likely be?
- What is the likelihood that James would be assessed and treated for any other conditions or problems than his presenting symptoms (i.e., burning on urination)?

SUMMARY

In this chapter, we have reviewed risk factors for several major health problems (LBW, asthma, overweight and obesity, and STIs) experienced by children and youth. Although there are risk factors that are unique to each of these health problems, two major risk factors are common across health problems: poverty and living in socially and physically unhealthy environments (Fraser, 2004; Moniz & Gorin, 2014). Access to care, which includes both access to health insurance and availability of coordinated and integrated systems of care, plays a major role in decreasing the risk for poor health outcomes and protecting children and youth from developing health problems.

U.S. health-care policy has increased children's access to health services through the creation of public health insurance programs such as Medicaid and CHIP and now through the Affordable Care Act (ACA). Through Title V of the Social Security Act and provisions of the ACA, the federal government has supported the development of a more coordinated and comprehensive service system. The medical home and school-based health centers are examples of efforts at coordination and integration. School-based health centers are a promising example of integration of primary care, behavioral health, and prevention services provided in a location that is accessible to children and youth enrolled in schools. However, attempts to fully integrate services for children and youth across major service systems (health, mental health, education, child welfare, and juvenile justice) are still in their infancy, and much remains to be accomplished. Furthermore, federal policy has had very limited success in reducing the number of children living in poverty or near poverty or ensuring that children and youth live in healthy environments. To truly make a significant difference in the health of children and youth, federal policy cannot be constrained to the creation of coordinated and integrated systems of care, although this would be a substantial achievement. National policy must also address the poverty and social inequities that contribute to poor health and well-being.

QUESTIONS FOR DISCUSSION

1. How do socioeconomic inequalities and physical and social environments contribute to health outcomes of children and youth? Given the existence of these inequalities, what effect will the full implementation of the Affordable Care Act, which expands insurance coverage to the uninsured and thereby increases access to medical care, have on the existing health disparities among children and youth?

2. Given the success of school-based health clinics in integrating service systems for children and youth, why has their establishment not been more widespread?

3. What other models are you aware of that integrate service systems, including health care for children and youth? What policies and environmental factors need to be in place for these service delivery models to be developed, implemented and sustained?

REFERENCES

Agency for Healthcare Research and Quality (n.d.). *Patient centered medical home resource center: Defining the PCMH*. Retrieved from http://pcmh.ahrq.gov/page/defining-pcmh

Ahmad, N., Biswas, S., Bae, S., Meador, K. E., Huang, R., & Singh, K. P. (2009). Association between obesity and asthma in US children and adolescents. *Journal of Asthma, 46*, 642–646. doi:10.1080/02770900802503123

Akinbami, L. J., Moorman, J. E., Garbe, P. L., & Sondik, E. J. (2009). Status of childhood asthma in the United States, 1980–2007. *Pediatrics, 123*, S131–S145. doi:10.1542/peds.2008-2233C

American Academy of Pediatrics. (2012). *What is a medical home?* Retrieved from http:www.medical-homeinfo.org/about/medical_home/

American Lung Association. (2012). *Asthma and children fact sheet*. Retrieved from http://www.lung.org/lung-disease/asthma/resources/facts-and-figures/asthma-children-fact-sheet.html#8

Anderson, R. M. (1995). Revisiting the behavioral model and access to medical care: Does it matter? *Journal of Health and Social Behavior, 36*, 1–10. doi:10.2307/2137284

Baena-Cagnani, C. E., Gomez, R. M., Baena-Cagnani, R., & Canonica, G. W. (2009). Impact of environmental tobacco smoke and active tobacco smoking on the development and outcomes of asthma and rhinitis. *Current Opinion in Allergy and Clinical Immunology, 9*, 136–140. doi:10.1097/ACI.0b013e3283294038

Bailey, B. A., McCook, J. G., Hodge, A., & McGrady, L. (2012). Infant birth outcomes among substance using women: Why quitting smoking during pregnancy is just as important as quitting illicit drug use. *Maternal and Child Health Journal, 16*, 414–422. doi:10.1007/s10995-011-0776-y

Barlow, S. E., & Expert Committee. (2007). Expert committee recommendations regarding the prevention, assessment, and treatment of child and adolescent overweight and obesity: Summary report. *Pediatrics, 120*, S164-192. doi:10.1542/peds.2007-2329C

Barnet, B., Arroyo, C., Devoe, M., & Duggan, A. K. (2004). Reduced school dropout rates among adolescent mothers receiving school-based prenatal care. *Archives of Pediatrics & Adolescent Medicine, 158*, 262–268. doi:10.1001/archpedi.158.3.262

Barnet, B., Duggan, A. K., & Devoe, M. (2003). Reduced low birth weight for teenagers receiving prenatal care at a school-based health center: Effect of access and comprehensive care. *Journal of Adolescent Health, 33*, 349–358. doi:10.1016/S1054-139X(03)00211-8

Barr, D. A., Lee, P. R., & Benjamin, A. E. (2003). Health care and health care policy in a changing world. In H. M. Wallace, G. Green, & K. Jaros (Eds.), *Health and welfare for families in the 21st century* (2nd ed., pp. 262–42). Boston, MA: Jones & Bartlett.

Bethell, C. D., Read, D., Blumber, S. J., & Newacheck, P. (2008). What is the prevalence of children with special health care needs: Towards an understanding of variations in findings and methods across three national surveys. *MCH Journal, 12*, 1–14. doi:10.1007/s10995-007-0220-5.

Black, M. H., Zhou, H., Takayanagi, M., Jacobsen, S. J., & Koebnick, C. (2013). Increased asthma risk and asthma-related health care complications associated with childhood obesity. *American Journal of Epidemiology, 178*, 1120–1128. doi:10.1093/aje/kwt093

Boonstra, H. D. (2009). Advocates call for a new approach after the era of "abstinence-only" sex education. *Guttmacher Policy Review, 12*(1), 6–11. Retrieved from http://www.guttmacher.org/pubs/gpr/12/1/gpr120106.html

Boulet, S. L., Schieve, L. A., Nannini, A., Ferre, C., Devine, O., Cohen, B., . . . Macaluso, M. (2008). Perinatal outcomes of twin births conceived using assisted reproduction technology: A population-based study. *Human Reproduction, 23*, 1941–1948. doi:10.1093/humrep/den169

Brindis, C. D., Klein, J., Schlitt, J., Santelli, J., Juszcak, L., & Nystrom, R. (2003). School-based health centers: Accessibility and accountability. *Journal of Adolescent Health, 32S,* 98–107. doi:10.1016/S1054-139X(03)00069-7

Brown, M. B., & Bolen, L. M. (2012). School-based health centers. In *Encyclopedia of adolescence.* (pp. 2506–2511). New York, NY: Springer.

Cassedy, A., Fairbrother, G., & Newacheck, P. W. (2008). The impact of insurance instability on children's access, utilization, and satisfaction with health care. *Ambulatory Pediatrics.* 8(5), 321–328. doi:10.1016/j.ambp.2008.04.007

Catalano, P. M., Farrell, K., Thomas, A., Huston-Presley, L., Mencin, P., de Mouzon, S. H., & Amini, S. B. (2009). Perinatal risk factors for childhood obesity and metabolic dysregulation. *American Journal of Clinical Nutrition, 90,* 1303–1313. doi:10.3945/ajcn.2008.27416

Centers for Disease Control and Prevention. (2012). *Sexually transmitted diseases surveillance 2011.* Atlanta, GA: U.S. Department of Health and Human Services.

Centers for Disease Control and Prevention. (2013a). *Summary health statistics for U.S. children: National Health Interview Survey, 2012.* Retrieved from http://www.cdc.gov/nchs/data/series/sr_10/sr10_258.pdf

Centers for Disease Control and Prevention. (2013b). *Results from the School Health Policies and Practices Study 2012.* Retrieved from http://www.cdc.gov/healthyyouth/shpps/2012/pdf/shpps-results_2012.pdf#page=27

Centers for Disease Control and Prevention. (2014a). *2012 National Health Interview Survey (NHIS) data.* Retrieved from http://www.cdc.gov/Asthma/nhis/2012/data.htm

Centers for Disease Control and Prevention. (2014b). *Sexually transmitted diseases surveillance 2012.* Retrieved from http://www.cdc.gov/std/stats12/Surv2012.pdf

Centers for Disease Control and Prevention. (2014c). *HIV among youth.* Retrieved from http://www.cdc.gov/hiv/pdf/risk_youth_fact_sheet_final.pdf

Chen, X. K., Wen, S. W., Fleming, N., Yang, Q., & Walker, M. C. (2008). Increased risks of neonatal and post-neonatal mortality associated with teenage pregnancy had different explanations. *Journal of Clinical Epidemiology, 61,* 688–694. doi:10.1016/j.jclinepi.2007.08.009

Child and Adolescent Health Measurement Initiative. (2013). *Who are children with special health care needs (CSHCN).* Data Resource Center, supported by Cooperative Agreement 1-U59-MC06980-01 from the U.S. Department of Health and Human Services, Health Resources and Services Administration (HRSA), Maternal and Child Health Bureau (MCHB). Retrieved from www.childhealthdata.org.

Chin, H. B., Sipe, T. A., Elder, R., Mercer, S. L., Chattopadhyay, S. K., Jacob, V.,…Santelli, J. (2012). The effectiveness of group-based comprehensive risk-reduction and abstinence education interventions to prevent or reduce the risk of adolescent pregnancy, human immunodeficiency virus, and sexually transmitted infections: Two systematic reviews for the guide to community preventive services. *American Journal of Preventive Medicine, 42,* 272–294. doi:10.1016/j.amepre.2011.11.006

Dabelea, D. (2007). The predisposition to obesity and diabetes in offspring of diabetic mothers. *Diabetes Care, 30,* S169-S174. doi:10.2337/dc07-s211

DeVoe, J. E., Baez, A., Angier, H., Krois, L., Edlund, C., & Carney, P. A. (2007). Insurance + access not equal to health care: Typology of barriers to health care access for low-income families. *Annals of Family Medicine, 5,* 511–518. doi:10.1370/afm.748

DeVoe, J. E., Petering, R., & Krois, L. (2008). A usual source of care: Supplement or substitute for health insurance among low-income children? *Medical Care, 46,* 1041–1048. doi:10.1097/MLR.0b013e3181866443

DeVoe, J. E., Tillotson, C., & Wallace, L. S. (2008). Uninsured children and adolescents with insured parents. *Journal of the American Medical Association, 300,* 1904–1913. doi:10.1001/jama.2008.516

Dietz, P. M., England, L. J., Shapiro-Mendoza, C. K., Tong, V. T., Farr, S. L., & Callaghan, W. M. (2010). Infant morbidity and mortality attributable to prenatal smoking in the U.S. *American Journal of Preventive Medicine, 39*, 45–52. doi:10.1016/j.ampere.2010.03.009

Dominguez, T. P. (2008). Race, racism, and racial disparities in adverse birth outcomes. *Clinical Obstetrics and Gynecology, 51*, 2, 360–370. doi:10.1097/GRF.Ob013e31816f28de

Donabedian, A. (1973). *Aspects of medical care administration.* Cambridge, MA: Harvard University Press.

Elkington, K. S., Teplin, L. A., Mericle, A. A., Welty, L. J., Romero, E. G., & Abram, K. M. (2008). HIV/ sexually transmitted infection risk behaviors in delinquent youth with psychiatric disorders: A longitudinal study. *Journal of the American Academy of Child and Adolescent Psychiatry, 47*, 901–911. doi:10.1097/CHI.0b013e318179962b

Federico, S. G., Abrams, L., Everhart, R. M., Melinkovich, P., & Hambidge, S. J. (2010). Addressing adolescent immunization disparities: A retrospective analysis of school-based health center immunization delivery. *American Journal of Public Health, 100*, 1630–1634. doi:10.2105/ AJPH.2009.176628

Finer, L. B., & Zolna, M. R. (2011). Unintended pregnancy in the United States: incidence and disparities, 2006. *Contraception, 84*, 478–485. doi:10.1016/j.contraception.2011.07.013

First Focus. (2012). *Top 10 Affordable Care Act wins for kids.* Retrieved from http://www.firstfocus.net/ top-10-affordable-care-act-wins-for-kids-0%20

Fothergill, K., & Feijoo, A. (2000). Family planning services at school-based health centers: Findings from a national survey. *Journal of Adolescent Health, 27*, 166–169. doi:10.1016/S1054-139X(00)00122-1

Fraser, M. W. (2004). The ecology of childhood: A multisystems perspective. In M.W. (Ed.), *Risk and resilience in childhood: An ecological perspective* (2nd ed., pp. 1–12). Washington, DC: NASW Press.

Fraser, M. W., & Terzian, M. A. (2005). Risk and resilience in child development: Practice, principles, and strategies. In G. P. Mallon & P. McCartt Hess (Eds.), *Child welfare for the 21st century: A handbook of practices, policies, and programs.* New York, NY: Columbia University Press.

Freedman, D. S., Mei, Z., Srinivasan, S. R., Berenson, G. S., & Dietz, W. H. (2007). Cardiovascular risk factors and excess adiposity among overweight children and adolescents: The Bogalusa Heart Study. *Journal of Pediatrics, 150*, 12–17. doi:10.1016/j.jpeds.2006.08.042

Gerald, L. B., Gerald, J. K., Gibson, L., Patel, K., Zhang, S., & McClure, L. A. (2009). Changes in environmental tobacco smoke exposure and asthma morbidity among urban school children. *Chest, 135*, 911–916. doi:10.1378/chest.08–1869

Gibbs, C. M., Wendt, A., Peters, S., & Hogue, C. J. (2012). The impact of early age at first child birth on maternal and infant health. *Paediatric & Perinatal Epidemiology, 26*, S259-S284. doi:10.1111/j.1365-3016.2012.01290.x

Greydanus, D. E., Patel, D. R., & Greydanus, E. K. (2003). Adolescent health. In H. M. Wallace, G. Green, & K. Jaros (Eds.), *Health and welfare for families in the 21st century* (2nd ed., pp. 289–318). Boston, MA: Jones & Bartlett.

Guo, J. J., Wade, T. J., & Keller, K. N. (2008). Impact of school-based health centers on students with mental health problems. *Public Health Reports, 123*, 768–780.

Gustafson, E. M. (2005). History and overview of school-based health centers in the US. *Nursing Clinics of North America, 40*, 595–606. doi:10.1016/j.cnur.2005.08.001

Halfon, N., & Hochstein, M. (1997). Developing a system of care for all: What the needs of vulnerable children tell us. In R. E. K. Stein & P. Brooks (Eds.), *Health care for children: What's right, what's wrong, what's next* (pp. 303–338). New York, NY: United Hospital Fund.

Han, J. C., Lawlor, D. A., & Kimm, S. Y. (2010). Childhood obesity. *Lancet, 375*, 1737–1748. doi:10.1016/ S0140-6736(10)60171-7

He, M., Harris, S., Piché, L., & Beynon, C. (2009). Understanding screen-related sedentary behavior and its contributing factors among school-aged children: A social-ecologic exploration. *American Journal of Health Promotion, 23,* 299–308. doi:10.4278/ajhp.07070965

Hellerstedt, W. L. (2013). The Affordable Care Act: What are its goals and do we need it? *Healthy Generations, 2013*(Fall). University of Minnesota, Center for Leadership Education in Maternal and Child Public Health. Retrieved from http://www.epi.umn.edu/mch

Henry J. Kaiser Family Foundation. (2009). *Enrolling uninsured low-income children in Medicaid and SCHIP.* Retrieved from http://www.kff.org/medicaid/upload/2177_06.pdf

Holland, M. L., Kitzman, H., & Veazie, P. (2009). The effects of stress on birth weight in low-income, unmarried Black women. *Women's Health Issues, 19,* 390–397. doi:10.1016/j.whi.2009.07.005

Hossain, M., Coughlin, R., & Zickafoose, J. (2014). *CHIPRA quality demonstration: States help school-based health centers strengthen their medical home features.* Washington, DC: Agency for Healthcare Research and Quality. Retrieved from www.mathematica-mpr.com/≈/media/publications/pdfs/health/highlights08.pdf

Institute of Medicine of the National Academies. (2006). *Preterm birth: Causes, consequences and prevention.* Washington, DC: National Academies Press. Retrieved from http://www.iom.edu/Reports.aspx?Topic1 = {6203D9D4-6BBB-471C-862A-BEAA79A8580B}&Search = preterm%20birth

Institute of Medicine of the National Academies. (2012). *Best care at lower cost: The path to continuously learning health care in America.* Retrieved from http://wwww.iom.edu/Reports/2012/Best-Care-at-Lower-Cost-The-Path-to-Continuously-Learning-Health-Care-in-America.aspx

Jepson, L., Juszczak, L., & Fisher, M. (1998). Mental health care in a high school based health service. *Adolescence, 33,* 1–15.

Jimenez-Pavon, D., Kelly, J., & Reilly, J. J. (2010). Associations between objectively measured habitual physical activity and adiposity in children and adolescents: Systematic review. *International Journal of Pediatric Obesity, 5,* 3–18. doi:10.3109/17477160903067601

Kaiser Commission on Medicaid and the Uninsured. (2013). *The uninsured a primer: Key facts about health insurance on the eve of health reform.* Retrieved from http://kaiserfamilyfoundation.files.wordpress.com/2013/10/7451-09-the-uninsured-a-primer-key-facts-about-health-insurance.pdf

Kann, L., Kinchen, S., Shanklin, S. L., Flint, K. H., Kawkins, J., Harris, W. A., . . . Zaza, S. (2014). Youth risk behavior surveillance—United States, 2013. *MMWR: Surveillance Summaries, 63*(SS-04), 1–168.

Keeton, V., Soleimanpour, S., & Brindis, C. D. (2012). School-based health centers in an era of health care reform: Building on history. *Current Problems in Pediatric and Adolescent Health Care, 42,* 132–158. doi:10.1016/j.cppeds.2012.03.002

Kempe, A., Beaty, B. L., Crane, L. A., Stokstad, J., Barrow, J., Belman, S., & Steiner, J. F. (2005). Changes in access, utilization, and quality of care after enrollment into a state child health insurance plan. *Pediatrics, 115,* 364–371. doi:10.1542/peds.2004–0475

Kessel, W., Jaros, K., & Harker, P. T. (2003). The Social Security Act and maternal and child health services: Securing a bright future. In H. M. Wallace, G. Green, & K. Jaros (Eds.), *Health and welfare for families in the 21st century* (2nd ed., pp. 164–170). Boston, MA: Jones & Bartlett.

Kohler, P. K., Manhart, L. E., & Lafferty, W. E. (2008). Abstinence-only and comprehensive sex education and the initiation of sexual activity and teen pregnancy. *Journal of Adolescent Health, 42,* 344–351. doi:10.1016/j.jadohealth.2007.08.026

Kost, K., & Henshaw, S. (2014). *U.S. teenage pregnancies, births and abortions, 2010: National and state trends by age, race and ethnicity.* New York, NY: Guttmacher Institute.

Kral, J. G., Biron, S., Simard, S., Hould, F. S., Lebel, S., Marceau, S., & Marceau, P. (2006). Large maternal weight loss from obesity surgery prevents transmission of obesity to children who were followed for 2 to 18 years. *Pediatrics, 118,* e1644–e1649. doi:10.1542/peds.2006-1379

Kramer, K. L., & Lancaster, J. B. (2010). Teen motherhood in cross cultural perspective. *Annals of Human Biology, 37,* 613–628. doi:10.3109/03014460903563434

Lalor, K., & McElvaney, R. (2010). Child sexual abuse, links to later sexual exploitation/high-risk sexual behavior, and prevention/treatment programs. *Trauma, Violence, & Abuse, 11*(4), 159–177. doi:10.1177/1524838010378299

Lawlor, D. A., Timpson, N. J., Harbord, R. M., Leary, S., Ness, A., McCarthy, M. I., . . . Smith, G. D. (2008). Exploring the developmental overnutrition hypothesis using parental–offspring associations and FTO as an instrumental variable. *PLoS Medicine, 5,* e33. doi:10.1371/journal.pmed.0050033

Lawson, J. A., Janssen, I., Bruner, M. W., Hossain, A., & Pickett, W. (2014). Asthma incidence and risk factors in a national longitudinal sample of adolescent Canadians: A prospective cohort study. *BMC Pulmonary Medicine, 14,* 51. doi:10.1186/1471-2466-14-51

Lee, S. H., O'Riordan, M. A., & Lazebnik, R. (2009). Relationships among depressive symptoms, sexually transmitted infections, and pregnancy in African-American adolescent girls. *Journal of Pediatric and Adolescent Gynecology, 22,* 19–23. doi:10.1016/j.jpag.2007.12.003

Liu, P. C., Kieckhefer, G. M., & Gau, B. S. (2013). A systematic review of the association between obesity and asthma in children. *Journal of Advanced Nursing, 69,* 1446–1465. doi:10.1111/jan.12129

Lofink, H., Kuebler, J., Juszczak, L., Schlitt, J., Even, M., Rosenberg, J., & White, I. (2013). *2010-2011 School-Based Health Alliance Census Report.* Washington, DC: School-Based Health Alliance.

Love, C., David, R. J., Rankin, K. M., & Collins, J.W. (2010). Exploring weathering: Effects of lifelong economic environment and maternal age on low birth weight, small for gestational age, and preterm birth in African-American and White women. *American Journal of Epidemiology, 172,* 2, 127–134. doi:10.1093/aje/kwq109.

Lu, M. C., Kotelchuck, M., Hogan, V., Jones, L., Wright, K., & Halfon, N. (2010). Closing the Black-White gap in birth outcomes: A life-course approach. *Ethnicity & Disease, 20,* (Suppl 2), 62–76.

Manlove, J., Terry-Humen, E., & Ikramullah, E. (2006). Young teenagers and older sexual partners: Correlates and consequences for males and females. *Perspectives on Sexual and Reproductive Health, 38,* 197–207. doi:10.1363/psrh.38.197.06

Mansour, M. E., Rose, B., Toole, K., Luzader, C. P., & Atherton, H. D. (2008). Pursuing perfection: An asthma quality improvement initiative in school-based health centers with community partners. *Public Health Reports, 123,* 717–730.

March of Dimes Foundation. (2014). *The impact of premature birth on society.* Retrieved from http://www.marchofdimes.com/mission/the-economic-and-societal-costs.aspx

Margolis, L. H., & Kotch, J. B. (2013). Tracing the historical foundations of maternal and child health to contemporary times. In J. B. Kotch (Ed.), *Maternal and child health: Programs, problems, and policy in public health* (3rd ed., pp. 11–34). Burlington, MA: Jones & Bartlett Learning.

Marshall, S. J., Biddle, S. J., Gorely, T., Cameron, N., & Murdey, I. (2004). Relationships between media use, body fatness and physical activity in children and youth: A meta-analysis. *International Journal of Obesity, 28,* 1238–1246. doi:10.1038/sj.ijo.0802706

Martin, J. A., Hamilton, B. E., Osterman, M. J. K., Curtin, S. C., & Mathews, T. J. (2013). Births: Final data for 2012. *National Vital Statistics Reports, 62,* 9. Hyattsville, MD: National Center for Health Statistics. Retrieved from http://www.cdc.gov/nchs/data/nvsr62/nvsr62_09.pdf

Maternal and Child Health Bureau. (n.d.). *Programs: Title V block grant to states.* Retrieved from http://mchb.hrsa.gov/programs/

McPherson, M., Arango, P., Fox, H., Lauver, C., McManus, M., Newacheck, P. W., . . . Strickland, B. (1998). A new definition of children with special health care needs. *Pediatrics, 102,* 137–140. doi:10.1542/peds.102.1.137

Midodzi, W. K., Rowe, B. H., Majaesic, C. M., Saunders, L. D., & Senthilselvan, A. (2010). Early life factors associated with incidence of physician-diagnosed asthma in preschool children: Results from the

Canadian Early Childhood Development cohort study. *Journal of Asthma, 47,* 7–13. doi:10.3109/02770900903380996

Monasterio, E., Hwang, L. Y., & Shafer, M. A. (2007). Adolescent sexual health. *Current Problems in Pediatric and Adolescent Health Care, 37,* 302–325. doi:10.1016/j.cppeds.2007.07.006

Moniz, C., & Gorin, S. (2014). *Health care policy and practice: A biopsychosocial perspective.* (4th ed.). New York, NY: Routledge.

Moreno, L. A., & Rodríguez, G. (2007). Dietary risk factors for development of childhood obesity. *Current Opinion in Clinical Nutrition & Metabolic Care, 10,* 336–341. doi:10.1097/MCO.0b013e3280a94f59

Morrison-Beedy, D., Carey, M. P., Feng, C., & Tu, X. M. (2008). Predicting sexual risk behaviors among adolescent and young women using a prospective diary method. *Research in Nursing & Health, 31,* 329–340. doi:10.1002/nur.20263

Nardin, R., Zallman, L., McCormick, D., Woolhandler, S., & Himelssem, D. (2013). *The uninsured after implementation of the Affordable Care Act: A demographic and geographic analysis.* Retrieved from http://healthaffairs.org/blog/2013/06/06/the-uninsured-after-implementation-of-the-affordable-care-act-a-demographic-and-geographic-analysis/

National Campaign to Prevent Teen and Unplanned Pregnancy. (2010). *Latest developments from the Obama administration and Capitol Hill.* Retrieved from http://www.thenationalcampaign.org/federalfunding/latest.aspx

National Center for Health Statistics. (2014). *Health, United States, 2013: With special feature on prescription drugs.* Retrieved from http://www.cdc.gov/nchs/hus.htm

Newacheck, P. W., Brindis, C. D., Cart, C. U., Marchi, K., & Irwin, C. E., Jr. (1999). Adolescent health insurance coverage: Recent changes and access to care. *Pediatrics, 104,* 195–202. doi:10.1542/peds.104.2.195

Newacheck, P. W., Hung, Y. Y., Park, M. J., Brindis, C. D., & Irwin, C. E., Jr. (2003). Disparities in adolescent health and health care: Does socioeconomic status matter? *Health Services Research, 38,* 1235–1252. doi:10.1111/1475–6773.00174

Newacheck, P. W., Pearl, M., Hughes, D. C., & Halfon, N. (1998). The role of Medicaid in ensuring children's access to care. *Journal of the American Medical Association, 280,* 1789–1793. doi:10.1001/jama.280.20.1789.

Ogden, C. L., & Carroll, M. D. (2010). *Prevalence of obesity among children and adolescents: United States, trends 1963–1965 through 2007–2008.* Retrieved from http://www.cdc.gov/nchs/data/hestat/obesity_child_07_08/obesity_child_07_08.pdf

Ogden, C. L., Carroll, M. D., Kit, B. K., & Flegal, K. M. (2014). Prevalence of childhood and adult obesity in the United States, 2011–2012. *Journal of the American Medical Association, 311,* 806–814. doi:10.1001/jama.2014.6228

Ogden, C. L., Lamb, M. M., Carroll, M. D., & Flegal, K. M. (2010). *Obesity and socioeconomic status in children and adolescents: United States, 2005–2008.* Retrieved from http://www.cdc.gov/nchs/data/databriefs/db51.pdf

Osypuk, T. L., & Acevedo-Garcia, D. (2008). Are racial disparities in preterm birth larger in hypersegregated areas? *American Journal of Epidemiology, 167,* 1295–1304. doi:10.1093/aje/kwn043

Pastore, D. R., Juszczak, L., Fisher, M. M., & Friedman, S. B. (1998). School-based health center utilization: A survey of users and nonusers. *Archives of Pediatrics & Adolescent Medicine, 152,* 763–767. doi:10.1001/archpedi.152.8.763

Pastore, D., & Techow, B. (2004). Adolescent school-based health care: A description of two sites in their 20th year of service. *Mount Sinai Journal of Medicine, 71,* 191–196.

Perkins, J., & Singh, D. (2014). ACA litigation continues: A primer of major cases. *Health Advocate: E-Newsletter of the National Health Law Program, 26.* Retrieved from http://www.healthlaw.org/issues/health-care-reform/health-advocate-july-2014#.U9LXhSjEdUQ

Powell, L. M., & Bao, Y. (2009). Food prices, access to food outlets and child weight. *Economics and Human Biology, 7*(1), 64–72. doi:10.1016/j.ehb.2009.01.004

Reuner, G., Hassenpflug, A., Pietz, J., & Philippi, H. (2009). Long-term development of low-risk low birth weight preterm born infants: Neurodevelopmental aspects from childhood to late adolescence. *Early Human Development, 85*, 409–413. doi:10.1016/j.earlhumdev.2009.01.007

Rogers, J. M. (2008). Tobacco and pregnancy: Overview of exposures and effects. *Birth Defects Research Part C: Embryo Today: Reviews, 84*, 1–15. doi:10.1002/bdrc.20119

Rosenbach, M. L., & Gavin, N. I. (1998). Early and periodic screening, diagnosis, and treatment and managed care. *Annual Review of Public Health, 19*, 507–525. doi:10.1146/annurev.publhealth.19.1.507

Rosenbaum, J. E. (2009). Patient teenagers? A comparison of the sexual behavior of virginity pledgers and matched nonpledgers. *Pediatrics, 123*(1), e110–e120. doi:10.1542/peds.2008–0407

Rosenthal, L., & Lobel, M. (2011). Explaining racial disparities in adverse birth outcomes: Unique sources of stress for Black American women. *Social Science & Medicine, 72*, 977–983. doi:10.1016/j.socscimed.2011.01.013

Rounds, K. A. (2004). Preventing sexually transmitted infections among adolescents. In M. W. Fraser (Ed.), *Risk and resilience in childhood: An ecological perspective* (2nd ed., pp. 251–280). Washington, DC: NASW Press.

Salam, M. T., Li, Y. F., Langholz, B., & Gilliland, F. D. (2004). Early-life environmental risk factors for asthma: Findings from the children's health study. *Environmental Health Perspectives, 112*, 760–765. doi:10.1289/ehp.6662

Santelli, J., Kouzis, A., & Newcomer, S. (1996). School-based health centers and adolescent use of primary care and hospital care. *Journal of Adolescent Health, 19*, 267–275. doi:10.1016/S1054-139X(96)00088-2

Sardell, A., & Johnson, K. (1998). The politics of EPSDT policy in the 1990s: Policy entrepreneurs, political streams, and children's health benefits. *Milbank Quarterly, 76*, 175–205. doi:10.1111/1468-0009.00086

School-Based Health Alliance. (n.d.) *Position statement: School-based health centers and the patient-centered medical home.* Retrieved from http://www.sbh4all.org/site/c.ckLQKbOVLkK6E/b.8943407/k.C6F6/PatientCentered_Medical_Home.htm

Senn, T. E., Carey, M. P., & Vanable, P. A. (2008). Childhood and adolescent sexual abuse and subsequent sexual risk behavior: Evidence from controlled studies, methodological critique, and suggestions for research. *Clinical Psychology Review, 28*, 711–735. doi:10.1016/j.cpr.2007.10.002

Sexuality Information and Education Council of the United States. (2012). *A brief history of federal funding for more comprehensive approaches to sex education FY10.* Retrieved from http://www.siecus.org/index.cfm?fuseaction = page.viewPage&pageID = 1341&nodeID = 1

Shi, L., & Singh, D. (2001). *Delivering health care in America: A systems approach* (2nd ed.). Gaithersburg, MD: Aspen.

Shone, L. P., Dick, A. W., Klein, J. D., Zwanziger, J., & Szilagyi, P. G. (2005). Reduction in racial and ethnic disparities after enrollment in the State Children's Health Insurance Program. *Pediatrics, 115*, e697–705. doi:10.1542/peds.2004–1726

Sia, C., Tonniges, T. F., Osterhus, E., & Taba, S. (2004). History of the medical home concept. *Pediatrics, 113*, 1473–1478.

Simpson, W. J. (1957). A preliminary report on cigarette smoking and the incidence of prematurity. *American Journal of Obstetrics and Gynecology, 73*, 808–815.

Soni, A. (2014). *The five most costly children's conditions, 2011: Estimates for the U.S. civilian noninstitutionalized children, ages 0-17.* Retrieved from http://meps.ahrq.gov/mepsweb/data_files/publications/st434/stat434.shtml

Starfield, B. (2008). Access, primary care, and the medical home: Rights of passage. *Medical Care, 46*, 1015–1016. doi:10.1097/MLR.0b013e31817fae3c

Stein, R. E. K. (1997). Changing the lens: Why focus on children's health? In R. E. K. Stein & P. Brooks (Eds.), *Health care for children: What's right, what's wrong, what's next?* (pp. 1–12). New York, NY: United Hospital Fund.

Strickland, B., McPherson, M., Weissman, G., van Dyck, P., Huang, Z. J., & Newacheck, P. (2004). Access to the medical home: Results of the National Survey of Children with Special Health Care Needs. *Pediatrics, 113,* 1485–1492.

Subbarao, P., Mandhane, P. J., & Sears, M. R. (2009). Asthma: Epidemiology, etiology and risk factors. *Canadian Medical Association Journal, 181,* E181–E190. doi:10.1503/cmaj.080612

Sutherland, E. R. (2008). Obesity and asthma. *Immunology and Allergy Clinics of North America, 28,* 589–602. doi:10.1016/j.iac.2008.03.003

Swartz, M. B., & Puhl, R. (2003). Childhood obesity: A societal problem to solve. *Obesity Reviews, 4,* 57–71. doi:10.1046/j.1467-789X.2003.00093.x

Szilagyi, P. G., Schuster, M. A., & Cheng, T. L. (2009). The scientific evidence for child health insurance. *Academic Pediatrics, 9*(1), 4–6. doi:10.1016/j.acap.2008.12.002

Taylor, E. D., Theim, K. R., & Mirch, M. C., (2006). Orthopedic complications of overweight in children and adolescents. *Pediatrics, 117,* 2167–2174. doi:10.1542/peds.2005-1832

Thakur, N., Oh, S. S., Nguyen, E. A., Martin, M., Roth, L. A., Galanter, J., . . . Burchard, E. G. (2013). Socioeconomic status and childhood asthma in urban minority youths. The GALA II and SAGE II Studies. *American Journal of Respiratory and Critical Care Medicine, 188,* 1202–1209. doi:10.1164/rccm.201306-1016OC

Tong, V. T., Dietz, P. M., Morrow, B., D'Angelo, D. V., Farr, S. L., Rockhill, K. M., & England, L. (2013). Trends in smoking before, during, and after pregnancy—Pregnancy risk assessment monitoring system, United States, 40 sites, 2000–2010. Retrieved from http://www.cdc.gov/mmwr/preview/mmwrhtml/ss6206a1.htm?utm_source = rss&utm_medium = rss&utm_campaign = trends-in-smoking-before-during-and-after-pregnancy-pregnancy-risk-assessment-monitoring-system-united-states-40-sites-20002010

U.S. Department of Health and Human Services. (2011). *The Affordable Care Act and the school-based health center capital program.* Retrieved from http://www.hhs.gov/healthcare/facts/factsheets/2011/12/sbhc.html

U.S. Department of Health and Human Services. (n.d.) *Healthy People 2020.* Retrieved from http://healthypeople.gov/2020/topicsobjectives2020/DataDetails.aspx?hp2020id = MICH-30.2

Wang, J., Visness, C. M., Calatroni, A., Gergen, P. J., Mitchell, H. E., & Sampson, H. A. (2009). Effect of environmental allergen sensitization on asthma morbidity in inner-city asthmatic children. *Clinical and Experimental Allergy,39,* 1381–1389. doi:10.1111/j.1365-2222.2009.03225.x

Williams, D. R., Sternthal, M., & Wright, R. J. (2009). Social determinants: Taking the social context of asthma seriously. *Pediatrics, 123,* S174–S184. doi:10.1542/peds.2008-2233H

Workowski, K., & Berman, S. (2010). STD treatment guidelines, 2010. *Morbidity and Mortality Weekly Reports, 59* (RR12), 1–110 Retrieved from http://www.cdc.gov/mmwr/preview/mmwrhtml/rr5912a1.htm

Wu, A. C., Smith, L., Bokhour, B., Hohman, K. H., & Lieu, T. A. (2008). Racial/ethnic variation in parent perceptions of asthma. *Ambulatory Pediatrics, 8*(2), 89–97. doi:10.1016/j.ambp.2007.10.007

ADDITIONAL READING

Center for Leadership Education in Maternal and Child Public Health. (2013). The Affordable Care Act: Goals and mechanisms/Implications of the Affordable Care Act on MCH populations and public health services. *Healthy Generations, 2013*(Fall), 1–40. Available from http://www.epi.umn.edu/mch/wp-content/uploads/2012/05/HG_Fall20132.pdf

Sparks, P. J. (2009). Do biological, sociodemographic, and behavioral characteristics explain racial/ethnic disparities in preterm births? *Social Science & Medicine, 68,* 1667–1675. doi:10.1016/j.socscimed.2009.02.026

Strolin-Goltzman, J. (2010). The relationship between school-based health centers and the learning environment. *Journal of School Health, 80,* 153–159. doi:10.1111/j.1746-1561.2009.00480.x

WEB-BASED RESOURCES

Association of Maternal and Child Health Programs (AMCHP), http://www.amchp.org/

Center for Health and Health Care in Schools, http://www.healthinschools.org

Centers for Disease Control and Prevention, http://www.cdc.gov/

Child Trends DataBank, http://www.childtrendsdatabank.org

Children's Defense Fund (CDF), http://www.childrensdefense.org/policy-priorities/childrens-health/

Families USA, http://www.familiesusa.org

The Future of Children, http://www.futureofchildren.org

Henry J. Kaiser Family Foundation, http://kff.org/health-reform/

March of Dimes, http://www.modimes.org/

Maternal and Child Health Bureau, http://mchb.hrsa.gov/

Maternal and Child Health Information Resource Center, Maternal and Child Health Bureau, http://www.mchb.hrsa.gov/mchirc/

The National Assembly on School Based Health Care, http://www.nasbhc.org/

The Robert Wood Johnson Foundation, http://www.rwjf.org/

CHAPTER 7

Policies and Programs for Children and Youth With Disabilities

Susan L. Parish

Alison W. Saville

Jamie G. Swaine

Leah Igdalsky

Children with disabilities (i.e., conditions producing functional limitations in mobility, self-care, communication, or learning) make up about 13% of the U.S. population between the ages of 5 and 17 years old (U.S. Department of Education, 2013). In addition, many more children younger than 5 years old have impairments of this level of severity. Although the increasing prevalence of childhood disability is well documented (Boyle et al., 2011), the reasons for this increase are not fully understood. Medical and technological advances have enabled more children with disabilities to survive, which has increased the prevalence of these conditions. However, increased public awareness has led to a greater identification of impairments, also contributing to the increased prevalence. The prevalence of disability is higher among African Americans than Whites. Studies attribute racial disparities in disability prevalence to the increased likelihood of African American children living in poverty (e.g., Newacheck, Hung, Park, Brindis, & Irwin, 2003); however, these findings must be substantiated with further research. The prevalence of disability also varies by gender and disability condition. For example, autism is more common among males (Jacquemont et al., 2014), whereas Rett Syndrome is found almost exclusively among females.

Most programs for children with disabilities determine eligibility based on a child's diagnosis or disability category, which may vary over the life course. In addition, how a policy or program defines disability can significantly affect the number of children who are deemed eligible to receive services. In the absence of a uniform definition of disability, children who are eligible for one program based on their diagnosis may not be eligible for another program, even if its mission is to serve children with the same disabilities (Beers, Kemeny, Sherritt, & Palfrey, 2003). Differential eligibility is more noticeable in state-run programs such as maternal and child health services because these services are administered under Title V of the Social Security Act, which gives states substantial latitude in determining program structures and processes (Beers et al., 2003).

Terminology. When a child does not reach expected benchmarks or developmental milestones such as turning over, crawling, walking, or talking, this is referred to as a *developmental delay*. Developmental delays are frequently found in young children before a specific condition is formally diagnosed. These delays may be a temporary or a lifelong condition. *Developmental disabilities* are lifelong impairments that manifest during childhood and result in substantial functional limitations, including intellectual disabilities, autism, cerebral palsy, Down syndrome, and other related disorders. Young adults with one or more of these disorders who are transitioning out of high school are often described as having a developmental disability, which is used as a general diagnostic category.

INCREASING PREVALENCE OF DISABILITY

Medical and technological advances during the latter half of the 20th century substantially improved prenatal and perinatal care and brought about dramatic changes in the survival rates of children born with impairments. For example, between 1990 and 2010, there was a 50% reduction in maternal mortality worldwide (World Health Organization, UNICEF, UNFPA, & The World Bank, 2012). These advances have translated into increased numbers of children with disabilities living into adolescence and adulthood and explain, at least in part, the increasing prevalence of disability among children worldwide.

Children with developmental disabilities often need a lifetime of assistance, including a developmentally appropriate sequence of special services and individualized supports (Developmental Disabilities Assistance and Bill of Rights Act of 2000). Conditions such as autism, sickle cell anemia, cystic fibrosis, and cerebral palsy result in elevated needs for both primary medical care and specialized therapeutic care. To maximize their cognitive, emotional, academic, and physical development, these children may need rehabilitation therapies, environmental adaptations, assistive devices, personal assistance, and mental health, home health, or respite care (Perrin, 2002). Ongoing therapies, specialized interventions, and ancillary and supportive services play a pivotal role in allowing children to maximize their capacity for independence and fully participate in daily activities and community life. Furthermore, ancillary and supportive services such as respite care and other family support services enable parents to care for their children at home rather than seek expensive out-of-home care, which is usually publicly financed (Abelson, 1999; Bruns & Burchard, 2000; Curran, Sharples, White, & Knapp, 2001).

A wide array of policies governs the services that children with disabilities and their families receive. Some policies are designed for children with disabilities (e.g., special education, disability income transfers), and others are designed for a broader population of children (e.g., provision of health-related services to children eligible for Medicaid). Policies directed at families often provide supports intended to reduce out-of-home placements and mitigate the physical, emotional, and financial burdens associated with caring for children with disabilities.

Although the overarching goal of these policies is to enhance development and adaptation, the service system for children with disabilities can best be characterized as fragmented. Numerous organizations control the delivery of services (e.g., local school districts, state disability offices, state or county social service agencies), and revenues typically come from two or more levels of government (i.e., federal, state, county, and/or local). Poor coordination and collaboration across agencies complicate the challenges families face in seeking assistance, and the barriers often seem insurmountable.

In the subsequent sections of this chapter, we review risk and protective factors related to childhood disability and outline the major social policies that have been directed toward children with disabilities and their families. The conceptualization of risk and protection within these policies is examined. Finally, recommendations to promote greater service integration are presented. However, before plunging into these tasks, we briefly describe the theoretical models that guide our analysis.

THREE THEORETICAL FRAMEWORKS

Three theoretical frameworks underpin this chapter: the ecological model, models of risk and protective factors, and the social or minority model of disability. The ecological model espoused by Bronfenbrenner (1979, 1986) posited that individual development occurs and can be understood only within a larger family and social-environmental context. In this model, understanding the interplay of factors at the level of the individual, the family, and the environment is necessary to comprehend what appear to be individual behavior and individual outcomes. Child developmental outcomes arise from the complex interplay of these interwoven elements.

Conceptually, risk and protective factors are those elements that influence the chances of adverse outcomes and optimal development, respectively (Fraser, Kirby, & Smokowski, 2004). We build our analysis from the elaboration of the risk and resilience framework presented by Fraser and his colleagues (2004) and the introductory chapter of this volume. The ecological perspective requires identifying and analyzing risk and protective factors at the levels of the child, the child's family, and the broader society. This analytic scheme is also consistent with recent disability studies that have identified a *social model of disability,* which distinguishes between individual impairment and disability. *Impairment* is an individual's biological condition, whereas *disability* is what accrues to an individual when society's attitudes, expectations, and built environments do not accommodate a full range of human difference. Davis (2000) succinctly described the relationship between disability and impairment:

> Disability is not so much the lack of a sense or the presence of a physical or mental impairment as it is the reception and construction of that difference. . . . An impairment is a physical fact, but a disability is a social construction. For example, lack of mobility is an impairment, but an environment without ramps turns that impairment into a disability. (p. 56)

This social model of disability is entirely consistent with an emancipatory and empowerment perspective. The goal of this chapter, then, is not to understand how individual impairments place children at risk but to evaluate how the larger environment—and especially society's response to impairment, as codified in public policy—increases the risk of adverse development or, alternatively, promotes the optimal development of children with disabilities. We turn first to the risk and protective factors associated with childhood disabilities.

RISK AND PROTECTIVE FACTORS FOR PROBLEMS EXPERIENCED BY CHILDREN WITH DISABILITIES

Risk Factors

In addition to living in poverty, a number of important risk factors are associated with childhood disability, including likelihood of experiencing abuse, social isolation, and ostracism from peers and the larger society, difficulty accessing needed supportive services, and problems obtaining medical care when it is needed.

Poverty and childhood disability status are compellingly related. About 38% of special needs children live in households with incomes below the federal poverty level (Parish, Shattuck, & Rose, 2009), which is a dramatically higher rate than the 22% of all US children who live in poverty (DeNavas-Walt, Proctor, & Smith, 2013). In general, child poverty rates tend to be highest among African American and Hispanic children, and households of any race or ethnicity that are headed by a single parent are much more likely to live in poverty than households headed by married parents (DeNavas-Walt et al., 2013).

The elevated risk of living in poverty for children with disabilities is a phenomenon that has been widely described by researchers and policy analysts, but it is not well understood. Even more disturbing, the prevalence of disability increased between the early 1980s and the mid-1990s among families living in poverty or those headed by a single mother (Fujiura & Yamaki, 2000). Furthermore, family income below the federal poverty level is associated with a higher prevalence of developmental disabilities (Boyle et al., 2011). Causal ambiguity precludes understanding the direction of effects, and further research is needed to determine the nature of the causal relationship between poverty and disability. A case for effects in both directions can be made. Low-income families are less likely to have access to sufficient food, adequate prenatal and other medical care, and decent safe housing, all of which are factors that can be implicated in increasing the risk of childhood disability. However, the extensive care needs of children with disabilities are likely to prohibit their parents from obtaining or maintaining sufficient employment necessary to bring the household out of poverty (Emerson, 2007).

Regardless of the direction of the relationship between poverty and disability, the fact that so many children with disabilities live in poverty has serious implications for their well-being. For children generally, living in poverty is associated with a host of negative consequences, including poor physical health, increased emotional and behavioral problems, diminished cognitive abilities, and reduced educational attainment (Brooks-Gunn & Duncan,

1997; Magnuson & Votruba-Drzal, 2009). However, concern is mounting that poverty is likely to have more deleterious effects for children with disabilities than it does for typically developing children (Park, Turnbull, & Turnbull, 2002). This is because children with disabilities require greater care and stimulation to achieve proper development, prevent regression, and avert the development of secondary conditions.

Costs of Disability

Research into how poverty influences child development is still in its infancy, and it will likely take some time before risk-inducing relationships and their applicability to children with disabilities are clear. We do know that the disability-related costs of raising a child are extremely high in the United States (Stabile & Allin, 2012; Parish, Seltzer, Greenberg, & Floyd, 2004). Families of children with disabilities face unique financial burdens, such as increased therapy costs and home adaptations (Newacheck & Kim, 2005; Parish & Cloud, 2006). These increased costs are particularly burdensome for lower-income families (Lukemeyer, Meyers, & Smeeding, 2000; Parish et al., 2009). Mothers of children with disabilities often have to reduce the number of hours they work or quit work outside the home completely to provide adequate care for their children with special needs (Parish et al., 2004). This phenomenon is subsequently associated with reduced income and lower asset accumulation over time (Parish et al., 2004).

Public income transfer and insurance programs do not cover most disability-related expenses (General Accounting Office, 1999). Impoverished families of children with disabilities have few choices or resources for meeting their child's impairment-related needs (Scorgie, Wilgosh, & McDonald, 1998). Inadequate financial resources are associated with diminished parental ability to cope with the extra health and daily care needs of children with disabilities (Yau & Li-Tsang, 1999). Moreover, evidence suggests that families raising children with disabilities often experience significant hardships (e.g., food insecurity, housing instability, foregone medical care). These hardships and deprivation extend well into the middle-class stratum of families raising children with disabilities; this finding is important because this pattern of hardship is not found among families of nondisabled children (Parish, Rose, Andrews, Grinstein-Weiss, & Richman, 2008).

Generally, poverty has a direct negative influence on maternal behavior and on the quality of parenting (Brooks-Gunn, Klebanov, & Liaw, 1995). We would expect to find similar relationships in the behavior of low-income mothers of children with disabilities; however, this issue has not been studied directly. High rates of abuse and neglect also place children with disabilities at risk. Child abuse is widely recognized as placing victimized children at considerable risk for adverse social, developmental, educational, and behavioral outcomes. Although it is difficult to determine the rates of abuse for the general population (see Chapter 3; Pagelow, 1984), it is even more problematic to ascertain abuse rates for children with disabilities because their impairments in cognitive and language skills make detection of abuse substantially more difficult (Sobsey, 1994). Rates of physical, sexual, and emotional abuse for children with disabilities are significantly higher than those for nondisabled children (Child Welfare Information Gateway, 2012). However, many in the field have argued that this estimate is quite low (Sobsey, 2004), and the U.S. Department of Health and

Human Services reports that 11% of child maltreatment victims have a disability (U.S. Department of Health and Human Services, 2010).

Serious risks to emotional well-being are associated with the social isolation of children with disabilities as well as their encounters with ostracism from peers and the larger society. The history of discriminatory and prejudicial treatment of people with disabilities of all ages is a dismal and pervasive aspect of Western history (Braddock & Parish, 2001). Unfortunately, contemporary reports of children with disabilities have indicated that these attitudes have not materially diminished. There is long-standing evidence that children interact differently with rejected and ignored classmates (Chazan, Laing, Jones, Harper, & Bolton, 1983; Dodge, 1983) and even the youngest children with disabilities experience bullying (Son, Parish & Peterson, 2012). Given these different patterns of interactions, children with disabilities, and particularly those with severe impairments, often have limited opportunities for friendships and integration with their peers.

Social isolation—having few friendships, limited reciprocal relationships, and minimal peer interactions—follows children with disabilities from early childhood into adolescence and adulthood (Keogh & Bernheimer, 1987; Keogh, Bernheimer, & Guthrie, 2004; Matheson, Olsen, Weisner, & Dykens, 2007). Although the long-term effects of this isolation have not been widely studied in children with disabilities, in general, children's social skills, networks, and relationships predict later adjustment (Kupersmidt, Coie, & Dodge, 1990; Meyer, Cole, McQuarter, & Reichle, 1990). In addition, childhood disability is associated with negative personal and employment outcomes (Edgar & Levine, 1987; Sitlington, Frank, & Carson, 1992; Whitney-Thomas & Moloney, 2001). Moreover, adolescents and children with disabilities express great dissatisfaction related to their lack of friends and social integration (Keogh et al., 2004).

Evidence has converged to indicate that parents encounter ongoing stress and family disruption over the life course of caring for their children with disabilities (e.g., Farber, 1960; Turnbull, Brotherson, & Summers, 1986; Williamson & Perkins, 2014). These stresses may result from the child's behavior problems, nighttime disturbance caused by the child's care needs, social isolation, family chaos, multiple child impairments, chronic ill health, and financial concerns (Singer & Irvin, 1989). However, compelling evidence also exists that parents who cope well with their child's needs enhance the child's cognitive and social adjustment and minimize further family disruption and distress (Bourke-Taylor, Pallant, Law, & Howie, 2012; Crnic, Friedrich, & Greenberg, 1983; Landesman, Jaccard, & Gunderson, 1989; Summers, Behr, & Turnbull, 1989). Successful parental adaptation and coping contributes to what is arguably the most critical protective factor related to childhood disability: strong parental support.

Parental support for children with disabilities takes a number of forms across childhood and often into adulthood. Because of the nature and organization of disability policy in the United States, parents are compelled to serve both as their child's advocate and as the child's case manager. When parents aggressively champion their child's needs, the child is much more likely to receive the services and supports to which he or she is entitled. Parental support also bolsters the child's self-esteem, creating resilience to the rejection that most children with disabilities encounter from peers and society.

A closely related protective factor is the competence and mastery that parents develop as their child ages; these capacities are gained through surmounting the adversity that they face in securing services for their child and in coming to terms with their child's impairment. For parents of young children with disabilities, a common developmental trajectory begins at the point of diagnosis with mourning for the nondisabled child they had anticipated. After this mourning period, most parents report increasing levels of satisfaction with their caregiving abilities and identify their caregiving role as a positive part of their self-identity. However, over the course of their child's development, parents might revisit grief and depression during transition periods (e.g., entry into kindergarten, high school graduation). For some parents, these transition points represent jarring reminders that the child's impairment has altered his or her developmental trajectory. Even so, parents also overwhelmingly report that their children with disabilities contribute emotionally, socially, and intellectually to the richness of family life (Summers et al., 1989; Trute & Hiebert-Murphy, 2002).

Protective Factors

Research on protective and promotive factors associated with childhood disability is far more limited. The most likely explanation for this deficit is that the medical model of disability that prevailed for much of the 20th century still informs policy and services for children with disabilities. The most important protective factors associated with childhood disability are those that emerge from the family and community context: parental competence as advocates, case managers, and caregivers for their children; supportive networks of peers, extended families, and communities; inclusion in activities of daily life and community life; and adequate and available medical, educational, and financial resources to enable parents to provide appropriate care for their children.

Extrafamilial protective factors include supportive schools, faith-based organizations such as churches or synagogues, and communities, as well as adequate levels of family support services, including support from disability and advocacy organizations that address the needs of children with disabilities and their families. Having sufficient and appropriate supports available is a critical factor in helping parents positively adapt to their child's disability (Ha, Greenberg, & Seltzer, 2011; Singer & Irvin, 1989). The policies that structure such supports are discussed in the next section. However, little research has been conducted investigating the mechanisms by which these risk and protective factors directly affect children with disabilities and their families. Although limited, some evidence supports our hypothesis that these protective factors (parental and other supports, responsive public policies, nurturing communities) are directly involved in building resilience among children with disabilities (McConnell, Savage, & Breitkreuz, 2014).

In summary, the life circumstances and development of children with disabilities are shaped by risk and protective factors that emerge from the environments in which these children live. These environmental factors emerge from within the family, the community, and the larger society and are manifested in the public policies that contribute to different facets of child and family life. Table 7.1 summarizes these significant factors.

Table 7.1   Risk and Protective Factors for Problems Experienced by Children With Disabilities

Risk Factors	Protective Factors
Poverty	Parental competence as advocates, case managers, and caregivers
Increased abuse and neglect	Supportive peer networks, extended families, and communities
Social isolation	Inclusion in community life and activities
Difficulty obtaining supportive services and medical care	Adequate medical, financial, and educational resources to enable parents to meet their children's needs
Ostracism by community and peers	

RISK, RESILIENCE, AND PROTECTION IN POLICIES FOR CHILDREN WITH DISABILITIES

Over the course of the last century, extraordinary changes occurred in policies for children with disabilities. At the outset of the 20th century, policy was organized at the state level and provided limited custodial care in segregated institutions to the exclusion of nearly all other services. Beginning in the 1930s, small-scale experimental programs in extra-institutional long-term care were implemented in New York and Ohio, but this approach did not take hold nationally. In response to the lack of services for children with disabilities, parents began organizing their own educational systems for their special-needs children, and by the early 1940s, fledgling parent advocacy groups had been established. Parent advocacy had a lasting impact on the service system and ultimately exerted greater influence than any other force over the shape of services for children with disabilities (Braddock & Parish, 2001).

Over the past four decades, assertive and effective advocacy by parents of children with disabilities has precipitated the development of policies that support services tailored to the individual needs of the child with disabilities and meet the needs of the entire family (Braddock & Parish, 2001). In addition, in the decades since the 1970s, parent advocacy culminated in the closure of hundreds of custodial institutions across the United States and led to the 1975 passage of legislation mandating education for children with disabilities. As parents emerged as champions for their children with disabilities, adult activists with disabilities also began to demand their civil rights, following the trail blazed by African American leaders in the civil rights movement.

These enormous changes resulted in two significant transformations. First, the service system, particularly in education and long-term care, began to reject the prevailing medical model, which held that individuals with disabilities were inherently defective and in need of professional cures. As noted previously, supporters of the social model of disability argued for the thorough inclusion of people with disabilities in all aspects of society, one that accommodates the full range of human differences. Advocacy by those with disabilities and their allies ultimately contributed to the successful passage of the Americans with

Disabilities Act of 1990, which prohibits discrimination in public settings and requires employers to accommodate people with disabilities (Braddock & Parish, 2001).

A second major transformation was the federal government's entry into the service and policy arena for children with disabilities, which began on a large scale in the 1970s. Even when the Social Security Act of 1935 was passed, the federal government's role was minimal and limited to funding supports or services for people with disabilities (i.e., money allocated through Title X of the act provided limited income transfers to the blind). The only exceptions to federal noninvolvement were income transfer and vocational rehabilitation provisions for veterans. For children with disabilities, the federal government continued its role of noninvolvement through much of the 20th century. However, the federal role changed in the 1970s when Medicaid was amended to allow federal reimbursement for medical and long-term care services for children and adults with mental retardation; federal law mandated education of children with disabilities, and the disability income transfer program (Supplemental Security Income [SSI]) was expanded to cover children.

These policy transformations evolved concurrently with practice changes. Consistent with the medical model of disability, which was strongly followed at the beginning of the 20th century, people with disabilities were considered deviants, and social policy responded with segregation and sterilization to prevent a perceived group of undesirables from procreating. Through most of that century, negative attitudes toward people with disabilities prevailed, and practice models encouraged parents to institutionalize young children with disabilities, surrendering them to warehouse-like facilities that provided rudimentary care (Braddock & Parish, 2001). As attitudes toward people with disabilities shifted, a civil and human rights perspective emerged, and practices began shifting to focus on supporting parents in providing at home care for their children with disabilities (Braddock & Parish, 2001).

At the outset of the 21st century, a number of disparate public policies influenced children with disabilities and their families. We describe key federal policies that address income support, education and early intervention, maternal and child health services, and family support. Medical care, which is also critically important for children with disabilities, is discussed in Chapter 6 of this volume.

Income Transfers

Children with disabilities and their families can receive income transfer payments through several different programs: initiatives designed specifically for people with disabilities and initiatives designed for low-income people in general. The two major disability income transfer programs in the United States are Social Security Disability Insurance and Supplemental Security Income (SSI). The disability insurance program targets workers who become disabled (and their dependents), and the program is not a major source of income for children with disabilities. In contrast, SSI stipulates provision of assistance specifically for children with disabilities. Generally, the largest cash assistance program for low-income families is the Temporary Assistance to Needy Families (TANF) program, the nation's welfare program, which states administer and jointly fund with the federal government.

SSI is a means-tested, monthly income program for the elderly and people with disabilities. The program is federally financed and administered, although some states supplement federal payments and a few states administer their own programs directly. Children with disabilities have received SSI since the program's inception in 1972 (Social Security Administration [SSA], 2000). Eligibility is based on the child's functional limitations and on parental income and assets relative to family size. For example, in 2014, a single child with disabilities living in a two-parent home could receive SSI payments if parental household income did not exceed $4,092 per month.

A total of 1.3 million children with disabilities younger than 18 years of age received SSI benefits in October 2012 (Ruffing & Pavetti, 2012). For 2012, the average monthly SSI benefit payment for children was $615 (Ruffing & Pavetti, 2012), which translates to an annual rate of $7,380. In 2014, the federal poverty threshold was $11,670 for one person (U.S. Department of Health and Human Services, 2014). Therefore, the SSI payment level for one individual was 37% below the federal poverty level. Although nearly 26% of children receiving SSI still live below the federal poverty level (Grad, 2000), the SSI program plays a vital role in reducing the extent of poverty experienced by these children. Two thirds of SSI beneficiaries receive at least half of their total income from SSI; Social Security benefits are responsible for reducing the poverty gap for SSI recipients by an average of 60% (Grad, 2000). Although the level of support provided by SSI is limited, reduced poverty for many children with disabilities and their families is an important protective factor.

However, the protective benefits of SSI have been eroded by the Personal Responsibility and Work Opportunity Reconciliation Act (PRWORA) of 1996. PRWORA catalyzed important changes in SSI for children with disabilities by constricting child SSI eligibility rules. Following new guidelines for eligibility, SSI retrenchment associated with PRWORA had dire consequences for children with disabilities and their families. Between 1996 and 2000, the number of child SSI beneficiaries with mental retardation declined by nearly 22% (or 76,000 individuals) and declined by 12% for children with all other disabilities (Parish, 2003). To compensate for the loss of their children's SSI income, some parents entered the workforce or increased their work hours (Inkelas, Rowe, Karoly, & Rogowski, 1999). However, increased work activity did not prevent total income from declining for most families, some of whom had to seek other forms of public assistance to compensate for the loss of SSI benefits (Davies, Iams, & Rupp, 2000; Inkelas et al., 1999).

Low-income families of children with disabilities can also receive income transfers through TANF, which was reauthorized by the Deficit Reduction Act of 2005. TANF, which replaced the earlier welfare program, Aid to Families with Dependent Children (AFDC), represented a major policy shift in public assistance. Under AFDC, parents raising children with disabilities were generally exempted from work requirements, whereas TANF requires participants to be involved in either work or job training; TANF also limits receipt of cash benefits to a lifetime maximum of 60 months (Thompson, Holcomb, Loprest, & Brennan, 1998). When Congress was debating the PRWORA legislation, the National Commission on Childhood Disability (1995) recommended exempting one parent of a child with disabilities from mandatory work requirements, excluding parents from being removed from welfare for 2 years following a child's termination from SSI, and prohibiting states from counting children's SSI benefits when assessing families' welfare eligibility. However, these recommendations were rejected in the final version of PRWORA. Current TANF policies allow states to exempt a parent caring for a family member with a disability from working if the person with a disability is living at home and is not a full-time student; however, states also have the discretion to establish more strict work participation rules than those set by the federal legislation (Parrott et al., 2007). Recent analyses have found that TANF has had a limited effect on low-income mothers of children with disabilities. Although TANF's stated purposes included increasing marriage and employment to reduce welfare reliance, evaluation of the program's effects show limited employment gains, no marriage increases, and no reduction in overall welfare use among low-income mothers of children with disabilities (Parish, Rose, & Andrews, 2010).

A real and urgent need exists for policies that accommodate the responsibilities of parents caring for children with disabilities. First, these parents face many barriers to maintaining employment, including children's ongoing and episodic needs for affordable and appropriate care (Rosman, McCarthy, & Woolverton, 2001; Shearn & Todd, 2000). In addition, low-income families, which are overrepresented among those raising children with disabilities, pay for most child care out-of-pocket; child care for children with disabilities is more expensive than routine child care, and the burden of these costs contributes substantially to the poverty of these families (Lukemeyer et al., 2000; Meyers, Han, Waldfogel, & Garfinkel, 2001; Meyers & Heintze, 1999). The elevated care needs of children with disabilities and the extraordinary caregiving responsibilities assumed by their parents place these parents at elevated risk of unemployment and underemployment, both of which are directly associated with family poverty (Parish et al., 2004; Lichter & Eggebeen, 1994).

The system of income transfers in the United States provides critical support to children with disabilities and their families. These programs directly address the increased risk of living in poverty for children with disabilities and attempt, albeit in a limited way, to ameliorate the high costs of raising children with disabilities. Although SSI alone does not provide sufficient resources to raise family income above the federal poverty level, its provisions are important protective factors for the thousands of families who receive it.

EDUCATION AND EARLY INTERVENTION

The Individuals with Disabilities Education Act (IDEA) began as the Education for All Handicapped Children Act of 1975 (PL 94-142) and gave all children with disabilities the right to a free and appropriate public education. This watershed civil rights law resulted from sustained advocacy by parents of children with disabilities. IDEA was reauthorized in 2004 under the Individuals with Disabilities Education Improvement Act (IDEIA).

Special education has been shaped by the six core principles that formed the nucleus of the Education for All Handicapped Children Act:

1. Zero reject means schools cannot exclude any children with disabilities from instruction.

2. Nondiscriminatory evaluation guarantees every child an individualized, culturally and linguistically appropriate evaluation before being placed in special education.

3. Individualized Education Plans (IEPs) delineate current performance, progress on past objectives, goals and services for the school year, and evaluation of outcomes.

4. Least restrictive environment describes the goal that children with disabilities are educated to the extent possible in settings with children without disabilities.

5. Due process codifies the legal steps to ensure school fairness and accountability in meeting a child's needs and how parents can obtain relief via a hearing or second opinions.

6. Parental participation gives parents the right to access their child's education records and participate in IEP planning. (Adapted from Kirk, Gallagher, & Anastasiow, 1993, pp. 51–52.)

These principles have remained fixtures of the act since its initial passage in 1975. However, the act has also changed over the years in response to litigation and reauthorizing statutes. We will describe least restrictive environment, IEPs, and some of the issues that have emerged, including school district responsibility to fund and provide needed services, procedures to plan for a child's transition out of school, and reliance on parents to serve as advocates for their children.

Least Restrictive Environment

The notion of least restrictive environment exists to ensure that children are served in inclusive and integrated settings and are not segregated from typically developing peers. However, because this is a recommendation and not a requirement of IDEA, there is great variability among school districts in the proportion of children with disabilities who are educated in inclusive settings. Furthermore, parents and teachers have reported mixed feelings about mainstreaming children with disabilities into least restrictive environments. Although regular education teachers generally support mainstreaming, their endorsement appears to deteriorate when they address their own willingness to include children with disabilities in their classrooms (Scruggs & Mastropieri, 1996). Moreover, teachers often are ill equipped or unwilling to adequately include children with special needs in classroom activities. Concerns about mainstreaming are common to parents whether raising children with or without disabilities. Some parents of typically developing children fear mainstreaming will mean that time will be taken away from their children's learning experiences, and some parents of children with disabilities fear their children will not receive the level of attention available in segregated classes (Rallis & Anderson, 1994). Despite this controversy, many agree that mainstreaming is critical for children with disabilities because it allows them to develop interpersonal and life skills and concurrently allows children without disabilities to learn to accept those with disabilities (Osborne & Dimattia, 1994).

Individualized Education Plans

The IEP is a legal document developed for each student with a disability. The IEP is developed by a multidisciplinary team, including the student, his or her parents, teachers, social workers, speech and physical therapists, psychologists, and other support people as necessary given the child's needs. The IEP is intended to ensure that the child receives an appropriate education in the least restrictive environment. It is a malleable document that is supposed to be revised annually, or more often if the child's needs change. IEPs address current educational performance levels, goals, services to support mainstreaming, and other considerations warranted by the child's particular abilities and needs (Sopko, 2003). Although IEPs were mandated by IDEIA and its IDEA forerunner, parents and teachers recognize numerous barriers in developing appropriate IEPs for children with disabilities. For example, IEPs take considerable time and skill to develop and involve varying perceptions and attitudes about interpretations of inclusion and the responsibilities of educators (Sopko, 2003).

Since 1997, IEPs have been required to include plans for the transition from school to adult life. This mandate was passed in response to overwhelming evidence of negative outcomes for children with disabilities who left high school. The goal of transition planning is to enable children with disabilities to become active and productive citizens by helping them bridge the distance between closely supervised, sheltered educational settings and the less-structured adult world. School districts can begin including transition planning in a child's IEP as early as age 14 years. Transition plans should address instruction, community involvement, employment, and other adult life objectives and should incorporate the child's individual interests and preferences (Sopko, 2003).

Although IDEIA guarantees children with disabilities the right to a free appropriate public education, there is frequent disagreement between parents and professionals regarding what constitutes an appropriate education. Schools often contest the education and support services requested by parents, and challenges are more common when school districts are asked to provide related services such as transportation, assistive technology, and medical services to assist children in obtaining an education (Katsiyannis & Yell, 2000).

Expensive health services for students with chronic health problems are often among the most controversial issues. The U.S. Supreme Court ruling in *Cedar Rapids Community School District v. Garret F.* (1999) required the school district to provide a specially trained nurse as part of a child's special education plan when having the nurse available was necessary for the child's participation in school (Katsiyannis & Yell, 2000). This ruling was an important victory for children whose impairments necessitate ongoing medical care. For all children with disabilities, this ruling represents a clear statement from the Supreme Court that schools are responsible for the provision of needed ancillary and supportive services.

Extensive litigation surrounding IDEIA and ongoing challenges by schools to the rights of children with disabilities has created a system in which parents must be assertive advocates. The burden parents undertake in being their child's advocates and the level of sophistication and resources they must bring to bear to secure their child's education are considerable. Part of the parental role in IEP planning is to safeguard their child's educational rights, which engenders an inherently adversarial relationship between parents and schools. Parents are expected to be active members of their child's IEP team (NICHCY, 2010). Although this expectation that parents will be vigorous advocate for their children has produced important outcomes such as the *Garret F.* decision, it is unrealistic and unreasonable to expect all parents to be effective advocates. Many parents, and particularly low-income parents, lack the educational and financial resources to effectively champion their children's needs. Children with disabilities who lack a resourceful parent-advocate may be denied their right to an education.

The second part of IDEIA that is critically important for children with disabilities is early intervention, which aims to provide prevention and treatment services to improve cognitive, social, and emotional development of children younger than 3 years old. Children may receive early intervention services if they are considered either at risk for delayed development or have been identified as having a developmental disability (NICHCY, 2014). Early intervention services have long been recognized as important for helping children with disabilities achieve their developmental potential. Best practices for early intervention programs involve a range of family-centered services that focus on meeting the needs of the child within the context of his or her family and larger environment. For example, in the course of early intervention, parents may be referred to job assistance or adult education and may receive assistance in obtaining housing and health care.

The philosophy undergirding early intervention is grounded in the concepts of protective and promotive factors. Ideally, early intervention services promote well-being and optimal development by providing comprehensive community-based support services to help improve developmental outcomes. Even young children with disabilities are at risk of developing further complications that may exacerbate their impairments or cause secondary conditions (Zipper & Simeonsson, 2004). Early intervention in the United States has been structured by a federal mandate since 1986, when Part H (now Part C) was added to the Education for All Handicapped Children Act, mandating the provision of early intervention services (PL 99-457). The act's early intervention mandate is to provide comprehensive services to families of children from birth to age 3 (Richmond & Ayoub, 1993).

When possible, early intervention services should be provided in the most appropriate natural setting, which includes the home or other community setting. The emphasis on community-based intervention is intended to promote children's integration and inclusion in their home communities (Graham & Bryant, 1993). Between 2003 and 2004, about 80% of early intervention programs were provided in children's homes (U.S. Department of Education, 2009). Broad-based early intervention services are essential for the cognitive, social, and emotional development of young children (e.g., NECTAC, 2011).

Multidisciplinary supports and programs scaffold the early intervention system, including audiology services, nutrition, family training and counseling, social work, physical and occupational therapy, and services providing assistive technology devices. At a minimum, states must identify infants and toddlers who are deemed to be at risk for or who already have identified developmental delays. Among other requirements, states are required to obtain Individualized Family Service Plans and provide data collection methods and evaluation procedures. When a child enters early intervention, assessments are conducted of child and family strengths and risk factors (Ramey & Ramey, 1998). Parents and professionals collaboratively develop the Individualized Family Service Plan, which addresses the child and family as a unit (Ramey & Ramey, 1998). This collaborative effort is important for adequately assessing risk and protective factors within the family structure and larger social environment.

Despite higher rates of disability and poverty among African American and Hispanic children, non-Hispanic White children are more likely to receive early intervention services than their peers (U.S. Department of Education, 2009). The disparity represents problems minority families face in accessing early intervention services and are not indicative of decreased need. After age 6, the likelihood that an African American child is enrolled in services increases as the child moves from early intervention into special education.

However, Hispanic children remain less likely to receive needed services than children from other racial/ethnic groups (U.S. Department of Education, 2009). The reasons for this trend are not fully understood and warrant further investigation.

TITLE V OF THE SOCIAL SECURITY ACT: MATERNAL AND CHILD HEALTH

Title V of the Social Security Act, also known as the Maternal and Child Health Services Block Grant, is a federal–state partnership program that is aimed at improving the health of all mothers and children. Title V is not an entitlement program, and eligibility criteria and how and what programs are funded vary widely across states (Beers et al., 2003; Maternal and Child Health Bureau, n.d.; Rosenbaum, Proser, Schneder, & Sonosky, 2002). Title V provides funds to states as block grants that allow the states autonomy to determine how to spend funds within general guidelines and goals. For every $4 in federal funds for the program, states are expected to spend $3 in matching funds. In general, states allocate funds to four levels of services:

- direct health-care services, such as health services for children with special health-care needs;

- enabling services, such as transportation, respite care, and health education;

- population-based services, such as newborn screening and immunization; and

- infrastructure building services, such as policy development, training, and applied research. (U.S. Department of Health and Human Services, 2008)

In fiscal year 2009, the total budget for the Federal–State Partnership Block Grant exceeded $5 billion. Of that money, almost 50% was earmarked for children with special health-care needs, which includes children with disabilities. However, there was a great deal of variation among states in spending their Title V budgets on children with special health-care needs, ranging from 6% in Illinois to 83% in California. States also varied in what level of service they chose to fund. For example, Tennessee allocated more than 72% of its total budget to direct health services, whereas Missouri allocated only 4% of its budget for such services (Maternal and Child Health Bureau, n.d.).

FAMILY SUPPORT

Families bear the greatest responsibility for caring for children with disabilities, and parents constitute the largest group of care providers (Hogan & Msall, 2002). Family support services are often provided over a child's life course and include respite care, environmental adaptations, assistive devices, personal assistance, mental health, and crisis intervention. These supports enable families to care for their children with disabilities at home rather than seek out-of-home care (Bruns & Burchard, 2000; Curran et al., 2001). In addition, these supports play a significant role in reducing the burden and stress associated with caring for children with disabilities at home (Floyd & Gallagher, 1997; Freedman & Boyer, 2000; Haveman, van Berkum, Reijinder, & Heller, 1997), and they help families obtain services for unmet needs (Heller, Miller, & Hsieh, 1999).

Despite the extent of care that families provide for their children with disabilities, none of the states provide any more than a meager level of family support. For example, spending for family support services to serve both children and adults with developmental disabilities and their families totaled just less than $2 billion in 2004; this was far short of the $39 billion spent for the entire developmental disabilities service system in all the states (Rizzolo, Hemp, & Braddock, 2006). Family support services across the United States are usually jointly financed by the federal and state governments, often using Medicaid resources that are typically administered by state or county governments. Levels of funding dedicated for family support and the types of services available vary greatly between the states (Parish, Pomeranz, & Braddock, 2003).

Even families who receive support services encounter difficulty in obtaining all the services they need to care for children with disabilities. Freedman and Boyer (2000) found that supports, such as respite care, demonstrably enhanced family well-being and were critically important to families. However, barriers to securing needed support services include a lack of flexibility in the types and frequency of services families received, and critical access difficulties, such as services being unavailable when they were most needed (Freedman & Boyer, 2000).

We have reviewed the major public policies that influence the lives of children with disabilities and their families in the United States: income transfers, education, early intervention, and family supports. Considerable variation exists in the extent to which knowledge of risk and resilience has informed the development of these policies. However, despite contention about their effectiveness, these policies are significant in the lives of children with disabilities and their families. The policies are contributing—although not yet optimally—to promoting child development and the successful adjustment of children with disabilities. Table 7.2 provides an overview of these policies and their features.

USING KNOWLEDGE OF RISK, PROTECTION, AND RESILIENCE TO ACHIEVE SERVICE INTEGRATION IN DISABILITIES POLICY

Two features define policies related to children with disabilities: (1) the reliance on parents to be advocates, case managers, and caregivers for their children; and (2) the fragmentation of policy across service domains. Parents are expected to have a central role in providing care for their children from the point of diagnosis to entry into early intervention, to obtaining support services, to enrolling in the education system, and through transition planning and beyond. In some policies, this parental role is explicit: early intervention programs have for decades embraced collaboration between parents and professionals, and the partnership has long been regarded as a best practice for infants, toddlers, and preschoolers with disabilities (Blue-Banning, Summers, Frankland, Nelson, & Beegle, 2004).

However, many parents lack the time, knowledge, and financial and emotional resources required to be full or effective partners in this endeavor. Within the formal education system,

Table 7.2 Major Policy Approaches Related to Children and Youth With Disabilities

	Income Transfers	Education	Early Intervention	Family Support	Maternal and Child Health (Title V)
Policy Authority	Temporary Assistance to Needy Families (TANF); Personal Responsibility and Work Opportunity Reconciliation Act of 1996 (federal); Supplemental Security Income benefits: Social Security Act, amended 1972 (federal)	Education for All Handicapped Children Act of 1975; replaced by Individuals with Disabilities Education Act (IDEA)	Part H added to Education for All Handicapped Children Act in 1986; replaced by Part C	Varies by state; federal Medicaid funds available to states through Home and Community Based Services Waiver (authorized by the Omnibus Budget Reconciliation Act of 1981)	Social Security Act of 1935; converted to a federal Maternal and Child Health block grant through the Omnibus Budget Reconciliation Act of 1981
Funding	TANF: State and federal; SSI: federal	Local and state; limited federal funding	Local and state; limited federal funding	State; Medicaid programs financed jointly by federal and state	State and federal
Core Features	TANF: time-limited cash assistance to low-income families; work requirements for parents; SSI: monthly payments to low-income children; eligibility based on child disability and family income	Children with disabilities entitled to free, appropriate public education in least restrictive environment; Individualized Education Plan (IEP) guides child's education; parents serve as advocates	Children with disabilities and possible developmental delays eligible to receive services to promote their development; Individualized Family Service Plan guides services to entire family	Varies by state; some states offer cash to families; others offer services like respite, parent support groups, etc.; eligibility requirements and breadth/depth of services vary by state	Aims to improve health of all mothers and children; services and eligibility vary by state; major services funded include direct health, enabling, population-based, and infrastructure building services

IDEIA has established ground rules through which parents can enter an adversarial role with their children's schools to obtain needed services. Parents speak poignantly of their advocacy at every step of their child's development to ensure that needed services are secured. Although over time sustained advocacy often helps parents become masters in navigating bureaucracies and securing services, such efforts are by no means the optimal way for children with disabilities to obtain what they need. Parents face enough stress in meeting their children's physical and emotional care needs and should not also have to fulfill roles as advocates and case managers.

Fragmentation of services remains an ongoing challenge for children with disabilities. Often, to obtain the services their children need, parents must navigate numerous different bureaucracies, with separate institutions governing income transfers, early intervention and education, family support, and medical care. All of these programs have different eligibility criteria, paperwork requirements, definitions of disability, revenue sources, and administrative entities. Despite considerable redundancy requiring parents to "prove" that their child has an impairment, streamlined applications or coordination across providers typically does not exist.

Juanita: A Case Example

To further illustrate the fragmentation and parental advocacy that are hallmarks of disability policy, we considered the experiences of a young girl, Juanita, who has cerebral palsy and intellectual disabilities. Cerebral palsy is a nonprogressive group of chronic conditions that results from a brain injury, which affects muscle coordination and motor development. Cerebral palsy was formerly included in the category of mental retardation, although cerebral palsy does not always include intellectual disabilities. Intellectual disabilities are characterized as below-average intelligence.

Juanita

Juanita is a 9-year-old who lives with her mother. Juanita's father has not had contact with the family since the girl's diagnosis with cerebral palsy at 20 months of age. Their extended family lives out of state. Juanita was slower than other young children to reach developmental milestones, and her pediatrician's referral to a neurologist established the diagnosis for cerebral palsy. Juanita was in a center-based early intervention program until she entered public school. Juanita is in a self-contained classroom with other children with disabilities, but her mother would prefer for her to be mainstreamed into a regular education classroom. Juanita walks with crutches, has difficulty grasping objects, and has limited speech that is difficult to understand. She is incontinent. She is very friendly and outgoing and is well liked by her teacher, classmates, and other children in her neighborhood. She has a great sense of humor and likes to tell jokes. Juanita's mother has a close relationship with one neighbor, but this neighbor is not comfortable providing child care for Juanita. Juanita's mother has had to limit her work to part-time employment because she cannot find afterschool care for Juanita, and she must drive and accompany Juanita to frequent medical appointments. Juanita's father does not pay child support, and because her mother's income is low, Juanita qualifies for monthly SSI payments and Medicaid. Over the past few years, when her mother's income temporarily increased because of work bonuses, Juanita's SSI benefits were reevaluated and terminated. Although her mother appealed those termination decisions, the appeals process took several weeks in each case. The appeals process is confusing, and Juanita's mother was not aware that she could ask for aid pending the outcome of the appeals.

Juanita's current IEP recommends only one specialized service, which is speech therapy that she receives in a group setting with several other classmates. Juanita's earlier IEP had also recommended physical therapy, but those services were discontinued 2 years ago when her IEP team, with the exception of her mother, decided the therapy was no longer necessary because she had made limited progress. Since that time, Juanita's physical functioning has deteriorated, but the IEP team rejected her mother's initial appeal to have the physical therapy put back into her IEP. Her mother wants to pursue this appeal further but needs to learn how to initiate further appeals.

During her early childhood, Juanita had a number of orthopedic surgeries to increase her physical functioning. Although she has Medicaid, the only health-care providers in the region who accept Medicaid are in a county clinic. Because of the practice structure of the county clinic, Juanita and her mother always have lengthy waits for care, and she usually sees different providers at each visit. Juanita needs adaptive devices to help her manipulate tools and independently complete activities of daily living (e.g., feeding, personal hygiene). To give Juanita greater independence in self-care, her mother has applied through the clinic's pediatrician for a number of these devices. Medicaid has denied these applications, but her mother is appealing those decisions. Medicaid does not cover the cost of Juanita's diapers, which are expensive. The mother has also applied for a cash subsidy to cover the cost of purchasing the adaptive devices Juanita needs, but she was told that she is ineligible because the household income is too high.

Juanita's mother contacted the regional office of the state's developmental disabilities department to request respite services. She would like to use the respite services for Juanita's afterschool care so she could work more hours. Although she has completed the application, it cannot be submitted until the clinic pediatrician finalizes the paperwork certifying Juanita's disability. Even if the application is approved, Juanita will be placed on the waiting list. The regional office told the mother the wait for respite services averages 18 months, and once services are available, she will be eligible to receive a maximum of 10 hours respite care a month. After receiving respite services for 1 year, she will again be wait-listed so that other families can receive the respite service. Given the long wait, Juanita's mother is anxious to get the application submitted. However, over the past 2 months, she has called the clinic weekly to check on the pediatrician's progress with this paperwork, but it has not yet been completed. No one has given her a reason for the delay.

Juanita and her mother's situation, like so many others, illustrates the complexity involved in navigating a fragmented and unresponsive service delivery system.

Policy Recommendations

Children with disabilities and their families are protected by policies that are designed to enhance family functioning and to provide services and therapies that maximize independence and inclusion in society. At present, family support and early intervention are based on principles of risk and protective factors. Special education was developed within a civil rights framework: Children with disabilities were entitled to the same educational opportunities as their nondisabled peers. Like SSI payments for children, special education offers some protective benefits, but such benefits are limited in scope. On balance, the accrued benefits do not mitigate the risks associated with childhood disability.

The limited availability of family support services across the United States translates into few benefits for most families. The model of early intervention, in which service provision is driven by collaborative parent–professional partnerships, has much to offer the broader arena of disability policy for children. In this model, the focus is the whole family rather than just the child with disabilities, and the goal is to meet the needs of the whole family across a spectrum of domains. Compelled by a single Individualized Family Support Plan (IFSP), care and services are typically coordinated to meet the full constellation of family needs. Our central policy recommendation is related to using an IFSP model to integrate and coordinate services across all service and support domains. Expanding the rubric of the IFSP to include family support services from all funding sources, including income transfers and Medicaid, would minimize the avenues and channels parents must navigate to obtain the services a child needs and to which he or she may be entitled. A "one-stop shopping" approach would also reduce the fragmentation in services and create a cohesive service structure. If the IFSP model were incorporated in children's education plans, a holistic framework of serving children with disabilities within the context of their families would replace the current fractured focus on child deficits and skills.

SUMMARY

We have described five of the major policies that influence the well-being of children with disabilities and their families: (1) income transfers, (2) education, (3) early intervention, (4) Title V Maternal and Child Health Services, and (5) family support services. We have shown that these policies place a burden on parents to function as advocates and case managers, and, more broadly, that the services produced by these policies function in similar ways but have inherent differences.

Understanding and accessing programs is difficult because of the lack of communication between systems, different eligibility criteria, and an array of separate (and competing) revenue sources. Although concepts of risk and protective factors are fundamental in early intervention and family support policies, they are applied in very limited ways to education and income transfer policies. In addition, family support is so inadequately funded that it has little meaning or impact for most families raising children with disabilities. Therefore, our final recommendations stem from a desire to enable families to meet the care needs of their children, at a minimum. To accomplish this objective, early intervention must be fully funded, and funding for family support and income transfers should be increased to meet the true needs of low-income families.

QUESTIONS FOR DISCUSSION

1. What are the implications of categorically based eligibility criteria for efforts to integrate policies for children with developmental disabilities with other child and family policies?

2. What policy changes would you recommend to better provide an integrated service delivery system for children and youth with developmental disabilities and their families?

3. How will the transition away from a medical model of disability to a social model of disability influence the delivery of services for children and youth with developmental disabilities and their families in the coming decades?

REFERENCES

Abelson, A. G. (1999). Respite care needs of parents of children with developmental disabilities. *Focus on Autism & Other Developmental Disabilities, 14,* 96–101. doi:10.1177/108835769901400204

Beers, N., Kemeny, A., Sherritt, L., & Palfrey, J. (2003). Variations in state-level definitions: Children with special health care needs. *Public Health Reports, 118,* 434–447.

Blue-Banning, M., Summers, J. A., Frankland, H. C., Nelson, L. L., & Beegle, G. (2004). Dimensions of family and professional partnerships: Constructive guidelines for collaboration. *Exceptional Children, 70,* 167–184.

Bourke-Taylor, H., Pallant, J. F., Law, M., & Howie, L. (2012). Predicting mental health among mothers of school-aged children with developmental disabilities: the relative contribution of child, maternal and environmental factors. *Research in Developmental Disabilities, 33*(6), 1732–1740. doi:10.1016/j.ridd.2012.04.011

Boyle, C. A., Boulet, S., Schieve, L., Cohen, R. A., Blumberg, S. J., Yeargin-Allsopp, M., Visser, S., & Kogan, M. D. (2011). Trends in the prevalence of developmental disabilities in US children, 1997–2008. *Pediatrics, 127*(6), 1034–1042. doi:10.1542/peds.2010-2989.

Braddock, D., & Parish, S. (2001). Disability history from antiquity to the Americans with Disabilities Act. In G. L. Albrecht, K. D. Seelman, & M. Bury (Eds.), *Handbook of disability studies* (pp. 11–68). Thousand Oaks, CA: Sage.

Bronfenbrenner, U. (1979). *The ecology of human development: Experiments by nature and design.* Cambridge, MA: Harvard University Press.

Bronfenbrenner, U. (1986). Ecology of the family as a context to human development: Research perspectives. *Development Psychology, 22,* 723–742. doi:10.1037/0012–1649.22.6.723

Brooks-Gunn, J., & Duncan, G. J. (1997). The effects of poverty on children. *Future of Children, 7,* 55–71. doi:10.2307/1602387

Brooks-Gunn, J., Klebanov, P. K., & Liaw, F. (1995). The learning, physical, and emotional environment of the home in the context of poverty: The Infant Health and Development program. *Children and Youth Services Review, 17,* 251–276. doi:10.1016/0190–7409(95)00011-Z

Bruns, E. J., & Burchard, J. D. (2000). Impact of respite care services for families with children experiencing emotional and behavioral problems. *Children's Services: Social Policy, Research, & Practice, 3,* 39–61. doi:10.1207/S15326918CS0301_3

Cedar Rapids Community School District v. Garret F., 526 U.S. 66 (1999). Retrieved from http://supreme .justia.com/us/526/66/

Chazan, M., Laing, A., Jones, J., Harper, G., & Bolton, J. (1983). The management of behavior problems in your children. *Early Childhood Development and Care, 11*, 227–244. doi:10.1080/0300443830110302

Child Welfare Information Gateway. (2012). *The risk and prevention of maltreatment of children with disabilites.* Washington, DC: U.S. Department of Health and Human Services, Children's Bureau.

Crnic, K. A., Friedrich, W. N., & Greenberg, M. T. (1983). Adaptation of families with mentally retarded children. *American Journal of Mental Deficiency, 88,* 125–138.

Curran, A. L., Sharples, P. M., White, C., & Knapp, M. (2001). Time costs of caring for children with severe disabilities compared with caring for children without disabilities. *Developmental Medicine & Child Neurology, 43,* 529–533. doi:10.1017/S0012162201000962

Davies, P., Iams, H., & Rupp, K. (2000). The effect of welfare reform on SSA's disability programs: Design of policy evaluation and early evidence. *Social Security Bulletin, 63,* 3–11.

Davis, L. (2000). Dr. Johnson, Amelia, and the discourse of disability in the eighteenth century. In H. Deutsch & F. Nussbaum (Eds.), *"Defects": Engendering the modern body* (pp. 54–74). Ann Arbor: University of Michigan Press.

DeNavas-Walt, C., Proctor, B. D, & Smith, J. C. (2013). *U.S. Census Bureau, current population reports, P60-245, income, poverty, and health insurance coverage in the United States: 2012.* Washington, DC: U.S. Government Printing Office..

Developmental Disabilities Assistance and Bill of Rights Act of 2000, PL 106-402. Retrieved from http://www.acf.hhs.gov/programs/add/ddact/DDACT2.html

Dodge, K. A. (1983). Behavioral antecedents of peer social status. *Child Development, 54,* 1386–1399.

Edgar, E., & Levine, P. (1987). *A longitudinal follow-along study of graduates of special education.* Seattle: University of Washington Child Development and Mental Retardation Center.

Emerson, E. (2007). Poverty and people with disabilities. *Mental Retardation and Developmental Disabilities Research Reviews, 13,* 107–113. doi:10.1002/mrdd.20144

Farber, B. (1960). Family organization and crisis: Maintenance of integration in families with a severely retarded child. *Monographs of the Society for Research in Child Development, 25,* 1–95. doi:10.2307/1165524

Floyd, F. J., & Gallagher, E. M. (1997). Parental stress, care demands, and use of support services for school-age children with disabilities and behavior problems. *Family Relations, 46,* 359–371. doi:10.2307/585096

Fraser, M. W., Kirby, L. D., & Smokowski, P. (2004). Risk and resilience in childhood. In M. W. Fraser (Ed.), *Risk and resilience in childhood: An ecological perspective* (pp. 13–66). Washington, DC: NASW Press.

Freedman, R. I., & Boyer, N. C. (2000). The power to choose: Supports for families caring for individuals with developmental disabilities. *Health & Social Work, 25,* 59–68.

Fujiura, G. T., & Yamaki, K. (2000). Trends in demography of childhood poverty and disability. *Exceptional Children, 66,* 187–199.

General Accounting Office. (1999, June). *SSI children: Multiple factors affect families' costs for disability-related services* (GAO/HEHS-99-99). Washington, DC: Author.

Grad, S. (2000, December 15). *The role of disability benefits in the economic well-being of beneficiaries.* Paper presented at the National Academy of Social Insurance Conference, Disability Income Policy: Opportunities and Challenges in the Next Decade, Washington, DC.

Graham, M., & Bryant, D. (1993). Characteristics of quality, effective service delivery systems for children with special needs. In D. Bryant & M. Graham (Eds.), *Implementing early intervention: From research to effective practice* (pp. 233–254). New York: Guilford Press.

Ha, J., Greenberg, J.S., & Seltzer, M.M. (2011). Parenting a child with a disability: The role of social support for African American parents. *Supportive Relationships, 92*(4), 405–411.

Haveman, M., van Berkum, G., Reijinder, R., & Heller, T. (1997). Differences in service needs, time demands, and caregiving burden among parents of persons with mental retardation across the life cycle. *Family Relations, 46,* 417–425. doi:10.2307/585101

Heller, T., Miller, A. B., & Hsieh, K. (1999). Impact of a consumer-directed family support program on adults with developmental disabilities and their family caregivers. *Family Relations, 48,* 419–427. doi:10.2307/585250

Hogan, D. P., & Msall, M. E. (2002). Family structure and resources and the parenting of children with disabilities and functional limitations. In J. G. Borkowski, S. L. Ramey, & M. Bristol-Power (Eds.), *Parenting and the child's world: Influences on academic, intellectual, and social-emotional development* (pp. 311–328). Mahwah, NJ: Lawrence Erlbaum.

Inkelas, M., Rowe, M., Karoly, L., & Rogowski, J. (1999). *Policy evaluation of the effects of the 1996 welfare reform legislation on SSI benefits for disabled children: First round case study findings.* Santa Monica, CA: Rand.

Jacquemont, S., Coe, B. P., Hersch M., Duyzend, M. H., Krumm N., Bergmann S., Beckmann J. S., Rosenfeld J. A., & Eichler E. E. (2014). A higher mutational burden in females supports a "Female Protective Model" in neurodevelopmental disorders. *The American Journal of Human Genetics, 94*(3), 415–425.

Katsiyannis, A., & Yell, M. L. (2000). The Supreme Court and school health services: *Cedar Rapids v. Garret F. Exceptional Children, 66,* 317–326.

Keogh, B. K., & Bernheimer, L. P. (1987). Developmental delays in preschool children: Assessment over time. *European Journal of Special Needs Education, 2,* 211–220. doi:10.1080/0885625870020401

Keogh, B. K., Bernheimer, L. P., & Guthrie, D. (2004). Children with developmental delays twenty years later: Where are they? How are they? *American Journal on Mental Retardation, 109,* 219–230. doi:10.1352/0895–8017(2004)109 < 219:CWDDTY > 2.0.CO;2

Kirk, S., Gallagher, J., & Asastasiow, N. (1993). *Educating exceptional children* (7th ed). Boston: Houghton Mifflin.

Kupersmidt, J. B., Coie, J. D., & Dodge, K. A. (1990). The role of peer relationships in the development of disorder. In S. R. Asher & J. D. Coie (Eds.), *Peer rejections in childhood* (pp. 17–59). New York: Cambridge University Press.

Landesman, S., Jaccard, J., & Gunderson, V. (1989). The family environment: The combined influences of family behavior, goals, strategies, resources, and individual experiences. In M. Lewis & S. Feinman (Eds.), *Social influences on development* (pp. 63–96). New York: Plenum Press.

Lichter, D. T., & Eggebeen, D. J. (1994). The effect of parental employment on child poverty. *Journal of Marriage and the Family, 56,* 633–645. doi:10.2307/352874

Lukemeyer, A., Meyers, M. K., & Smeeding, T. (2000). Expensive kids in poor families: Out of pocket expenditures for the care of disabled and chronically ill children and welfare reform. *Journal of Marriage and the Family, 62,* 399–415. doi:10.1111/j.1741–3737.2000.00399.x

Magnuson, K., & Votruba-Drzal, E. (2009). Enduring influences of childhood poverty. *Focus, 26*(2), 32–37.

Maternal and Child Health Bureau. (n.d.). *Title V information system.* Retrieved from https://perfdata .hrsa.gov/mchb/TVISReports/Default.aspx

Matheson, C., Olsen, R. J., Weisner, T., & Dykens, E. (2007). A good friend is hard to find: Friendship among adolescents with disabilities. *American Journal on Mental Retardation, 112*(5), 319–329. doi:10.1352/0895-8017(2007)112[0319:AGFIHT]2.0.CO;2

McConnell, D., Savage, A., & Breitkreuz, R. (2014). Resilience in families raising children with disabilities and behavior problems. *Research in Developmental Disabilities, 35*(4), 833–848. doi:http:// dx.doi.org/10.1016/j.ridd.2014.01.015

Meyer, L., Cole, D. A., McQuarter, R., & Reichle, J. (1990). Validation of the assessment of social competence for children and young adults with developmental disabilities. *Journal of the Association for Persons with Severe Handicaps, 15,* 57–68.

Meyers, M. K., Han, W. J., Waldfogel, J., & Garfinkel, I. (2001). Child care in the wake of welfare reform: The impact of government subsidies on the economic well-being of single-mother families. *Social Service Review, 75,* 29–59. doi:10.1086/591881

Meyers, M. K., & Heintze, T. (1999). The child care subsidy shortfall: Is the subsidy system working? *Social Service Review, 73,* 37–64. doi:10.1086/515796

National Commission on Childhood Disability. (1995, October). *Supplemental Security Income for children with disabilities: Report to Congress.* Washington, DC: Author.

National Early Childhood Technical Assistance Center (NECTAC). (2011). *The importance of early intervention for infants and toddlers with disabilities and their families.* Retrieved from: http://www.cdd.unm.edu/ecln/ECLNSpecial/common/pdfs/eifactsheet_2pg.pdf

Newacheck, P. W., Hung, Y. Y., Park, M. J., Brindis, C. D., & Irwin, C. E., Jr. (2003). Disparities in adolescent health and health care: Does socioeconomic status matter? *Health Services Research, 38*(5), 1235–52.

Newacheck, P. W., & Kim, S. E. (2005). A national profile of healthcare utilization and expenditures for children with special health care needs. *Archives of Pediatric and Adolescent Medicine, 159,* 10–17. doi:10.1001/archpedi.159.1.10

NICHCY. (2010). *Parents on the IEP team.* Retrieved from: http://www.parentcenterhub.org/repository/iep-parents/

NICHCY. (2014). *Overview of early intervention.* Retrieved from: http://www.parentcenterhub.org/repository/ei-overview/

Osborne, A. G., & Dimattia, P. (1994). The IDEA's least restrictive environment mandate: Legal implications. *Exceptional Children, 61,* 6–14.

Pagelow, M. D. (1984). *Family violence.* New York: Praeger.

Parish, S. L. (2003). Mental retardation and federal income transfers: The political and economic context. *Mental Retardation, 41,* 446–459. doi:10.1352/0047–6765(2003)41 < 446:FIPAMR > 2.0.CO;2

Parish, S. L., & Cloud, J. M. (2006). Financial well-being of young children with disabilities and their families. *Social Work, 51,* 223–232.

Parish, S. L., Pomeranz, A. E., & Braddock, D. (2003). Family support in the United States: Financing trends and emerging initiatives. *Mental Retardation, 41,* 174–187. doi:10.1352/0047–6765(2003)41 < 174:FSITUS > 2.0.CO;2

Parish, S. L., Rose, R. A., & Andrews, M. E. (2010). TANF and the employment, marriage, and welfare use of low-income mothers raising children with disabilities. *Exceptional Children, 76,* 234–253.

Parish, S. L., Rose, R. A., Andrews, M. E., Grinstein-Weiss, M., & Richman, E. L. (2008). Material hardship among U.S. families raising children with disabilities. *Exceptional Children, 75,* 71–92.

Parish, S. L., Seltzer, M. M., Greenberg, J. S., & Floyd, F. J. (2004). Economic implications of caregiving at midlife: Comparing parents of children with developmental disabilities to other parents. *Mental Retardation, 42,* 413–426.

Parish, S.L., Shattuck, P. T., & Rose, R. A. (2009). Financial burden of raising CSHCN: Association with state policy choices. *Pediatrics, 124,* Supplement 6, S435–S442. [doi:10.1542/peds.2009-1255P]

Park, J., Turnbull, A. P., & Turnbull, H. R. (2002). Impacts of poverty on quality of life in families of children with disabilities. *Exceptional Children, 68,* 151–170.

Parrott, S., Schott, L., Sweeney, E., Baider, A., Ganzglass, E., Greenberg, M., . . . Turetsky, V. (2007). *Implementing the TANF changes in the Deficit Reduction Act: "Win-win" solutions for families and states* (2nd ed.). Washington, DC: Center on Budget and Policy Priorities and Center for Law and Social Policy. Retrieved from http://www.cbpp.org/cms/?fa = view&id = 1176

Perrin, J. M. (2002). Health services research for children with disabilities. *The Milbank Quarterly, 80,* 303–324. doi:10.1111/1468–0009.t01-1-00005

Rallis, S. F., & Anderson, G. (1994). *Building inclusive schools: Places where all children can learn* (Occasional Paper Series, Vol. 9, No. 2). Andover, MA: Regional Laboratory for Educational Improvement of the Northeast & Islands.

Ramey, C. T., & Ramey, S. L. (1998). Early intervention and early experience. *American Psychologist, 53,* 109–120. doi:10.1037/0003–066X.53.2.109

Richmond, J., & Ayoub, C.C. (1993). Evolution of early intervention philosophy. In D. M. Bryant & M. A. Graham (Eds.), *Implementing early intervention: From research to effective practice* (pp. 1–17). New York: Guilford Press.

Rizzolo, M. C., Hemp, R., & Braddock, D. (2006). Family support services in the United States. *Policy Research Brief, 17*(1), Minneapolis: University of Minnesota.

Rosenbaum, S., Proser, M., Schneider, A., & Sonosky, C. (2002). *Using the Title V Maternal and Child Health Services Block Grant to support child development services.* Washington, DC: The Commonwealth Fund. Retrieved from http://www.commonwealthfund.org/usr_doc/rosenbaum_titlev_481.pdf

Rosman, E., McCarthy, J., & Woolverton, M. (2001). *Child care: Adults with mental health needs and children with special needs.* Washington, DC: Georgetown University Child Development Center.

Ruffing, K., & Pavetti, D. (2012). *SSI and children with disabilities: Just the facts.* Washington, DC: Center on Budget and Policy Priorities.

Scorgie, K., Wilgosh, L., & McDonald, L. (1998). Stress and coping in families of children with disabilities: An examination of recent literature. *Developmental Disabilities Bulletin, 26,* 22–42.

Scruggs, T. E., & Mastropieri, M. (1996). Teacher perceptions of mainstreaming/ inclusion, 1958–1995: A research synthesis. *Exceptional Children, 63,* 59–74.

Shearn, J., & Todd, S. (2000). Maternal employment and family responsibilities: The perspectives of mothers of children with learning disabilities. *Journal of Applied Research in Intellectual Disabilities, 13,* 109–131.

Singer, G. H., & Irvin, L. K. (1989). Family caregiving, stress, and support. In G. H. Singer & L. K. Irvin (Eds.), *Support for caregiving families: Enabling positive adaptation to disability* (pp. 207–219). Baltimore, MD: Brookes.

Sitlington, P., Frank, A., & Carson, R. (1992). Adult adjustment among high school graduates with mild disabilities. *Exceptional Children, 59,* 221–233.

Sobsey, D. (1994). *Violence and abuse in the lives of people with disabilities: The end of silent acceptance?* Baltimore, MD: Brookes.

Social Security Administration. (2000, September 11). Supplemental Security Income: Determining disability for a child under 18. Final rules. *Federal Register, 65,* 54747–54790. Retrieved from http://frwebgate.access.gpo.gov/cgi-bin/getdoc.cgi?dbname = 2000_register&docid = 00–22753-filed.pdf

Sopko, K. M. (2003). *The IEP: A synthesis of current literature since 1997.* Alexandria, VA: National Association of State Directors of Special Education.

Son, E., Parish, S. L., & Peterson, N.A. (2012). National prevalence of peer victimization among young children with disabilities in the United States. *Children & Youth Services Review, 34,* 1540–1545.

Stabile, M., & Allin, S. (2012). The economic costs of childhood disability. *The Future of Children, 22*(1), 65–96.

Summers, J. A., Behr, S. K., & Turnbull, A. P. (1989). Positive adaptation and coping strengths of families who have children with disabilities. In G. H. S. Singer & L. K. Irvin (Eds.), *Support for caregiving families* (pp. 27–40). Baltimore, MD: Brookes.

Thompson, T. S., Holcomb, P. A., Loprest, P., & Brennan, K. (1998). *State welfare-to-work policies for people with disabilities.* Washington, DC: Urban Institute.

Trute, B., & Hiebert-Murphy, D. (2002). Family adjustment to childhood developmental disability: A measure of parent appraisal of family impacts. *Journal of Pediatric Psychology, 27*(3), 271–280. doi:10.1093/jpepsy/27.3.271

Turnbull, A. P., Brotherson, M. J., & Summers, J. A. (1986). Family lifecycle: Theoretical and empirical implications and future directions for families with mentally retarded members. In J. J. Gallagher & P. M. Vietze (Eds.), *Families of handicapped persons: Research, programs and policy issues* (pp. 45–66). Baltimore, MD: Brookes.

U.S. Department of Education. (2009). *Twenty-eighth annual report to Congress on the implementation of the Individuals with Disabilities Education Act, 2006.* Washington, DC: Author.

U.S. Department of Education, National Center for Education Statistics. (2013). *Digest of Education Statistics, 2012* (NCES 2014-015), Washington, DC: Author.

U.S. Department of Health and Human Services. (2008). *State Medicaid-MCH coordination: A review of Title V and Title XIX interagency agreements* (2nd ed.). Washington DC: Author.

U.S. Department of Health and Human Services. (2014, January 22). *Annual update of the HHS poverty guidelines.* Retrieved from https://federalregister.gov/a/2014-01303

U.S. Department of Health and Human Services, Administration for Children and Families, Administration on Children, Youth and Families, Children's Bureau. (2010). *Child maltreatment 2009.* Retrieved from http://archive.acf.hhs.gov/programs/cb/pubs/cm09/cm09.pdf

Whitney-Thomas, J., & Moloney, M. (2001). "Who I am and what I want": Adolescents' self-definition and struggles. *Exceptional Children, 67,* 375–389.

Williamson, H. J., & Perkins, E. A. (2014). Family caregivers of adults with intellectual and developmental disabilities: outcomes associated with U.S. services and supports. *Intellectual and Developmental Disabilities, 52*(2), 147–159. doi:10.1352/1934-9556-52.2.147

World Health Organization, UNICEF, UNFPA, & The World Bank. (2012). *Trends in maternal mortality: 1990 to 2010.* Geneva, Switzerland: Author.

Yau, M. K., & Li-Tsang, C. W. (1999). Adjustment and adaptation in parents of children with developmental disabilities in two-parent families: A review of the characteristics ancillary attributes. *British Journal of Developmental Disability, 45,* 38–51.

Zipper, I., & Simeonsson, R. J. (2004). Promoting the development and well-being of young children with disabilities. In M. Fraser (Ed.), *Risk and resilience in childhood: An ecological perspective* (pp. 244–264). Washington, DC: NASW Press.

ADDITIONAL READING

Davis, L. (2013). *The disability studies reader* (4th ed.). New York: Routledge.

Hogan, D. (2012). *The family consequences of children's disability.* New York: Russell Sage Foundation.

Naseef, R.A. (2013). *Autism in the family: Caring and coping together.* Baltimore: Brookes.

WEB-BASED RESOURCES

The Arc, http://www.thearc.org/

Bazelon Center for Mental Health Law, http://www.bazelon.org/

Children's Defense Fund, http://www.childrensdefense.org/

Family Voices, http://www.familyvoices.org/

Institute for Community Inclusion, http://www.communityinclusion.org/

Kids Together, Inc., http://www.kidstogether.org/

Tash, Equal Opportunity and Inclusion for People with Disabilities, http://www.tash.org/

CHAPTER 8

Policies and Programs for Adolescent Substance Abuse

Elizabeth K. Anthony

Jeffrey M. Jenson

Matthew O. Howard

Adolescent substance abuse has been the subject of frequent discussion in local, state, and federal policy circles since the 1960s. Substance abuse among children and youth has also attracted the attention of the American public. A recent opinion poll conducted by the Gallup Organization revealed that 68% of Americans viewed drug use as one of the most serious problems facing teenagers (Gallup Organization, 2009). About 53% of respondents believe that the federal government has made little or no progress in preventing drug use in the past several years.

The visible and often devastating effects of substance use on individuals—coupled with the societal and economic costs associated with abuse—have been the targets of repeated social intervention in the past century. Demands for policy and program reform have come from a range of constituents and organizations. A report published at the beginning of the past decade by Physician Leadership on National Drug Policy (2002) outlined the need for more policy directives aimed at preventing adolescent substance abuse in the United States. Recent reports from the National Institute on Drug Abuse (NIDA) and the Substance Abuse and Mental Health Services Administration (SAMHSA) place considerable emphasis on informing practitioners about efficacious ways to prevent and treat adolescent substance abuse (NIDA, 2009; SAMHSA, 2010). It is significant that researchers and policy officials are working together to apply knowledge about the risk and protective factors associated with the onset and use of alcohol and illicit drugs to social interventions and policies for children and families (Hawkins, 2006; Liddle & Rowe, 2006; Scheier, 2010; Woolf, 2008).

In this chapter, we describe risk and protective factors related to substance use and abuse. In addition, we review past and current policy and program responses to treating and preventing substance abuse in adolescence. The utility of a public health framework that emphasizes risk, protection, and resilience for the development of innovative policy and programs is examined. We begin with a brief discussion of recent trends in adolescent substance use.

TRENDS IN ADOLESCENT SUBSTANCE USE

Adolescent substance use exists on a continuum that includes no use, nonproblematic use, abuse, and dependence. Substance abuse and dependence represent the most serious concerns to practitioners and policymakers. However, even low levels of drug use by children and youth can be problematic, given the many developmental tasks they encounter at school and in the community. Our review of trends in substance use, therefore, includes reports of experimental and regular use.

The nation's most accurate prevalence estimates for adolescent substance use come from the Monitoring the Future (MTF) study (Johnston, O'Malley, Bachman, & Schulenberg, 2013), sponsored by NIDA and the University of Michigan. MTF is an annual assessment of alcohol and drug use in a random sample of about 16,000 public and private high school students. In-school surveys with nationally representative samples of high school seniors have been conducted since 1975. Eighth- and 10th-grade students have been surveyed since 1991.

There have been several notable trends in adolescent substance use since the 1970s. Lifetime illicit drug use—including the use of marijuana, hallucinogens, cocaine, heroin, and other opiates as well as stimulants, barbiturates, or tranquilizers that are not under a doctor's order—peaked among seniors in 1981. About 66% of 12th graders in 1981 used an illicit drug at least once in their lives; 43% used an illicit drug other than marijuana. Lifetime use of illicit drugs reached its lowest point in 1992; only 41% of seniors used any illicit drug, and 25% used an illicit drug other than marijuana. In 1993, seniors reversed a decade-long pattern of declining illicit drug use.

Rates of illicit drug use rose for 6 consecutive years, and by 1999, 55% of seniors reported using illicit drugs. A 10-year trend of declining rates of illicit drug use among high school seniors began in 2000. By 2009, only 47% of seniors reported illicit drug use in their lifetime. This rate rose slightly to 50% by 2013.

Lifetime alcohol and tobacco use by seniors reached their highest levels in the late 1970s and early 1980s. About 93% of seniors reported lifetime alcohol use between 1977 and 1985. In 2013, 68% of seniors reported lifetime alcohol use. Interestingly, lifetime cigarette smoking among young people peaked in 1977. About 76% of seniors smoked cigarettes in 1977, compared with 38% in 2013.

Substance use among younger adolescents is of particular concern to policymakers and practitioners because early initiation is positively related to later problem use. The number of 8th-grade students reporting lifetime use of any illicit drug decreased from a high of 31% in 1996 to 20% in 2013. About 39% of 10th grade students used illicit drugs in 2013.

Adolescent males continue to use most drugs at higher rates than females. There are a few exceptions, with girls in eighth grade having slightly higher rates of use of some substances, such as inhalants and amphetamines. Gender differences in use, with males using at a higher rate for most substances, tend to appear and stabilize as students grow older. Historically, MTF results have indicated that alcohol and drug use are more prevalent among White students than among African American or Hispanic students (Johnston et al., 2013a). However, in 2012, the annual prevalence of illicit drug use among 12th graders was 41% for Hispanic students, 40% for White students, and 35% for African American students. In addition to this shift for Hispanic students, the more recent narrowing of the difference among African American students is driven largely by an increase in marijuana use. Overall, African American students still maintain lower levels of use for the majority of licit and illicit drugs in 8th, 10th, and 12th grades (Johnston et al., 2013a).

MTF results provide a fairly accurate picture of substance use among American youth. However, it is important to acknowledge that the MTF study may underestimate the magnitude of substance use among youth in the United States because it does not include school dropouts (an estimated 15% to 20% of students in this age group), a group at high risk for alcohol and drug use. Estimates of drug and alcohol use among minority groups may be particularly affected because more American Indian and Hispanic high school seniors drop out of school than African American, Asian American, or White seniors (Johnston et al., 2013a).

Trends in adolescent substance use point to the need for a continuum of policy and practice responses. Prevention strategies are needed to delay initiation and to interrupt the progression of substance use that often begins with alcohol or tobacco and culminates with more serious drug use. Conversely, treatment options are necessary for individuals exhibiting symptoms of abuse or dependence. In recent years, policy and program approaches aimed at preventing and treating adolescent substance abuse have been based on etiological models that emphasize principles of risk, protection, and resilience.

THE ETIOLOGY OF ADOLESCENT SUBSTANCE ABUSE: PRINCIPLES OF RISK, PROTECTION, AND RESILIENCE

Knowledge generated by investigations examining the relationship among risk and protective factors and adolescent substance use has led to significant advancements in the etiology, assessment, and prevention of drug abuse (for a review of such investigations, see Belcher & Shinitzky, 1998; Brook, Brook, & Pahl, 2006; Hawkins, Catalano, & Miller, 1992; Jenson, 2004; Kim, 2009; Schinke, Fang, & Cole, 2008). Yet, definitions and policy applications underlying concepts of risk and protection are clouded with controversy. Most researchers, practitioners, and public health specialists agree that risk factors for adolescent substance use can be empirically identified. As noted in Chapter 1, there is considerably less agreement about the concept and definition of protection. Some authors (Luthar, 2003) have asserted that risk and protective factors act as polar opposites of one another. Other investigators (Fraser, 2004; Rossa, 2002; Rutter, 2000) have argued that protective factors are characteristics and conditions that moderate or mediate levels of risk for problem behaviors like substance abuse. The following discussion of protective factors, consistent with the interpretation presented in Chapter 1, is based on the view that protective factors are traits, conditions, and characteristics that influence or modify the risk of substance abuse.

Risk Factors

Risk factors for adolescent substance abuse occur at environmental, interpersonal, social, and individual levels. These factors are summarized next and in Table 8.1.

Table 8.1   Risk Factors for Adolescent Substance Abuse

Environmental Factors
Low taxation and weak regulation of alcohol and drugs
Permissive cultural and social norms about substance use
Availability of alcohol and drugs
Poverty
Limited economic opportunity
Neighborhood disorganization
Low neighborhood attachment
High rates of residential mobility
High rates of adult criminality
High population density
Interpersonal and Social Factors
Family conflict
Poor family management practices
Dysfunctional family communication patterns
Parent and sibling substance use
Poor parent–child bonding
School failure
Low commitment to school
Rejection by conforming peer groups
Association with drug-using friends
Individual Factors
Family history of alcoholism
Sensation-seeking orientation
Poor impulse control
Attention deficits
Hyperactivity

Source: Table adapted from Jenson (2004).

Environmental Risk Factors

Community laws and norms favorable to drug use, such as low legal drinking ages and low taxes on alcoholic beverages, increase the risk of substance use during adolescence (Joksch, 1988). Studies examining the relationship between legal drinking age and adolescent drinking and driving have shown that lowering the drinking age increases underage drinking and teen traffic fatalities (Saffer & Grossman, 1987). Laws and norms that express intolerance for use of alcohol and illicit drugs by adolescents are associated with a lower prevalence of alcohol and drug use (Johnston, 1991).

Child poverty rates have increased in the last few years; 23% of children under the age of 18 lived in conditions of poverty in 2012 (Annie E. Casey Foundation, 2013). Poverty is associated with many adverse adolescent outcomes, including conduct problems, delinquency, and unwanted pregnancy (Cauce, Stewart, Rodriguez, Cochran, & Ginzler, 2003; Hannon, 2003). Poverty may also have an indirect effect on adolescent substance use. Family income is associated with many other risk factors for drug use (e.g., parenting practices and academic difficulties); low family income may affect drug use indirectly through such risk factors.

Low neighborhood attachment, school transitions, and residential mobility are associated with drug and alcohol abuse (Murray, 1983). Neighborhoods with high population density and high rates of adult crime also have high rates of adolescent crime and drug use (Simcha-Fagan & Schwartz, 1986). Neighborhood disorganization may also indirectly affect risk for drug abuse by eroding the ability of parents to supervise and control their children.

Interpersonal and Social Risk Factors

Interpersonal and social risk factors for adolescent substance abuse occur in family, school, and peer settings. Children whose parents or siblings engage in serious alcohol or illicit drug use are themselves at greater risk for these behaviors (Biederman, Faraone, Monuteaux, & Feighner, 2000). Children raised in families with lax supervision, excessively severe or inconsistent disciplinary practices, and little communication and involvement between parents and children are also at high risk for later substance abuse (Hill, Shen, Lowers, & Locke, 2000). Similarly, studies have shown that parental conflict is related to subsequent alcohol or drug use by adolescent family members (Brook, Whiteman, Gordon, & Brook, 1988).

School failure, low degree of commitment to education, and lack of attachment to school are school-related factors that increase the risk of substance abuse during adolescence (Holmberg, 1985). Adolescent drug users are more likely to skip classes, be absent from school, and perform poorly than non-drug users (Gottfredson, 1981).

Association with friends who use drugs is among the strongest predictors of adolescent substance abuse (Fergusson & Horwood, 1999; Reinherz, Giaconia, Hauf, Wasserman, & Paradis, 2000). Peer rejection in elementary grades is associated with school problems and delinquency (Coie, 1990; Kupersmidt, Coie, & Dodge, 1990), which are also risk factors for drug abuse. Some investigators have hypothesized that rejected children form friendships with other rejected children and that such groups become delinquent or engage in drug use during adolescence (Patterson, 2002; Patterson, Reid, & Eddy, 2002).

Individual Risk Factors

Psychosocial and biological factors are related to drug and alcohol abuse during adolescence. For example, evidence from adoption, twin, and half-sibling studies supports the notion that alcoholism is an inherited disorder (Cadoret, Cain, & Grove, 1980). Several studies have found that a sensation-seeking orientation predicts initiation and continued use of alcohol and other drugs (Cicchetti & Rogosch, 1999; Cloninger, Sigvardsson, & Bohman, 1988). Research also indicates that attention deficit disorders, hyperactivity, and poor impulse control before the age of 12 predict the age of onset of drinking and drug use (Shedler & Block, 1990).

Jenson and Potter (2003) found three distinct patterns of co-occurring mental health and substance use patterns in a longitudinal investigation of 154 detained youths. Adolescents who were most likely to abuse alcohol and other drugs also had high levels of self-reported depression, paranoia, hostility, and suicidal ideation. This and other investigations (Loeber, Farrington, Stouthamer-Loeber, & van Kammen, 1998; Vaughn, Freedenthal, Jenson, & Howard, 2007; Vaughn, Wallace, Davis, Fernandes, & Howard, 2008) suggest that mental health problems may play an important role in a youth's decision to experiment with and to persistently use alcohol or other drugs.

Protective Factors

Many adolescents develop healthy relationships and succeed in school and the community despite being exposed to multiple risk factors. Empirical research devoted to identifying individual and environmental characteristics that protect youth from substance abuse has lagged behind similar efforts aimed at identifying risk factors for drug use. However, an increasing number of investigators have begun to examine the relationship between protective factors and substance use in recent years (Brook et al., 2006; Jenson, 2004). When identified in children and adolescents, protective factors can be established or enhanced to reduce risks for substance abuse. Protective factors for alcohol and other drug use are summarized next and in Table 8.2.

Table 8.2   Protective Factors Against Adolescent Substance Abuse

Environmental, Interpersonal, and Social Factors
Being a firstborn child
Being raised in a small family
Low parental conflict
Caring relationships with siblings
Caring relationships with extended family members
Attachment to parents
Social support from nonfamily members
Commitment to school
Involvement in conventional activities
Belief in prosocial norms

Individual Factors
Social and problem-solving skills
Positive attitude
Positive temperament
High intelligence
Low childhood stress

Source: Table adapted from Jenson (2004).

Environmental, Interpersonal, and Social Protective Factors

Environmental, interpersonal, and social protective factors are attributes that buffer community, neighborhood, family, school, and peer risk factors. The most comprehensive study of protective factors among children was conducted by Werner and colleagues. Werner and Smith (1989) began following a cohort of high-risk children in Kauai, Hawaii, in 1955. Analysis of the children's outcomes as adolescents and adults has contributed to knowledge about factors that prevent youth from abusing alcohol and other drugs.

Werner (1994) found that being raised in a family with four or fewer children, experiencing low parental conflict, and being a firstborn child reduce the effects of poverty and other risk factors for substance abuse. Children who abstained from drug use during adolescence and early adulthood had positive parent–child relationships in early childhood and caring relationships with siblings and grandparents. Children who abstained from alcohol and other drugs also received social support and frequent counsel from teachers, ministers, and neighbors (Werner, 1994).

A positive family milieu and community supports are protective factors for drug abuse among children exposed to multiple risk factors. Garmezy (1985) found low childhood stress among high-risk children living in supportive family environments and among adolescents who had strong external support systems. Because stress increases the risk of drug use in later adolescence and early adulthood (Rutter, 2000), such findings have implications for preventing childhood and early adolescent drug abuse.

Strong social bonds to parents, teachers, and prosocial peers are significant factors in children's resistance to drug use (Berrueta-Clement, Schweinhart, Barnett, Epstein, & Weikhard, 1984). Four elements of the social bond have been found to be inversely related to adolescent drug abuse: (1) strong attachments to parents (Brook et al., 2006), (2) commitment to school (Friedman, 1983), (3) involvement in prosocial activities such as church or community organizations (Miller, Davies, & Grenwald, 2000), and (4) belief in the generalized norms and values of society (Jenson & Howard, 1999).

Understanding the processes by which strong social bonds develop is necessary to develop strategies that increase healthy bonding in high-risk youth. Social learning (Bandura, 1989) and social development (Catalano & Hawkins, 1996) theorists have suggested that three conditions are critical to the formation of strong social bonds: (1) opportunities for involvement in prosocial activities, (2) possession of the requisite behavioral and cognitive skills necessary to achieve success in such activities, and (3) rewards or recognition for positive behaviors. To promote healthy bonds, policies should support intervention strategies that provide opportunities, enhance skills, and offer rewards to high-risk youth.

Individual Protective Factors

Individual protective factors are psychosocial and biomedical characteristics that inhibit drug use. Competence in social and problem-solving situations is associated with abstinence and reductions in teenage drug use and delinquency. In a sample of high-risk urban children, Rutter (2000) found that problem-solving skills and strong self-efficacy were associated with successful adolescent outcomes. Youth who possessed adequate problem-solving skills and the ability to use skills were less likely to engage in drug use and delinquency. Jenson, Wells, Plotnick, Hawkins, and Catalano (1993) found that strong self-efficacy decreased the likelihood of drug use 6 months following drug treatment among adjudicated delinquents. These findings suggest that social and problem-solving skills moderate the effects of multiple risk factors for drug abuse and other adolescent outcomes.

Attitude and temperament are protective factors for substance abuse. Positive social orientation and positive temperament reduce the likelihood of adolescent drug abuse in several studies of high-risk youth (e.g., Jenson & Howard, 1999). Low intelligence (Werner, 1994) is also related to drug use.

Resilience

In Chapter 1 of this volume, Jenson and Fraser note the importance of resilience—an individual's ability to succeed in the face of adverse life circumstances—in the prevention of adolescent problem behaviors such as substance abuse. Anecdotal accounts detailing a person's ability to overcome substance abuse and addiction are common in American popular literature (Burroughs, 2003; Hamill, 1994; Knapp, 1996). However, the concept of resilience as an empirical construct in the explanation, prevention, or treatment of adolescent substance use remains a relatively new area of investigation (Luthar, 2003; Meschke & Patterson, 2003).

Studies indicate that some children and adolescents display high levels of functioning despite being surrounded by adverse familial or environmental influences (Fergusson & Horwood, 2003; Zucker, Wong, Puttler, & Fitzgerald, 2003). Zucker et al. (2003) examined the relationship between levels of resilience and subsequent childhood and adolescent outcomes among sons of alcoholic fathers and found that resilient youth were significantly more likely than nonresilient youth to resist substance use and other antisocial behaviors. Other studies have focused on the role of resilience in overcoming conditions of poverty (Cauce et al., 2003) and exposure to violence (Gorman-Smith & Tolan, 2003). Additional research is needed to better understand the direct and indirect effects of resilience on substance use.

Summary

Risk factors for substance use have been shown to be relatively stable over the past several decades. The factors summarized earlier consistently predict alcohol and drug use even though social norms about the acceptability of substance use have changed several times during this period. This suggests that policies and programs should encourage the development of strategies that target risk factors at multiple levels, including differential vulnerability, poor child-rearing practices, school achievement, social influences, social learning, and broad social norms.

Protection and resilience hold great promise in understanding, preventing, and treating substance abuse. Knowledge gained from studies examining the complex relationships among risk, protection, and resilience should be considered in policy and program design.

RISK, PROTECTION, AND RESILIENCE IN SUBSTANCE ABUSE POLICY

The Evolution of Drug Policy: A Brief Overview

Drug policy in the United States reflects cultural beliefs about the risks associated with substance use and the role of governmental regulation in people's personal and social lives. Cultural beliefs about substance use and opinions about the best way to prevent or treat substance abuse are in turn affected by a host of social, political, and economic conditions (DuPont & Voth, 1995). The evolving nature of these beliefs may best be seen in the underlying tension that is evident between policy approaches favoring control and regulation and those favoring prevention and treatment. The relative emphasis placed on control strategies versus prevention and treatment alternatives has a significant impact on the nature of policies, programs, and services for children and adolescents available at any given point in time (McBride, VanderWaal, & Terry-McElrath, 2001; Musto, 1996). The good news for prevention and treatment advocates may be that increases in federal funding for adolescent health have led to a greater array of substance abuse prevention and treatment alternatives for children and youth (Dougherty, 1993; Irwin, Burg, & Cart, 2002). Of particular note, beginning in 2010, the Obama administration's approach to reducing drug use and the consequences of drug use has shifted the historical enforcement approach ("war on drugs") to the use of science and evidence-based public health and safety, focusing on prevention, treatment, and recovery (Office of National Drug Control Policy [ONDCP], 2014). In the current economic climate, however, there is considerable competition for funds, and efforts to reduce substance abuse among youth must demonstrate evidence of effectiveness. Major American drug policies of the past century are reviewed next and are shown in Table 8.3.

Early Drug Policy

American drug policy emerged at the turn of the century with the passage of several important acts. The Pure Food and Drug Act of 1906 required labeling of all drugs sold in the country. The Harrison Narcotics Act of 1914 and the 1919 Volstead Act prohibited the sale of narcotics and alcohol (DuPont & Voth, 1995). Prohibition against illicit drugs was used as a public policy approach well into the 1950s, when the federal government implemented drug trafficking laws and enacted strict penalties for drug violations.

1960–1980

The "drug revolution" of the 1960s and 1970s created an increase in demand for illicit drugs that was unparalleled in prior years. Changing social norms reflecting greater tolerance for experimental drug use led to a shift from the predominantly punitive stance that was common before 1960 to an interest in decriminalizing marijuana and other less serious drugs. As "recreational" and experimental drug use became more common, increased public awareness of the health risks associated with substance use coincided with the development of prevention and treatment strategies for illicit drug abuse (McBride et al., 2001). Passage of the Narcotic Addict Rehabilitation Act of 1966 reflected

Table 8.3 Major Federal Substance Abuse Policies for Children and Families, 1990 to Present

Legislation	Purpose
1906 Pure Food and Drug Act	Required the patent medicine industry to list product ingredients
1914 Harrison Narcotics Act	Prohibited the manufacture, sale, and possession of narcotics
1919 Volstead Act and Eighteenth Amendment to the Constitution	Prohibited the sale of alcohol
1937 Marijuana Tax Act	Prohibited the nonmedical use of marijuana
1966 Narcotic Addict Rehabilitation Act	Established civil commitment system (treatment) for federal offenders rather than prosecution
1970 Comprehensive Drug Abuse Prevention and Control Act	Consolidated previous drug laws and reduced penalties for marijuana possession; included the Controlled Substances Act, which established five schedules for regulating drugs based on medicinal value and potential for addiction or abuse
1986 and 1988 Anti-Drug Abuse Acts	Emphasized law enforcement in general, with the 1988 act also attending to treatment and prevention; created the Office of National Drug Control Policy (ONDCP) and the Substance Abuse and Mental Health Services Administration (SAMHSA)
1997 Title XXI (SSA), State Child Health Insurance (SCHIP) established	Expanded health insurance coverage for children and allowed flexibility in resource distribution
2008 Mental Health Parity and Addiction Equity Act (MHPAEA)	Required equity with all medical/surgical benefits for financial requirements and treatment limitations for mental health or substance use disorder benefits
Patient Protection and Affordable Care Act (ACA) of 2010	Among the other major changes to national health-care delivery, the 2014 expansion builds on the MHPAEA and requires coverage of mental health and substance use disorders services at parity with medical and surgical benefits for all new small group and individual market plans.

society's desire to help individuals suffering from addiction. And, in 1967, the American Medical Association endorsed the disease theory as the predominant explanation of alcohol addiction, a change that was to have a profound effect on American social policy (Freeman, 2001).

The 1970s witnessed several key pieces of drug-related legislation. Predating President Richard Nixon's declaration calling for a "war on drugs" by just 1 year, Congress passed the Comprehensive Drug Abuse Prevention and Control Act in 1970. The act consolidated several previous federal laws and categorized addictive drugs for purposes of control and regulation. While reducing the penalties for certain types of possession offenses, the act also strengthened law enforcement efforts. The emphasis on rehabilitation, however, remained an important part of the 1970 legislation.

1980–Present

An increase in drug use among the nation's youth at the end of the 1970s marked a reversal in public opinion about the nature of substance use policy. "Get-tough" approaches began to replace policies favoring community-based treatment, and the subsequent passage of the Anti-Drug Abuse Acts of 1986 and 1988 reinforced a return to policies favoring law enforcement and control (McBride et al., 2001). The federal Office of National Drug Control Policy (ONDCP) was created in 1988 to better coordinate drug policy across states and international borders. By the late 1980s, all states raised the legal drinking age to 21 in response to growing concerns about the dangers and consequences of adolescent alcohol abuse. Arrest, conviction, and incarceration rates for drug-related offenses—particularly among poor youth and youth of color—increased following tougher policy provisions passed in the 1980s (Snyder, 1990).

Some policy experts noted a return to drug policies favoring prevention and rehabilitation in the past decade (Physician Leadership on National Drug Policy, 2002). As one important example, treatment parity with other health conditions from an insurance perspective has long been sought by mental health and substance-related disorder advocates. When the Mental Health Parity Act was first introduced in 1996, it provided parity for mental health benefits, in terms of aggregate lifetime and annual dollar limits, when compared with medical/surgical benefits. Substance abuse or chemical dependency was excluded, however. When the Mental Health Parity and Addiction Equity Act (MHPAEA) was passed in 2008, it required equity for mental health and substance use-disorder benefits when these services are provided. Specifically, the financial requirements such as copays or deductibles and limitations set on treatment must be "no more restrictive" than the limitations set for all medical/surgical benefits (U.S. Department of Labor, 2010). Building on the MHPAEA and beginning in 2014, the implementation of the Patient Protection and Affordable Care Act (2010) requires coverage of mental health and substance use-disorder services and requires that these services be provided at parity with medical and surgical benefits by insurers and group health plans (Beronio, Po, Skopec, & Glied, 2013).

This change coincides with a newfound interest in viewing adolescent substance abuse as a public health problem and applying principles of risk and protection to substance policy and programs. The Obama Administration's reform of drug policy that began in 2010 emphasizes the prevention of drug abuse as a public health issue in addition to a criminal justice issue. As a consequence, federal drug-control spending has decreased funds for supply reduction while increasing funds for demand reduction in recent years (ONDCP, 2014). Next, we discuss specific federal policies across the domains of law enforcement, prevention, and treatment. These selected policies highlight major trends in policy approaches aimed at adolescent substance abuse.

Law Enforcement

Law enforcement has always been a critical component of American drug policy (Morin & Collins, 2000; Physician Leadership on National Drug Policy, 2002). Funding for law enforcement efforts aimed at combating adolescent substance abuse has increased substantially nearly every year since 1980. Federal spending for the control of illicit drugs alone increased from $1.5 billion in 1981 to $17.9 billion in 1999 (Robert Wood Johnson Foundation, 2001). Historically, more than 75% of federal funds distributed to state and local communities for the control of illicit drug use were devoted to law enforcement activities (Kleiman, 1998).

The 2014 National Drug Control Strategy earmarked approximately 60% of the $25 billion drug control budget for the supply-reduction strategies of international, interdiction, and domestic law enforcement. The remaining 40% of the overall budget was allocated to prevention and treatment (ONDCP, 2014). As Figure 8.1 demonstrates, despite recent shifts, federal spending for supply reduction remains disproportionate to spending levels for prevention and treatment (ONDCP, 2014). However, federal funding for prevention and treatment has increased under the Obama administration from 2013 to the proposed budget for 2015.

Domestic and international law enforcement and interdiction policies constitute what is known as a *supply-reduction strategy*. Intended to disrupt the drug trade market and to limit access to drugs, supply reduction relies on practices such as taxation and law enforcement to control alcohol and illicit drug use. Initiatives to dismantle illicit drug trafficking networks are also included in supply-reduction strategies. The federal drug-control budget

Figure 8.1 Federal Drug Control Resources by Function

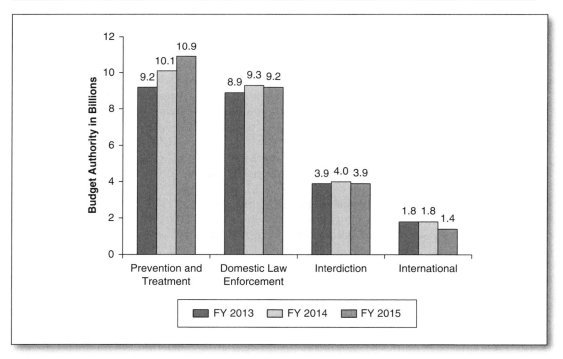

Source: This figure is adapted from the *National Drug Control Budget, FY 2015 Funding Highlights,* by ONDCP, 2014, Washington, DC: The White House.

provides funding through various initiatives to increase the capacity of organizations such as the Drug Enforcement Administration, Federal Bureau of Investigation, U.S. Customs Service, Border Patrol, and Coast Guard to implement these approaches. Federal initiatives to disrupt international illegal markets, particularly through partnerships with Colombian and Mexican governments, were major goals of the Bush administration (ONDCP, 2009).

The effectiveness of law enforcement and drug interdiction can be evaluated by assessing the cost of illicit drugs and by monitoring rates of adolescent substance use. Based on these outcome measures, the results of law enforcement and drug interdiction efforts have achieved limited success. Although the United States has spent more than $18 billion a year on international law enforcement and interdiction, evidence suggests that the relative price of many "hard drugs" has actually decreased in recent years (Bach & Lantos, 1999; Kleiman, 1998) and that access to illicit drugs has not diminished (Robert Wood Johnson Foundation, 2001). In 2013, about 50% of adolescents had tried an illicit substance by the time they graduated from 12th grade (Johnston et al., 2013b), a finding that offers at least cursory evidence to suggest that law enforcement and interdiction efforts alone are not effective in reducing adolescent substance use.

Supply-reduction strategies restricting access and increasing taxes for alcohol and other drugs appear to have produced greater success in reducing substance abuse. For example, an increase in the minimum drinking age is associated with a decline in alcohol consumption and in alcohol-related auto fatalities (Cook & Tauchen, 1984). Furthermore, federal taxes on alcohol and tobacco have generated government revenue that has been used to fund efficacious prevention and treatment services in many states (Robert Wood Johnson Foundation, 2001).

Many experts assert that policy debates about the merits of supply reduction strategies do not lie in the specific findings regarding the effectiveness of law enforcement, interdiction, taxation, and restrictive access strategies (Caulkins, Reuter, Iguchi, & Chiesa, 2005; Kleiman, 1998; Morin & Collins, 2000). Rather, the primary concern of many policy officials is the disproportionate allocation of federal funding, which has historically relegated prevention and treatment alternatives to a secondary priority. Continuing to increase funding for law enforcement and interdiction during periods of limited funding for prevention and treatment illustrates this source of major policy contention. Given the enormous cost of interdiction and enforcement and the ongoing increases necessary to reduce the illicit drug trade, many public-health officials continue to advocate for higher levels of funding for prevention and treatment.

Prevention

The history of adolescent substance abuse prevention efforts dates to at least the 1960s (Jenson & Bender, 2014). Early prevention efforts educated children and youth about different types of drugs and informed young people about the physical effects of using alcohol and other substances. These "information-only" programs fell short of providing interactive experiences to young people and relied on didactic learning approaches to educate them about substance abuse. Other programs employed "scared-straight" tactics to warn adolescents about the adverse individual and social consequences of alcohol and illicit drugs. Perhaps not surprisingly, programs relaying only information about alcohol and other drugs or exposing youth to the risks of drug use produced few positive results (Hawkins, 2006; Jenson, 2010).

The evolution of substance abuse prevention advanced slowly following the early 1970s. It was not until the mid-1980s that an emerging group of prevention researchers began to introduce and test school-based curricula as a new approach to prevent substance abuse (Botvin, 2004; Catalano, 2007). These curricula were based on known correlates of substance abuse and relied on interactive and structured activities that involved children in the concept of prevention. Subsequent longitudinal studies of these interventions revealed that well-designed prevention curricula could effectively prevent the initiation of drug use among young people (e.g., Hansen, 1992). The common thread among the programs was the use of a risk and protective factor framework as a guiding source of program design.

Policies and programs supporting substance abuse prevention have increased significantly since the initial program evaluations of the mid-1980s. The FY 2015 national drug-control budget proposes a 4.5% increase ($58.1 million) over the FY 2014 budget for prevention efforts (ONDCP, 2014). It is widely agreed that the adoption of the risk-based prevention paradigm is largely responsible for the increased attention to prevention policy and prevention research (Robertson, David, & Rao, 2003). NIDA, SAMHSA, and governmental entities such as the Office of Juvenile Justice and Delinquency Prevention (OJJDP) all recognize the utility of a public health framework for prevention and have taken efforts to implement principles of risk, protection, and resilience in their program and policy initiatives (Howell, 2003; Robertson et al., 2003; Schinke, Brounstein, & Gardner, 2002). Programs targeting factors that increase and guard against the risk of substance abuse now represent the most commonly used prevention strategy in the United States (American Academy of Pediatrics, 2001; Centers for Disease Control and Prevention, 2008; Jenson, 2010). The results from a number of longitudinal investigations of risk-based prevention programs implemented in school, family, and community settings reveal positive outcomes with regard to substance use (for reviews, see Biglan & Smolkowski, 2002; Foxcroft, Ireland, Lister-Sharp, Lowe, & Breen, 2003; Pentz, 2010).

Federal Policy Initiatives

Several important federal policy directives support the use of a public health framework for substance abuse prevention. The Drug-Free Communities Program, initiated in 1997, supports community and anti-drug coalitions that create collaborative efforts among prevention agencies and organizations (ONDCP, 2010). The Department of Education and SAMHSA provide funds for school- and community-based prevention programs under this initiative.

Changing social norms about substance use is a primary objective of several media campaigns and education programs that have received generous federal support. In 1998, the National Youth Anti-Drug Media Campaign received $195 million in federal funding and $2 billion in public and private funds to combat media images promoting substance use (Kelder, Maiback, Worden, Biglan, & Levitt, 2000).

The National Youth Anti-Drug Media Campaign has been one of the most visible and widespread prevention strategies in the country. Partnership for Drug-Free Kids (formerly known as Partnership for a Drug-Free America) was founded in 1987 as a collaboration with the Ad Council. The program's primary objective was to educate children, youth, and parents about drug use and to promote young people's ability to reject illegal drugs through personal and social skill development (ONDCP, 1997). The campaign aimed to change social norms about drug use by communicating messages about youth who do not use substances, discussing the negative effects of drugs, and portraying the positive aspects of a drug-free lifestyle (ONDCP, 1997). An evaluation of the campaign revealed that nearly 80% of youth and 70% of parents who were polled about the campaign recalled seeing at least one message delivered through media sources each week (Westat & the Annenberg School for Communication, 2003). However, like the information-only effort before it, the media campaign in this format produced little direct evidence of reducing substance use. Some modifications have been made to the overall strategy since 2005 through the "Above the Influence" (ATI) (http://www.abovetheinfluence.com/) teen-targeted campaign, which is based on commercial advertising and marketing principles (ONDCP, 2012). The ad and campaign messages were developed and tracked through research and testing phases. The 2010 relaunch increased the scope of the ATI brand with national television, print, and Internet exposure in addition to local advertising. The results of several evaluations suggested that exposure to ATI predicted a reduction in the initiation of marijuana use (Slater, Kelly, Lawrence, Stanley, & Cornello, 2011); a reduction in marijuana use among eighth-grade girls (Carpenter and Pechmann, 2011; Farrelly, Davis, Haviland, Messeri, & Healton, 2005); and improvements in anti-drug beliefs, drug use intentions, and marijuana use for the target audience of the ATI campaign (Scheier, Grenard, & Holtz, 2011).

Public schools have been a primary location of substance abuse prevention activities. Funding for school-based drug education formally began in the 1980s, when Congress allocated about $500 million a year for prevention activities (Burke, 2002; Wyrick, Wyrick, Bibeau, & Fearnow-Kenney, 2001). Federal government involvement in substance abuse prevention, however, has had an uneven history. In the late 1980s and early 1990s, significant amounts of government dollars were devoted to a drug abuse resistance education program called Project D.A.R.E. The popular program brought police officers and law enforcement officials to school classrooms. Officers warned children about the dangers of alcohol and other drugs and worked to reduce negative stereotypes of law enforcement. Evaluations of Project D.A.R.E. revealed that the program was no more effective than routine prevention approaches being used in the nation's schools and classrooms to prevent substance use (Lynam et al., 1999). To their credit, the developers of D.A.R.E. used these findings to retool the program to include more interactive and skills-based teaching strategies in the curriculum. Still, the enormous sum of money allocated to an ineffective program has been a stark lesson to policymakers about the risk of funding untested prevention approaches.

In 1997, the U.S. Department of Education's Safe and Drug-Free School and Communities Program took an important step in prevention policy by requiring all programs that receive federal funds to select and implement interventions that had demonstrated some degree of effectiveness in preventing substance use. Efforts to increase the number of empirically supported interventions in prevention settings have positively affected the quality and outcomes of school-based prevention programs since 1997 (Burke, 2002). NIDA supports considerable substance abuse prevention research and has developed specific action steps for school and community-based programs that are based on principles of risk and protection (Robertson et al., 2003).

Prevention research continues to advance what is known about effective ways to delay or prevent substance use initiation. Efforts are now underway to implement efficacious programs on a larger scale across school districts and communities. No matter how effective such efforts become, the need for treatment services for children and youth experiencing more serious substance use problems must also be an important part of a policy and program continuum.

Treatment

As the Affordable Care Act is fully implemented, more adolescents should become eligible for substance use disorder services as an identified "essential health benefit" via expansion of dependent coverage, Medicaid and Children's Health Insurance Program (CHIP), and the health insurance marketplace (Pilkey et al., 2013). Health insurance eligibility is an important part of substance abuse treatment services; however, several other treatment barriers still exist. Several public health organizations, including Physician Leadership on Drug Policy and the American Academy of Pediatrics (2000), were at the forefront of advocacy efforts aimed at increasing funding for substance abuse treatment. A position paper on adolescent drug policy that was published by Physician Leadership on National Drug Policy (2002) called for the use of evidence-based interventions in drug treatment. The group also suggested that levels of substance abuse funding should be similar to funds provided for diseases such as diabetes and heart disease. Physician Leadership on National Drug Policy continues to argue that the long-standing federal emphasis on law enforcement policy has mitigated the potential of treatment as a means of reducing substance abuse problems. Importantly for prevention and treatment efforts, the Obama Administration's approach to drug control acknowledges drug addiction as a preventable and treatable disease rather than a moral failing (ONDCP, 2014).

There is currently no national standard of care for treating adolescent substance abusers in the United States. Substance abuse treatment varies by region, state, and locality and is generally considered to be poorly funded and difficult to access. Recent estimates from SAMHSA's National Survey on Drug Use and Health reveal that about 1.6 million young people require treatment for an illicit drug or alcohol use problem annually but only 157,000 received treatment in a specialty facility (SAMHSA, 2013). Other reports have indicated that as few as one in every 10 adolescents who need substance abuse treatment actually receive it and that only 25% of those participating in treatment receive the appropriate type and level of assistance (Center for Substance Abuse Treatment, 2002; NIDA, 2009). Historically, access to care appears to be strongly related to inadequate health insurance coverage and to complicated managed-care regulations that limit time allotted for treatment (American Academy of Pediatrics, 2001). While the Patient Protection and Affordable Care Act (2010) expands health insurance coverage for uninsured adolescents and School-Based Health Centers under the Act show promise for access to treatment, there are many barriers to providing treatment that is tailored to the needs of adolescents.

A major concern affecting access to care for many children and adolescents is the fragmented nature of substance abuse treatment. Policies and programs supporting adolescent substance abuse treatment come from such disparate domains as education, juvenile justice, child welfare, labor, and health. Each system has its own eligibility criteria, and each operates independently from the other. The result is a fragmented system of care in which many youth may be shuffled from program to program with little coordination across service sectors.

Youth with substance abuse problems are also more likely to experience other mental health problems. In many cases, treatment facilities in one system are not equipped to handle multiple problems. For example, estimates indicate that 60% to 80% of youth involved in the juvenile justice system also have a substance use disorder (Washburn et al., 2008). Few resources currently exist to treat youth who have multiple problems.

Public sources provide funding for alcohol and drug treatment through a combination of Medicaid and state and local funds. Funds for public substance abuse treatment are limited, and restrictions placed on the type of eligible service often prevent integration across systems of care (Physician Leadership on National Drug Policy, 2002). The Medicaid program provides health insurance coverage for more than 16.4 million children. However, Medicaid programs display considerable variation in the services they fund, ranging from comprehensive treatment benefits in some states to only inpatient detoxification in other states (Gehshan, 1999). Medicaid reimbursement rates are also typically quite low, which has led to less incentive to provide treatment services (American Academy of Pediatrics, 2001).

Expansion of health-care coverage for low-income children was included as a provision in a 1997 bill that created the State Children's Health Insurance Program (SCHIP), now simply referred to as Children's Health Insurance Program (CHIP). This program allows states to access federal funds for children who are not eligible for other coverage. Funds are provided via the Medicaid program or through a separate program established specifically for CHIP participants. Although coverage still varies considerably by state, all states using CHIP have generally paid for detoxification and for some types of outpatient substance abuse treatment (Gehshan, 1999).

Medicaid and CHIP are required to implement the Early and Periodic Screening, Diagnosis, and Treatment Program (EPSDT). Many experts believe that EPSDT could be an effective way to increase substance abuse treatment services for troubled youth (Rosenbaum, Johnson, Snonsky, Markus, & DeGraw, 1998). However, a general lack of awareness about EPSDT in the professional community has led to underutilization. Weak coordination between Medicaid and SCHIP has also limited use of EPSDT as a referral source for substance abuse treatment.

Federal block grants provide resources that seek to improve access to substance abuse treatment services. These grants typically provide funds that are channeled through federal and state agencies. For example, prevention services funded by the Substance Abuse Prevention and Treatment Block Grant are administered by the Center for Substance Abuse Prevention. Corresponding treatment services are funded and administered by the Center for Substance Abuse Treatment, SAMHSA, and the U.S. Department of Health and Human Services. With many states rolling block-grant money into specialty "carve-out" arrangements, one policy concern is that substance abuse services may be inappropriately offered by mental health providers rather than by trained substance abuse treatment specialists.

Finally, financial barriers to substance abuse treatment exist. The Affordable Care Act of 2010 now requires parity for mental health and substance use disorder services; however, access to services and availability of developmentally appropriate services is still a concern. Several public health organizations have recently made policy recommendations calling for a more thoughtful and integrated continuum of care in adolescent substance abuse prevention and treatment (American Academy of Pediatrics, 2010; Robert Wood Johnson Foundation, 2010). We explore these and other ideas more fully in the next section.

USING KNOWLEDGE OF RISK, PROTECTION, AND RESILIENCE TO ACHIEVE SERVICE INTEGRATION

Principles of risk, protection, and resilience are key components of effective substance abuse intervention. The potential of these principles for public policy has yet to be fully realized. To be effective, knowledge of risk, protection, and resilience should undergird policy and programs in all systems of care for children and youth.

A Continuum of Substance Abuse Policy

Substance use disorders are prevalent among children and youth in nearly all public sectors of care in the United States. Aarons, Brown, Hough, Garland, and Wood (2001) examined prevalence rates for substance use disorders among adolescents who were receiving care in five service systems in San Diego County. Prevalence estimates ranged from 19% for youth in the child welfare system to 41% and 62% for adolescents in the mental health and juvenile justice systems, respectively. More recent estimates reveal that as many as 49% of children in foster care (Vaughn, Ollie, McMillen, Scott, & Munson, 2007), 80% of youth in the juvenile justice system (Washburn et al., 2008), and 50% of youth with serious mental health problems use alcohol and illicit drugs (James, 2007). The high prevalence of substance abuse across systems of care points to the need for better integration and coordination of prevention and treatment policy and programs.

Policies aimed at adolescent substance abuse, like policies targeting other childhood and adolescent problems, have largely been incremental and fragmented. That is, programs and interventions tend to develop as a result of localized conditions that fail to consider national trends vis-à-vis substance abuse or empirical evidence regarding the relative effectiveness of prevention and treatment approaches. To confound matters, service sectors for high-risk youth develop responses to problems that tend to be very similar to one another. Creating an integrated continuum of care must begin with assessment and screening policies and practices.

Assessment and Screening Policies

An integrated system of care for children and youth must first acknowledge the need to assess and screen youth for a variety of problem behaviors, including substance abuse. Once appropriate assessment data are collected, appropriate placements and sanctions can be more easily determined. Policies are needed to create centralized assessment centers that serve diagnostic and referral needs across major service systems for children and adolescents. Provisions of these policies should include standardized diagnostic tools that offer interpretative guidelines for juvenile justice, mental health, child welfare, and substance abuse practitioners. Standardized assessment procedures might also lead to more systematic placement criteria and decision-making and would allow cross-system comparisons of risk and protective factors found to be prevalent among youth and their family members. Knowledge of these factors, in turn, could be used to inform the direction of prevention and treatment programs.

Prevention Policies

Perhaps the single greatest policy need in substance abuse prevention lies in funding. Prevention has historically been underfunded when compared with competing demands made by treatment providers and law enforcement (Catalano, 2007; Jenson & Bender, 2014). In recent years, longitudinal studies have indicated that some prevention programs are effective in preventing and reducing substance abuse and are more cost-effective than treatment and law enforcement approaches (Aos, Lieb, Mayfield, Miller, & Pennucci, 2004). The availability of effective programs through the dissemination efforts of entities such as SAMHSA's National Registry of Effective Programs, the Center for the Study and Prevention of Violence, and interdisciplinary groups dedicated to advancing evidence-based practice such as the Cochrane Collaboration and the Campbell Collaboration is further argument for the adoption of prevention policy as a national priority for children and families.

To reach more children and families, prevention policy must bring effective programs to scale at the school, neighborhood, and community levels. One method of increasing the use of effective programs in community settings is found in the Communities That Care (CTC) intervention (Hawkins, Catalano, & Associates, 1992). In the CTC model, coalitions are formed to engage in systematic prevention planning that requires communities to identify prevalent risk and protective factors for adolescent problems in their localities. Following the assessment of such factors, communities are encouraged to select, implement, and evaluate prevention strategies on the basis of available empirical evidence. Recent findings from a longitudinal study called the Community Youth Development Study, a randomized trial that uses principles of CTC, have revealed significantly lower rates of delinquency and drug use among students in experimental communities compared with control communities (Hawkins et al., 2008). These promising results have led the Center for Substance Abuse Prevention (2010) to recommend CTC as a key component in its overall prevention strategy.

A Prevention Case Example

Bishopville, a (fictitious) suburban community on the East Coast, has recently become alarmed about increases in adolescent substance abuse. Anecdotal reports about all-night drug parties (i.e., raves) involving alcohol, marijuana, and hallucinogens have surfaced in local schools and neighborhoods. A recent party led to the arrest of six teenagers and alerted officials that action steps were necessary.

(Continued)

(Continued)

Officials chose the Communities That Care (CTC) model (Hawkins et al., 1992) as a means of better understanding and addressing the problem of adolescent substance abuse in Bishopville. Using the model, Bishopville employed the following action steps that led to the creation of a city-wide prevention policy:

Step 1: *Organizing and mobilizing.* Leaders of Bishopville selected key individuals to guide the prevention planning process. These included the mayor, educators, business representatives, and other elected officials. The group subsequently formed a community prevention board that was charged with organizing and mobilizing other community advocates and constituency groups.

Step 2: *Developing a community profile of strengths, resources, and challenges.* Risk and protective factors for adolescent substance use were assessed using a CTC survey with a random sample of children and adolescents in Grades 6 to 12. Survey results were used to rank the most common risk and protective factors found among children and youth in Bishopville. A community-needs assessment aimed at identifying existing and needed services for children and youth was also conducted in this phase.

Step 3: *Creating a strategic prevention plan.* In this phase, the Bishopville Community Prevention Board reviewed and selected several efficacious prevention strategies that will be implemented in their local schools and neighborhoods. A school-based curriculum that targets the early onset of substance use and a community-level media campaign were among the strategies selected for implementation.

Step 4: *Evaluating and monitoring the plan.* Steps were identified to monitor and evaluate the prevention strategies selected by the board. Outcome measures and other methodological decisions were made in consultation with local and national experts to ensure a rigorous evaluation process.

Please see Hawkins, Catalano, and Associates (1992) and Hawkins et al. (2008) for a more detailed description of using the CTC model in a community setting.

Treatment Policies

Historically, treatment for young people has mirrored that for adults; 12-step and self-help interventions based on a disease model of addiction have dominated the field (Liddle & Rowe, 2006). Reviews of adolescent substance abuse treatment have identified relatively few controlled trials in the past two decades (Deas & Thomas, 2001; Jenson, Howard, & Vaughn, 2004; Vaughn & Howard, 2004). Meta-analytic studies assessing treatment outcomes for young drug abusers have suggested that cognitive-behavioral interventions promoting skill development and family-based therapeutic approaches are among the most effective treatment strategies for adolescents (Vaughn & Howard, 2004). Additional controlled studies of adolescent substance use treatment are needed to create the knowledge base necessary to recommend and disseminate efficacious programs to the practice community. Only limited empirical evidence is available to form the basis of a policy continuum reflecting different levels of treatment for adolescent substance abuse. Standards of care for treatment connected to evidence-based interventions also need to be made available to professionals in the treatment community.

Years of anecdotal evidence suggest that a lack of communication between drug treatment agencies and poor coordination across service systems have interacted to create a mix of programs that have not adequately met the needs of adolescent substance abusers like the case shown here. Several treatment initiatives have shown promise with regard to improving the disjointed treatment system. Drug courts, an initiative funded by the federal government under the National Drug Control Strategy (ONDCP, 2009) are one alternative for juvenile offenders with substance abuse problems. As part of the program, youth may be referred to treatment and receive mandatory drug sanctions in lieu of traditional case-processing. The Tribal Youth program administered by OJJDP (2000) emerged in response to the problem of violent crime and co-occurring substance use disorders among American Indian youth. The departments of Health and Human Services, Education, Interior, and Justice collaborated to design the program. Program objectives include providing a range of assessment and treatment strategies aimed at addressing the unique needs of substance-abusing American Indian youth. The Tribal Youth initiative represents the type of cross-system coordination needed to implement integrated policies and services for troubled youth.

These initiatives represent only the surface of adolescent substance abuse treatment needs in the United States. Efficacy trials of treatment approaches, community advocacy efforts, and standards of care are needed to inform the direction of substance abuse treatment. Coordination across agencies and the development of systems of care should be a top priority in treatment policy discussions.

SUMMARY

Principles of risk, protection, and resilience hold great promise for substance abuse programs and policies. A prevention-and-treatment continuum based on risk and protective factors offers a cogent solution to legislators and policy officials charged with developing effective ways to prevent and reduce adolescent substance abuse. A public health model that incorporates risk and protection as guiding principles is also consistent with the current evidence-based practice movement.

Efforts toward integrating substance abuse policy might benefit by examining overlapping initiatives in juvenile justice and mental health. Co-occurring drug use and mental health problems are well documented among young people. Many youth with concomitant problems are subsequently placed in the nation's juvenile justice and mental health systems. Efforts to improve coordination must also include the array of treatment providers who contract for services with public agencies. Community-based programs that offer outpatient care, day treatment, and residential care must be added to policy discussions across the multiple service systems for children, youth, and families. A public health approach emphasizing risk, protection, and resilience may provide a common language and effective organizing framework for adolescent substance programs and policies.

A Treatment Case Example

A case history. Johnny is a 16-year-old boy who is currently under the jurisdiction and supervision of the juvenile justice system. He has a history of property offending dating back some 6 years to when he was arrested for stealing. In recent years, Johnny's behavior escalated to more serious offenses, including assault. He first experimented with alcohol and marijuana at age 12 and now admits to using marijuana, cocaine, and hallucinogens "whenever and wherever" they are available. Johnny was placed in the juvenile justice system for assaulting a boy in his neighborhood. He reports that he had been drinking and was high on cocaine at the time of the incident.

Johnny's family life had been unstable. His father left home when Johnny was 5 years old; the family has had relatively little contact with him since that time. Johnny has heard from other relatives that his father frequently uses alcohol and that he has been incarcerated on several occasions. Johnny's mother has worked a series of low-paying jobs but has no history of substance abuse. Two years ago, his mother invited her boyfriend into the family home. Johnny was initially resentful of this decision and has adapted to the situation by largely ignoring the boyfriend. Johnny has two sisters, both of whom are younger. Johnny's mother reports that Johnny tends to be withdrawn and sad much of the time. He spends long periods of time alone in his room and has recently stopped seeing many of his friends.

System response. Johnny's case represents a profile that is common among youth in the juvenile justice system. Perhaps what is most typical is the presence of multiple and overlapping behavior problems. Johnny's problems include antisocial conduct, substance abuse, and undiagnosed symptoms of depression.

Theoretically, the presence of these problems could logically lead to placement in the juvenile justice system for antisocial conduct, the substance abuse treatment network for drug-using behaviors, or the mental health system for symptoms of depression. The challenge for treating Johnny—and the thousands of young people like him—lies in integrating system responses and treatments in a manner that addresses Johnny's multiple problems. In Johnny's case, policies that create and support a centralized assessment process might best lead to a coordinated response across multiple service systems.

QUESTIONS FOR DISCUSSION

1. What have been the dominant public policy approaches to adolescent substance abuse in the past four decades? Which strategy has received the greatest percentage of funding?

2. What are the financial and organizational implications of a shift to a public health approach to substance abuse prevention and treatment?

3. What are the challenges in integrating service systems for the delivery of adolescent substance abuse treatment and prevention?

4. What policy recommendations would you make to address the disjointed delivery system?

REFERENCES

Aarons, G. A., Brown, S. A., Hough, R. L., Garland, A. F., & Wood, P. A. (2001). Prevalence of adolescent substance use across five sectors of care. *Journal of the American Academy of Child & Adolescent Psychiatry, 40,* 419–426.

American Academy of Pediatrics. (2000). Insurance coverage of mental health and substance abuse services for children and adolescents: A consensus statement. *Pediatrics, 106,* 860–862.

American Academy of Pediatrics. (2001). Improving substance abuse prevention, assessment, and treatment financing for children and adolescents. *Pediatrics, 108,* 1025–1029.

American Academy of Pediatrics. (2010). About us. Retrieved from http://www.aap.org/visit/cmte35.htm

Annie E. Casey Foundation. (2013). *National KIDS COUNT.* Retrieved from http://www.kidscount.org/datacenter/

Aos, S., Lieb, R., Mayfield, J., Miller, M., & Pennucci, A. (2004). *Benefits and costs of prevention and early intervention programs for youth.* Olympia: Washington State Institute for Public Policy.

Bach, P. B., & Lantos, J. (1999). Methadone dosing, heroin affordability and the severity of addiction. *American Journal of Public Health, 89,* 662–665.

Bandura, A. (1989). Human agency in social cognitive theory. *American Psychologist, 14,* 1175–1184.

Belcher, H. M., & Shinitzky, H. E. (1998). Substance abuse in children: Prediction, protection, and prevention. *Archives of Pediatrics and Adolescent Medicine, 152,* 952–960.

Beronio, K., Po, R., Skopec, L., & Glied, S. (2013). *Affordable Care Act will expand mental health and substance use disorder benefits and parity protections for 62 million Americans.* ASPE Research Brief. Washington, DC: Department of Health and Human Services, Office of the Assistant Secretary for Planning and Evaluation.

Berrueta-Clement, J. R., Schweinhart, L. J., Barnett, W. S., Epstein, A. S., & Weikhard, D. P. (1984). *Changed lives: The effects of the Perry Preschool Program on youths through age 19.* Ypsilanti, MI: High/Scope Press.

Biederman, J., Faraone, S. V., Monuteaux, M. C., & Feighner, J. A. (2000). Patterns of alcohol and drug use in adolescents can be predicted by parental substance use disorders. *Pediatrics, 106,* 792–797.

Biglan, A., & Smolkowski, K. (2002). Intervention effects on adolescent drug use and critical influences on the development of problem behavior. In D. B. Kandel (Ed.). *Stages and pathways of drug involvement: Examining the gateway hypothesis* (pp. 158–183). New York: Cambridge University Press.

Botvin, G. J. (2004). Advancing prevention science and practice: Challenges, critical issues, and future directions. *Prevention Science, 5,* 69–72.

Brook, J. S., Brook, D. W., & Pahl, K. (2006). The developmental context for adolescent substance abuse intervention. In H. A. Liddle & C. L. Rowe (Eds.), *Adolescent substance abuse: Research and clinical advances* (pp. 25–51). New York: Cambridge University Press.

Brook, J. S., Whiteman, M., Gordon, A. S., & Brook, D. W. (1988). The role of older brothers in younger brothers' drug use viewed in the context of parent and peer influences. *Journal of Genetic Psychology, 151,* 59–75.

Burke, M. R. (2002). School-based substance abuse prevention: Political finger-pointing does not work. *Federal Probation, 66,* 66–71.

Burroughs, A. (2003). *Dry: A memoir.* New York: St. Martin's Press.

Cadoret, R. J., Cain, C. A., & Grove, W. M. (1980). Development of alcoholism in adoptees raised apart from alcoholic biologic relatives. *Archives of General Psychiatry, 37,* 561–563.

Carpenter, C. S., & Pechmann, C. (2011). Exposure to the "Above the Influence" antidrug advertisements and adolescent marijuana use in the United States, 2006–2008. *American Journal of Public Health, 101*(5), 948–54.

Catalano, R. F. (2007). Prevention is a sound public and private investment. *Criminology and Public Policy, 6,* 377–398. doi: 10.1111/j.1745-9133.2007.00443.x

Catalano, R. F., & Hawkins, J. D. (1996). The social development model: A theory of antisocial behavior. In J. D. Hawkins (Ed.), *Delinquency and crime: Current theories* (pp. 149–197). New York: Cambridge University Press.

Cauce, A. M., Stewart, A., Rodriguez, M. D., Cochran, B., & Ginzler, J. (2003). Overcoming the odds? Adolescent development in the context of urban poverty. In S. S. Luthar (Ed.), *Resilience and vulnerability: Adaptation in the context of childhood adversities* (pp. 343–363). Cambridge, UK: Cambridge University Press.

Caulkins, J. P., Reuter, P., Iguchi, M. Y., & Chiesa, J. (2005). *How goes the "war on drugs"? An assessment of U.S. drug problems and policy.* Santa Monica, CA: RAND Corporation.

Center for Substance Abuse Treatment. (2002). *Treatment episode data set, 2002.* Retrieved from www .icpsr.umich.edu/SAMHDA/das.html.

Center for Substance Abuse Prevention. (2010). *Communities That Care® community planning system.* Rockville, MD: Author.

Centers for Disease Control and Prevention. (2008). *Understanding youth violence: Fact sheet.* Atlanta: Author.

Cicchetti, D., & Rogosch, F. A. (1999). Psychopathology as risk for adolescent substance use disorders: A developmental psychopathology perspective. *Journal of Clinical Child Psychology, 28,* 355–365.

Cloninger, C. R., Sigvardsson, S., & Bohman, M. (1988). Childhood personality predicts alcohol abuse in young adults. *Alcoholism: Clinical and Experimental Research, 12,* 494–503.

Coie, J. D. (1990). Towards a theory of peer rejection. In S. R. Asher & J. D. Coie (Eds.), *Peer rejection in childhood* (pp. 365–398). New York: Cambridge University Press.

Cook, P. J., & Tauchen, G. (1984). The effect of minimum drinking age legislation on youthful auto fatalities, 1970–1977. *Journal of Legal Studies, 13,* 169–190.

Deas, D., & Thomas, S. E. (2001). An overview of controlled studies of adolescent substance abuse treatment. *The American Journal on Addictions, 10,* 178–189.

Dougherty, D. M. (1993). Adolescent health: Reflections on a report to the U.S. Congress. *American Psychologist, 48,* 193–201.

DuPont, R. L., & Voth, E. A. (1995). Drug legalization, harm reduction, and drug policy. *Annals of Internal Medicine, 123,* 461–465.

Farrelly, M. C., Davis, K. C., Haviland, M. L., Messeri, P., & Healton, C. G. (2005). Evidence of a dose-response relationship between "truth" antismoking ads and youth smoking prevalence. *American Journal of Public Health, 95*(3), 425–431.

Fergusson, D. M., & Horwood, L. J. (1999). Prospective childhood predictors of deviant peer affiliations in adolescence. *Journal of Child Psychology and Psychiatry and Allied Disciplines, 40,* 581–592.

Fergusson, D. M., & Horwood, L. J. (2003). Resilience in childhood adversity: Results of a 21-year study. In S. S. Luthar (Ed.), *Resilience and vulnerability: Adaptation in the context of childhood adversities* (pp. 130–155). New York: Cambridge University Press.

Foxcroft, D. R., Ireland, D., Lister-Sharp, D. J., Lowe, G., & Breen, R. (2003). Longer term primary prevention for alcohol misuse in young people: A systematic review. *Addiction, 98,* 397–411.

Fraser, M. W. (Ed.). (2004). *Risk and resilience in childhood: An ecological perspective* (2nd ed.). Washington, DC: NASW.

Freeman, E. M. (2001). *Substance abuse intervention, prevention, rehabilitation, and systems change strategies: Helping individuals, families, and groups to empower themselves.* New York: Columbia University Press.

Friedman, A. S. (1983). *Clinical research notes.* Rockville, MD: National Institute on Drug Abuse.

Gallup Organization. (2009). *Illegal drugs.* Retrieved from http://www.gallup.com/poll/1657/illegal-drugsw.aspx

Garmezy, N. (1985). Stress-resistant children: The search for protective factors. In J. E. Stevenson (Ed.), *Recent research in developmental psychology* (pp. 213–233). Oxford, UK: Pergamon Press.

Gehshan, S. (1999). *Substance abuse treatment in state children's health insurance programs.* Washington, DC: National Conference of State Legislatures.

Gorman-Smith, D., & Tolan, P. H. (2003). Positive adaptation among youth exposed to community violence. In S. S. Luthar (Ed.), *Resilience and vulnerability: Adaptation in the context of childhood adversities* (pp. 392–413). New York: Cambridge University Press.

Gottfredson, G. D. (1981). Schooling and delinquency. In S. E. Martin, L. B. Sechrest, & R. Redner (Eds.), *New directions in the rehabilitation of criminal offenders* (pp. 424–469). Washington, DC: National Academy Press.

Hamill, P. (1994). *A drinking life: A memoir.* Boston: Little, Brown.

Hannon, L. (2003). Poverty, delinquency, and educational attainment: Cumulative disadvantage or disadvantage saturation? *Sociological Inquiry, 73,* 576–594.

Hansen, W. B. (1992). School-based substance abuse prevention: A review of the state of the art in curriculum: 1980–1990. *Health Education Research, 7,* 403–430.

Hawkins, J. D. (2006). Science, social work, prevention: Finding the intersections. *Social Work Research,* 137–152.

Hawkins, J. D., Brown, E. C., Oesterle, S., Arthur, M. W., Abbot, R. D., & Catalano, R. F. (2008). Early effects of Communities that Care on targeted risks and initiation of delinquent behavior and substance use. *Journal of Adolescent Health, 43,* 15–22.

Hawkins, J. D., Catalano, R. F., & Associates. (1992). *Communities That Care: Action for drug abuse prevention.* San Francisco: Jossey-Bass.

Hawkins, J. D., Catalano, R. F., & Miller, J. Y. (1992). Risk and protective factors for alcohol and other drug problems in adolescence and early adulthood: Implications for substance abuse prevention. *Psychological Bulletin, 112,* 64–105.

Hill, S. Y., Shen, S., Lowers, L., & Locke, J. (2000). Factors predicting the onset of adolescent drinking in families at high risk for developing alcoholism. *Biological Psychiatry, 48,* 265–275.

Holmberg, M. B. (1985). Longitudinal studies of drug abuse in a fifteen-year-old population. I. Drug career. *Acta Psychiatrica Scandinavia, 71,* 67–79.

Howell, J. C. (2003). *Preventing and reducing juvenile delinquency: A comprehensive framework.* Thousand Oaks, CA: Sage.

Irwin, C. E., Burg, S. J., Cart, C. U. (2002). America's adolescents: Where have we been, where are we going? *Journal of Adolescent Health, 31,* 91–121.

James, A. (2007). Mental health in childhood and adolescence. *The Lancet, 369,* 1251–1252.

Jenson, J. M. (2004). Risk and protective factors for alcohol and other drug use in childhood and adolescence. In M. W. Fraser (Ed.), *Risk and resilience in childhood: An ecological perspective* (2nd ed., pp. 183–208). Washington, DC: NASW.

Jenson, J. M. (2010). Advances in preventing childhood and adolescent problem behavior. *Research on Social Work Practice, 20*(6), 701–713.

Jenson, J. M., & Bender, K. A. (2014). *Preventing child and adolescent problem behavior. Evidence-based strategies in schools, families, and communities.* New York: Oxford University Press.

Jenson, J. M., & Howard, M. O. (1999). Hallucinogen use among juvenile probationers: Prevalence and characteristics. *Criminal Justice and Behavior, 26,* 357–372.

Jenson, J. M., Howard, M. O., & Vaughn, M. G. (2004). Assessing social work's contribution to controlled studies of adolescent substance abuse treatment. *Journal of Social Work in the Addictions, 4,* 54–66.

Jenson, J. M., & Potter, C. C. (2003). The effects of cross-system collaboration on mental health and substance abuse problems of detained youth. *Research on Social Work Practice, 13,* 588–607.

Jenson, J. M., Wells, E. A., Plotnick, R. D., Hawkins, J. D., & Catalano, R. F. (1993). The effects of skills and intentions to use drugs on posttreatment drug use of adolescents. *American Journal of Drug and Alcohol Abuse, 19,* 1–17.

Johnston, L. D. (1991). Toward a theory of drug epidemics. In L. Donohew, H. E. Sypher, & W. J. Bukoski (Eds.), *Pervasive communication and drug abuse prevention* (pp. 93–131). Hillsdale, NJ: Lawrence Erlbaum.

Johnston, L. D., O'Malley, P. M., Bachman, J. G., & Schulenberg, J. E. (2013a). *Demographic subgroup trends among adolescents for fifty-one classes of licit and illicit drugs, 1975–2012.* Ann Arbor, MI: Institute for Social Research, The University of Michigan.

Johnston, L. D., O'Malley, P. M., Miech, R. A., Bachman, J. G., & Schulenberg, J. E. (2013b). *Monitoring the Future. National survey results on drug use, 1975–2013.* Bethesda, MD: National Institute of Drug Abuse.

Joksch, H. C. (1988). *The impact of severe penalties on drinking and driving.* Washington, DC: AAA Foundation for Traffic Safety.

Kelder, S. H., Maibach, E., Worden, J. K., Biglan, A., & Levitt, A. (2000). Planning and initiation of the ONDCP National Youth Anti-Drug Media Campaign. *Journal of Public Health Management Practice, 6,* 14–26.

Kim, K. J. (2009). Risk and protective factors for drug use among American youth. In J. A. Mancini & K. A. Roberto (Eds.), *Pathways of human development: Explorations of change* (pp. 113–126). Lanham, MD: Lexington Books.

Kleiman, M. A. (1998). Drugs and drug policy: The case for a slow fix. *Issues in Science and Technology, 15,* 45–52.

Knapp, C. (1996). *Drinking: A love story.* New York: Delta.

Kupersmidt, J. B., Coie, J. D., & Dodge, K. A. (1990). The role of poor peer relationships in the development of disorder. In S. R. Asher & J. D. Coie (Eds.), *Peer rejection in childhood* (pp. 274–305). New York: Cambridge University Press.

Liddle, H. A., & Rowe, C. L. (Eds.). (2006). *Adolescent substance abuse: Research and clinical advances.* New York: Cambridge University Press.

Loeber, R., Farrington, D. P., Stouthamer-Loeber, M., & van Kammen, W. B. (1998). *Antisocial behavior and mental health problems: Explanatory factors in childhood and adolescence.* Mahwah, NJ: Lawrence Erlbaum.

Luthar, S. S. (Ed.). (2003). *Resilience and vulnerability: Adaptation in the context of childhood adversities.* Cambridge, UK: Cambridge University Press.

Lynam, D. R., Milich, R., Zimmerman, R., Novak, S. P., Logan, T. K., Martin, C., & Leukefeld, C., & Clayton, R. (1999). Project DARE: No effects at 10-year follow-up. *Journal of Consulting and Clinical Psychology, 67,* 590–593.

McBride, D. C., VanderWaal, C. J., & Terry-McElrath, Y. M. (2001). *The drug-crime wars: Past, present and future directions in theory, policy and program interventions* (Research Paper Series 14). Washington, DC: The National Institute of Justice.

Meschke, L. L., & Patterson, J. M. (2003). Resilience as a theoretical base for substance abuse prevention. *The Journal of Primary Prevention, 23,* 483–514.

Miller, L., Davies, M., & Greenwald, S. (2000). Religiosity and substance use and abuse among adolescents in the National Comorbidity Survey. *Journal of the American Academy of Child and Adolescent Psychiatry, 39,* 1190–1197.

Morin, S. F., & Collins, C. (2000). Substance abuse prevention: Moving from science to policy. *Addictive Behaviors, 25,* 975–983.

Murray, C. A. (1983). The physical environment and community control of crime. In J. Q. Wilson (Ed.), *Crime and public policy* (pp. 67–91). San Francisco: Institute for Contemporary Studies.

Musto, D. F. (1996). Alcohol in American history. *Scientific American, 274,* 78–82.

National Institute on Drug Abuse. (2009). *Principles of drug addiction treatment: A research-based guide* (2nd ed., NIH Publication No. 09–4180). Washington, DC: U.S. Department of Health and Human Services.

Office of Juvenile Justice and Delinquency Prevention. (2000). *Tribal youth program.* Washington, DC: U.S. Department of Justice, Office of Justice Programs, Office of Juvenile Justice and Delinquency Prevention.

Office of National Drug Control Policy. (1997). *The national youth anti-drug media campaign: Communication strategy statement.* Washington, DC: Author.

Office of National Drug Control Policy. (2009). *The president's national drug control strategy, 2009.* Washington, DC: Executive Office of the President.

Office of National Drug Control Policy. (2010). *Drug free communities support program.* Retrieved from http://www.whitehouse.gov/ondcp/drug-free-communities-support-program

Office of National Drug Control Policy. (2012). *Above the influence.* Retrieved from http://www.whitehouse.gov/sites/default/files/page/files/ati_fact_sheet_6-26-12.pdf

Office of National Drug Control Policy. (2014). *2013 National drug control strategy.* www.whitehouse.gov/ondcp/national-drug-control-strategy

Patient Protection and Affordable Care Act, PL 111-148, §2702, 124 Stat. 199, 318–319 (2010).

Patterson, G. R. (2002). The early development of coercive family process. In J. B. Reid, G. R. Patterson, & J. Snyder (Eds.), *Antisocial behavior in children and adolescents: A developmental analysis and model for intervention* (pp. 25–44). Washington, DC: American Psychological Association.

Patterson, G. R., Reid, J. B., & Eddy, J. M. (2002). A brief history of the Oregon model. In J. B. Reid, G. R. Patterson, & J. Snyder (Eds.), *Antisocial behavior in children and adolescents: A developmental analysis and model for intervention* (pp. 3–24). Washington, DC: American Psychological Association.

Pentz, M. A. (2010). Translating research into practice and practice into research for drug use prevention. In L. Scheier (Ed.). *Handbook of drug use etiology: Theory, methods, and empirical findings* (pp. 581–596). Washington, DC: American Psychological Association.

Physician Leadership on National Drug Policy. (2002). *Adolescent substance abuse: A public health priority: An evidence-based, comprehensive, and integrative approach.* Providence, RI: Brown University, Center for Alcohol and Addiction Studies.

Pilkey, D., Skopec, L., Gee, E., Finegold, K., Amaya, K., & Robinson, W. (2013). *The Affordable Care Act and adolescents. ASPE Research Brief.* Washington, DC: U. S. Department of Health & Human Services, Office of the Assistance Secretary for Planning and Evaluation.

Reinherz, H. Z., Giaconia, R. M., Hauf, A. M., Wasserman, M. S., & Paradis, A. D. (2000). General and specific childhood risk factors for depression and drug disorders by early childhood. *Journal of the American Academy of Child and Adolescent Psychiatry, 39,* 223–231.

Robertson, E. B., David, S. L., & Rao, S. A. (2003). *Preventing drug use among children and adolescents: A research-based guide for parents, educators, and community leaders* (2nd ed.). Bethesda, MD: U.S. Department of Health and Human Services.

Robert Wood Johnson Foundation. (2001). *Substance abuse: The nation's number one health problem. Key indicators for policy.* Princeton, NJ: Author.

Robert Wood Johnson Foundation. (2010). *Publications and research: Addictions.* Retrieved from http://www.rwjf.org/pr/topic.jsp?topicid = 1006

Rosenbaum, S., Johnson, K., Snonsky, C., Markus, A., & DeGraw, C. (1998). The children's hour: The state of children's health insurance program. *Health Affairs, 17,* 75–89.

Rossa, M. W. (2002). Some thoughts about resilience versus positive development, main effects, versus interaction effects and the value of resilience. *Child Development, 71,* 567–569.

Rutter, M. (2000). Psychosocial influences: Critiques, findings, and research needs. *Development and Psychopathology, 12,* 375–405.

Saffer, H., & Grossman, M. (1987). Beer taxes, the legal drinking age, and youth motor vehicle fatalities. *Journal of Legal Studies, 16,* 351–374.

Scheier, L. (Ed.). (2010). *Handbook of drug use etiology: Theory, methods, and empirical findings.* Washington, DC: American Psychological Association.

Scheier, L. M., Grenard, J. L., & Holtz, K. D. (2011). An empirical assessment of the "Above the Influence" advertising campaign. *Journal of Public Health, 95*(3), 425–431.

Schinke, S., Brounstein, P., & Gardner, S. (2002). *Science-based prevention programs and principles, 2002* (DHHS Pub No. SMA 03-3764). Rockville, MD: Substance Abuse and Mental Health Services Administration.

Schinke, S. P., Fang, L., & Cole, K. C. A. (2008). Substance use among early adolescent girls: Risk and protective factors. *Journal of Adolescent Health, 43,* 191–194.

Shedler, J., & Block, J. (1990). Adolescent drug use and psychological health: A longitudinal inquiry. *American Psychologist, 45,* 612–630.

Simcha-Fagan, O., & Schwartz, J. E. (1986). Neighborhood and delinquency: An assessment of contextual effects. *Criminology, 24,* 667–703.

Slater, M.D., Kelly, K. J., Lawrence, F. R., Stanley, L. R., & Cornello, M. L. (2011). Assessing media campaigns linking marijuana non-use with autonomy and aspirations: "Be Under Your Own Influence" and ONDCP's "Above the Influence." *Prevention Science, 12*(1), 12–22.

Snyder, H. (1990). *Growth in minority detentions attributed to drug law violators.* Washington, DC: Office of Juvenile Justice and Delinquency Prevention.

Substance Abuse and Mental Health Services Administration. (2010). *National registry of effective programs.* Retrieved from http://www.nrepp.samhsa.gov/

Substance Abuse and Mental Health Services Administration. (2013). *Results from the 2012 National Survey on Drug Use and Health: Summary of national findings,* NSDUH Series H-46, HHS Publication No. (SMA) 13-4795. Rockville, MD: Author.

U.S. Department of Labor. (2010). *Frequently asked questions about the Mental Health Parity Act.* Retrieved from http://www.dol.gov/ebsa/faqs/faq_consumer_ mentalhealthparity.html

Vaughn, M. G., Freedenthal, S., Jenson, J. M., & Howard, M. O. (2007). Psychiatric symptoms and substance use among juvenile offenders. *Criminal Justice and Behavior, 34,* 1296–1312.

Vaughn, M. G., & Howard, M. O. (2004). Adolescent substance abuse treatment: A synthesis of controlled evaluations. *Research on Social Work Practice, 14,* 325–335.

Vaughn, M. G., Ollie, M. T., McMillen, J. C., Scott, L., & Munson, M. (2007). Substance use and abuse among older youth in foster care. *Addictive Behaviors, 32,* 1929–1935.

Vaughn, M. G., Wallace, J. M., Davis, L., Fernandes, G. T., & Howard, M. O. (2008). Variations in mental health problems, substance use, and delinquency between African American and Caucasian juvenile offenders. *International Journal of Offender Therapy and Comparative Criminology, 52,* 311–329.

Washburn, J. J., Teplin, L. A., Voss, L. S., Simon, C. D., Abram, K. M., & McCelland, G. M. (2008). Pyschiatric disorders among detained youths: A comparison of youths processed in juvenile court and adult criminal court. *Psychiatric Services, 59,* 965–973.

Werner, E. E. (1994). Overcoming the odds. *Developmental and Behavioral Pediatrics, 15,* 131–136.

Werner, E. E., & Smith, R. S. (1989). *Vulnerable but invincible: A longitudinal study of resilient children and youth.* New York: Adams, Bannister, and Cox.

Westat & the Annenberg School for Communication. (2003). *Evaluation of the National Youth Anti-Drug Media Campaign: 2003 report of findings executive summary* (Contract No: N01DA-8-5063). Washington, DC: National Institute on Drug Abuse.

Woolf, S. H. (2008). The power of prevention and what it requires. *Journal of the American Medical Association, 299,* 2437–2439.

Wyrick, D., Wyrick, C. H., Bibeau, D. L., & Fearnow-Kenney, M. (2001). Coverage of adolescent substance use prevention in state frameworks for health education. *Journal of School Health, 71,* 437–442.

Zucker, R. A., Wong, M. M., Puttler, L. I., & Fitzgerald, H. E. (2003). Resilience and vulnerability among sons of alcoholics: Relationship to developmental outcomes between early childhood and adolescence. In S. S. Luthar (Ed.), *Resilience and vulnerability: Adaptation in the context of childhood adversities* (pp. 76–103). New York: Cambridge University Press.

ADDITIONAL READING

Jenson, J. M., & Bender, K. A. (2014). *Preventing child and adolescent problem behavior. Evidence-based strategies in schools, families, and communities.* New York: Oxford University Press.

Liddle, H. A., & Rowe, C. L. (Eds.). (2006). *Adolescent substance abuse: Research and clinical advances.* New York: Cambridge University Press.

Scheier, L. (Ed.). (2010). *Handbook of drug use etiology: Theory, methods, and empirical findings.* Washington, DC: American Psychological Association.

Springer, D. W., & Rubin, A. (Eds.). (2009). *Substance abuse treatment for youth and adults.* Hoboken, NJ: John Wiley.

Tolan, P., Szapocznik, J., & Sambrano, S. (Eds.). (2007). *Preventing youth substance abuse: Science-based programs for children and adolescents.* Washington, DC: American Psychological Association.

WEB-BASED RESOURCES

The Campbell Collaboration, www.campbellcollaboration.org

The Cochrane Collaboration, www.cochrane.org

Monitoring the Future, www.monitoringthefuture.org

National Institute on Drug Abuse, www.nida.nih.gov

Physician Leadership on National Drug Policy, www.PLNDP.org

Robert Wood Johnson Foundation, www.impacteen.org

Social Development Research Group, www.sdrg.u.washington.edu

Substance Abuse and Mental Health Services Administration, www.samhsa.gov

CHAPTER 9

Juvenile Justice Policies and Programs

William H. Barton

The knowledge, events, and values specific to any given point in time exert a profound influence on juvenile justice policy and practices. After decades of "getting tough" with young offenders and flirting with the treatment model du jour, the juvenile justice system now finds itself at a policy and programmatic crossroad. Recent advances in theory, research, and practice based on principles of risk, protection, and resilience hold promise for a more rational, comprehensive set of juvenile justice policies and practices. Nevertheless, such optimism must be tempered by the inevitable role played by societal values, politics, and public perceptions and by limitations in the knowledge base itself.

This chapter provides an outline of this conceptual advance in juvenile justice policy, places it in a historical context, and suggests ways it can be used to improve current and future policies and practices. The first section presents an overview of the goals and stakeholders involved in juvenile justice policy. The second section reviews current patterns of delinquency prevalence and incidence. The third section outlines the risk and protective factors associated with delinquent behavior. The fourth section traces the history of juvenile justice policies, noting the extent to which presumed risk and protective factors have exerted an influence. The final section applies what we have learned about risk, protection, and resilience to juvenile justice policies and practices and concludes that this knowledge base can provide a foundation for more effective and efficient ways to address delinquency through the promotion of positive youth development.

PURPOSE AND OVERVIEW OF JUVENILE JUSTICE POLICY

Prior to the 20th century, the United States did not have a juvenile justice policy per se. Although age was considered a factor in mitigating punishment, the adult court had jurisdiction over children who committed crimes. The first juvenile court was established in Chicago in 1899, and by 1925, all but two states had followed suit (Bernard &

Kurlychek, 2010). The juvenile court was the expression of the first formal juvenile justice policy, which held that juveniles were distinct from adults and that the system should act in the best interests of the child. Specialized juvenile probation services emerged to monitor juveniles who were under the jurisdiction of the court (National Center for Juvenile Justice, 1991).

This two-tiered court system created a tension between the goals of rehabilitation and punishment that continues to this day. As described later in this chapter, the parade of policy reforms since the founding of the juvenile court has reflected alternating emphases on these two primary goals. Historically, relatively lenient policies favoring treatment have alternated with "get tough" policies mandating punishment. Table 9.1 summarizes events that have shaped juvenile justice policy since the founding of the first juvenile court.

Table 9.1   Chronology of Events Affecting U.S. Juvenile Justice Policy

Date	Event	Comments
<1899		Children treated the same as adults under the law
1899	First juvenile court established in Cook County, Illinois	*Parents patriae* philosophy—juvenile court was to act in the best interests of the child
1900–1950	All states establish juvenile courts	
1960s–1980s	Interest in delinquency prevention, diversion, and deinstitutionalization programs	Community organization approaches (e.g., Mobilization for Youth), diversion, and deinstitutionalization are implemented (see 1974 JJDPA below)
1966	*Kent v. United States*	Courts must provide the "essentials of due process" in transferring juveniles to the adult system
1967	*In re* Gault	In hearings that could result in commitment to an institution, juveniles have four basic constitutional rights (notice, counsel, questioning witnesses, protection against self-incrimination)
1968	Juvenile Delinquency Prevention and Control Act	Children charged with status offenses were to be handled outside the court system
1970	*In re* Winship	In delinquency matters, the state must prove its case beyond a reasonable doubt
1971	*McKeiver v. Pennsylvania*	Jury trials are not constitutionally required in juvenile court hearings
1974	Juvenile Justice and Delinquency Prevention Act (JJDPA)	Deinstitutionalization of status offenders; separation of juvenile and adult offenders

(Continued)

Table 9.1 (Continued)

Date	Event	Comments
1975	Lipton, Martinson, & Wilks report	Results misinterpreted by most as indicating that "nothing works" in juvenile corrections
1975	*Breed v. Jones*	Waiver to criminal court following adjudication in juvenile court constitutes double jeopardy
1977–1979	*Oklahoma Publishing Co. v. District Court/Smith v. Daily Mail*	The press may report juvenile court proceedings under certain circumstances
1980	Amendment to the JJDPA	Juveniles removed from adult jails and lockups
1982	*Eddings v. Oklahoma*	Reversed the death sentence of a 16-year-old tried in adult court; ruled that a defendant's young age should be considered a mitigating factor
1984	*Schall v. Martin*	Preventive "pretrial" detention of juveniles is allowable under certain circumstances
1988	Maloney, Romig, & Armstrong introduce the "balanced approach"	Some juvenile justice jurisdictions adopt the three goals of public safety protection, accountability, and competency development
1988	*Thompson v. Oklahoma*	Ruled that the Eighth Amendment prohibits the death penalty for persons younger than 16 years old
1989	*Stanford v. Kentucky*	Ruled that the Eighth Amendment does not prohibit the death penalty for persons who committed capital crimes when 16 or 17 years old
1980s–1990s	Several highly publicized violent acts by juveniles; states "toughen" juvenile codes	More juveniles are transferred to the adult system; many states adopt mandatory sentences; juvenile court confidentiality provisions are weakened; special programs target serious juvenile offenders; "Scared-Straight" and boot camp programs proliferate
1990s	Many states adopt blended sentencing policies	Extends sanctions beyond upper age of juvenile court jurisdiction; creates a middle ground between juvenile and adult sanctions
1990s	Many schools adopt "zero-tolerance" policies	More youths excluded from school; often end up in the juvenile justice system
1993	Office of Juvenile Justice and Delinquency Prevention (OJJDP) introduces its "comprehensive strategy"	Approach favors prevention, risk assessment and classification, and adoption of evidence-based treatment programs; adopted by several states
1995	OJJDP launches "balanced & restorative justice" project	Restorative justice philosophy begins to appear in some jurisdictions (e.g., victim–offender mediation, family group conferences, teen courts)

Date	Event	Comments
1995–2010	The rate of juvenile crime declines; Annie E. Casey Foundation's Juvenile Detention Alternatives Initiative spreads; "What Works" initiative is marketed to jurisdictions to encourage use of evidence-based interventions; major federal re-entry initiatives launched (Serious and Violent Offender Re-entry Initiative)	Despite juvenile crime reductions, formal court processing continues to increase and "get tough" policies remain; use of secure detention and post-adjudication incarceration decrease slightly; some jurisdictions adopt evidence-based interventions
2005	*Roper v. Simmons*	U.S. Supreme Court ruled that the Eighth Amendment prohibits imposing the death penalty on all juveniles under the age of 18
2010–2012	*Graham v. Florida; Miller v. Alabama; Jackson v. Hobbs*	U.S. Supreme Court ruled that the Eighth Amendment does not allow a juvenile offender to be sentenced to life in prison without parole for a non-homicide offense
2011–2014	The rate of juvenile crime remains low. The National Research Council of the National Academy of Sciences issues a major report calling for a developmental approach to juvenile justice. The National Campaign to Reform State Juvenile Justice Systems releases a report titled *The Fourth Wave*.	These reports represent the culmination of the incorporation of concepts of risk, resilience, and developmental science into juvenile justice. While vestiges of the "get tough" policies remain, many jurisdictions are changing their approaches as a result of these conceptual advances and in response to shrinking resources.

Sources: Bazemore and Umbreit (1995); Bernard and Kurlychek (2010); Latessa (2004); Lattimore et al. (2004); McNeese (1998); National Research Council (2013); Skiba et al. (2003); Snyder and Sickmund (1999, 2006); Stanfield (1999); Weiss (2013); Wilson and Howell (1993).

To whom do juvenile justice policies apply? The juvenile court has jurisdiction over young people who meet the definition of a juvenile in a given state and against whom a petition is filed alleging a delinquent act (behavior that would be a crime if committed by an adult) or a status offense (behavior that would not be considered criminal if committed by an adult, e.g., school truancy or running away from home). Once a petition is filed, the juvenile probation department prepares a predisposition report summarizing the facts and context of the case and containing recommendations to the judge for corrective action. Should the judge *adjudicate* the child as delinquent, which is analogous to a determination of guilt in adult criminal court, dispositional options might include probation supervision, placement in a nonresidential program, or residential placements of varying restrictiveness.

The definition of a juvenile, that is, one who comes under the jurisdiction of the juvenile court, varies from state to state. In most states, the upper age limit of juvenile court jurisdiction is 17 years, but in New York and North Carolina, that limit is 15 years; in 10 other states, including Georgia, Massachusetts, Michigan, and Texas, it is 16 years; and in Connecticut, the age limit was raised from 15 to 17 years in 2012 (Office of Juvenile Justice and Delinquency Prevention [OJJDP], 2013a). Further complicating the definition of a juvenile, policies in some states extend juvenile court jurisdiction to age 20 years for status offenses, and most states (32) allow extended juvenile court supervision of placements of delinquents through age 20 (or even older in a few states, including through age 24 in California, Montana, Oregon, and Wisconsin) (OJJDP, 2013b).

States have long been able to use judicial waiver to transfer young offenders to adult court jurisdiction under certain conditions. In the 1990s, many states modified their juvenile codes to redefine young people who commit certain crimes as adults, even though their age would otherwise define them as juveniles. For example, in many states, 14- or 15-year-olds charged with murder or certain other serious crimes can be processed automatically in adult court. In addition, most states have other mechanisms of transferring jurisdiction from juvenile to adult court by judicial waiver, prosecutorial discretion, or both.

Juvenile justice policies affect many other stakeholders, including the family members of young offenders, the neighborhoods in which they live, the broader community, and the public and private service providers who administer juvenile justice programs. Thus, as juvenile justice policies shift emphases among the system's goals, there are ongoing implications for family stability, neighborhood social capital, and the economy. Taxpayers pay for the majority of juvenile justice services. In recent years, the cost of such services has been rapidly increasing, led by treatments that are more intensive, settings that are most restrictive (i.e., requiring greater security measures), and services that are of greater duration.

DELINQUENCY AND DELINQUENTS: PREVALENCE AND TRENDS

As noted earlier, the term *delinquency* technically refers to acts committed by juveniles that would be crimes if committed by adults. However, delinquency often colloquially refers to the full range of problem behaviors exhibited by young people that could result in their appearance in juvenile court. A complication emerges when we realize that delinquency is a concept defined through a combination of behavioral indicators and societal definitions and responses, and these definitions and responses tend to change over time. Indeed, some behaviors that are currently not considered as delinquency may have once fit the definition, whereas some contemporary constructions of delinquent behavior might not have been labeled as problematic in other times. For example, in earlier eras, delinquency included simply being seen near an unsavory establishment or being poor and congregating in public with other poor children (Bernard & Kurlychek, 2010). More recently, some altercations among youth that previously would have been ignored or handled informally by parents, neighbors, or schools now lead to formal charges. The dynamic nature of the concept of delinquency poses some problems for a discussion of risk and protective factors because there is at least an implicit assumption that the outcome being "predicted" is at the individual level.

Despite the preceding caveat, describing the current prevalence and distribution of delinquency provides a sense of its scope. There are two ways to approach this task. First, given the focus of this chapter on juvenile justice policies and how they apply to those who become involved with the juvenile justice system, we summarize recent data on juvenile arrests and court processing. Then, because not all delinquent behavior is detected or formally processed but is, at least in large part, presumably related to the same etiological factors, we summarize what is known from self-report delinquency studies.

In 2011, the most recent year for which data are available, 1.47 million people younger than 18 years of age were arrested in the United States, accounting for 20% of all arrests for property crimes and 13% of arrests for violent crimes (Puzzanchera, 2013). Most U.S. crimes are committed by people between the ages of 10 and 49 years old, 20% of whom are between 10 and 17 years old, according to the 2010 Census (Howden & Meyer, 2013). Thus, juveniles are overrepresented in arrests for such crimes as arson (42%), vandalism (29%), robbery (22%), burglary (21%), and motor vehicle theft (21%) but are underrepresented in arrests for such crimes as murder (8%), aggravated assault (10%), drug abuse violations (10%), and forcible rape (14%) (Puzzanchera, 2013). In 2011, females were involved in about one third (29%) of juvenile arrests (Puzzanchera, 2013). Although African Americans make up just 17% of the U.S. population between the ages of 10 and 17 years old, African American youth accounted for much higher percentages of juvenile arrests for nearly all offense categories (e.g., violent crimes, 51%; property crimes, 35%; drug abuse violations, 23%) (Puzzanchera, 2013). Similar arrest data are not available for Hispanic youth. However, there is evidence that Hispanic youth are slightly overrepresented at other points in the juvenile justice system. In 2011, about 21% of the U.S. population between 10 and 17 years old was Hispanic (author calculation, based on data tables in U.S. Census Bureau, 2013); in a 1-day census in 2011, Hispanic youth accounted for 25% of those detained and 22% of those in residential juvenile correctional placement (Sickmund, Sladky, Kang, & Puzzanchera, 2013).

Another way to look at juvenile offense patterns is to consider the proportion of juvenile arrests accounted for by various crimes. Of the 1.47 million juvenile arrests in 2011, 4.6% were for violent index offenses (e.g., murder, non-negligent manslaughter, forcible rape, robbery, aggravated assault); 23% were for property crime index offenses (e.g., burglary, larceny-theft, motor vehicle theft, arson); 13% were for other assaults; 10% were for drug offenses; 9% were for disorderly conduct; 7% were for alcohol offenses; 5% were for vandalism; and the remaining 28% were for other nonindex offenses (based on Puzzanchera, 2013). Juvenile arrest rates for nearly all crimes have decreased noticeably since a high point in the mid-1990s, with an overall decline of 31% from 2002 to 2011, and are at their lowest levels since 1980 (Puzzanchera, 2013). The decline has been even more pronounced for African American youth than for White youth, excluding a brief uptick between 2004 and 2008 (Puzzanchera, 2013).

Of course, police do not refer all arrested youth to juvenile courts. In 2011, police referred 68% of arrested youth to juvenile courts and 7% directly to adult courts, while releasing 22%, with the remaining 3% referred to some other service (Puzzanchera, 2013). In 2010, juvenile courts processed about 1.4 million delinquency cases (Puzzanchera & Robson, 2014). In contrast to juvenile arrest trends, juvenile court delinquency caseloads increased 17% from 1985 to 2010, although they declined 19% from 2001 to 2010 (Puzzanchera & Robson, 2014). Of the delinquency cases brought before juvenile courts in

2010, more than half (54%) resulted in formal petitions, about one-third (31%) were adjudicated delinquent, and about 8% were placed out of the home (Puzzanchera & Robson, 2014). The large majority of all cases (about 67%), whether formally petitioned or not, received some form of consequence (or service), including probation, placement, or some other sanction (Puzzanchera & Robson, 2014).

The official record data described above reflect the volume of delinquency brought to the attention of law enforcement and the courts. However, juvenile arrest and court data do not give a good estimate of the overall incidence or prevalence of delinquent behavior. Much delinquent activity goes undetected or unprocessed by the system. Moreover, arrests are case-specific rather than person-specific or crime-specific. That is, the same juvenile may account for several arrests, a single arrest may result from several crimes committed by an individual, and a single crime may result in the arrest of multiple individuals (Puzzanchera, 2013). Therefore, studies of self-reported delinquency can be a useful supplement to official data.

Self-report delinquency studies have a long history in criminology research, with the consensus being that youths' self-reports of delinquent activity are reasonably reliable and valid when collected under appropriate conditions of anonymity or confidentiality (Elliott & Ageton, 1980; Farrington, Loeber, Stouthamer-Loeber, Van Kammen, & Schmidt, 1996; Hindelang, Hirschi, & Weis, 1981; O'Malley, Bachman, & Johnston, 1983). Studies based on samples of general school populations have consistently shown that about 80% of adolescents report having engaged in behavior that could have gotten them in trouble with the law if detected. A relatively high number of adolescents report use of alcohol and illegal substances, truancy, and minor fights (Elliott, Huizinga, & Ageton, 1985; Farrington et al., 1996). A smaller number of adolescents report involvement in serious offenses against people or property. Relatively few adolescents report frequently committing such offenses, and most do not go on to commit crimes as adults (Elliott et al., 1985; Farrington et al., 1996; Moffitt & Caspi, 2001). Thus, although a large majority of youth engages in some misconduct, relatively few—only 6% to 8%—are the chronic, serious juvenile offenders who account for most of the serious juvenile crime (Hamparian, 1978; Wolfgang, Figlio, & Sellin, 1972; Wolfgang, Thornberry, & Figlio, 1987). Risk and protective factors for delinquent conduct are described next.

Risk and Protective Factors for Delinquency

The risk and protection framework for understanding delinquency has evolved from separate lines of research and theory. Some researchers have adopted an epidemiological approach to the study of youth problem behaviors, such as psychopathology, substance abuse (Hawkins, Catalano, & Miller, 1992), delinquency (Dryfoos, 1990; Elliott, 1994; Thornberry, Huizinga, & Loeber, 1995; Tremblay & Craig, 1995), school dropout (Wehlage, Rutter, Smith, Lesko, & Fernandez, 1989), and teenage pregnancy (Dryfoos, 1990; Franklin, Grant, Corcoran, O'Dell, & Bultman, 1995). From a different perspective, other researchers have attempted to understand why some individuals achieve positive developmental outcomes despite resembling those at highest risk for failure (Anthony, 1987; Rutter, 1985; Werner & Smith, 2001). In recent decades, these streams of research and theory have converged to identify a common set of risk and protective factors associated with various developmental outcomes.

Risk factors have been defined by Fraser, Kirby, and Smokowski (2004) as "any influences that increase the chances for harm or, more specifically, influences that increase the probability of onset, digression to a more serious state, or maintenance of a problem condition" (p. 14). Regarding *protective factors*, some scholars make a distinction between *direct* protective factors that predict low involvement in problem behaviors with or without the presence of risk and *indirect* or *buffering* factors that operate in the presence of risk to mediate or buffer the effect of risk, thus enhancing positive adaptation (Garmezy, 1985; Lösel & Farrington, 2012; Masten, 1994; Rutter, 1985). Others suggest using the term *promotive factors* for those influences associated with positive developmental outcomes for all people, reserving the term *protective factors* for those that operate only or more strongly in the presence of risk (Fraser et al., 2004; Fraser & Terzian, 2005; Sameroff, 1999). Risk, promotive, and protective factors each may operate in either domain-specific (i.e., related to specific developmental outcomes) or general ways.

Most research on risk, promotive, and protective factors usually focuses on linking variation in these potentially predictive factors with variation in outcomes such as delinquency, other youth problems, and/or positive developmental trajectories. Also important to an understanding of risk, resilience, and juvenile justice is the growing understanding of what may be considered a universal risk of adolescence as a developmental stage. Studies of adolescent brain development since the late 1990s have produced a growing consensus that "adolescence" is defined less by chronological age than by a combination of biological markers and social roles, brain development does not proceed at the same pace for everyone and may not be complete until one's mid-20s, the frontal lobe (responsible for decision-making) develops last, and significant hormonal changes occur that are linked to emotionality and aggression (Dahl, 2004; Weinberger, Elvevag, & Giedd, 2005). Accordingly, impulsive behavior is essentially normal for adolescents, some of this impulsivity may lead to engagement in delinquent behavior, and, in turn, such behavior may lead to encounters with law enforcement and the juvenile justice system (Coalition for Juvenile Justice, 2006). Of course, how these developmental patterns play out for individual youth depends upon a complex interplay of the variable ecological influences discussed below.

Several recent reviews summarized the research regarding risk factors, protective factors, and resilience in general (Durlak, 1998; Fraser et al., 2004; Werner & Smith, 2001) and for delinquency and violence in particular (Hawkins et al., 2000; Howell, 2003; Lipsey & Derzon, 1998; Lösel & Farrington, 2012; Office of the Surgeon General, 2001; Stouthamer-Loeber, Loeber, Wei, Farrington, & Wikström, 2002; Williams, Ayers, Van Dorn, & Arthur, 2004). Table 9.2 lists risk, protective, and promotive factors identified at various ecological levels in those reviews.

Individual Level

Some risk and protective factors are biological or genetic in origin. For example, males are at higher risk than females for antisocial behavior (e.g., Patterson, Reid, & Dishion, 1992). Recent work suggests that the absence of the genetically controlled monoamine

Table 9.2 Risk, Protective, and Promotive Factors for Juvenile Delinquency

Level	Risk Factors	Protective/Promotive Factors
Individual: Biological and Genetic	Gender (male)[abcd] Absence of MAOA gene[af] Neuropsychological defects[e] Cognitive defects—low IQ[bcdefh] Difficult temperament[ce] Hyperactivity/ADHD[bdef] Perinatal trauma[eh] Neurotoxins[e] Maternal alcohol or drug use in pregnancy[e]	Gender (female)[e] High heart rate[f] High IQ[adfgh] Easy temperament[aefh]
Individual: Psychological and Behavioral	Aggression[bcd] Beliefs favorable to deviance[cd] Alienation[cde] Rebelliousness[e] Impulsiveness[cf] Risk-taking[bc]	Assertiveness[h] Prosocial attitudes/beliefs[defg] Social problem-solving skills[hi] Self-efficacy[afi] Self-esteem[a] Internal locus of control[fh] Religious/spiritual orientation[f]
Family	Family management problems[abcde] Family conflict[acde] Lack of parental involvement[bcde] Low level of parental education[h] Low family SES[f] Child maltreatment[abcdh] Family history of crime[bcde] Parental antisocial personality[e] Parental psychopathology[ah] Parental attitudes favoring deviance[d] Parent–child separation[bcdh] Divorce[cdeh] Large family size[c]	Positive discipline techniques[ce] Supportive relationships[aefghi] Monitoring and supervision[ef] Parent with high school education or more[h] Low parental stress[f] Above average family SES[f] Good communication[g] Family advocacy[e] Achievement orientation[ef] Strong spiritual values[e] Racial pride[e] Extended family bonds[e] Fewer siblings[g]
Other Adults		Presence of caring adult[ah]
Peers	Antisocial peers[bcdef] Delinquent siblings[b] Gang membership[bd]	Prosocial peer group[efghi] Social isolation[f]
School	Early academic failure[bcdeh] Low school commitment[bcde] Aggressive behavior in school[e] Poor-quality schools[c] Truancy[bc] Frequent school transitions[b]	Academic success[aefgh] Positive bonding to school[defgh] Positive school climate[f] High-quality schools[i]

Neighborhood	High population density[e] High population mobility[e] Physical deterioration[ce] High crime rates[bd] Availability of drugs/weapons[be] Lack of social cohesion[e] Low resident attachment[e]	Collective efficacy[a] Non-disadvantaged neighborhood[fg] Low neighborhood crime/low violence[fg]
Society/Community	Antisocial community norms/laws[e] Exposure to violence[b] Racial prejudice and discrimination[ab] Few education/employment opportunities[a] Poverty[abcdeh]	Prosocial community norms/laws[ei] Support[e] Empowerment[e] Many education/employment opportunities[a] Boundaries and expectations[e] Constructive use of time[e] Regular church involvement[h]

a. Fraser, Kirby, and Smokowski (2004).

b. Hawkins et al. (2000).

c. Lipsey and Derzon (1998).

d. Office of the Surgeon General (2001).

e. Williams et al. (2004).

f. Lösel & Farrington (2012).

g. Stouthamer-Loeber et al. (2002).

h. Werner and Smith (2001).

i. Durlak (1998).

oxidase (MAOA) enzyme is associated with aggressive behavior (Rowe, 2001) and that its presence can buffer the risks associated with early child maltreatment (Kim-Cohen et al., 2006). Several researchers have identified the role of temperament in resilience, finding that, from an early age, children with an "easy" temperament fare better than do those with a "difficult" temperament (Moffitt & Caspi, 2001; Werner & Smith, 2001). Presumably, the child's natural temperament elicits responses in kind from parents and others. Hyperactivity in young children is associated with later behavioral problems and delinquency (Loeber, Farrington, & Petechuk, 2003). Intelligence, as measured with IQ tests, can be seen as a protective factor when high (Masten, 1994) and a risk factor when low (Loeber, Farrington, Stouthamer-Loeber, & van Kammen, 1998). Hawkins, Catalano, and Miller (1992) reported a relationship between a mother's alcohol and drug use during pregnancy and a child's later delinquency.

Other factors at the individual level are psychological or behavioral. Risk factors include early aggressive behavior (Farrington, 1991; Hawkins et al., 2000), rebelliousness, and alienation (Williams et al., 2004). Attitudes and beliefs favorable to deviance are a risk factor (Hawkins et al., 2000), whereas prosocial attitudes act as a protective factor (Lösel & Farrington, 2012; Office of the Surgeon General, 2001; Williams et al., 2004). Other protective or promotive factors include high levels of internal locus of control and asser-tiveness (Werner & Smith, 2001), social problem-solving skills (Durlak, 1998; Werner & Smith, 2001; Williams et al., 2004), self-efficacy, self-esteem (Fraser et al., 2004), and hav-ing a religious or spiritual orientation (Lösel & Farrington, 2012).

Family Level

The family represents the most salient social context for children; therefore, it is not surprising that the literature identifies a number of important risk and protective or promo-tive factors within the family. A relatively consistent picture emerges. Through attachment and modeling, the family exerts a profound effect on children's behavior. Nearly all authors of systematic reviews have noted inconsistent or harsh discipline practices, parental crim-inality, child maltreatment, lack of parental involvement, and divorce as risk factors and concurrently mentioned warm relationships with prosocial parents who are involved in their children's lives and who provide consistent monitoring and discipline as perhaps the strongest protective or promotive factor (Durlak, 1998; Fraser et al., 2004; Hawkins et al., 2000; Lipsey & Derzon, 1998; Lösel & Farrington, 2012; Office of the Surgeon General, 2001; Stouthamer-Loeber et al., 2002; Werner & Smith, 2001; Williams et al., 2004). Werner and Smith (2001) noted the role of parental education in preventing antisocial conduct and found that parents with a high school education represented the line tipping the scale from a risk factor to a protective factor. However, a more recent study by Theokas and Lerner (2006) suggested that the strongest family factor protecting against adolescent risk behav-iors is not parental education but rather "collective activity," such as eating dinner together. Williams et al. (2004) mentioned several protective factors that appear to apply specifically to African American families, including a strong achievement orientation, presence of strong spiritual values, racial pride, and bonds to extended family members.

From a meta-analysis of 119 studies that examined relationships between various fam-ily characteristics and concurrent or later problem behaviors, Derzon (2010) concluded that family factors (including family SES, discord, stability, warmth and relationship, and child-rearing skills, among others) may play a more complex role. As an example, Derzon (2010) notes,

> ...the lack of care-giver warmth may, on its own, modestly increase the likelihood of youth antisocial behavior. However, in the presence of other risk factors (e.g., gang membership, drug use, low impulse control), warm relationships between care-giver and child likely reduces the influence of these factors while the lack of warmth may significantly amplify the impact of those risk factors in generating antisocial behavior. (p. 290)

Peers

Association with delinquent peers is a frequently cited and relatively strong correlate of delinquency, which appears to apply more to adolescents than to younger children (Hawkins et al., 2000; Moffitt, 1993; Office of the Surgeon General, 2001). It would seem logical that delinquent peers can both model and reinforce antisocial behavior, although it may also be the case that delinquent youth select delinquent friends. Lösel and Farrington (2012), however, cautioned that delinquent peers may be a marker rather than a cause of delinquency. Interestingly, in a multisite study, Henry, Tolan, Gorman-Smith, and Schoeny (2012) found that peer deviance was a significant risk only for White youth and not for African American or Latino youth. On the other hand, Haggerty, Skinner, McGlynn-Wright, Catalano, and Crutchfield (2013) found no race differences in predictors of teen violence. There appears to be a consensus that association with prosocial peers functions as a protective or promotive factor regardless of race (Durlak, 1998; Lösel & Farrington, 2012; Stouthamer-Loeber et al., 2002; Werner & Smith, 2001).

Other Adults

A relationship with a caring adult outside of the immediate family is an important protective factor or asset (Eccles & Gootman, 2002; Fraser et al., 2004; Scales & Leffert, 1999; Werner & Smith, 2001). Such a relationship may emerge naturally with an extended family member, a neighbor, or teacher. Alternatively, this relationship may be arranged in formal mentoring programs, such as the Big Brothers and Big Sisters program. This program has been successful in reducing recidivism among young offenders (Tierney, Grossman, & Resch, 1995).

Schools

Next to the family, schools are the most important social arena for children and adolescents. The literature consistently indicates that school commitment and academic performance are linked to developmental outcomes. Low commitment and poor performance are consistently identified as risk factors, and strong commitment and good performance are identified as protective factors (Fraser et al., 2004; Hawkins et al., 2000; Henry et al., 2012; Lipsey & Derzon, 1998; Lösel & Farrington, 2012; Mann & Reynolds, 2006; Office of the Surgeon General, 2001; Richart, Brooks, & Soler, 2003; Stouthamer-Loeber et al., 2002; Werner & Smith, 2001; Williams et al., 2004). Moreover, there is evidence that the quality of the school environment plays an important role in the onset and prevention of delinquency (Durlak, 1998; Gottfredson, 2000; Lipsey & Derzon, 1998).

Neighborhood and Community

Poverty is one of the most frequently cited correlates of delinquency (Fraser et al., 2004; Hawkins, Catalano, & Miller, 1992; Hawkins et al., 2000; Lipsey & Derzon, 1998; Office of the Surgeon General, 2001; Werner & Smith, 2001). The availability of drugs and weapons, exposure to violence, and neighborhood disorganization in general (e.g., high population mobility, physical deterioration, high crime rates, and lack of social cohesion) are risk factors for delinquency (Aisenberg & Herrenkohl, 2008; Hawkins et al., 2000; Nash & Bowen, 1999; Sampson, Raudenbush, & Earls, 1997; Williams et al., 2004). On the other hand, communities and neighborhoods with high collective efficacy are presumed to exert informal social control that helps protect against delinquency (Fraser et al., 2004; Lösel & Farrington, 2012; Nash & Bowen, 1999; Sampson et al., 1997).

Community norms broadly affect delinquency through formal laws and policies as well as informal means (Durlak, 1998; Hawkins, Catalano, & Miller, 1992; Williams et al., 2004). For example, a community that vigorously pursues enforcement of age limits for the purchase of alcohol might be expected to have lower delinquency rates. Fraser et al. (2004) noted that limited opportunities for education and employment and the presence of racial discrimination are risk factors for delinquency, whereas the presence of opportunities for education and employment provides protection from delinquency.

Race and Ethnicity

When considering risk and resilience, it is challenging to disentangle race and ethnicity from socioeconomic status. It is clear that African American and Latino youth in particular show higher rates of involvement in youth problem behaviors generally (Cauce, Cruz, Corona, & Conger, 2011) and in delinquency in particular, as described previously in this chapter. African American and Latino youth are much more likely than White youth to reside in high-poverty neighborhoods, which in turn exposes them to much higher levels of the community-level risk factors listed above (e.g., low social cohesion, exposure to violence, availability of drugs and weapons, etc.) and places families at higher levels of stress. In addition to facing the neighborhood conditions just mentioned, many African American and Latino families are headed by single parents, many parents struggle to find work (or, if working, struggle to find adequate time to supervise children), and many families lack other childcare resources, all of which may negatively affect parenting practices (Cauce et al., 2011). While research in general indicates that parental warmth, engagement, and support provide strong protection regardless of race or ethnicity (Fraser et al., 2004; Li, Nussbaum, & Richards, 2007; Williams et al., 2004) and that authoritarian parenting styles are less effective, there is evidence that strong discipline may be effective in buffering many of the low-income neighborhood risks in African American and Latino households (Cauce et al., 2011). Finally, as will be argued below, the juvenile justice system itself may be viewed as a risk factor, and youth of color are clearly overrepresented throughout the system (a review of the extensive literature on Disproportionate Minority Contact is beyond the scope of this chapter; for a quick summary, see Bell & Ridolfi, 2008; National Council on Crime and Delinquency, 2007).

Gender Differences

A recent meta-analysis of predictors of delinquency among girls documented important gender differences in risk and needs profiles (Hubbard & Pratt, 2002). The results indicated that even though many of the strong predictors were the same as those for boys (e.g., history of antisocial behavior, antisocial peers, antisocial attitudes, and antisocial personality), the role of other predictors was more pronounced among girls. These gender-dependent factors included IQ, family dysfunction, trauma and sexual abuse, mental health and substance abuse problems, high-risk sexual behaviors, and school problems (Hubbard & Pratt, 2002). These findings were consistent with those of a recent study of 672 girls in detention, which determined that most of the girls had experienced trauma (84%), met criteria for mental health problems (78%), reported having a parent or close friend with criminal justice system involvement (61%), and had been sexually active (76%) (Lederman, Dakof,

Larrea, & Li, 2004). In another study, detained girls were significantly more likely than were detained boys to exhibit risks and needs related to family and parenting, mental health, traumatic events, physical health, psychopathy, accountability, and peer relationships (Gavazzi, Yarcheck, & Chesney-Lind, 2006).

Although these differences suggest the need for gender-specific programming, the evidence supporting the effectiveness of gender-specific programming is not yet compelling. Zahn and colleagues, in a recent systematic review of evaluations of gender-specific and gender-neutral programs, concluded that (a) there were very few strong studies available, (b) there was no evidence that gender-specific programs were more effective than other programs in reducing recidivism, and (c) there was evidence that programs with a strong history of success with boys also worked well for girls (Zahn, Day, Mihalic, & Tichavsky, 2009). However, the investigators noted that gender-specific programs showed positive results on measures related to empowerment and quality of life, including education, employment, relationships, self-esteem, and self-efficacy (Zahn et al., 2009).

Summary

In addition to illustrating the ecological nature of risk and protection, several key themes emerge from this review:

- Many risk, promotive, and protective factors are malleable (e.g., the presence of social support, the development of social skills, parenting skills); others are not subject to change (e.g., IQ, temperament, gender).

- The effect of risk factors is not necessarily linear; that is, the presence of multiple risk factors can increase the probability of undesirable outcomes exponentially (Lösel & Farrington, 2012; Pollard, Hawkins, & Arthur, 1999; Rutter, 2001).

- There is both overlap—among the risk, protective, and promotive factors—and co-occurrence—among adolescent problem behaviors—with a set of common risk and protective factors associated with a range of problems (Dryfoos, 1990; Hawkins, Catalano, & Miller, 1992; Huizinga, Loeber, Thornberry, & Cothern, 2000).

- The effect of some risk and protective factors is developmentally specific (Hawkins et al., 2000; Office of the Surgeon General, 2001).

- Risk and protective factors generally appear to operate similarly across cultural and ethnic groups (Elliott, Huizinga, & Menard, 1989; Haggerty et al., 2013; Hawkins, Laub, & Lauritsen, 1998; Williams, Ayers, Abbott, Hawkins, & Catalano, 1999), with some exceptions (Cauce et al., 2011; Henry et al., 2012); however, there are gender differences as noted above.

- Risk factors can combine either simultaneously or cumulatively over time and, in either case, increase the probability of undesirable outcomes.

- In general, risk factors and protective factors are inversely distributed across social strata; that is, those at highest risk generally have fewer natural protections than those at lower risk (Cauce et al., 2011; Pollard et al., 1999).

A useful theoretical framework for summarizing knowledge of risk, protection, resilience, and developmental outcomes comes from the social development model (Catalano & Hawkins, 1996), which is a synthesis of social control theory, social learning theory, and differential association theory. Although developed as an explanation for antisocial behavior, the social developmental model is more broadly applicable to developmental outcomes. Catalano and Hawkins (1996) outlined the four purported socialization processes affecting children that constitute the heart of the model:

> (1) perceived opportunities for involvement in activities and interactions with others, (2) the degree of involvement and interaction, (3) the skills to participate in these involvements and interactions, and (4) the reinforcement they perceive as forthcoming from performance in activities and interactions. (p. 156)

Through these processes, the child develops a social bond with the socializing unit, with its strength dependent on the consistency of the socializing processes. Bonding, which consists of attachment, commitment, and beliefs, then influences the child's subsequent behavior as he or she seeks to maintain the connection. Antisocial behavior results from (a) a weakening of the bond with prosocial socialization agents; (b) a situation in which, even in the presence of a prosocial bond, the situational inducements to deviance are sufficiently compelling; or (c) a situation in which the child develops a strong bond to antisocial socialization agents, including parents or peers. Finally, the social developmental model contains developmentally specific submodels that reflect changes in the child's salient socialization agents at different ages (e.g., the progression from family to school). From this model, it can be seen that behavior emerges from the ecological interplay of individual characteristics, social interactions, and environmental supports/constraints; the direction of the developmental trajectory (prosocial or antisocial) is dependent on the array of risk, protective, and promotive factors.

Notwithstanding the substantial advances in research and theory regarding risk and resilience, no one should assume that knowledge of risk and protective profiles can predict long-term developmental outcomes with pinpoint accuracy. For example, attempts to quantify the effect sizes of various risk factors have shown that the predictive power of even the most powerful risk factors is modest (Hawkins et al., 2000; Office of the Surgeon General, 2001). Evidence from longitudinal studies suggests that turning points, such as military service and, especially, marriage, can have a profound effect on positively redirecting developmental trajectories (Laub & Sampson, 2003; Werner & Smith, 2001). The error variance in predictive models may be due to incomplete specification of the predictors, or it may indicate that chance, personal agency, and individuals' interpretation of the immediate context play major roles in eliciting behavior. As Lösel and Bender (2003) noted, "errors in prediction of antisociality in childhood and adolescence should not just be viewed as a technical deficit. They are also indicators of the general phenomena of multifinality and equifinality in development" (p. 131). In sum, although the growing knowledge base of the risk and resilience framework may have great relevance for policies and practices, that knowledge must be applied cautiously and with recognition of its limits.

RISK, PROTECTION, AND RESILIENCE IN JUVENILE JUSTICE POLICY

Until recently, knowledge of risk, protection, and resilience had not influenced juvenile justice policies and programs in profound ways. This lack of influence in itself is not surprising because this knowledge base has emerged only within the last few decades. Instead, policies and practices appear to have primarily reflected concepts such as deterrence, incapacitation, and retribution, with an occasional dose of developmental psychology. Juvenile justice policies and programs have sought to protect the community and to reform offenders by teaching offenders that delinquency leads to unpleasant consequences. This lesson has been implemented by either closely supervising offenders' behavior or placing offenders in restrictive settings, keeping them off the streets for some time.

In the century since the founding of the juvenile court, juvenile justice policies have evolved amid the dialectic between the goals of punishment and rehabilitation of young offenders. Bernard and Kurlychek (2010) have captured this fluctuating history well, describing the "cycle of juvenile justice" as beginning with the observation that delinquency is a serious and escalating problem, blaming the problem on the current tenor of policies (either "get tough" or lenient), advocating reforms moving to the other pole, discovering that the problem remains unsolved, blaming the then-current tenor of policies, switching to the other pole again, and so on.

Juvenile courts were meant to function in the best interests of the child, and early juvenile correctional programs were supposed to be treatment programs rather than prisons. However, when high rates of delinquency and recidivism continued, the juvenile court and juvenile correctional practices became tougher. Specifically, the court's discretionary powers, which were intended to reduce the punitiveness of the adult courts, became suspect because juveniles lacked many due process protections. A series of U.S. Supreme Court challenges gradually brought many of those due process protections into the juvenile court by the latter part of the 20th century (Bernard & Kurlychek, 2010; Snyder & Sickmund, 1999). However, the increasing formality of the juvenile court system has rendered it more like the adult system and perhaps paved the way for policies such as "three strikes," mandatory sentences for some offenses, and the increasing use of transfer to the adult system via judicial waiver, prosecutorial direct file, or statutory exclusion.

JUVENILE JUSTICE SYSTEM INVOLVEMENT AND INCARCERATION AS RISK FACTORS

Throughout its checkered history, the juvenile justice system has continually relied on secure, residential placements, both before adjudication (detention) and after adjudication (training schools and private secure residential facilities). In recent years, a number of studies have documented major problems with the use of such facilities (for a recent vivid qualitative examination, see Bernstein, 2014). Specifically:

1. Secure facilities are overused; many youths in secure residential facilities are not serious or chronic offenders and could be placed in less restrictive settings (Snyder & Sickmund, 1999, 2006).

2. Many secure residential facilities house youths in poor conditions characterized by overcrowding (Livesy, Sickmund, & Sladky, 2009), sexual abuse (Beck, Harrison, & Guerino, 2010), or otherwise unsafe environments (Lerner, 1986; Parent et al., 1994).

3. Secure residential facilities are relatively ineffective; that is, gains made during incarceration, if any, tend to dissipate when youths return to the community, and recidivism outcomes are often no better—or even worse—than would be found in less restrictive, community-based settings (Gatti, Tremblay, & Vitaro, 2009; Holman & Ziedenberg, 2006; Lipsey, 1992; Loeber & Farrington, 1998; Loughran et al., 2009).

Treatment programming in juvenile corrections has used behavioral contingencies and, more recently, cognitive-behavioral approaches to modify behavior and thinking patterns that are presumed to lead to offending behavior. Within the field, there has been some recognition of the importance of peer influences on adolescents, as expressed in treatment models such as *guided group interaction* (McCorkle, Elias, & Bixby, 1958) and *positive peer culture* (Vorath & Brendtro, 1974). However, whatever the treatment modality, recidivism has remained high, with studies finding that between 50% and 90% of youths are reincarcerated in juvenile or adult facilities within 1 to 3 years of their release from juvenile correctional facilities (Howell, 2003; Minor, Wells, & Angel, 2008; Trulson, Marquart, Mullings, & Caeti, 2005).

Considerable evidence has accumulated to suggest that juvenile justice system involvement is itself a risk factor for poor developmental outcomes. The iatrogenic effects (i.e., unintentional detrimental or harmful effects) of involvement with the juvenile justice system include, but are not limited to, future offending. For example, even after controlling for offense-related and demographic factors, both the use of secure detention and the decision to formally process a case have been linked to more restrictive dispositions and higher levels of recidivism (Feld, 1991; Frazier & Bishop, 1985; Frazier & Cochran, 1986). Similarly, the research cited above about the iatrogenic effects of incarceration is compelling (Gatti et al., 2009; Holman & Ziedenberg, 2006; Lipsey, 1992; Loeber & Farrington, 1998; Loughran et al., 2009). Social learning theory (Akers, 1985) provides one theoretical explanation for these relationships; exposure to other delinquent peers occurs in most juvenile justice interventions, especially incarceration, and it results in peer-deviancy training (Dishion, McCord, & Poulin, 1999; Dishion, Spracklen, & Patterson, 1996; Dodge, Dishion, & Lansford, 2006). Alternatively, labeling theory (Becker, 1963; Bernburg, Krohn, & Rivera, 2006; Lemert, 1951) suggests that others respond to the label of *delinquent* by expecting the youth to behave accordingly, and youth who are labeled as delinquent might also internalize that label. In addition to being a risk factor for recidivism, juvenile justice system involvement during adolescence is associated with limited educational, employment, and financial outcomes as well as adult mental health disorders and substance abuse (Fagan & Freeman, 1999; Moffitt, Caspi, Harrington, & Milne, 2002). For a recent review of the evidence regarding the deleterious social, developmental, and fiscal consequences of incarcerating juveniles, see a recent report from the Justice Policy Institute (Petteruti, Walsh, & Velázquez, 2009).

RISK, RESILIENCE, AND RECENT REFORM EFFORTS

Despite the "get tough" climate of juvenile justice policies initiated since the latter part of the 20th century, some policy officials have recognized the ineffectiveness and expense of relying on incarceration to reform offenders. Therefore, some policymakers have advocated for greater use of community-based programs at all stages of the juvenile justice system. In many instances, community-based responses have served to divert youths from formal processing through the system. In other instances, community-based resources have served as integral parts of the formal system (e.g., probation) or as complementary components (e.g., community-based treatment programs). For a review of community-based programs in juvenile justice, see Barton (2002).

In an attempt to move beyond the punishment–rehabilitation dialectic, Maloney, Romig, and Armstrong (1988) provided a major advance in conceptualizing juvenile justice goals by articulating the "balanced approach" to probation. According to this approach, juvenile justice policymakers must consciously balance concern for three system goals: (1) public safety protection, (2) accountability (of the juvenile and the system), and (3) competency development. In other words, every decision point in the system must consider and account for these three goals. Several states subsequently adopted the balanced approach in their juvenile codes or agency mission statements.

More recently, advocates of restorative justice (e.g., Bazemore & Terry, 1997; Bazemore & Umbreit, 1995) have sought to replace the traditional retributive paradigm of juvenile justice, which views crimes as offenses committed against society, with a new paradigm that views crimes as upsetting the balance of rights and obligations, with victims and offenders seeking a mediated restoration of that balance. Although the restorative justice paradigm has not been adopted fully in most places, elements of restorative justice have increasingly appeared, usually targeting minor or first-time offenders, including such practices as family-group conferences (McGarrell, Olivares, Crawford, & Kroovand, 2000) and teen courts (Butts, Buck, & Coggeshall, 2002). In many ways, the restorative justice approach is consistent with the principles of risk, protection, and resilience.

Since the mid-1990s, knowledge about risk and protective factors has found its way into mainstream juvenile justice policy discussions and has been heavily promoted by the Office of Juvenile Justice and Delinquency Prevention in its comprehensive strategy (Howell, 1995; Wilson & Howell, 1993). This strategy combines an emphasis on prevention strategies, which attempt to reduce community risk factors and enhance protective factors, with the application of community-based interventions (and less use of incarceration) and evidence-based treatment models in the juvenile justice system. Although not limited to jurisdictions adopting the comprehensive strategy, an increasingly common application of risk principles (albeit not resilience) to juvenile justice has been the use of structured risk-assessment instruments (Howell, 2003; Wiebush, Baird, Krisberg, & Onek, 1995). Many jurisdictions now use such instruments at various points in the juvenile justice system to guide decisions regarding placement in secure detention, probation supervision levels, dispositional placement restrictiveness, and aftercare planning (Wiebush et al., 1995).

Risk, protection, and resilience are explicitly ecological concepts; however, the tendency is to apply them primarily at the individual level. Thus, we see the contemporary extension of the typological enterprise, with an emphasis on developing risk and need profiles of individual youths and making juvenile justice system decisions (e.g., detention placements, treatment plans) at least partly based on these assessments. This approach may or may not be much of an improvement. The evidence suggests that although risk and protective factors have some explanatory power at the aggregate level, these factors do not do a very good job of predicting outcomes at the individual level (Laub & Sampson, 2003; Office of the Surgeon General, 2001; White, Moffitt, Earls, Robins, & Silva, 1990). The use of risk profiles represents an improvement over pure chance predictions, but the rate of false-positive and false-negative predictions is high. False-positive predictions are characterized by individuals with high-risk profiles who do not go on to commit more offenses. Conversely, false-negative predictions involve youths with low-risk profiles who do go on to commit crimes. In some sense, the advances in risk and protective factor research may have provided juvenile justice policymakers and practitioners with an exaggerated sense of confidence that their decisions are evidence-based decisions.

RISK, RESILIENCE, AND EVIDENCE-BASED PROGRAMS

A burgeoning literature on "what works" in juvenile justice has emerged in recent decades as a counter to the now infamously misinterpreted "nothing works" mantra of the 1970s (Lipton, Martinson, & Wilks, 1975). Major reviews and meta-analyses of juvenile correctional treatment programs have indicated that many approaches, if implemented correctly and targeted toward the appropriate youths, can reduce recidivism (Andrews et al., 1990; Lipsey, 1992; Lipsey & Wilson, 1998). Several websites list prevention and intervention programs with research-based evidence of effectiveness. For example, The Blueprints for Violence Prevention (Center for the Study and Prevention of Violence [CSPV], 2014) considers model programs to be those that meet the following criteria: evidence of a deterrent effect with a strong research design, sustained effect, and multiple site replications. Promising programs meet only the first criterion. As of this writing, the Blueprints website lists nine model programs and 23 promising programs addressing youth risk or protective factors related to delinquency.

The financial burden of programs is also an important consideration. The Washington State Institute for Public Policy (WSIPP) has applied a sophisticated cost–benefit analysis based on meta-analyses of a wide range of crime-prevention and intervention programs for juveniles and adults (Drake, Aos, & Miller, 2009). The WSIPP analysis found that many prevention and intervention programs are cost-effective, whereas others are not. Table 9.3 presents a listing of several juvenile programs and indicates whether they are Blueprint model programs and whether the program has been determined as cost-effective by the WSIPP.

In the WSIPP model, benefits are estimated per participant and reflect the combined savings to taxpayers from reduced criminal justice processing costs (if any) and the value of crime victim benefits based on the program's estimated effect on preventing future crimes, net of program costs (Drake et al., 2009). Programs with poor economic returns include "Scared Straight" programs, wilderness challenge programs, intensive probation or parole programs, and boot camps, none of which is even remotely informed by the

Table 9.3   Model and/or Cost-Effective Prevention/Intervention Programs

Program	Model Program[a]	Cost-Effective[b]
Functional Family Therapy (FFT)	Yes	Yes
Life Skills Training (LST)	Yes	Yes
Multisystemic Therapy (MST)	Yes	Yes
Nurse-Family Partnership	Yes	Yes
Multidimensional Treatment Foster Care (MTFC)	Yes	Yes
New Beginnings (Intervention for Children of Divorce)	Yes	
Positive Action *(School-based program)*	Yes	
Promoting Alternative Thinking Strategies (PATHS)	Yes	
Project Towards No Drug Abuse	Yes	
Aggression Replacement Therapy		Yes
Multidimensional Family Therapy (MDTF) for substance abusers		Yes
Restorative justice for low-risk offenders		Yes
Teen courts		Yes
Drug court		Yes
Family integrated transitions		Yes
Adolescent diversion project		Yes
Interagency coordination programs		Yes
Early childhood education for low-income 3- and 4-year-olds		Yes

a. Center for the Study and Prevention of Violence (2014).

b. Aos and Drake (2013); Drake, Aos, and Miller (2009).

risk and resilience framework. In contrast, prevention programs that strengthen families, provide mentoring, and foster school success and social skills, along with intervention programs that are either explicitly ecological or target key risk factors, were found to be highly cost effective (Drake et al., 2009). Examples of highly cost-effective programs included Multisystemic Therapy, Functional Family Therapy, and coordinated services (i.e., comprehensive, coordinated services also called *wraparound* services). Drake and colleagues (2009), with a partial, more recent update (Aos & Drake, 2013), reported that these programs offered combined benefits per participant, ranging from about $15,000 to as much as $88,000 (see above for how benefits were calculated). It is no accident that these cost-effective approaches are either informed by or consistent with the risk and resilience framework.

Although much of the research base on risk and protection uses the presence or absence of delinquency as the primary dependent variable, merely preventing delinquent or anti-social behavior may not be the only positive goal of risk- and resilience-based interventions. The resilience literature and positive youth development literature remind us that being "problem-free isn't fully prepared" (Pittman & Irby, 1996, p. 3). The juvenile justice system is primarily concerned with preventing the recurrence of delinquency. However, that system might be more successful if it were to embrace the universal goals of positive youth development, which focus on promoting competence, character, connections, confidence, and contribution (Hamilton, Hamilton, & Pittman, 2004). In this way, communities would have the opportunity not only to prevent youth problem behaviors but also to promote long-term, healthy development.

Clearly, formal juvenile justice system involvement, particularly incarceration, interrupts the normal course of adolescent development. It disrupts adolescents' ability to complete developmental tasks by removing them from the supports and opportunities available in the community to their nondelinquent peers (Altschuler, 2005; Chung, Little, & Steinberg, 2005). Although the risk and resilience framework has increasingly informed juvenile justice policies and programs, its full potential has yet to be realized. It can provide a foundation for more fundamental changes in juvenile justice policies and practices. These changes would incorporate the truly ecological nature of risk and resilience, broaden the system goals from merely controlling delinquent behavior to promoting positive youth development, and rely on and further promote coordination among the various service systems that affect the lives of adolescents, as advocated by Jenson and Fraser (2006). The next section explores what some of those changes might look like and highlights some efforts that are currently underway.

USING KNOWLEDGE OF RISK, PROTECTION, AND RESILIENCE TO ENHANCE JUVENILE JUSTICE POLICY AND PRACTICES

Based on the risk and resilience framework, Fraser and Terzian (2005) outlined three basic practice principles: (1) strengthen protection and reduce risk (both must be addressed); (2) understand the effect of the social and developmental context on protection and risk; and (3) identify and disrupt risk mechanisms, that is, the "sequencing of events that elevate risk" (p. 20). The Blueprint model programs and the cost-effective programs identified by WSIPP, along with the following discussion of additional ways to incorporate the risk and resilience framework into juvenile justice, are congruent with these practice principles.

Changing the Culture of Juvenile Justice

Thorough application of the risk and resilience framework would require a change in the prevailing juvenile justice culture, and that traditional culture is deeply entrenched. It is difficult for justice system actors to transcend long-standing beliefs in the effectiveness of deterrence and punishment, despite evidence to the contrary. It is also difficult for those working in the current juvenile justice system to take an ecological view when confronted with a steady stream of individuals. The culture of many juvenile justice agencies is "passive-defensive," with routinized procedures, resistance to innovation, and "climates characterized by depersonalization, emotional exhaustion, role overload, and role conflict" (Hemmelgarn, Glisson, & James, 2006, pp. 76–77). The effects of this culture and climate include low morale, high rates of staff turnover, and cookie-cutter approaches to case planning and interventions. The poor outcomes have been documented previously in this chapter.

In the last few years, interest in incorporating positive youth development principles into juvenile justice has grown, albeit not without recognition of the challenges facing such a transformation (Barton, 2004; Butts, Bazemore, & Meroe, 2010; Butts, Mayer, & Ruth, 2005; Frabutt, Di Luca, & Graves, 2008; Schwartz, 2001; Torbet & Thomas, 2005). There are some juvenile justice settings in which the positive youth development perspective has taken root, and although strong evidence of effectiveness is not yet available, these settings tend to produce more positive climates, less staff turnover, and much lower rates of recidivism (Barton & Butts, 2008; Barton & Mackin, 2012; Barton, Mackin, & Fields, 2008; Kurtz & Linnemann, 2006). The comments of an administrator who shepherded such a transformation are provided in Box 1.

Several factors appear to promote the successful transformation of an agency's culture:

- A hospitable community culture—the values in relatively progressive communities are more likely to be congruent with positive youth development principles;

- The commitment of leadership—establishing and championing a vision, facilitating and empowering staff to adopt innovation, and staying the course;

- Adopting the strengths perspective as the practice model;

- Encouraging early adopters to serve as role models and peer trainers;

- Thorough training, followed by periodic "booster" trainings;

- Intentional hiring—bringing on staff already familiar with positive youth development principles and/or strength-based practice, or at least those who do not have to "unlearn" the traditional approaches;

- Integration into bureaucratic processing—make the paperwork reflect the goals and practice principles (more details on this point appear below);

- Consistent reinforcement through regular staff supervision;

- Collaboration with other agencies in the community—organizational permeability helps to prevent a return to the isolated correctional culture;

- Using feedback from data on youth outcomes for continuous quality improvement and to help "sell" the new approach. (Barton & Butts, 2008, pp. 43–45)

The integration of positive youth development principles and the strengths perspective into the bureaucratic processing of juvenile justice agencies is especially critical. This integration can be, and should be, completed at two levels: individual practice and program accountability. Integration at the level of individual practice requires the adoption of a structured strengths assessment. Some of the risk assessment instruments mentioned previously include some coverage of strengths but typically address strengths as an afterthought, and seldom do the strengths inform case planning in any meaningful way. There are instruments that staff can use to assess strengths, including the Behavioral and Emotional Rating Scale (Epstein & Sharma, 1998), Child and Adolescent Needs and Strengths (Lyons, Griffin, Fazio, & Lyons, 1999), and the Youth Competency Assessment (Mackin, Weller, Tarte, & Nissen, 2005; Nissen, Mackin, Weller, & Tarte, 2005). These instruments encourage staff to create truly individualized intervention plans, and the process of administering the assessment also enables staff to develop stronger relationships with the youths; such relationships are at the heart of producing positive change (Barton & Butts, 2008).

To promote program accountability congruent with the risk and resilience and positive youth development frameworks, program design and evaluation should be based on explicit program theory, which highlights the role of the positive youth development principles as both intermediate and longer term outcomes. An evaluation of an out-of-school-time program provides an example of the application of such a logic model (Anthony, Alter, & Jenson, 2009). This model begins with the identification of risks at multiple ecological levels and then designs interventions to provide protections intended to build resilience and produce intermediate outcomes related to positive youth development (competence, confidence, character, and connection), which, in turn, are expected to produce long-term outcomes including not only reduced antisocial behavior but milestones of positive development (educational achievement and economic self-sufficiency; Anthony et al., 2009, p. 49). Making explicit the linkages between risk, resilience, positive youth development, and long-term promotion of positive developmental outcomes (and reduction of the probability of negative developmental outcomes), models such as this one encourage program stakeholders to focus rationally on strategies that risk and resilience theory and research suggest will be most effective.

Comments of a County Juvenile Probation Administrator About Changing the Culture

I would say that, . . . commonly in our field, there are two different mindsets. One is that these kids are doing things that are harmful to other people, to society, and that's true. And so people who have that view of these kids—harmful to society—they often have a lot of compassion for victims, and they take a point of view that the only way to approach that is to control that, to contain that, and that might mean removing kids from the community or restricting [kids]; this whole restrictive-punitive notion of how you deal with that. And then there are the other people who [think that] these are kids who you need to support, develop, and help. And I think that the most significant realization that we can come to is that they are not mutually exclusive, incompatible approaches, and that there is another way—which acknowledges that the kids have hurt society and have created victims and hurt people—but at the same time acknowledges that they have the capabilities and strengths and capacities that haven't been tapped; and that the approach is that you can do all of these things at one time. . . . Just because you have identified a kid's strengths doesn't mean that you . . . say, "We accept the things you've done." And I think it's the same thing for parents or running any organization. There are certain things that are not acceptable—and you have to be very clear about what those are—but at the same time you acknowledge that there are a lot of things in each individual that are very strong, and you point those to success. So I think that it's that bifocal frame of reference that you have to overcome: it's not either-or.

I think the only way you can overcome it—[because] you *don't* go into a big room of 400 people or your big staff and tell them that, you *don't* preach it. I could probably say better what you *don't* do; I know what you don't do—What you do is first of all [have] patience and recognize that organizational change takes years, and that you need to [be] very explicit. . . . I approach things [with] fairly long-range plans, long-range vision and constantly communicate that vision. [I am] very clear about what that [vision] is; it's not very complicated. It can be very simple, and you pretty much keep saying the same things over and over again. You can see it here; we are pretty clear about what our values are. We defined what they are, we make decisions of hiring based on those values, we incorporate them at every level. You model them, and then you see change over the course of the years.

Source: [Name withheld], from interview transcript with this author, October 11, 2006. This county department had adopted a strength-based, positive youth development approach in 2001. By 2004, its rate of delinquency petitions was substantially lower than that of the other large counties in its state. Its recidivism rate of 25% was lower than the state average and had fallen faster than that in the rest of the state.

JUVENILE JUSTICE INTERVENTIONS

As noted previously, efforts within the core of the juvenile justice system to incorporate knowledge of risk, protection, and resilience in policy and practice have been limited. Nevertheless, there are some promising ways that the risk and resilience perspective can inform juvenile justice policies and practices. Chief among these is the use of truly individualized, collaborative case coordination in system of care (SOC) (Duchnowski, Kutash, & Friedman, 2002; Stroul & Friedman, 1986) or wraparound service models (Burchard, Bruns, & Burchard, 2002; Goldman, 1999; VanDenBerg & Grealish, 1996). The wraparound approach explicitly values culturally competent, strengths-based assessment and practice (Saleebey, 2013); involves youths, parents, informal sources of support, and professionals as partners in service planning; and operates through a formal collaboration among provider agencies that span traditional service arenas and use blended funding streams (Goldman, 1999). A growing body of evidence supports the promise of wraparound services (Burchard et al., 2002) and indicates that this approach is cost-effective (Aos, Phipps, Barnoski, & Lieb, 2001).

Models of individualized wraparound service can be applied to juvenile justice (Kendziora & Osher, 2004). Wraparound programs such as Wraparound Milwaukee (Kamradt, 2000;

Wraparound Milwaukee, n.d.) and the Dawn Project in Indianapolis (Choices, 2010) serve youth with mental health or substance abuse needs who enter the juvenile justice system. These programs have reported promising results in terms of reduced residential placements and lowered recidivism (Kamradt, 2000; Wisconsin Council on Children and Families, 2010; Wright & Anderson, 2005). Most, if not all, cases currently entering the juvenile justice system or transitioning from residential placements could benefit from wraparound services. The intensity of services could vary based on the assessed needs and strengths of the individuals, their families, and contexts. Not all would require lengthy and expensive services, and the use of and length of stay in costly residential placements would likely decrease.

The Annie E. Casey Foundation's Juvenile Detention Alternatives Initiative (JDAI) is another vehicle that has triggered culture shifts in several jurisdictions. Using a detailed blueprint to guide detention reform, JDAI encourages stakeholders to adopt values consistent with the risk and resilience framework to reshape their understanding of detention and, by extension, the broader juvenile justice system. Formally launched in five sites in 1993, JDAI had expanded to more than 250 sites in 39 states by 2013, covering about one-third of the nation's youths (Mendel, 2014). Although the initiative has not been successful or sustained in all sites, a recent evaluation documented dramatic reductions in the use of secure detention (50% or more) in many sites, with no concomitant increases in juvenile crime or failures to appear for court hearings (Mendel, 2014). Moreover, the JDAI approach has been credited with other system improvements beyond reductions in secure detention use, including reduced disproportionate minority contact, fewer commitments to state juvenile correctional institutions, enhancements to community-based intervention alternatives, and greater collaboration among system stakeholders (Mendel, 2014). From personal experience with several JDAI sites, I have been struck by changes in the way JDAI site stakeholders view and talk about youth, including greater recognition of the applicability of a strengths-based, positive youth development lens that focuses as much on enhancing protective factors as on controlling risk factors.

In the last few years, the cumulative research on risk and resilience, coupled with advances in developmental science, appears to have reached a broader audience of policymakers and practitioners, fueling some promising, holistic proposals for transforming the juvenile justice system. For example, the National Research Council (2013) and the National Campaign to Reform State Juvenile Justice Systems (Weiss, 2013) have offered comprehensive strategies and pointed to several exemplary programs and jurisdictions. Not only do these approaches rest on convincing evidence of effectiveness, but they promise to be less costly. Perhaps some of the impetus for embracing these approaches comes from jurisdictions' recent fiscal constraints, but perhaps it also reflects the eventual translation of research into practice. It remains to be seen whether these perspectives, what Weiss (2013) has termed the "Fourth Wave" of juvenile justice reforms, will take root, promote the culture change in juvenile justice described in the previous section, and be sustained, or turn out simply to be another pendulum swing in the cycle of juvenile justice (Bernard & Kurlychek, 2010).

A more radical way of embracing the risk and resilience framework might be to divorce the juvenile justice system from treatment programming altogether. Others have advocated splitting the legal and social welfare programming aspects of the court (e.g., Feld, 1999), but for slightly different reasons. Recall the three goals of juvenile justice articulated in the balanced approach as described earlier (Maloney et al., 1988). Perhaps the juvenile justice system should concentrate on what it could do best—public safety protection and account-ability enforcement from a *just deserts* framework, transferring responsibility for compe-tency development to community service providers more aligned with the risk and resilience framework. That is, there would still be juvenile court proceedings, probation oversight, and enforcement of the terms of accountability. However, probation would work in partnership with community service providers and other community stakeholders, who would both participate in the development of dispositional recommendations to the court and provide the individualized case management services.

Prevention

Knowledge of risk, protection, and resilience may be most useful for juvenile justice at the periphery of the system, where the corrosive influence of the traditional juvenile justice culture is either absent or minimal. The best example is prevention, where this knowledge can inform efforts to lower the risks and increase the protection in entire communities or focus efforts on targeting risks and strengthening protection in the more specific contexts of schools or families. The *Communities That Care* (CTC) approach of Hawkins, Catalano, and Associates (1992) is an example of community-wide prevention that is developed in considerable detail. CTC components include a framework for community mobilization, local assessment of risk and protective factors, and a menu of evidence-based programs that can be tailored to meet specific communities' needs. An evaluation of CTC in several Pennsylvania communities showed CTC counties with modestly reduced delinquency rates even though implementation was inconsistent (Greenberg & Feinberg, 2002). More recently, a CTC evaluation that used a randomized, county-level design in several states showed promising early results in terms of reductions in targeted risk factors and delayed onset of delinquent behavior among youth in CTC sites (Hawkins et al., 2008) and CTC appears on the most recent WSIPP list of evidence-based, general prevention programs (WSIPP, 2014).

There is evidence that school-based prevention programs targeting risk factors can be effective (CSPV, 2014; Hawkins & Herrenkohl, 2003). These programs address the major school-based risks, including early aggressive behavior, academic failure, and low commit-ment to school. The promising approaches that Hawkins and Herrenkohl reviewed included attempts to improve organizational climate and classroom management, to engage families in supporting academic achievement, to increase opportunities for school bonding, to teach emotional skills for self-control and social interaction, and to promote prosocial norms.

Similarly, Tremblay and Japel (2003) reviewed a number of programs that appeared effec-tive in preventing delinquency by improving parents' skills and supports, addressing chil-dren's cognitive skills, and reducing early disruptive behavior among children. Tremblay and Japel's review showed that several perinatal and preschool programs effectively changed parenting behavior in at-risk families (e.g., communication, attitudes, discipline techniques) in ways that would appear to reduce risks and strengthen protection. Another group of stud-ies included in Tremblay and Japel's review supported the notion that very early interven-tions with at-risk families, including parent training, environmental stimulation, and parent support could improve children's cognitive functioning and reduce early disruptive behaviors. Tremblay and Japel (2003) concluded, "The general impression from the review of the twenty-eight prevention experiments is that early childhood interventions can have a positive impact on the three most important risk factors for juvenile delinquency: disruptive behavior, cognitive skills, and parenting" (p. 237).

More recently, Hall, Simon, Lee, and Mercy (2012) identified several promising youth violence prevention approaches that emphasize community collaborations targeting locally specified risk and protective factors. In addition, the Office of Justice Programs and Centers for Disease Control and Prevention published a comprehensive approach to gang prevention (Simon, Ritter, & Mahendra, 2013) that builds upon the ecological risk and resilience and positive youth development frameworks discussed in this chapter.

Aftercare

Another key opportunity for incorporating the risk and resilience framework at the periphery of juvenile justice is aftercare, as best exemplified by the Intensive Aftercare Program model (IAP) developed by Altschuler and Armstrong (1991, 1998). IAP includes the following key components:

- case management services;
- a collaborative network of community services;
- services that are "backed in" to the residential facility (i.e., the case manager meets with the youth, conducts an assessment, develops a release plan, and arranges for relevant community-based service providers to visit the youth in the facility prior to release);
- a "step-down" process, in which youths move first into a transition phase, gradually experiencing more community interaction during the last weeks of incarceration, and then go on to closely supervised release, and finally to decreased supervision; and
- a system of graduated sanctions to help control behavior during aftercare. (Altschuler & Armstrong, 1998)

The Boys & Girls Clubs of America has recently attempted to blend IAP and strengths-based principles in juvenile aftercare programs in several sites (Barton, 2006). A case example illustrating ways to incorporate strengths into aftercare programming is discussed in Box 2.

Evidence for the effectiveness of juvenile aftercare programs is mixed. The National Council on Crime and Delinquency (NCCD) evaluated three IAP pilot sites over a 5-year period, using an experimental design that included random assignment to IAP and a control group in each site (Wiebush, Wagner, McNulty, Wang, & Le, 2005). The study concluded that recidivism rates were high for both the IAP and control groups. These disappointing results were tempered somewhat by cautions related to small sample sizes and by the observation that many youths in the control groups may have received enhanced parole services as well. Finally, there was some evidence that among the IAP participants, those who received higher levels of services both prerelease and postrelease showed lower rates of recidivism (Wiebush et al., 2005). A more recent evaluation of the Boys & Girls Clubs of America's juvenile reentry programs, which are also based on the IAP model, produced findings similar to those of the NCCD study (Barton, Jarjoura, & Rosay, 2014). The authors attributed the lack of strong evidence for effectiveness to many daunting implementation challenges faced by the sites. However, Aos (2004) found promising results in a quasi-experimental evaluation of Washington State's Family Integrated Transitions (FIT) program. Although not identical to the IAP model, the FIT program shares many important elements, including family involvement, a collaborative team approach to case management, and continuity between prerelease and postrelease phases.

Incorporating Strengths in Juvenile Aftercare

When Raymond was a 12-year-old, he was committed for possession of a firearm on school property. He was sent to one of two maximum security facilities for boys in the state. He struggled with the program at the facility and spent 2 years at the facility before he was released on 6 months parole and allowed to live with his mother. Just after he completed his parole, while staying with his father in a nearby county, he was arrested on a battery charge. He was placed back with his mother and ordered to serve home detention for 3 months. The day after he was released from home detention, he left the house without permission. He used drugs he stole from his aunt, who also lived in the house, and his mother reported him to the police. He resisted arrest and was committed back to the state, being sent to a second maximum security facility as a 15-year-old.

This time, he completed the treatment program at the state facility with few problems. Although he could have been released after 10 months, there were concerns about him living with either parent. The mother lived in a trailer with four children and a husband. The father owned a strip club and was at work every night for the entire night. Consequently, Raymond would have been without supervision in his father's home. Raymond preferred to live with his father; his mother resented this and acted to prevent it. Their relationship was very strained as a result, and they broke off all contact. Raymond no longer knows how to get in touch with his mother. Finally, arrangements were made for Raymond to be released to a group home. He spent 7 days at the group home before he was arrested for shoplifting. He was recommitted to the secure care facility. He is now 17 years old and expects to be released this fall.

He currently has access to an aftercare program that began working with him in the secure care facility. In addition to many risk factors (early involvement with the system, aggression, broken home, strained relationship with his mother, negative peer involvement), his aftercare worker has identified several strengths in Raymond. He is strong academically; is a skilled athlete; is competent in using assertiveness to avoid peer pressure; is eager to please adults and people in authority; is developing

(Continued)

(Continued)

skills in decision-making and problem-solving; and is able to reflect critically on his own thinking, choices, and behavior. He has demonstrated good insights into his relationships with his family, has expressed that he wants to work with a mentor, and has been open to asking for assistance. He enjoys working on service projects and willingly takes a leadership role, if allowed.

Raymond and his father have a good relationship, and each cares about the other. His father is planning to remarry soon. A placement with his father may be possible this time, if the father's new wife is willing and able to help with evening supervision. Raymond expects to complete his GED while in the facility and wants to go to college. His aftercare worker will help him apply to the local technical college. Other components of his reentry plan include providing Raymond with an opportunity to participate in Youth as Resources service projects with other prosocial youth and perhaps to work at a Boys & Girls Club, where he can combine his athletic interests with his leadership skills. He will be referred for counseling to help him deal with his feelings about his relationship with his mother. An important aspect of this aftercare program is the continuity of the mentoring relationship with the aftercare worker begun in the facility and continuing into the community.

Source: Adapted from Dr. Roger Jarjoura, director, Aftercare for Indiana Through Mentoring, personal communication, June 10, 2004. Used with permission.

SUMMARY

Juvenile justice policies and practices are society's way of confronting and dealing with behavior beyond the social norms, that is, juvenile delinquency. The United States historically has vacillated between an emphasis on punishment and treatment of juvenile delinquents, with neither approach proving very effective. The juvenile court was established in 1899 to formally recognize that children were distinct from adults. However, since then, the vacillation between punishment and treatment emphases has intensified. To illustrate, the juvenile court has taken on more of the trappings of the adult system, and the end of the 20th century produced a wave of "get tough" policies such as zero tolerance and the increased use of transfers to the adult court, despite a decline in juvenile crime rates since the late 1990s.

An examination of juvenile justice policy and practice trends reveals little explicit connection to the research and theory that has grown from the risk and resilience perspective until very recently. Its impact may finally be growing, as evidenced by several major policy initiatives. The risk and resilience framework evolved from two initially separate streams of research: developmental psychopathology, using epidemiological methods to identify the causes of youth problem behaviors, and longitudinal studies of resilience seeking to understand why some people attain positive developmental outcomes in the face of high risk or adversity. A reasonable consensus has emerged regarding an array of risk and protective or promotive factors at various ecological levels—the individual, family, peers, school, neighborhood, community, and society—that influence the probability of delinquency and other youth problems.

It is logical to assume that this knowledge can help the juvenile justice system develop policies and practices that, by reducing risk and enhancing protection, prevent delinquency or its recurrence. At present, the most common application of this framework has been the proliferation of risk-assessment instruments to guide placement or treatment decisions at various points in the juvenile justice process. This chapter has argued that despite the impressive aggregate claims of the risk and resilience research, this risk-assessment approach, although perhaps an improvement over purely discretionary, clinical judgment, has limitations because it primarily presumes a degree of predictive accuracy at the individual level that does not exist.

This chapter has presented several promising strategies for incorporating risk and resilience into the juvenile justice system, including community-wide prevention initiatives, targeted prevention in schools or with families, and interventions such as individualized wraparound services and aftercare programs that aim to work across system boundaries. Truly meaningful change in juvenile justice policies and practices requires a culture shift in the way system actors view youth and the goals of the system. This shift should be based on the ecological risk and resilience framework, pursue positive youth development goals in addition to the prevention and control of delinquency, and incorporate a strengths-based, collaborative approach to practice. This chapter highlighted some recent attempts to transform the juvenile justice culture, including the explicit adoption of a strength-based, positive youth development approach in some jurisdictions; the Annie E. Casey Foundation's JDAI; and recent national proposals to reform juvenile justice using concepts of risk, resilience, and developmental science. All of these strategies include making the boundaries of the juvenile justice system more permeable through formal collaborations with other community entities. In this way, the partnering agencies and stakeholders can reinforce the application of the risk and resilience framework, thereby enhancing the juvenile justice system's ability to achieve all three of its goals: public safety protection, accountability, *and* competency development.

QUESTIONS FOR DISCUSSION

1. What are the main obstacles to incorporating the principles of risk, protection, and resilience into juvenile justice policies and practices?

2. In what ways is the strengths perspective compatible with the principles of risk, protection, and resilience?

3. What are the major factors leading to reforms or modifications of juvenile justice policies and practices? Which, if any, are most apt to lead to sustained changes? Why?

4. How do risk and protective factors for juvenile delinquency compare with those identified for other youth problems, such as substance abuse or poor school adjustment?

5. Do you think the "Fourth Wave" of juvenile justice reforms emerging in recent years will spread? Why or why not? If such reforms do become widely adopted, do you think they will be sustained or be overtaken by a subsequent round of "get tough" policies and practices?

REFERENCES

Aisenberg, E., & Herrenkohl, T. (2008). Community violence in context: Risk and resilience in children and families. *Journal of Interpersonal Violence, 23,* 296–315. doi:10.1177/0886260507312287

Akers, R. L. (1985). *Deviant behavior: A social learning approach* (3rd ed.). Belmont, CA: Wadsworth.

Altschuler, D. M. (2005). Policy and program perspectives on the transition to adulthood for adolescents in the juvenile justice system. In D. W. Osgood, E. M. Foster, C. Flanagan, & G. R. Ruth (Eds.), *On your own without a net: The transition to adulthood for vulnerable populations* (pp. 92–113). Chicago: University of Chicago Press.

Altschuler, D. M., & Armstrong, T. L. (1991). *Intensive community-based aftercare prototype: Policies and procedures.* Baltimore: The Johns Hopkins University, Institute for Policy Studies.

Altschuler, D. M., & Armstrong, T. L. (1998). Recent developments in juvenile aftercare: Assessment, findings, and promising programs. In A. R. Roberts (Ed.), *Juvenile justice: Policies, programs, and services* (2nd ed., pp. 448–472). Chicago: Nelson-Hall.

Andrews, D. A., Zinger, I., Hoge, R. D., Bonta, J., Gendreau, P., & Cullen, F. T. (1990). Does correctional treatment work? A clinically relevant and psychologically informed meta-analysis. *Criminology, 28,* 369–404. doi:10.1111/j.1745-9125.1990.tb01330.x

Anthony, E. J. (1987). Children at high risk for psychosis growing up successfully. In E. J. Anthony & B. J. Cohler (Eds.). *The invulnerable child* (pp. 147–184). New York: Guilford Press.

Anthony, E. K., Alter, C. F., & Jenson, J. M. (2009). Development of a risk and resilience-based out-of-school time program for children and youths. *Social Work, 54,* 45–55.

Aos, S. (2004). *Washington State's Family Integrated Transitions program for juvenile offenders: Outcome evaluation and benefit-cost analysis.* Olympia: Washington State Institute for Public Policy. Retrieved from http://www.wsipp.wa.gov/ReportFile/888/Wsipp_Washington-State-s-Family-Integrated-Transitions-Program-for-Juvenile-Offenders-Outcome-Evaluation-and-Benefit-Cost-Analysis_Full-Report.pdf

Aos, S., & Drake, E. (2013). *Prison, police, and programs: Evidence-based options that reduce crime and save money* (Doc. No. 13-11-1901). Olympia: Washington State Institute for Public Policy.

Aos, S., Phipps, P., Barnoski, R., & Lieb, R. (2001). *The comparative costs and benefits of programs to reduce crime: Version 4.0.* Olympia: Washington State Institute for Public Policy.

Barton, W. H. (2002). Juvenile justice: Community treatment. In J. Dressler (Ed.-in-chief), *Encyclopedia of crime and justice* (2nd ed., pp. 917–927). New York: Macmillan Reference.

Barton, W. H. (2004). Bridging juvenile justice and positive youth development. In S. F. Hamilton & M. A. Hamilton (Eds.), *The youth development handbook: Coming of age in American communities* (pp. 77–102). Thousand Oaks, CA: Sage.

Barton, W. H. (2006). Incorporating the strengths perspective into intensive juvenile aftercare. *Western Criminology Review, 7*(2), 48–61.

Barton, W. H., & Butts, J. A. (2008). *Building on strength: Positive youth development in juvenile justice programs.* Chicago: Chapin Hall Center for Children at the University of Chicago. Retrieved from http://jeffreybutts.files.wordpress.com/2008/08/building.pdf

Barton, W. H., Jarjoura, G. R., & Rosay, A. B. (2014). Evaluating a juvenile reentry program: An elusive target. In M. S. Crow & J. O. Smykla (Eds.), *Offender reentry: Rethinking criminology and criminal justice* (pp. 307–329). Burlington, MA: Jones & Bartlett Learning.

Barton, W. H., & Mackin, J. R. (2012). Towards a strength-based juvenile correctional facility: Sustainability and effects of an institutional transformation. *Journal of Offender Rehabilitation, 51,* 435–452. doi:10.1080/10509674.2012.700688

Barton, W. H., Mackin, J. R., & Fields, J. (2008). Assessing youth strengths in a residential juvenile correctional program. *Residential Treatment for Children & Youth, 23*(3/4), 11–36. doi:10.1080/08865710802071770

Bazemore, G., & Terry, W. C. (1997). Developing delinquent youths: A reintegrative model for rehabilitation and a new role for the juvenile justice system. *Child Welfare, 76,* 665–716.

Bazemore, G., & Umbreit, M. (1995). *Balanced and restorative justice: Program summary* (NCJ 149727). Washington, DC: U.S. Department of Justice, Office of Juvenile Justice and Delinquency Prevention.

Beck, A. J., Harrison, P. M., & Guerino, P. (2010). Sexual victimization in juvenile facilities reported by youth, 2008–09. *Bureau of Justice Statistics Special Report.* Washington, DC: U.S. Department of Justice, Office of Justice Programs, Bureau of Justice Statistics. Retrieved from http://bjs.ojp.usdoj.gov/index.cfm?ty = pbdetail&iid = 2113

Becker, H. S. (1963). *Outsiders: Studies in the sociology of deviance.* New York: Free Press.

Bell, J., & Ridolfi, L. A. (2008). *Adoration of the question: Reflections on the failure to reduce racial & ethnic disparities in the juvenile justice system.* San Francisco, CA: The W. Hayward Burns Institute.

Bernard, T. J., & Kurlychek, M. C. (2010). *The cycle of juvenile justice* (2nd ed.). New York: Oxford University Press.

Bernburg, J. G., Krohn, M., & Rivera, C. J. (2006). Official labeling, criminal embeddedness, and subsequent delinquency: A longitudinal test of labeling theory. *Journal of Research in Crime and Delinquency, 43,* 67–88. doi:10.1177/0022427805280068

Bernstein, N. (2014). *Burning down the house: The end of juvenile prison.* New York, NY: The New Press.

Burchard, J. D., Bruns, E. J., & Burchard, S. N. (2002). The wraparound approach. In B. J. Burns & K. Hoagwood (Eds.), *Community treatment for youth: Evidence-based interventions for severe emotional and behavioral disorders* (pp. 69–90). New York: Oxford University Press.

Butts, J. A., Bazemore, G., & Meroe, A. S. (2010). *Positive youth justice: Framing justice interventions using the concepts of positive youth development.* Washington, DC: Coalition for Juvenile Justice.

Butts, J. A., Buck, J., & Coggeshall, M. B. (2002). *The impact of teen court on young offenders.* Washington, DC: Urban Institute, Justice Policy Center.

Butts, J., Mayer, S., & Ruth, G. (2005). *Focusing juvenile justice on positive youth development.* Chicago: Chapin Hall Center for Children at the University of Chicago.

Catalano, R. F., & Hawkins, J. D. (1996). The social development model: A theory of antisocial behavior. In J. D. Hawkins (Ed.), *Delinquency and crime: Current theories* (pp. 149–197). Cambridge, UK: Cambridge University Press.

Cauce, A. M., Cruz, R., Corona, M., & Conger, R. (2011). The face of the future: Risk and resilience in minority youth. In G. Carlo, L. J. Crockett, & M. A. Carranza (Eds.), *Health disparities in youth and families: Research and Applications* (pp. 13–32). Nebraska Symposium on Motivation 57. New York, NY: Springer. doi:10.1007/978-1-4419-7092-3_2

Center for the Study and Prevention of Violence. (2014). *Blueprints for violence prevention.* Boulder: University of Colorado, Center for the Study and Prevention of Violence. Retrieved from http://www.blueprintsprograms.com/allPrograms.php

Choices, Inc. (2010). *Fiscal and clinical models of Choices.* Indianapolis, IN: Author. Retrieved from http://www.choicesteam.org/documents/whitepapers/ChoicesFiscalReport.pdf

Chung, H. L., Little, M., & Steinberg, L. (2005). The transition to adulthood for adolescents in the juvenile justice system: A developmental perspective. In D. W. Osgood, E. M. Foster, C. Flanagan, & G. R. Ruth (Eds.), *On your own without a net: The transition to adulthood for vulnerable populations* (pp. 68–91). Chicago: University of Chicago Press.

Coalition for Juvenile Justice. (2006). *What are the implications of adolescent brain development for juvenile justice?* Washington, DC: Author.

Dahl, R. E. (2004). Adolescent brain development: A period of vulnerabilities and opportunities. *Annals of the New York Academy of Sciences, 1021,* 1–22. doi:10.1196/annals.1308.001

Derzon, J. H. (2010). The correspondence of family features with problem, aggressive, criminal, and violent behavior: A meta-analysis. *Journal of Experimental Criminology, 6,* 263–292. doi:10.1007/s11292-010-9098-0

Dishion, T. J., McCord, J., & Poulin, F. (1999). When interventions harm. Peer groups and problem behavior. *American Psychologist, 34,* 755–764. doi:10.1037/0003-066X.54.9.755

Dishion, T. J., Spracklen, K. M., & Patterson, G. R. (1996). Deviancy training in male adolescent friendships. *Behavior Therapy, 27,* 373–390. doi:10.1016/S0005-7894(96)80023-2

Dodge, K. A., Dishion, T. J., & Lansford, J. E. (2006). Deviant peer influences in intervention and public policy for youth. *Social Policy Report, 20*(1), Retrieved from http://www.srcd.org/sites/default/files/documents/spr20-1.pdf

Drake, E. K., Aos, S., & Miller, M. G. (2009). Evidence-based public policy options to reduce crime and criminal justice costs: Implications for Washington State. *Victims and Offenders, 4,* 170–196. doi:10.1080/15564880802612615

Dryfoos, J. G. (1990). *Adolescents at risk: Prevalence and prevention.* New York: Oxford University Press.

Duchnowski, A. J., Kutash, K., & Friedman, R. M. (2002). Community-based interventions in a system of care and outcomes framework. In B. J. Burns & K. Hoagwood (Eds.), *Community treatment for youth: Evidence-based interventions for severe emotional and behavioral disorders* (pp. 16–37). New York: Oxford University Press.

Durlak, J. A. (1998). Common risk and protective factors in successful prevention programs. *American Journal of Orthopsychiatry, 68,* 512–520. doi:10.1037/h0080360

Eccles, J., & Gootman, J. A. (Eds.). (2002). *Community programs to promote youth development.* Washington, DC: National Academy Press.

Elliott, D. S. (1994). Serious violent offenders: Onset, developmental course, and termination—The American Society of Criminology 1993 presidential address. *Criminology, 32,* 1–21. doi:10.1111/j.1745-9125.1994.tb01144.x

Elliott, D. S., & Ageton, S. (1980). Reconciling race and class differences in self-reported and official estimates of delinquency. *American Sociological Review, 45,* 95–100. doi:10.2307/2095245

Elliott, D. S., Huizinga, D., & Ageton, S. (1985). *Explaining delinquency and drug use.* Beverly Hills, CA: Sage.

Elliott, D. S., Huizinga, D., & Menard, S. (1989). *Multiple problem youth: Delinquency, substance use and mental health problems.* New York: Springer-Verlag.

Epstein, M. H., & Sharma, J. M. (1998). *Behavioral and Emotional Rating Scale (BERS).* Austin, TX: PRO-ED.

Fagan, J., F., & Freeman, R. B. (1999). Crime and work. In M. Tonry (Ed.), *Crime and justice: A review of research* (pp. 225–290). Chicago: University of Chicago Press.

Farrington, D. P. (1991). Childhood aggression and adult violence. In D. Pepler & K. H. Rubin (Eds.), *The development and treatment of childhood aggression* (pp. 2–29). Hillsdale, NJ: Lawrence Erlbaum.

Farrington, D. P., Loeber, R., Stouthamer-Loeber, M., Van Kammen, W. B., & Schmidt, L. (1996). Self-reported delinquency and a combined delinquency seriousness scale based on boys, mothers, and teachers: Concurrent and predictive validity for African-Americans and Caucasians. *Criminology, 34,* 493–517. doi:10.1111/j.1745-9125.1996.tb01217.x

Feld, B. C. (1991). Justice by geography: Urban, suburban, and rural variations in juvenile justice administration. *Journal of Criminal Law and Criminology, 82*(1), 156–210. doi:10.2307/1143795

Feld, B. C. (1999). *Bad kids: Race and the transformation of the juvenile court.* New York: Oxford University Press.

Frabutt, J. M., Di Luca, K. L., & Graves, K. N. (2008). Envisioning a juvenile justice system that supports positive youth development. *Notre Dame Journal of Law, Ethics & Public Policy, 22,* 107–125.

Franklin, C., Grant, D., Corcoran, J., O'Dell, P., & Bultman, L. (1995). *Effectiveness of prevention programs for adolescent pregnancy: A meta-analysis.* Austin: University of Texas at Austin, School of Social Work.

Fraser, M. W., Kirby, L. D., & Smokowski, P. R. (2004). Risk and resilience in childhood. In M. W. Fraser (Ed.), *Risk and resilience in childhood: An ecological perspective* (2nd ed., pp. 13–66). Washington, DC: NASW Press.

Fraser, M. W., & Terzian, M. A. (2005). Risk and resilience in child development: Principles and strategies of practice. In G. P. Mallon & P. McCartt Hess (Eds.), *Child welfare for the twenty-first century: A handbook of practices, policies, and programs* (pp. 55–71). New York: Columbia University Press.

Frazier, C. E., & Bishop, D. M. (1985). The pretrial detention of juveniles and its impact on case dispositions. *Journal of Criminal Law and Criminology, 76*(4), 1132–1152. doi:10.2307/1143504

Frazier, C. E., & Cochran, J. C. (1986). Detention of juveniles: Its effects on subsequent juvenile court processing decisions. *Youth and Society, 17,* 286–305. doi:10.1177/0044118X86017003005

Garmezy, N. (1985). Stress-resistant children: The search for protective factors. In J. E. Stevenson (Ed.), *Recent research in developmental psychopathology* (pp. 213–233). New York: Pergamon Press.

Gatti, U., Tremblay, R. E., & Vitaro, F. (2009). Iatrogenic effect of juvenile justice. *Journal of Child Psychology and Psychiatry, 50,* 991–998. doi:10.1111/j.1469-7610.2008.02057.x

Gavazzi, S. M., Yarcheck, C. M., & Chesney-Lind, M. (2006). Global risk indicators and the role of gender in a juvenile detention sample. *Criminal Justice and Behavior, 33,* 597–612. doi:10.1177/0093854806288184

Goldman, S. K. (1999). The conceptual framework for wraparound: Definition, values, essential elements, and requirements for practice. In B. J. Burns & S. K. Goldman (Eds.), *Systems of care: Promising practices in children's mental health, 1998 Series* (Vol. 4, pp. 27–34). Washington, DC: Center for Effective Collaboration and Practice, American Institutes for Research.

Gottfredson, D. C. (2000). *Schools and delinquency.* New York: Cambridge University Press.

Greenberg, M., & Feinberg, M. (2002). *An evaluation of PCCD's Communities That Care delinquency prevention initiative: Final report* (NCJ 281283). Harrisburg: Pennsylvania State University, College of Human Development.

Haggerty, K. P., Skinner, M. L., McGlynn-Wright, A., Catalano, R. F., & Crutchfield, R. D. (2013). Parent and peer predictors of violent behavior of Black and White teens. *Violence and Victims, 28,* 145–160. doi:10.1891/0886-6708.28.1.145

Hall, J. E., Simon, T. R., Lee, R. D., & Mercy, J. A. (2012). Implications of direct protective factors for public health research and prevention strategies to reduce youth violence. *American Journal of Preventive Medicine, 43*(2S1), S76–S83. doi:10/1016/j.amapre.2012.019

Hamilton, S. F., Hamilton, M. A., & Pittman, K. (2004). Principles for youth development. In S. F. Hamilton & M. A. Hamilton (Eds.), *The youth development handbook: Coming of age in American communities* (pp. 3–22). Thousand Oaks, CA: Sage.

Hamparian, D. (1978). *The violent few: A study of dangerous juvenile offenders.* Lexington MA: Lexington Books.

Hawkins, D. F., Laub, J. H., & Lauritsen, J. L. (1998). Race, ethnicity, and serious juvenile offending. In R. Loeber & D. P. Farrington (Eds.), *Serious and violent juvenile offenders: Risk factors and successful interventions* (pp. 30–47). Thousand Oaks, CA: Sage.

Hawkins, J. D., Brown, E. C., Oesterle, S., Arthur, M. W., Abbott, R. D., & Catalano, R. F. (2008). Early effects of Communities That Care on targeted risks and initiation of delinquent behavior and substance use. *Journal of Adolescent Health, 43,* 15–22. doi:10.1016/j.jadohealth.2008.01.022

Hawkins, J. D., Catalano, R. F., & Associates. (1992). *Communities That Care: Action for drug abuse prevention.* San Francisco: Jossey-Bass.

Hawkins, J. D., Catalano, R. F., & Miller, J. Y. (1992). Risk and protective factors for alcohol and other drug problems in adolescence and early adulthood: Implications for substance abuse prevention. *Psychological Bulletin, 112,* 64–105. doi:10.1037/0033-2909.112.1.64

Hawkins, J. D., & Herrenkohl, T. I. (2003). Prevention in the school years. In D. P. Farrington & J. W. Coid (Eds.), *Early prevention of adult antisocial behaviour* (pp. 265–291). Cambridge, UK: Cambridge University Press. doi:10.1017/CB09780511489259.009

Hawkins, J. D., Herrenkohl, T. I., Farrington, D. P., Brewer, D., Catalano, R. F., Harachi, T. W., & Cothern, L. (2000). *Predictors of youth violence* (NCJ 179065). Washington, DC: U.S. Department of Justice, Office of Juvenile Justice and Delinquency Prevention.

Hemmelgarn, A. L., Glisson, C., & James, L. R. (2006). Organizational culture and climate: Implications for services and interventions research. *Clinical Psychology: Science and Practice, 13*, 73–89. doi:10.1111/j.1468–2850.2006.00008.x

Henry, D. B., Tolan, P. H., Gorman-Smith, D., & Schoeny, M. E. (2012). Risk and direct protective factors for youth violence: Results from the Centers for Disease Control and Prevention's Multisite Violence Prevention Project. *American Journal of Preventive Medicine, 43*(2S1), S67–S75. doi:10.1016/j.amepre.2012.04.025

Hindelang, M. J., Hirschi, T., & Weis, J. G. (1981). *Measuring delinquency.* Beverly Hills, CA: Sage.

Holman, B., & Ziedenberg, J. (2006). *The dangers of detention: The impact of incarcerating youth in detention and other secure facilities.* Washington, DC: Justice Policy Institute. Retrieved from http://www.justicepolicy.org/images/upload/06-11_rep_dangersofdetention_jj.pdf

Howden, L. M., & Meyer, J. A. (2011, May). Age and sex composition: 2010. *2010 Census Briefs.* Washington, DC: United States Census Bureau. Retrieved from http://www.census.gov/prod/cen2010/briefs/c2010br-03.pdf

Howell, J. C. (Ed.). (1995). *Guide for implementing the comprehensive strategy for serious, violent, and chronic offenders* (NCJ 153681). Washington, DC: U.S. Department of Justice, Office of Juvenile Justice and Delinquency Prevention.

Howell, J. C. (2003). *Preventing and reducing juvenile delinquency: A comprehensive framework.* Thousand Oaks, CA: Sage.

Hubbard, D. J., & Pratt, T. C. (2002). A meta-analysis of the predictors of delinquency among girls. *Journal of Offender Rehabilitation, 34*(3), 1–13. doi:10.1300/J076v34n03_01

Huizinga, D., Loeber, R., Thornberry, T. P., & Cothern, L. (2000). *Co-occurrence of delinquency and other problem behaviors* (NCJ 182211). Washington, DC: U.S. Department of Justice, Office of Juvenile Justice and Delinquency Prevention.

Jenson, J. M., & Fraser, M. W. (2006). Toward the integration of child, youth, and family policy: Applying principles of risk, resilience, and ecological theory. In J. M. Jenson & M. W. Fraser (Eds.), *Social policy for children and families: A risk and resilience perspective* (pp. 265–279). Thousand Oaks, CA: Sage.

Kamradt, B. (2000). Wraparound Milwaukee: Aiding youth with mental health needs. *Juvenile Justice Journal, 7.* Retrieved from https://www.ncjrs.gov/html/ojjdp/jjjnl_2000_4/wrap.html

Kendziora, K. T., & Osher, D. M. (2004). Fostering resilience among youth in the juvenile justice system. In C. S. Clauss-Ehlers & M. D. Wiest (Eds.), *Community planning to foster resilience in children* (pp. 177–195). New York: Kluwer Academic.

Kim-Cohen, J., Caspi, A., Taylor, A., Williams, B., Newcombe, R., Craig, I. W., & Moffitt, T. E. (2006). MAOA, maltreatment, and gene-environment interaction predicting children's mental health: New evidence and a meta-analysis. *Molecular Psychiatry, 11*, 903–913.

Kurtz, D., & Linnemann, T. (2006). Improving probation through client strengths: Evaluating strength based treatments for at-risk youth. *Western Criminology Review, 7*(1), 9–19.

Latessa, E. J. (2004). The challenge of change: Correctional programs and evidence-based practices. *Criminology and Public Policy, 3*, 547–559.

Lattimore, P. K., Brumbaugh, S., Visher, C., Lindquist, C. H., Winterfield, L., Salas, M., & Zweig, J. (2004). *National Portrait of the Serious and Violent Offender Reentry Initiative* (RTI Report 8805). Research

Triangle Park, NC: Research Triangle Institute. Retrieved from https://www.ncjrs.gov/pdffiles1/Archive/222766NCJRS.pdf

Laub, J. H., & Sampson, R. J. (2003). *Shared beginnings, divergent lives*. Cambridge, MA: Harvard University Press.

Lederman, C. S., Dakof, G. A., Larrea, M. A., & Li, H. (2004). Characteristics of adolescent females in juvenile detention. *International Journal of Law and Psychiatry, 27,* 321–337. doi:10.1016/j.ijlp.2004.03.009

Lemert, E. M. (1951). *Social pathology*. New York: McGraw-Hill.

Lerner, S. (1986). *Bodily harm: The pattern of fear and violence at the California Youth Authority*. Bolinas, CA: Common Knowledge Press.

Li, S. T., Nussbaum, K. M., & Richards, M. H. (2007). Risk and protective factors for urban African-American youth. *American Journal of Community Psychology, 39,* 21–35. doi:10.1007/s10464-007-9088-1

Lipsey, M. (1992). Juvenile delinquency treatment: A meta-analytic inquiry into the variability of effects. In T. D. Cook, H. Cooper, D. S. Cordray, H. Hartman, L. V. Hedges, R. J. Light, & F. Mosteller (Eds.), *Meta-analysis for explanation: A casebook* (pp. 83–127). New York: Russell Sage Foundation.

Lipsey, M. W., & Derzon, J. H. (1998). Predictors of violent and serious delinquency in adolescence and early adulthood: A synthesis of longitudinal research. In R. Loeber & D. P. Farrington (Eds.), *Serious and violent juvenile offenders: Risk factors and successful interventions* (pp. 86–105). Thousand Oaks, CA: Sage.

Lipsey, M. W., & Wilson, D. B. (1998). Effective intervention for serious juvenile offenders: A synthesis of research. In R. Loeber & D. P. Farrington (Eds.), *Serious and violent juvenile offenders: Risk factors and successful interventions* (pp. 313–345). Thousand Oaks, CA: Sage.

Lipton, D., Martinson, R., & Wilks, J. (1975). *The effectiveness of correctional treatment: A survey of treatment evaluation studies*. New York: Praeger.

Livesy, S., Sickmund, M., & Sladky, A. (2009). *Juvenile residential facility census, 2004: Selected findings* (NCJ 222721). Washington, DC: U.S. Department of Justice, Office of Justice Programs, Office of Juvenile Justice and Delinquency Prevention.

Loeber, R., & Farrington, D. P. (Eds.). (1998). *Serious & violent juvenile offenders: Risk factors and successful interventions*. Thousand Oaks, CA: Sage.

Loeber, R., Farrington, D. P., & Petechuk, D. (2003). *Child delinquency: Early intervention and prevention* (NCJ 186162). Washington, DC: Office of Juvenile Justice and Delinquency Prevention. Retrieved May 19, 2004, from https://www.ncjrs.gov/pdffiles1/ojjdp/186162.pdf

Loeber, R., Farrington, D. P., Stouthamer-Loeber, M., & van Kammen, W. B. (1998). *Antisocial behavior and mental health problems: Explanatory factors in childhood and adolescence*. Mahwah, NJ: Lawrence Erlbaum.

Lösel, F., & Bender, D. (2003). Protective factors and resilience. In D. P. Farrington & J. W. Coid (Eds.), *Early prevention of adult antisocial behaviour* (pp. 130–204). Cambridge, UK: Cambridge University Press. doi:10.1017/CBO9780511489259.006

Lösel, F., & Farrington, D. P. (2012). Direct protective and buffering protective factors in the development of youth violence. *American Journal of Preventive Medicine, 43*(2S1), S8–S23.

Loughran, T. A., Mulvey, E. P., Schubert, C. A., Fagan, J., Piquero, A. R., & Losoya, S. H. (2009). Estimating a dose–response relationship between length of stay and future recidivism in serious juvenile offenders. *Criminology, 47,* 699–740. doi:10.1111/j.1745-9125.2009.00165.x

Lyons, J. S., Griffin, E., Fazio, M., & Lyons, M. B. (1999). *Child and adolescent needs and strengths: An information integration tool for children and adolescents with mental health challenges (CANS-MH). Manual*. Chicago: Buddin Praed Foundation.

Mackin, J. R., Weller, J. M, Tarte, J. M., & Nissen, L. B. (2005). Breaking new ground in juvenile justice settings: Assessing for competencies in juvenile offenders. *Juvenile and Family Court Journal,* 25–37. doi:10.1111/j.1755–6988.2005.tb00104.x

Maloney, D., Romig, D., & Armstrong, T. (1988). Juvenile probation: The balanced approach. *Juvenile and Family Court Journal, 39,* 1–62. doi:10.1111/j.1755–6988.1988.tb00623.x

Mann, E. A., & Reynolds, A. J. (2006). Early intervention and juvenile delinquency prevention: Evidence from the Chicago Longitudinal Study. *Social Work Research, 30,* 153–167.

Masten, A. S. (1994). Resilience in individual development: Successful adaptation despite risk and adversity. In M. C. Wang & E. W. Gordon (Eds.), *Educational resilience in inner-city America: Challenges and opportunities* (pp. 3–25). Hillsdale, NJ: Lawrence Erlbaum.

McCorkle, L. W., Elias, A., & Bixby, F. L. (1958). *The Highfields story: A unique experiment in the treatment of juvenile delinquents.* New York: Holt.

McGarrell, E. F., Olivares, K., Crawford, K., & Kroovand, N. (2000). *Returning justice to the community: The Indianapolis restorative justice experiment.* Indianapolis, IN: Hudson Institute, Crime Control Policy Center.

McNeese, C. A. (1998). Juvenile justice policy: Current trends and twenty-first century issues. In A. R. Roberts (Ed.), *Juvenile justice: Policies, programs, and services* (2nd ed., pp. 21–39). Chicago: Nelson-Hall.

Mendel, R. A. (2014). *Juvenile Detention Alternatives Initiative: Progress report 2014.* Baltimore: Annie E. Casey Foundation.

Minor, K. I., Wells, J. B., & Angel, E. (2008). Recidivism among juvenile offenders following release from residential placements: Multivariate predictors and gender differences. *Journal of Offender Rehabilitation, 46,* 171–188. doi:10.1080/10509670802143474

Moffitt, T. E. (1993). Adolescence-limited and lift-course-persistent antisocial behavior: A developmental taxonomy. *Psychological Review, 100,* 674–701. doi:10.1037/0033–295X.100.4.674

Moffitt, T. E., & Caspi, A. (2001). Childhood predictors differentiate life-course persistent and adolescence-limited antisocial pathways among males and females. *Development and Psychopathology, 132,* 355–375. doi:10.1017/S0954579401002097

Moffitt, T. E., Caspi, A., Harrington, H., & Milne, B. J. (2002). Males on the life-course-persistent and adolescence-limited antisocial pathways: Follow-up at 26 years. *Development and Psychopathology, 14,* 179–207. doi:10.1017/S0954579402001104

Nash, J. K., & Bowen, G. L., (1999). Perceived crime and informal social control in the neighborhood as a context for adolescent behavior: A risk and resilience perspective. *Social Work Research, 23,* 171–186.

National Center for Juvenile Justice. (1991). *Desktop guide to good juvenile probation practice.* Washington, DC: U.S. Department of Justice, Office of Juvenile Justice and Delinquency Prevention.

National Council on Crime and Delinquency. (2007, January). *And justice for some: Differential treatment of youth of color in the justice system.* Oakland, CA: Author. Retrieved from http://www.nccdglobal.org/sites/default/files/publication_pdf/justice-for-some.pdf

National Research Council. (2013). *Reforming juvenile justice: A developmental approach.* Committee on Assessing Juvenile Justice Reform, R. J. Bonnie, R. L. Johnson, B. M. Chemers, & J. A. Schuck (Eds.), Committee on Law and Justice, Division of Behavioral and Social Sciences and Education. Washington, DC: The National Academies Press.

Nissen, L. B., Mackin, J. R., Weller, J. M., & Tarte, J. M. (2005). Identifying strengths as fuel for change: A conceptual and theoretical framework for the Youth Competency Assessment. *Juvenile and Family Court Journal,* 1–15. doi:10.1111/j.1755–6988.2005.tb00099.x

Office of Juvenile Justice and Delinquency Prevention (OJJDP). (2013a, August 5). Jurisdictional boundaries; Upper and lower age of juvenile court delinquency and status offense jurisdiction, 2012.

OJJDP Statistical Briefing Book. Retrieved from http://www.ojjdp.gov/ojstatbb/structure_process/qa04102.asp?qaDate = 2012

Office of Juvenile Justice and Delinquency Prevention (OJJDP). (2013b, April 29). Jurisdictional boundaries: Extended age of juvenile court jurisdiction, 2012. *OJJDP Statistical Briefing Book*. Retrieved from http://www.ojjdp.gov/ojstatbb/structure_process/qa04106.asp?qaDate = 2012

Office of the Surgeon General. (2001). *Youth violence: A report of the Surgeon General*. Washington, DC: U.S. Department of Health and Human Services. Retrieved from http://www.surgeongeneral.gov/library/youthviolence/

O'Malley, P. M., Bachman, J. G., & Johnston, L. D. (1983). Reliability and consistency in self reports of drug use. *International Journal of Addictions, 18*, 805–824. doi:10.3109/10826088309033049

Parent, D. G., Leiter, V., Kennedy, S., Livens, L., Wentworth, D., & Wilcox, S. (1994). *Conditions of confinement: Juvenile detention and corrections facilities. Research summary* (NCJ 145793). Washington, DC: U.S. Department of Justice, Office of Juvenile Justice and Delinquency Prevention.

Patterson, G. R., Reid, J. B., & Dishion, T. J. (1992). *Antisocial boys*. Eugene, OR: Castalia.

Petteruti, A., Walsh, N., & Velázquez, T. (2009). *The cost of confinement: Why good juvenile justice policies make good fiscal sense*. Washington, DC: Justice Policy Institute. Retrieved from http://www.justicepolicy.org/images/upload/09_05_REP_CostsOfConfinement_JJ_PS.pdf

Pittman, K., & Irby, M. (1996). *Preventing problems or promoting development: Competing priorities or inseparable goals?* Baltimore: International Youth Foundation.

Pollard, J. A., Hawkins, J. D., & Arthur, M. W. (1999). Risk and protection: Are both necessary to understand diverse behavioral outcomes in adolescence? *Social Work Research, 23*, 145–158.

Puzzanchera, C. (2013, December). *Juvenile arrests 2011*. Washington, DC: Office of Juvenile Justice and Delinquency Prevention, Juvenile Offenders and Victims: National Report Series. Retrieved from http://www.ojjdp.gov/pubs/244476.pdf

Puzzanchera, C., & Robson, C. (2014, February). *Delinquency cases in juvenile court, 2010*. Washington, DC: Office of Juvenile Justice and Delinquency Prevention, Juvenile Offenders and Victims: National Report Series. Retrieved from http://www.ojjdp.gov/pubs/243041.pdf

Richart, D., Brooks, K., & Soler, M. (2003). *Unintended consequences: The impact of zero tolerance and other exclusionary polices on Kentucky students*. Washington, DC: Building Blocks for Youth. Retrieved from http://www.buildingblocks foryouth.org/kentucky/kentucky.pdf

Rowe, D. C. (2001). *Biology and crime*. Los Angeles: Roxbury Press.

Rutter, M. (1985). Resilience in the face of adversity: Protective factors and resistance to psychiatric disorders. *British Journal of Psychiatry, 147*, 598–611. doi:10.1192/bjp.147.6.598

Rutter, M. (2001). Psychosocial adversity: Risk, resilience and recovery. In J. M. Richman & M. W. Fraser (Eds.), *The context of youth violence: Resilience, risk, and protection* (pp. 13–41). Westport, CT: Praeger.

Saleebey, D. (Ed.). (2013). *The strengths perspective in social work practice* (6th ed.). Boston, MA: Pearson Education.

Sameroff, A. J. (1999). Ecological perspectives on developmental risk. In J. D. Osofsky & H. E. Fitzgerald (Eds.), *WAIMH handbook of infant mental health: Vol. 4. Infant mental health groups at high risk* (pp. 223–248). New York: Wiley.

Sampson, R. J., Raudenbush, S. W., & Earls, R. (1997). Neighborhoods and violent crime: A multilevel study of collective efficacy. *Science, 277*, 918–924.

Scales, P. C., & Leffert, N. (1999). *Developmental assets: A synthesis of scientific research on adolescent development*. Minneapolis, MN: Search Institute.

Schwartz, R. G. (2001). Juvenile justice and positive youth development. In P. L. Benson & K. Pittman (Eds.), *Trends in youth development: Visions, realities and challenges* (pp. 231–268). Boston: Kluwer Academic.

Sickmund, M., Sladky, T. J., Kang, W., & Puzzanchera, C. (2013). *Easy access to the census of juveniles in residential placement: 1997–2011.* Online. Retrieved from http://www.ojjdp.gov/ojstatbb/ezacjrp/

Simon, T. R., Ritter, N. M., & Mahendra, R. R. (Eds.). (2013). *Changing course: Preventing gang membership.* Washington, DC: U.S. Department of Justice, Office of Justice Programs. Retrieved from https://ncjrs.gov/pdffiles1/nij/239234.pdf

Skiba, R., Simmons, A., Staudinger L., Rausch, M., Dow, G., & Feggins, R. (2003, May). *Consistent removal: Contributions of school discipline to the school-prison pipeline.* Paper presented at the School to Prison Pipeline Conference, Harvard Civil Rights Project, Cambridge, MA.

Snyder, H. N., & Sickmund, M. (1999). *Juvenile offenders and victims: 1999 national report.* Pittsburgh, PA: National Center for Juvenile Justice.

Snyder, H. N., & Sickmund, M. (2006). *Juvenile offenders and victims: 2006 national report* (NCJ 212906). Washington, DC: U.S. Department of Justice, Office of Justice Programs, Office of Juvenile Justice and Delinquency Prevention.

Stanfield, R. (1999). The JDAI story: Building a better juvenile detention system. In *Pathways to Juvenile Detention Reform, Overview.* Baltimore, MD: Annie E. Casey Foundation.

Stouthamer-Loeber, M., Loeber, R., Wei, E., Farrington, D. P., & Wikström, P. H. (2002). Risk and promotive effects in the explanation of persistent serious delinquency in boys. *Journal of Consulting and Clinical Psychology, 70,* 111–123. doi:10.1037/0022-006X.70.1.111

Stroul, B. A., & Friedman, R. M. (1986). *A system of care for seriously emotionally disturbed children and youth.* Washington, DC: CASSP Technical Assistance Center, Georgetown University Child Development Center.

Theokas, C., & Lerner, R. M. (2006). Observed ecological assets in families, schools, and neighborhoods: Conceptualization, measurement, and relations with positive and negative developmental outcomes. *Applied Developmental Science, 10,* 61–74. doi:10.1207/s1532480xads1002_2

Thornberry, T. P., Huizinga, D., & Loeber, R. (1995). The prevention of serious delinquency and violence: Implications from the program of research on the causes and correlates of delinquency. In J. C. Howell, B. Krisberg, J. D. Hawkins, & J. J. Wilson (Eds.), *Serious, violent, and chronic juvenile offenders: A sourcebook* (pp. 213–237). Thousand Oaks, CA: Sage.

Tierney, J., Grossman, J., & Resch, N. (1995). *Making a difference: An impact study of Big Brothers/Big Sisters.* Philadelphia: Public/Private Ventures.

Torbet, P., & Thomas, D. (2005). *Advancing competency development: A white paper for Pennsylvania.* Pittsburgh, PA: National Center for Juvenile Justice.

Tremblay, R. E., & Craig, W. M. (1995). Developmental crime prevention. In M. Tonry & D. P. Farrington (Eds.), *Building a safer society: Strategic approaches to crime prevention* (pp. 151–236). Chicago: University of Chicago Press.

Tremblay, R. E., & Japel, C. (2003). Prevention during pregnancy, infancy, and the preschool years. In D. P. Farrington & J. W. Coid (Eds.), *Early prevention of adult antisocial behaviour* (pp. 205–264). Cambridge, UK: Cambridge University Press. doi:10.1017/CBO9780511489259.007

Trulson, C. R., Marquart, J. W., Mullings, J. L., & Caeti, T. J. (2005). In between adolescence and adulthood. Recidivism outcomes of a cohort of state delinquents. *Youth Violence and Juvenile Justice, 3,* 355–387. doi:10.1177/1541204005278802

U.S. Census Bureau. (2013, December). *Current population survey, annual social and economic supplement, 2012.* Washington, DC: Author. Retrieved from http://www.census.gov/population/hispanic/data/2012.html

VanDenBerg, J. E., & Grealish, M. E. (1996). Individualized services and supports through the wraparound process: Philosophy and procedures. *Journal of Child and Family Studies, 5,* 7–21. doi:10.1007/BF02234675

Vorath, H., & Brendtro, L. K. (1974). *Positive peer culture.* Chicago: Aldine.

Washington State Institute for Public Policy (WSIPP). (2014, January). *Inventory of evidence-based, research-based, and promising practices.* Retrieved from http://www.wsipp.wa.gov/Reports/PolicySubarea/3

Wehlage, G., Rutter, R. A., Smith, G. A., Lesko, N., & Fernandez, R. R. (1989). *Reducing the risk: Schools as communities of support.* London: Falmer Press.

Weinberger, D. R., Elvevag, B., & Giedd, J. N. (2005). *The adolescent brain: A work in progress.* Washington, DC: National Campaign to Prevent Teen Pregnancy.

Weiss, G. (2013). *The fourth wave: Juvenile justice reforms for the twenty-first century.* New York, NY: Public Interest Projects, National Campaign to Reform State Juvenile Justice Systems. Retrieved from http://www.publicinterestprojects.org/wp-content/uploads/2013/09/The-Fourth-Wave-Long.pdf

Werner, E. E., & Smith, R. S. (2001). *Journeys from childhood to midlife: Risk, resilience, and recovery.* Ithaca, NY: Cornell University Press.

White, J. L., Moffitt, T. E., Earls, F., Robins, L. N., & Silva, P. A. (1990). How early can we tell? Predictors of childhood conduct disorder and adolescent delinquency. *Criminology, 29,* 507–533. doi:10.1111/j.1745–9125.1990.tb01337.x

Wiebush, R. G., Baird, C., Krisberg, B., & Onek, D. (1995). Risk assessment and classification for serious, violent, and chronic juvenile offenders. In J. C. Howell, B. Krisberg, J. D. Hawkins, & J. J. Wilson (Eds.), *Serious, violent, & chronic juvenile offenders: A sourcebook* (pp. 171–212). Thousand Oaks, CA: Sage.

Wiebush, R. G., Wagner, D., McNulty, B., Wang, Y., & Le, T. N. (2005). *Implementation and outcome evaluation of the Intensive Aftercare Program: Final report* (NCJ 206177). Washington, DC: U.S. Department of Justice, Office of Juvenile Justice and Delinquency Prevention.

Williams, J. H., Ayers, C. D., Abbott, R. D., Hawkins, J. D., & Catalano, R. F. (1999). Racial differences in risk factors for delinquency and substance use among adolescents. *Social Work Research, 23,* 241–256.

Williams, J. H., Ayers, C. D., Van Dorn, R. A., & Arthur, M. W. (2004). Risk and protective factors in the development of delinquency and conduct disorder. In M. W. Fraser (Ed.), *Risk and resilience in childhood: An ecological perspective* (2nd ed., pp. 209–249). Washington, DC: NASW Press.

Wilson, J. J., & Howell, J. C. (1993). *A comprehensive strategy for serious, violent, and chronic juvenile offenders: Program summary* (NCJ 143453). Washington, DC: U.S. Department of Justice, Office of Juvenile Justice and Delinquency Prevention.

Wisconsin Council on Children and Families (2010). *Understanding wraparound: A study in recidivism.* Milwaukee, WI: Wraparound Milwaukee. Retrieved from http://county.milwaukee.gov/ImageLibrary/Groups/cntyHHS/Wraparound/UNDERSTANDINGRECIDIVISM2011.pdf

Wolfgang, M. E., Figlio, R. M., & Sellin, T. (1972). *Delinquency in a birth cohort.* Chicago: University of Chicago Press.

Wolfgang, M., Thornberry, T. P., & Figlio, R. M. (1987). *From boy to man, from delinquency to crime: Follow up to the Philadelphia birth cohort of 1945.* Chicago: University of Chicago Press.

Wraparound Milwaukee. (n.d.). *Wraparound: background and history.* Milwaukee, WI: Author. Retrieved from http://wraparoundmke.com/

Wright, E. R., & Anderson, J. A. (2005, September). *Sixth annual evaluation briefing of the Dawn Project Evaluation Study.* Indianapolis, IN: Indiana University, Indiana Consortium for Mental Health Services Research. Retrieved from http://www.choicesteam.org/documents/reports/DawnProjectEvaluationBriefing.pdf

Zahn, M. A., Day, J. C., Mihalic, S. F., & Tichavsky, L. (2009). Determining what works for girls in the juvenile justice system: A summary of evaluation evidence. *Crime & Delinquency, 55,* 266–293. doi:10.1177/0011128708330649

ADDITIONAL READING

Bazemore, G., & Walgrave, L. (Eds.). (1999). *Restorative juvenile justice: Repairing the harm of youth crime.* Monsey, NY: Criminal Justice Press.

Bernard, T. J., & Kurlychek, M. C. (2010). *The cycle of juvenile justice* (2nd ed.). New York: Oxford University Press.

Hamilton, S. F., Hamilton, M. A., & Pittman, K. (2004). Principles for youth development. In S. F. Hamilton & M. A. Hamilton (Eds.), *The youth development handbook: Coming of age in American communities* (pp. 3–22). Thousand Oaks, CA: Sage.

Howell, J. C. (2003). *Preventing and reducing juvenile delinquency: A comprehensive framework.* Thousand Oaks, CA: Sage.

National Research Council. (2013). *Reforming juvenile justice: A developmental approach.* Committee on Assessing Juvenile Justice Reform, R. J. Bonnie, R. L. Johnson, B. M. Chemers, & J. A. Schuck (Eds.), Committee on Law and Justice, Division of Behavioral and Social Sciences and Education. Washington, DC: The National Academies Press.

Weiss, G. (2013). *The fourth wave: Juvenile justice reforms for the twenty-first century.* New York, NY: Public Interest Projects, National Campaign to Reform State Juvenile Justice Systems. Retrieved from http://www.publicinterestprojects.org/wp-content/uploads/2013/09/The-Fourth-Wave-Long.pdf

WEB-BASED RESOURCES

Annie E. Casey Foundation, http://www.aecf.org/

Building Blocks for Youth, http://www.buildingblocksforyouth.org/

Center for the Study and Prevention of Violence (Blueprints), http://www.blueprintsprograms.com/

Office of Juvenile Justice and Delinquency Prevention (OJJDP), http://www.ojjdp.gov/

OJJDP: Model Programs Guide, http://www.ojjdp.gov/mpg

OJJDP: Statistical Briefing Book, http://www.ojjdp.gov/ojstatbb/default.asp

Washington State Institute for Public Policy, http://www.wsipp.wa.gov/intro.asp

CHAPTER 10

Toward the Integration of Child, Youth, and Family Policy

Applying Principles of Risk, Resilience, and Ecological Theory

Jeffrey M. Jenson

Mark W. Fraser

The chapters in this book describe policies and programs aimed at pressing problems facing American children and their families. These policies—and the services they have generated—represent a complex array of legislative, administrative, and judicial responses to social and health problems affecting children. Identifying and analyzing major policy responses to the challenges confronted by children and their families is a difficult undertaking for legislators, governmental officials, judges, scholars, and other experts. Imagine, then, the confusion experienced by a child, adolescent, or parent receiving assistance in one or more of the service systems reviewed in this book. Unfortunately, no road map exists to guide family members through the labyrinth of programs and agencies that provide services for children and youth. For many families, what we call the "service system" is not a system. Rather, it is a maze of programs and procedures with varying eligibility requirements and service definitions. In their complexity, these systems too often wind up compromising the good intentions of advocates, policymakers, and practitioners.

To try to make sense of public policies in terms of their historical development and current dimensions, chapter authors have applied a risk and resilience framework that is grounded in ecological theory. In the following section, we summarize their findings using the constructs of risk and protection. The second section outlines a developmental process to guide the creation and implementation of a logical continuum of policies and programs for children, youth, and families.

POLICIES AND PROGRAMS ACROSS SERVICE SYSTEMS

This book has traced the origins and evolution of public policies that define major American service systems for children, youth, and families. Chapter authors have used the principles of risk and resilience to describe and assess policy responses to a range of child and adolescent problems and conditions. Each chapter began with a review of risk and protective factors that were relevant to problem behaviors or to conditions within particular policy domains, such as child welfare and mental health.

Services in the areas of income maintenance, child welfare, developmental disabilities, education, health, juvenile justice, mental health, and substance abuse are usually developed vertically, with separate funding streams and administrative structures; however, the reader is likely to have been struck by the similarity of risk and protective factors across substantive domains. Prior reviews of risk and protection have also noted the overlap of risk and protective factors across problem domains (Fraser, Kirby, & Smokowski, 2004; Hawkins, Catalano, & Miller, 1992; Jenson & Bender, 2014; O'Connell, Boat, & Warner, 2009). The similarity of factors related to different service systems is a clue both to the complexity of public responses to issues confronting children and families and to the potential for reform. In Chapter 1, we identified common risk and protective factors for child and adolescent problems at the environmental, interpersonal, social, and individual levels of influence. These characteristics and conditions are ubiquitous across all of the policy domains discussed in the book.

The presence of common risk and protective factors for different child and adolescent behaviors and conditions affords a special opportunity to think organically about creating policies that address the root causes of problem behaviors. For example, the authors in this volume have indicated that a number of common environmental factors, such as poverty, poor parenting, and community disorganization, are associated with juvenile delinquency, substance abuse, and child maltreatment. It follows, then, that these risk factors should become the targets of coordinated and integrated policy and program responses in the juvenile justice, substance abuse, and child welfare systems.

A parallel theme that emerged from each chapter concerned the lack of attention in policy development that has been afforded to the underlying correlates of child and adolescent problems. On balance, chapters described an incremental and reactive approach to the creation of policies that collect over time to form the basis for programs in public service systems for children, youth, and families. Policies tend to be the product of reform cycles that stem from changes in the nature and prevalence of social and health problems. For example, the rubella epidemic of the mid-1960s increased the number of children with severe auditory and visual disabilities. The sudden increase in the population with special needs contributed to the reform of special education policies; through the Education for All Handicapped Children Act (PL 94-142) in 1975, public schools were provided with resources to serve children with disabling conditions that had once been considered so severe that only institutional care was thought appropriate. When incidence and prevalence rates increase dramatically, the attention of the public and policymakers is diverted to particular service systems or programs. When the prevalence of problems increases, policy reforms tend to be introduced at a fast pace, but often without adequate consideration of unintended consequences or long-term effects.

This pattern of hurried, inadequately considered policy formulation is common. In Chapter 9, Barton noted the cyclical nature of juvenile justice policy, which is characterized by a shifting emphasis on rehabilitation and punishment. This revolving cycle of policy has defined a myriad of reforms, ranging from the creation of probation in the first juvenile courts of the early 1900s to recent judicial waiver procedures that permit juvenile offenders to be tried in criminal courts and exposed to adult sanctions. Barton noted that officials in the juvenile justice system are currently debating the merits of policy changes made in the mid-1990s, which led to a greater emphasis on punishing young offenders. Similarly, Fraser and Lanier (Chapter 5) identified fluctuations in mental health policy based on evolving beliefs about the appropriate role of institutional and community-based care for persons with serious mental illnesses. In addition, Pecora and Harrison-Jackson (Chapter 3) traced the evolution of child welfare policy through periods that saw dramatic changes in social norms regarding child abuse and neglect. Examples of the cyclical and reformist nature of social policy for children and families are numerous.

Only the naive would not recognize the important contribution of social norms and public perceptions to public policy. After all, legislation is largely a result of the public's reaction to social conditions and problems. The discussion of the No Child Left Behind Act (PL 107-110) provided by Frey, Mandlawitz, Perry, and Walker in Chapter 4 illustrated the power of public perception in reshaping education. Public outcry for school reform and accountability in the past decade are reflected in many provisions of the act. Similar examples can be drawn from the evolution of public policies in the antipoverty field (as discussed by Williams Shanks and Danziger in Chapter 2) and the developmental disabilities field (as discussed by Parish, Saville, Swaine, and Igdalsky in Chapter 7).

The recent passage of the national Patient Protection and Affordable Care Act (ACA) (PL 11–148) demonstrates clearly the complexities inherent in balancing incremental change and public perception. Following 18 months of deliberation, the U.S. Senate and House of Representatives passed significant health-care legislation in March 2010. Congressional deliberations highlighted the tension between legislators who favored comprehensive reform and legislators who favored incremental change in health-care policy. Sentiment for comprehensive or incremental reform was also expressed in public actions taken by members of the medical profession, health insurance companies, and public interest groups. The ACA was the product of a long and contentious debate that led to a series of compromises between officials who held competing views on comprehensive and incremental change. Key provisions of the legislation are designed to make health care more affordable and accountable. The bill bans insurance companies from discriminating against individuals with preexisting health conditions and provides a means for uninsured people to obtain health care. Specific provisions of the law will be implemented in defined phases during the next several years. However, the effects of what many public officials perceive to be an ill-advised and radical change in health-care policy will likely be debated— and adjudicated—for many years. Rounds, Hall, and Huitron discuss initial effects of the ACA on health-care policies and practices in Chapter 6.

Public policy should be based on the confluence of public concern and research knowledge. However, the urgency created by public perception and pressure sometimes precipitates changes that produce reforms with unintended and negative side effects. When pressured to respond to real or apparent changes in the nature of a child or adolescent problem behavior, officials frequently turn to convenient policy solutions that address symptoms but fail to address the underlying risk and protective factors associated with that problem (Jenson & Bender, 2014). The result of this process is ineffective, fragmented, and short-lived programs that sometimes do more harm than good. Arguably the greatest and most damaging effect is that such programs add to bureaucratic inertia, making systems more complicated, slower to respond with true reform, and less fertile for creating innovations.

Few service systems for children, youth, and families have developed a deliberate or effective continuum of care. Nearly all chapter authors noted that primary care systems tend to offer a patchwork assortment of programs and services that are seldom delivered to children and families in a sequential or rational fashion. One exception might be the comprehensive strategy for the prevention, treatment, and control of juvenile delinquency, which was adopted by the juvenile justice system in the late 1990s. This strategy, developed and disseminated by the Office of Juvenile Justice and Delinquency Prevention (Howell, 2003; Zavlek, 2005), outlines a continuum of care and graduated sanctions (i.e., punishments related to the seriousness of offenses) that many states use as a framework for handling young offenders. The strategy emphasizes a continuum of service that matches the individual's needs, which are often identified through systematic risk assessment, and the individual's history of offending to appropriate interventions and sanctions. Recent studies indicate that a comprehensive approach to reducing recidivism among juvenile offenders is effective (e.g., Howell & Lipsey, 2012).

Finally, careful historical analysis reveals that untested and ineffective policies and programs are repeated over time. One example is the recurring use of media campaigns as a way to increase awareness about the dangers of substance use. Anthony, Jenson, and Howard note in Chapter 8 that this strategy had little effect on reducing substance use in the 1970s and early 1980s. However, recent public awareness of increasing drug use among adolescents has rekindled interest in media and information campaigns that alert young people and their parents to the dangers of alcohol and other illicit drug use. As Anthony and colleagues discussed, this interest is reflected in the large allocation of federal funds to a national media campaign in recent years.

Perhaps the most salient point in each author's historical review of public policy is the absence of a uniform underlying framework to guide policy development. No common model or framework for policy development could be found across the eight service systems reviewed by authors. We believe that principles of risk and resilience—grounded in ecological theory—offer a useful framework for considering the conditions that affect children and that, by applying a risk- and protective-factor perspective, we can better design social programs to address these conditions. Next, we offer some thoughts on how these principles might be used to develop policy for children, youth, and families.

RISK AND RESILIENCE: AN ECOLOGICAL PERSPECTIVE FOR DEVELOPING CHILD, YOUTH, AND FAMILY POLICY

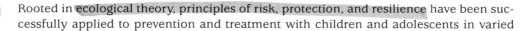
Rooted in ecological theory, principles of risk, protection, and resilience have been successfully applied to prevention and treatment with children and adolescents in varied

settings. In particular, substance abuse- and delinquency-prevention programs have been based on risk and protective factors occurring at levels of influence (e.g., environmental, interpersonal and individual) that are compatible with ecological theory (Germain, 1991). However, the full utility of risk, protection, and ecological theory for policy development remains untapped.

Using a risk- and protection-based approach to creating policies for children, youth, and families requires a step-by-step approach. These steps are outlined next and summarized in the developmental policy process shown in Figure 10.1.

Step 1: Evaluate Risk and Protective Factors

Policymaking begins with developing an understanding of the risk and protective factors associated with a targeted child or adolescent problem behavior. Consistent with ecological theory, factors should be assessed or summarized at environmental, interpersonal, social, and individual levels. Chapter authors have reviewed risk and protective factors associated with each of the problem behaviors and conditions discussed in this book. Because common risk and protective factors have been identified for many social and health problems, it may not always be necessary for policymakers to conduct basic risk or protective factor assessments. In many fields, research studies already specify predominant risk and protective factors (e.g., Fraser, 2004; Hawkins, 2006; Herrenkohl, Chung, & Catalano, 2004; Jenson & Bender, 2014; Woolf, 2008). However, differences in local environmental conditions may necessitate new assessments in some circumstances. For example, an urban center may be concerned about the disproportionate nature of poverty or the needs of racial/ethnic groups in certain geographic areas. The ways in which risk and protective factors vary by region, gender, and culture are the subject of much current research. Although some risk and protective factors are common, risk factors also clearly vary from the tribal lands of the mountain and plains states to the urban centers of the East and West coasts. These differences complicate risk assessment and pose a major challenge for policymakers.

Thinking about policy from a risk and protection perspective offers two advantages. First, the perspective allows for the use of a common language across policy domains. This gives policymakers, advocates, practitioners, and researchers a uniform vocabulary to use in describing related behaviors, setting program objectives, and assessing program outcomes. Second, because concepts of risk and protection emerged from research in several related fields—child development, mental health, prevention science, and public health in particular—we can build on diverse and cumulative scientific knowledge. This rapidly expanding knowledge base holds the potential—as demonstrated in many chapters of this book—to reform service systems across the country.

Step 2: Assign Policy Responsibility in Ways That Promote Service Integration Across Systems

Policies based on empirical evidence about the risk and protective factors associated with child and youth problems should be developed and implemented across the policy

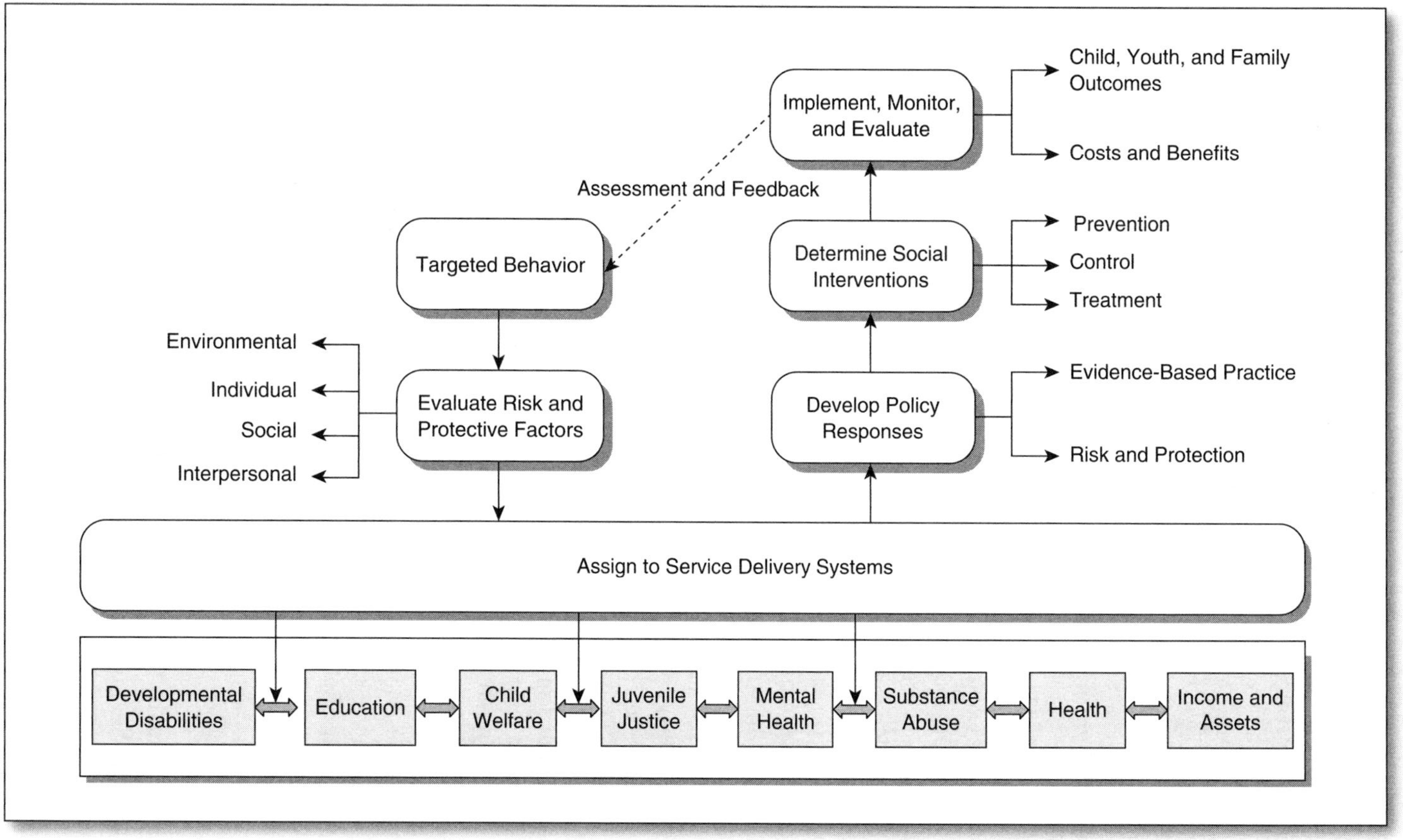

Figure 10.1 A Developmental Process of Child, Youth, and Family Policy

arenas addressed in this book. Integrating key programs and services identified or implied by policies across and within systems of care should be a priority. Critical questions that should be considered in the policy development and integration processes include the following:

1. Which service systems have primary responsibility for the programs and services defined or implied by the policy?

2. Where does fiscal accountability lie for the programs and services defined or implied by the stated policy?

3. Does the stated policy explicitly develop links between and within the major service systems for children, youth, and families?

4. Do adequate implementation resources exist within or across the primary systems to achieve service integration?

5. How can service systems integrate existing or new program resources, including staff, physical locations, training curricula, and evaluation tools and methods?

Locating and integrating program components defined by social and health policies within and across service systems are challenging undertakings. Collaborative partnerships between executive leadership, administrators, practitioners, and researchers are necessary to achieve the more fluid delivery and integration of policies aimed at children, youth, and families. Collaboration between service systems to prevent early and unwanted teen pregnancy illustrates policy and program efforts aimed at integration. See the accompanying box.[1]

A similar example illustrating the positive effects that system collaboration and integration can have on adolescent behavior is found in efforts to treat co-occurring substance abuse and mental health problems. Jenson and Potter (2003) tested an experimental intervention created to fill the mandate of legislation passed by the Colorado State Legislature. A legislative note mandated the mental health and juvenile justice systems to find innovative ways to treat co-occurring substance use and mental health problems among young offenders. The state systems responded by assessing risk and protective factors for adolescent substance abuse and mental health problems. An intervention was designed to place mental health case managers in juvenile justice facilities. Jenson and Potter conducted a longitudinal investigation of the program and found that the youth who received the intervention reported significant reductions in their levels of depression, anxiety, and substance use. This type of cross-system integration holds promise for reducing child and adolescent problem behaviors. Studies showing positive outcomes resulting from coordinated interventions involving systems from mental health, health, juvenile justice, and substance abuse domains illustrate the potential of social policies supporting programs that cross traditional boundaries (Finkelstein & Markoff, 2004; Graves, Frabutt, & Shelton, 2007; Kaufman et al., 2006). These findings are encouraging because they indicate that we are beginning to recognize the benefits of policies, programs, and services that use coordinated and collaborative efforts.

The Value of Collaboration and Integration: The Case of Early and Unwanted Teen Pregnancy

Early and unwanted adolescent pregnancy rates fell by 24% between 1996 and 2001 (Centers for Disease Control and Prevention, 2002). The decline, although likely influenced by a host of factors, was partially attributed to improvements in the coordination of policies and programs between the nation's health-care and educational systems. This collaborative effort included:

- The systematic dissemination of information by public health departments, government agencies, and schools aimed at educating and creating awareness among the public about the high rates of adolescent pregnancy in the United States.
- The implementation of school-based prevention efforts aimed at delaying the onset of adolescents' sexual activity and educating students about the risks associated with unprotected sex.
- The creation of school-based health clinics to reach adolescents who might not have access to medical care and thus were likely to be at highest risk for early and unwanted pregnancy.
- The allocation of targeted federal, state, and local funds to establish community-based health clinics that educate young men and women at risk for early, unwanted pregnancy and offer treatment for young families.

The decline in adolescent pregnancy rates came at a time of increased collaboration between the nation's health-care and educational systems. This successful collaboration demonstrated the potential of policy and program integration for reducing child and adolescent problems.

Step 3: Use Evidence to Create Public Policy Responses

Empirical evidence gained from studies of risk and protective factors should be used to create child, youth, and family public policies. Developing evidence-based policy, or at least evidence-informed policy, will require the dissemination of aggregate-level information about the etiology of child and adolescent problems to policymakers during the deliberation processes that lead to the creation of public policy. A critical step in dissemination is translating the empirical evidence in a manner that is immediately useable and practical for legislators and policy experts.

Recent developments in evidence-based practice (EBP) offer an opportunity to advance the notion of creating policies for children and families from an empirical framework. In the 1990s, EBP evolved in the medical profession from a concept to a movement to a professional imperative aimed at helping physicians select effective treatments for their patients. Definitions and perceptions of what EBP is—and what it is not—vary widely. In what is arguably the most accepted definition of EBP, Sackett and colleagues (Sackett, Straus, Richardson, Rosenberg, & Haynes, 2000) stated that EBP is "the integration of best research evidence with clinical expertise and [client] values" (p. 1). This definition implies that EBP is a process, characterized by specific steps and actions that require practitioners to locate, select, and implement the best available interventions for a targeted group or population.

An important parallel exists between the essential steps of EBP and the policy making process as illustrated in Figure 10.1. In both processes, the identification of risk and protective factors associated with specific problems lead to the design, selection, and testing of individual and social interventions. In an ideal setting, the best available interventions—meaning those with strong research evidence supporting their effectiveness—are then translated to broad-based social policies aimed at improving the lives of children and families.

Unfortunately, relatively few effective interventions manage to navigate the difficult path from implementation to policy. One recent exception is the Nurse-Family Partnership Program developed by David Olds and colleagues (Olds, Henderson, Tatelbaum, & Chamberlin, 1986). Aimed at guiding low-income mothers and their firstborn children toward successful futures, the program offers intensive home-visitation services during a woman's pregnancy and for 2 years after the birth of a first child. Controlled trials of the intervention have demonstrated positive effects in preventing child maltreatment and reducing maternal arrests (Olds et al., 2014). In addition, other evaluation studies have demonstrated reductions in child and adolescent conduct problems (Olds et al., 2009; Olds et al., 2010). More important, the program has recently been adopted by Colorado, among several other states, as part of a required set of interventions aimed at helping vulnerable young women and their families. The successful translation of evidence gained from intervention trials of the Nurse-Family Partnership to specific child and family policy may provide a template for other systems of care discussed in this book.

Step 4: Determine the Course of Specific Individual and Social Interventions

To determine the course of individual and social interventions, policy officials should consider evidence that identifies evidence-based programs and services for children and adolescents. Policy creation that integrates principles of risk, resilience, and EBP requires a comprehensive review of empirical evidence about the efficacy of alternative intervention approaches. In essence, determining the appropriate course of social intervention begs the old question, "What works best for whom under what conditions?"

Several outlets have surfaced as sources for obtaining information about effective interventions for children and youth. In Chapter 1, we noted the work of the University of Colorado's Center for the Study and Prevention of Violence. The center has identified a number of efficacious prevention programs that can be selected as the basis for a community or state's violence-prevention efforts (Center for the Study and Prevention of Violence, 2014). Similarly, the Substance Abuse and Mental Health Services Administration (2014) maintains the National Registry of Evidence-Based Programs and Practice, a comprehensive list of effective substance abuse and mental health programs. The Coalition for Evidence-Based Policy (2014) has compiled a compendium of early childhood, educational, and youth development programs that have been found effective in preventing violence and other childhood and adolescent problems. In addition, interdisciplinary groups such as the international Campbell and Cochrane Collaborations have provided public worldwide access to systematic reviews of the literature on treatment outcomes across a range of adolescent problems. These reviews offer a rich source of information for policy officials who are engaged in the process of recommending or selecting interventions for public systems of care (Campbell Collaboration Library, 2014; Cochrane Collaboration, 2014).

Decision makers are beginning to consider both program and cost-effectiveness when selecting interventions and creating policies for children and families. Historically, practitioners and policy officials have had little credible empirical evidence regarding the costs and benefits of social interventions to guide their decisions about which programs to select or to fund. Fortunately, this situation is changing through work conducted by numerous research teams, such as Aos and colleagues at the Washington State Institute for Public Policy (Aos, Lieb, Mayfield, Miller, & Pennucci, 2004; Lee, Aos, Drake, Pennucci, Miller, & Anderson, 2012). These researchers reviewed the benefits and costs of a wide range of prevention programs aimed at problems such as aggression, delinquency, school failure, and substance abuse. All of the programs included in their review had been previously tested in research using either an experimental design or a well-constructed quasi-experimental design. Findings from the study showed that some prevention programs yielded cost savings and effectively prevented or delayed the onset of problem behaviors. Equally important, Aos and associates produced tangible evidence in the form of a *benefit-per-dollar cost figure* for early childhood, prenatal and infant home visitation, youth development, mentoring, substance abuse, teen pregnancy, and juvenile offender programs. Benefits were greatest for juvenile offender programs. In these programs, the cost savings ranged from $1,900 to more than $31,000 per participant. Substantial benefits were also found among prenatal and infant home visitation programs, ranging from $6,200 to $17,200 in savings per individual youth. In addition, early childhood education programs and selected youth development programs were shown to produce significant benefits. The cost-saving figures generated by the Aos team point both to the importance of investing in effective programs and to the danger of funding ineffective programs. Policymakers and other decision makers are well advised to consider the findings and to implement the recommendations consistent with the growing evidence base. To make better use of the research literature on the effectiveness of interventions for children and adolescents (for a review, see Allen-Meares & Fraser, 2004) and to implement the kind of collaborative programs the authors have described in every chapter will require state and local officials to find ways of breaking down organizational barriers. In addition, policymakers will need to break through institutional isomorphism and exert leadership in overcoming the turf issues that have confounded previous reform efforts (e.g., the implementation of the Children's and Community Mental Health Services Improvement Act of 1992, which attempted to create systems of care within mental health). Unfortunately, many of the nation's educational systems, human services agencies, and state and community organizations fail to consider, select, or implement tested or effective programs. There continues to be a significant gap between what we know to be effective in preventing and treating childhood and family problems and what programs are actually implemented; this gap must be narrowed (Fixsen, Naoom, Blasé, Friedman, & Wallace, 2005). Policymakers should be encouraged to pay greater attention to the benefits gained by implementing proven and tested programs. Perceived barriers associated with replicating and implementing effective program strategies must be eliminated.

Step 5: Implement, Monitor, and Evaluate Policies and Interventions

The development of collaborative systems of care will also require greater emphasis on monitoring and evaluating the interventions. The energy and enthusiasm associated with reforms must be converted into systemic procedures that monitor the implementation of new programs, provide feedback, and articulate consequences for failed or inconsistent implementation. This level of accountability implies using fidelity checks to ensure that interventions are being implemented as intended, conducting cost–benefit analyses to assess the economic consequences of programs and policies, and assessing child, youth, and parent outcomes. Monitoring and evaluation allow legislators and others to determine the outcomes of policies and programs; effective efforts can be re-funded, and ineffective approaches can be redesigned.

SUMMARY

In this book, we have suggested that this country needs a new framework for child, youth, and family policy. Specifically, we have argued that a risk and resilience model, grounded in principles of ecological theory, offers potential for creating policies and programs that will lead to effective interventions for the problems that confront children and families in America.

The time is ripe for a new paradigm that will focus on the developmental processes—both risk and protective—related to the social and health problems that public policies are intended to address. Opinion polls assessing public willingness to fund early intervention and rehabilitation programs for children and youth have shown strong support for collaborative and community-based efforts (Baker, Metcalfe, Berenblum, Aviv, & Gertz, 2014; National Council on Crime and Delinquency, 2007). Advances in strengths-based practice, assets-oriented programming, and positive youth development have emerged, and they complement the risk, protection, and resilience framework set forth in this volume (Catalano, 2007; Maton, Schellenbach, Leadbeater, & Solarz, 2004). Although more research is needed to better understand the interactive processes inherent in these approaches, the potential of the risk and resilience model for policy development should not be understated. Finally, recent trends in the acceptance of evidence-based practice have brought researchers and policy experts together in ways that were unseen in past years.

The principles of risk and resilience arose from research on developmental psychopathology and prevention science. Major advances have occurred in these fields in the articulation of the developmental trajectories of children who drop out of school, become delinquent, use illicit substances, experience serious emotional disorders, or have other poor developmental outcomes. At the same time, this knowledge has been used to design effective prevention programs, many of which have been described in the previous chapters. These programs attempt to reduce risk, strengthen protection, and alter developmental trajectories. Findings from these programs are promising (Dodge, 2009; Jenson & Bender, 2014).

In the glow of promise from these programs, we ask, "Is it adequate to construct policy on the basis of risk factors alone?" We think risk reduction alone is an insufficient goal for public policy, although achieving risk reduction would be a significant step forward. It is the hope incumbent in the concept of resilience—where children at high risk prevail over adversity—that gives us pause. One driving force behind policy development must clearly be a moral imperative to reduce risk. However, from resilient children, we learn that risk reduction is defined, in part, by strategies that ameliorate or buffer adversities. In studying these protective processes, we often find that what protects children at risk also serves to promote positive developmental outcomes for all children (e.g., Fraser, 2004; Jenson, Alter, Nicotera, Anthony, & Forrest-Bank, 2013).

From this perspective, public policy for children and youths should be guided by attempts toward reducing risk *while* promoting protection. For all children (including those at risk), public policy should promote competence in social and academic settings, confidence in interpersonal relationship, and a self-efficacy in making life-course decisions. In addition, child policy should seek to foster connections to others who provide support and mentoring, the development of character or moral integrity regarding right and wrong behaviors, and feelings of caring or compassion for others who may be less fortunate (Catalano, Berglund, Ryan, Lonczak, & Hawkins, 2004; Catalano, Hawkins, Berglund, Pollard, & Arthur, 2002; Lerner, Almerigi, Theokas, & Lerner, 2005; Lerner, Fisher, & Weinberg, 2000). Too often, policy development is influenced by changes in problem rates or by catalyzing events such as epidemics or disasters. Of course, it is important to respond when rates rise or events create great need. However, public policy for children and youth should be proactive rather than reactive. It should promote protective processes that nurture developmental outcomes for all children, but especially those at great risk. In the sense of *Healthy People 2020* (U.S. Department of Health and Human Services, 2010), the intent of public policy for children, youth, and families should extend beyond the prevention of delinquency, substance abuse, or other social and health problems. Rather, the intent of policy should express health-promoting societal goals related to positive developmental outcomes for all children and the creation of widely accessible means for achieving those outcomes. Although highly structured and focused programs may always be needed to help children who have special needs (e.g., children who are victimized by individual disadvantage or tragic events), public policy for children should be rooted in core commitments that strengthen families, improve schools, and reinvigorate neighborhoods.

Much remains to be done to solve the fragmented nature of child, youth, and family policy in the United States. Individual service systems employ skilled practitioners, and each system can point to exemplary programs and innovative service delivery patterns. Despite those examples, child, youth, and family policies continue to suffer from the lack of an underlying and unifying framework that integrates services across problem domains and creates fully articulated systems of care. A risk and resilience perspective, coupled with ecological theory, holds promise as an organizing framework for future public policy efforts directed at the nation's young people. It is their future and our challenge.

NOTE

1. Biglan, Brennan, Foster, and Holder (2004) used a similar format with a different example to demonstrate the importance of collaboration in developing strategies for working with high-risk youth.

REFERENCES

Allen-Meares, P., & Fraser, M. W. (Eds.). (2004). *Intervention with children and adolescents: An interdisciplinary perspective.* Needham Heights, MA: Allyn & Bacon.

Aos, S., Lieb, R., Mayfield, J., Miller, M., & Pennucci, A. (2004). *Benefits and costs of prevention and early intervention programs for youth.* Olympia: Washington State Institute for Public Policy.

Baker, T., Metcalfe, C. F., Berenblum, T., Aviv, G., & Gertz, M. (2014). Examining public preferences for the allocation of resources to rehabilitative versus punitive crime policies. *Criminal Justice Policy Review.* Advance online publication. doi: 10.1177/0887403414521462.

Biglan, A., Brennan, P. A., Foster, S. L., & Holder, H. D. (2004). *Helping adolescents at risk. Prevention of multiple problems.* New York: Guilford Press.

Campbell Collaboration Library. (2014). *The Campbell Collaboration Library of systematic reviews.* Retrieved from http://www.campbellcollaboration.org/library.php.

Catalano, R. F. (2007). Prevention is a sound public and private investment. *Criminology and Public Policy, 6,* 377–398. doi: 10.1111/j.1745-9133.2007.00443.x

Catalano, R. F., Berglund, M. L., Ryan, J. A. M., Lonczak, H. S., & Hawkins, J. D. (2004). Positive youth development in the United States: Research findings on evaluations of positive youth development programs. *Annals of the American Academy of Political and Social Science, 591,* 98–124. doi:10.1177/0002716203260102

Catalano, R.F., Hawkins, J.D., Berglund, L., Pollard, J. A., & Arthur, M. W. (2002). Prevention science and positive youth development: Competitive or cooperative frameworks? *Journal of Adolescent Health, 31,* 230–239. doi:10.1016/S1054–139X(02)00496–2

Center for the Study and Prevention of Violence. (2014). *Blueprints for healthy youth development.* Retrieved from http://www.colorado.edu/cspv/

Centers for Disease Control and Prevention. (2002). *Special tabulations of first births from the 1997–2002 natality data sets* (Nos. 9–16, Series 21). Retrieved from http://wonder.cdc.gov/wonder/help/Natality.html.

Coalition for Evidence-Based Policy. (2014). *What works in social policy? Findings from well-conducted randomized controlled trials.* Retrieved from http://evidencebasedprograms.org

Cochrane Collaboration. (2014). *Cochrane reviews.* Retrieved from http://www.cochrane.org/cochrane-reviews.

Dodge, K. A. (2009). Community intervention and public policy in the prevention of antisocial behavior. *Journal of Child Psychology and Psychiatry, 50,* 194–200. doi:10.1111/j.1469–7610.2008.01985.x

Finkelstein, N., & Markoff, L. S. (2004). The Women Embracing Life and Living (WELL) Project: Using the relational model to develop integrated systems of care for women with alcohol/drug use and mental health disorders with histories of violence. *Alcoholism Treatment Quarterly, 22,* 63–80. doi:10.1300/J020v22n03_04

Fixsen, D. L., Naoom, S. F., Blasé, K. A., Friedman, R. M., & Wallace, F. (2005). *Implementation research: A synthesis of the literature* (FHMI Publication #231). Tampa: University of South Florida, Louis de la Parre Florida Mental Health Institute, National Implementation Research Network.

Fraser, M. W. (Ed.). (2004). *Risk and resilience in childhood: An ecological perspective* (2nd ed.). Washington, DC: NASW Press.

Fraser, M. W., Kirby, L. D., & Smokowski, P. R. (2004). Risk and resilience in childhood. In M. W. Fraser (Ed.), *Risk and resilience in childhood: An ecological perspective* (2nd ed., pp. 13–66). Washington, DC: NASW Press.

Germain, C. B. (1991). *Human behavior in the social environment: An ecological view.* New York: Columbia University Press.

Graves, K. N., Frabutt, J. M., & Shelton, T. L. (2007). Factors associated with mental health and juvenile justice involvement among children with severe emotional disturbance. *Youth Violence and Juvenile Justice, 5,* 147–167. doi:10.1177/1541204006292870

Hawkins, J. D. (2006). Science, social work, prevention: Finding the intersections. *Social Work Research,* 137–152. doi:10.1093/swr/30.3.137

Hawkins, J. D., Catalano, R. F., & Miller, J. Y. (1992). Risk and protective factors for alcohol and other drug problems in adolescence and early adulthood: Implications for substance abuse prevention. *Psychological Bulletin, 112,* 64–105. doi:10.1037/0033-2909.112.1.64

Herrenkohl, T. I., Chung, I. J., & Catalano, R. F. (2004). Review of research on predictors of youth violence and school-based and community-based prevention approaches. In P. Allen-Meares & M. W. Fraser (Eds.), *Intervention with children and adolescents: An interdisciplinary perspective* (pp. 449–476). Boston: Pearson Education.

Howell, J. C. (2003). *Preventing and reducing juvenile delinquency: A comprehensive framework.* Thousand Oaks, CA: Sage.

Howell, J. C., & Lipsey, M. W. (2012). Research-based guidelines for juvenile justice programs. *Justice Research and Policy, 14,* 17–34. doi: 10.3818/JRP.14.1.2012.17

Jenson, J. M., Alter, C. F., Nicotera, N., Anthony, E. K., & Forrest-Bank, S. S. (2013). *Risk, resilience, and positive youth development: Developing effective community programs for high-risk youth. Lessons from the Denver Bridge Project.* New York: Oxford University Press.

Jenson, J. M., & Bender, K. A. (2014). *Preventing child and adolescent behavior. Evidence-based strategies in schools, families, and communities.* New York: Oxford University Press.

Jenson, J. M., & Potter, C. A. (2003). The effects of cross-system collaboration on mental health and substance abuse problems of detained youth. *Research on Social Work Practice, 13,* 588–607. doi:10.1177/1049731503253405

Kaufman, J. S., Crusto, C. A., Quan, M., Ross, E., Friedman, S. R., O'Rielly, K., & Call, S. (2006). Utilizing program evaluation as a strategy to promote community change: Evaluation of a comprehensive, community-based, family violence initiative. *American Journal of Community Psychology, 38,* 191–200. doi:10.1007/s10464-006-9086-8

Lee, S., Aos, S., Drake, E., Pennucci, A., Miller, M., & Anderson, L. (2012). *Return on investment: Evidence-based options to improve statewide outcomes.* Olympia: Washington State Institute for Public Policy.

Lerner, R. M., Almerigi, J. B., Theokas, C., & Lerner, J. V. (2005). Positive youth development: A view of the issues. *The Journal of Early Adolescence, 25,* 10–16.

Lerner, R. M., Fisher, C. B., & Weinberg, R. A. (2000). Toward a science for and of the people: Promoting civil society through the application of developmental science. *Child Development, 71,* 11–20. doi:10.1111/1467-8624.00113

Maton, K. I., Schellenbach, C. J., Leadbeater, B. J., & Solarz, A. L. (2004). *Investing in children, youth, families, and communities. Strengths-based research and policy.* Washington, DC: American Psychological Association. doi:10.1037/10660-000

National Council on Crime and Delinquency. (2007). *New NCCD poll shows public strongly favors youth rehabilitation and treatment.* Retrieved from http://www.nccd-crc.org/nccd/pubs/zogbyPR0207 .pdf.

O'Connell, M. E., Boat, T., & Warner, K. E. (Eds.). (2009). *Preventing mental, emotional, and behavioral disorders among young people: Progress and possibilities.* Washington, DC: National Research Council and Institute of Medicine. The National Academies Press.

Olds, D. L, Eckenrode, J., Henderson, C., Kitzman, H., Cole, R., Luckey, D., Holmberg, J., & Baca, P. (2009). Preventing child abuse and neglect with home visiting by nurses. In K. A. Dodge & D. L.

Coleman (Eds.), *Preventing child maltreatment: Community approaches* (pp. 29–54). New York: Guilford Press.

Olds, D. L., Henderson, C. R., Tatelbaum, R., & Chamberlin, R. (1986). Improving the prenatal care and outcomes of pregnancy: A randomized trial of nurse home visitation, *Pediatrics, 77,* 16–28.

Olds, D. L., Kitzman, H., Cole, R., Hanks, C., Arcoleo, K., Anson, E., Luckey, D., Knudtson, M., Henderson, C., Bondy, J., & Stevenson, A. (2010). Enduring effects of prenatal and infancy home visiting by nurses on maternal life course and government spending: Follow-up of a randomized trial among children at age 12 years. *Archives of Pediatrics & Adolescent Medicine, 164,* 419–424. doi:10.1001/archpediatrics.2010.49.

Olds, D. L., Kitzman, H., Knudtson, M. S., Anson, E., Smith, J. A., & Cole, R. (2014). Effect of home visiting by nurses on maternal and child mortality. Results of a 2-decade follow-up of a randomized clinical trial. *JAMA Pediatrics.* Advance online publication. Retrieved from http://archpedi.jamanetwork.com/article.aspx?articleid = 1886653.

Sackett, D. L., Straus, S. E., Richardson, W. S., Rosenberg, W., & Haynes, R. B. (2000). *Evidence-based medicine: How to practice and teach EBM* (2nd ed.). New York: Churchill Livingstone.

Substance Abuse and Mental Health Services Administration. (2014). *NREPP: SAMHSA's national registry of evidence-based programs and practices.* Retrieved from http://www.nrepp.samhsa.gov/

U.S. Department of Health and Human Services. (2010). *Healthy people 2020: The road ahead.* Washington, DC: Government Printing Office.

Woolf, S. H. (2008). The power of prevention and what it requires. *Journal of the American Medical Association, 299,* 2437–2439. doi:10.1001/jama.299.20.2437

Zavlek, S. (2005). *Promoting community-based facilities for violent juvenile offenders as part of a system of graduated sanctions* (NCJ 209326; Juvenile Justice Practice Series). Washington, DC: U.S. Department of Justice, Office of Justice Programs, Office of Juvenile Justice and Delinquency Prevention.

Index

About the Editors

Jeffrey M. Jenson, PhD, is the Philip D. and Eleanor G. Winn Professor for Children and Youth at Risk in the Graduate School of Social Work, University of Denver. His research focuses on the application of a public health approach to preventing child and adolescent health and behavior problems and on the evaluation of preventive interventions aimed at promoting positive youth development. Dr. Jenson has published seven books and numerous articles and chapters on topics of prevention and child and adolescent development. His 2014 book (with K. Bender), *Preventing Child and Adolescent Problem Behavior: Evidence-Based Strategies in Schools, Families, and Communities* (Oxford University Press), is a comprehensive review of empirical evidence pertaining to the efficacy of universal, selected, and indicated preventive interventions for children and youth. Dr. Jenson has received several awards for his scholarship, including the Aaron Rosen Award from the Society for Social Work and Research. He is the recipient of Distinguished Scholar and University Lecturer awards from the University of Denver and is a former editor-in-chief of the journal *Social Work Research*. Dr. Jenson is a fellow of the American Academy of Social Work and Social Welfare and the Society for Social Work and Research.

Mark W. Fraser, PhD, holds the Tate Distinguished Professorship at the School of Social Work, University of North Carolina, where he serves as Associate Dean for Research. He has won numerous awards for research and teaching, including the Aaron Rosen Award and the Distinguished Achievement Award from the Society for Social Work and Research. His work focuses on risk and resilience, child behavior, child and family services, and research methods. He has published widely and, in addition to *Social Policy for Children and Families,* is the co-author or editor of eight books. These include *Families in Crisis,* a study of intensive family-centered services, and *Evaluating Family-Based Services,* a text on methods for family research. In *Risk and Resilience in Childhood,* he and his colleagues describe resilience-based perspectives for child maltreatment, substance abuse, and other social problems. In *Making Choices,* Dr. Fraser and his co-authors outline a program to help children build sustaining social relationships. In *The Context of Youth Violence,* he explores violence from the perspective of resilience, risk, and protection, and in *Intervention with Children and Adolescents,* he and his colleagues review advances in intervention knowledge for social and health problems. In *Intervention Research: Developing Social Programs,* he and his colleagues describe the design and development of social programs. His most recent book is *Propensity Score Analysis: Statistical Methods and Applications.* Dr. Fraser serves as editor of the *Journal of the Society for Social Work and Research.* He is a fellow of the National Academies of Practice, the Society for Social Work and Research, and the American Academy of Social Work and Social Welfare.

About the Contributors

Elizabeth K. Anthony, PhD, is an Associate Professor in the School of Social Work and a Research Faculty Affiliate of the Southwest Interdisciplinary Research Center at Arizona State University, where she teaches courses in applied research and clinical practice with children and adolescents. Dr. Anthony's research and publications focus on resilience among low-income adolescents and interventions to promote healthy outcomes among children and adolescents living in poverty. Prior to joining the faculty at Arizona State University, she served as Research Director on a longitudinal study of at-risk youth living in Denver public housing neighborhoods and as a postdoctoral fellow at the University of California, Berkeley.

William H. Barton, PhD, is Professor Emeritus in the Indiana University School of Social Work at Indiana University–Purdue University in Indianapolis, where he taught courses in juvenile justice policy, research methods, leadership, and the philosophy of science until his retirement in 2014. Dr. Barton's research interests include juvenile justice, delinquency prevention, youth development, and community practice. For more than 30 years, he has conducted evaluations of juvenile justice programs and policies throughout the United States. Among his many publications are numerous journal articles, book chapters, and two co-authored books.

Sandra K. Danziger, PhD, is a Professor of Social Work, School of Social Work, and Research Professor of Public Policy, Gerald R. Ford School of Public Policy, at the University of Michigan. Her primary research interests and publications examine the effects of public antipoverty and social service programs and policies on the well-being of disadvantaged families, particularly single mothers and their children. She is a Co-Investigator on the Michigan Recession and Recovery Study and was Principal Investigator on the Women's Employment Study that tracked the effects of the 1996 welfare reform. Professor Danziger was a 2009 Scholar in Residence at the Rockefeller Foundation Bellagio Center, Bellagio, Italy. She received the 2006 Society for Social Work Research Excellence in Research Award. She was a Visiting Scholar at the Russell Sage Foundation, New York, in 2002 to 2003, and, in 1994, was Visiting Research Scientist, Office of the Secretary, Assistant Secretary for Planning and Evaluation, U.S. Department of Health and Human Services, Washington, D.C.

Mary E. Fraser, DSW, has worked as a program and policy consultant to mental health departments in three states. Dr. Fraser wrote the Child and Adolescent Service System Program grant for the state of Utah in the early 1990s and served as that office's first director. She worked in the capacity of executive staff member to the North Carolina Legislative Oversight Committee on Mental Health Reform in 2000. Dr. Fraser's numerous publications focus on mental health policy and practice for children and families. She was previously a clinical adjunct professor in social work and psychiatry at the University of North Carolina at Chapel Hill.

Andy J. Frey, PhD, is a Professor and Chair of the school social work specialization in the Kent School of Social Work at the University of Louisville. Dr. Frey's research interests and publications address the provision of school-based mental health and school social work services and prevention and intervention for young children with challenging behavior. Prior to his appointment at the University of Louisville, he was a school social worker and behavioral consultant in Douglas County, Colorado.

William J. Hall, MSW, is a doctoral candidate at the School of Social Work, University of North Carolina at Chapel Hill. His research has included process evaluation for a school-based intervention for pediatric obesity and type-2 diabetes, school bullying and climate issues for sexual minority youth, and the evaluation of visual interventions for implicit ethnic bias among school and health-care professionals.

Markell Harrison-Jackson, PhD, is an Independent Educational Leadership and Child Welfare Consultant. In this role, he has developed programs for domestic and international child welfare, foster care, and educational systems. Dr. Jackson's work spans 16 years in educational settings and includes experience as a special education teacher, principal, and school administrator. He also teaches independent living skills to foster care youth and provides individual and group counseling to at-risk youth.

Matthew O. Howard, PhD, is the Frank A. Daniels Jr. Distinguished Professor of Human Services Policy Information in the School of Social Work and Faculty Research Fellow in the Cecil G. Sheps Center for Health Services Research at the University of North Carolina at Chapel Hill. Dr. Howard has published more than 220 articles in the field of substance abuse and is the recipient of three research grants from the National Institutes of Health aimed at understanding the natural history of inhalant abuse. Dr. Howard has served as Editor-in-Chief of *Social Work Research* and the *Journal of Social Service Research* and is currently North American Editor of the *British Journal of Social Work*. Dr. Howard was named a Fellow of the Society for Social Work and Research and a Fellow of the American Academy of Social Work and Social Welfare and received the University of North Carolina Excellence in Graduate Teaching Award in 2014.

Guadalupe V. Huitron, MSW, MPH is Country Director for Belize at Population Services International, a global health organization focusing on maternal and child health and HIV and AIDS.

Leah Igdalsky, BA, is a Research Associate at the Lurie Institute for Disability Policy in the Heller School for Social Policy and Management at Brandeis University. Her research interests include women's issues, aging, and disability policy.

Paul Lanier, PhD, is an Assistant Professor at the University of North Carolina at Chapel Hill School of Social Work, where he teaches courses in social policy and program evaluation. His research focuses on the prevention of child maltreatment, with an emphasis on improving the availability of evidence-based mental health services. Dr. Lanier received training as part of the Doris Duke Fellowship for the Promotion of Child Well-Being and the NIMH Pre-Doctoral Fellowship at the Center for Mental Health Services Research at the Brown School at Washington University in St. Louis. Dr. Lanier previously worked in an adolescent psychiatric treatment setting in North Carolina as an aftercare counselor.

Myrna R. Mandlawitz, JD, is president of MRM Associates, LLC, a Washington, D.C., lobbying firm, and has represented the School Social Work Association of America as its Director of Government Relations since 1999. She is a specialist in legal and policy issues related to special education and children's mental health. Prior to establishing her own government relations practice, Ms. Mandlawitz served as Government Relations Director for the National Association of State Directors of Special Education and spent 14 years as a classroom teacher in a large rural/suburban school district near Richmond, Virginia.

Susan L. Parish, PhD, MSW, is the Nancy Lurie Marks Professor of Disability Policy and Director, Lurie Institute for Disability Policy, at The Heller School for Social Policy and Management, Brandeis University. Her research examines the health and well-being of children and adults with disabilities and their caregiving families. She teaches courses in social policy and research methods.

Peter J. Pecora, PhD, is the Managing Director of Research Services for Casey Family Programs and Professor in the School of Social Work at the University of Washington. Dr. Pecora has worked with state departments of social services in the United States and in other countries to refine foster care programs, develop evaluation strategies, and implement intensive home-based services and risk assessment systems for child protective services. His co-authored books and articles focus on child welfare program design, administration, and research. In 2009, he was elected to the American Academy of Social Work and Social Welfare as a fellow and inaugural board member.

Armon R. Perry, PhD, is an Associate Professor in the Kent School of Social Work at the University of Louisville. Dr. Perry's research interests include fathers' involvement with their children and social welfare policy. Prior to his appointment at the University of Louisville, Dr. Perry was a child protective services social worker in Montgomery, Alabama.

Kathleen A. Rounds, PhD, is a Professor in the School of Social Work at the University of North Carolina at Chapel Hill. She is the Director of the Leadership in Public Health Social Work Program and Co-Chair of the dual degree program in social work and public health. Dr. Rounds's research has included evaluations of services for people with HIV, services for pregnant and postpartum women using substances, adolescent parenting programs, and interdisciplinary leadership and workforce development in maternal and child health.

Alison W. Saville, MSW, MSPH, is the Project Manager for the Children's Outcomes Research Program (COR) at University of Colorado–Denver. She currently manages an investigation funded by the National Institutes of Health entitled Population versus Practice-Based Interventions to Increase Immunizations.

Jamie G. Swaine, MSW, is a Clinical Instructor in the Developmental Disabilities Training Institute at the School of Social Work, University of North Carolina at Chapel Hill. She currently manages a project funded by the U.S. Department of Education that is testing the effectiveness of a community-based intervention to improve cervical and breast cancer screening rates for women with intellectual disabilities.

Hill M. Walker, PhD, is a Professor of Special Education, Co-Director of the Institute on Violence and Destructive Behavior, and Research Director of the Center on Human Development, in the College of Education at the University of Oregon. He has a longstanding interest in behavioral assessment and in the development of effective intervention procedures for use in school settings with a range of behavior disorders. His research interests include social skills assessment, curriculum development and intervention, longitudinal studies of aggression and antisocial behavior, and the development of early screening procedures for detecting students who are at risk for social-behavioral adjustment problems and/or later school dropout.

Trina R. Williams Shanks, PhD, is an Associate Professor in the School of Social Work at the University of Michigan. She is Co-Principal Investigator on the SEED impact assessment survey, a quasi-experimental study of children's savings accounts among preschool families. Her interests include asset-building policy and practice across the life cycle, the impact of poverty and wealth on child development outcomes, and community and economic development in urban areas.